PURE SPACE

EXPANDING THE PUBLIC SPHERE THROUGH PUBLIC SPACE TRANSFORMATIONS IN LATIN AMERICAN SPONTANEOUS SETTLEMENTS

PREFACE AND ACKNOWLEDGEMENTS

The arguments of the book acknowledge the key role of public space not only to improve the physical conditions of spontaneous settlements[1] in cities of Latin America and the Global South, but additionally as a tool to advance urban integration. Public policy on urban improvement in spontaneous settlements has too often focused solely on housing solutions which in reality can only represent a partial answer given the overwhelming number of people living in spontaneous settlements. Self-built homes have allowed families and individuals to resolve the unmet housing demand. They have also created communities that in many cases date back to anywhere between 60 and 100 years. Nonetheless, they remain marginal and segregated from city dynamics, revealing that improvement efforts alone have not been enough to lift the stigma from these territories. Access to work opportunities and the option to participate in the recreational and cultural activities cities offer is a human right. In this sense, spontaneous settlements need to be recognized as part of the city and become fully integrated within its symbolic and functional dimensions. The challenge is finding ways to promote and strengthen this recognition. Public space in communities not only benefits neighbors with access to recreation and gathering space, it is also a way for them to receive outside visitors so that people from other neighborhoods can feel welcome. It serves as a common platform people across the city share. Public space, however, is notoriously scarce in spontaneous settlements, which is why it is important to support projects that increase access to parks, plazas and open space in these territories. Furthermore, producing public space is also far less expensive than social housing projects and represents a cost-effective and viable vehicle to improve the livelihood of inhabitants. Most importantly, shared public space offers a strategy to incorporate spontaneous settlements, in an obvious and straight forward way, into a larger notion of the city.

Vibrant and healthy cities are well communicated and movement within them is fluid. Their neighborhoods are open and visible; they are accessible, through and through; and all are recognized as part of a whole. This is not the case in many Latin American cities, which tend to be fragmented and segregated in terms of social classes, economic status, as well as “formal” and “informal” territories. Urban public policies must begin to address these conditions more aggressively and provide all citizens with equal access to services and amenities. The private and non-for-profit sectors also have a great deal to contribute toward nudging a shift away from the construction of urban differences through social

1 Spontaneous settlements will be used to identify what is commonly called informal settlement and to avoid using pejorative terminologies. See note 3 of the introduction.

initiatives, events and programs. As economic inequality and the divide between citizens within the same city increases, building a case for the "complete city"[2] becomes all the more pertinent. A complete city is one that acknowledges all of its territories and takes advantage of its resources in terms of culture, demographics and urban spaces. Taking steps toward building one is a clear path toward redistributing and democratizing the knowledge and wealth that have historically attracted people to cities.

This research began in 2012 when I started to visit various cities in Latin America thanks to the Wheelwright Fellowship from Harvard University Graduate School of Design, awarded in 2011. I am deeply grateful to Harvard, my alma mater, for the opportunity to go deeper into an aspect of the built environment I felt very curious about and was eager to better understand. I am especially grateful to Jorge Silvetti, Mónica Ponce de León, Hashim Sarkis and Nader Tehrani for all the lessons learned and for your support. Each of the cities I visited had their own unique dynamic and required different amounts of time to understand and learn about the various initiatives that had been implemented over the past decades. I approached people involved in urban and social maters through various contacts. Some were pointed out by local government as in the cases of Guayaquil, Rio de Janeiro and Medellin; others were located through academic circles, as in the cases of Lima and Valparaiso. These visits produced a copious amount of information that took months to process and interiorize. After a great deal of reflection, what I found to be the most significant urban transformations I witnessed were the projects that included public spaces.

Most of the projects in this publication were identified as part of the Wheelwright experience. To these I added Villa Tranquila, in Buenos Aires, Argentina, which I visited in 2010, and in 2018, Miravalle in Mexico City. Two projects in Caracas, in which my office Enlace Arquitectura was directly or partially involved between 2014 and 2018 have also been incorporated in the publication. These last 4 projects expand the regional representation of the repertoire to a total of eight cities in eight different countries. Many of the projects included have not been previously published, nor are particularly well-known within their cities.

Since 2012 this research has been presented in four exhibitions which were designed and curated together with my office Enlace Arquitectura. In Caracas, it was presented as "Puro Espacio: transformaciones de espacio público en barrios de América Latina" at the Centro de Arte los Galpones de Los Chorros in November 2013. I am grateful to Manuel Torres and Raquel Ocariz for making the space available to us and supporting our work. The exhibition´s

2 See note 134 in the coda.

second iteration was titled "Tactical Resilience" and took place at the Eric Arthur Gallery of the Daniels Faculty of Architecture, Landscape and Design at the University of Toronto, in September 2014. I would like to extend a sincere thank you to Laura Miller for her curatorial work and advice in showcasing the projects. In November of the same year the work was presented in the exhibition "Latin American lessons in informal settlement rehabilitation" in the Architecture Museum of Buenos Aires. I am grateful to Rubén Ramírez, Representative of CAF in Argentina at the time, Juan Carlos Fried from SIUS-FADU, UBA and Flavio Jánchez from FADU, UBA who participated in the opening event. And I especially want to thank Martin Marcos, the Museum's director, Pablo Rossi for the exhibition´s design and installation, as well as Max Rohm for making the alliances and the event possible. "Pure Space: public space transformations in Latin American slums" was presented a fourth time at Florida International University (FIU) Miami Beach Urban Studios Design Gallery between September and November 2015. I am deeply grateful to Henry Rueda and Jason Chandler for inviting us to this exhibition space and to the FIU students Luca Di Giacomo, Patricia Elso, Giovanna Gallardo, Stephany Guinan and Matt Wasala for all their enthusiasm and support.

The arguments and justifications have shifted over the years and will likely continue to do so in years to come, since they are part of an emerging field of knowledge that is being constructed with new experiences, both failures and successes. In that sense, the content of this publication is a photograph of where the ideas stand today. It has made its way into a book format thanks to the financial support of the Graham Foundation for Advanced Studies in the Fine Arts and CAF development bank of Latin America. I am grateful to José Carrera, former Vice President of Social Development at CAF for believing in this body of research, as well as Hely Olivares, Pablo López, Andrés Sarache, Barbara Zamora and Andrés Zamora. Thank you as well to Ricardo Devesa of Actar Publishers for enthusiastically moving forward with this publication.

I am grateful to the people in each city who helped me navigate their maps and locate the various social initiatives and urban interventions built in spontaneous settlements. In 2010, I travelled to Buenos Aires and had the opportunity to visit Villa Tranquila with the project architect of the Vicente López Plaza, Max Rohm. Then in 2012, I spent some time in Chile before traveling to Lima and I would like to thank Antonio Lipthay for taking me along on a site visit to the Cerro El Toro and Cerro El Pino pavement projects. In Lima, Alexia León and Paulo Dam helped connect me with people in the city involved in social projects. Through an interview with Shariff Kahat I gained a much better understanding of the city´s social housing history. Artist Alejandra Ballón introduced me to Albina Ruiz, director of Ciudad Saludable. I am very grateful to Ramiro García of the NGO Desco, for a generous tour of the work they have done in Villa Santa Maria del Triunfo and Villa El Salvador. Diego Villarán, the founder of Alto Perú, thank you for allowing me to spend an evening with your students, and Matías Ballón, general director of Alto Perú for sharing information as we wrote the project´s case study.

In Rio de Janeiro I was very fortunate to be welcomed by Flavio Ferreira, who has been instrumental in many of the urban transformation projects in Rio de Janeiro, and his wife Heloisa and daughter Carolina. To my friend Anik Meyer-Weiner, thank you for all your support while in Rio. To Roberto Pacheco and Eve Bélanger of AfroReggae, thank you for coordinating a very thorough tour of the Vigário Geral headquarters. To Alan Brum Pinheiro of Raízes em Movimento in Complexo Alemão, thank you for a very illuminating conversation on how the cable car project was executed and the shortcoming it had with the community. To Daniele Ramalho, Vera Saboya, Alexandre Pimentel, and Sergio Magalhaes, I am grateful for showing me cultural projects in Rocinha and Manguinhos. Tiago Borba of the Rio de Janeiro Prefecture, thank you for a very insightful interview. To Jorge Mario Jauregui thank you for sharing information on your projects. Washington Fajardo, I am very grateful for your counsel and putting me in touch with key figures in the city. Alfredo Sirkis, Director of Rio de Janeiro's Environmental Department, thank you for sharing information on the Chapéu Mangueira project. In Medellín, I am grateful to Jorge Pérez Jaramillo who sat with me and mapped out every project I should visit on a large foldout map, as well as sharing his knowledge on the city´s transformation. Alejandro Echeverri, thank you for your time and inviting me visit the HP headquarters construction site, as well as conversations on your work during Mayor Sergio Fajardo´s administration period. To Natalia Castaño and Daniel Felipe Quiceno (Perro), thank you for a wonderful tour of the Comuna 13. Likewise, Juan Sebastian Bustamante, thank you for sharing information on EAFIT's projects. Carlos Rodriguez, thank you for a generous interview. Thank you to Carolina Gómez- Cortés, of the Buen Comienzo program and Antonio José Toro of the City´s housing authority. I am grateful to Luisa Elena Torres for giving me a thorough tour of Santo Domingo Savio and the area around the Juan Bobo Creek. Alfredo Vasquez, coordinator of the Botero Library and Cielo María Holguín, who worked at the Moravia Cultural Center, thank you for your interviews. I am grateful to Jeisson "Jeihhco" Castaño for sharing information on the Casa Kolacho initiative. In Guayaquil, I would like to thank Italia Delgado from CAF BEDE for coordinating visits and contacting key people in the city, as well as Constanza Calderón from CAF for her support. To Mario Pérez of the CAF BEDE Unit thank you for information on Guayaquil´s Urban Regeneration Project. Jenny Poveda Saltos, thank you for showing me the municipality's social projects for Cerro Santa Ana. Washington Villacís, Borys Pinargote, Genaro Cubillo and Jorge Berrezueta, thank you for taking me to see so many of the urban interventions that have been built in the city over the past decade.

The Mexico City project in Iztapalapa came into the publication more recently. I had a chance to visit Miravalle in September 2018. Thank you to Jorge Carvajal and Edgar Pichard for sharing their knowledge on the history of the Miravalle projects and the community organization that has made them possible. Thank you to Nicolás Montecchi-Palazzi for all the support as well. The projects featured in Caracas are directly related to work by Enlace Arquitectura. The "El Calvario Puertas Abiertas" initiative has been led by Cheo Carvajal and community leader José González. Thank you for sharing the experience as it has evolved over four successful editions. And also thank you for including us in more than one of those editions. To the people of Fudep, María Gloria Olivo, Rosalba Gil, Victor Guerrero, Marlene Jairala and Francia Sierralta, thank you for sharing your knowledge, for the opportunity to work together on meaningful projects in Venezuela.

The entire office of Enlace Arquitectura has been instrumental in producing the drawings for the publication, compiling research on each specific project as well as writing them into case studies. I am grateful for the support of María Virginia Millán who has been a key figure in tackling all the information gathered over so many years and succinctly building it into texts that describe each of the projects. I also want to thank Sergio Dos Santos, Valentina Caradonna, Verónica González, Jenirée Calderón, Sofía Paz, Vanesa Malpica and Eduardo Mouthar for all the work they put into the drawings, plans and maps of each of the 23 projects. And I would like to thank everyone that helped put the exhibitions together over the years, Sergio Dos Santos, Valentina Caradonna, Katherine Aguilar, Lisimar Campero, Ana Mosquera, Leonardo Jerez, Roselys Acosta, Odette Galavis and Ray Coello. You have been a constant source of motivation and energy to pursue this research and push it forward all the way through publication.

Along the way conversations with colleagues at the Department of Architecture and Art at the Simón Bolívar University and friends both in and outside the field of design, have been very stimulating. Silvia Soonets, Yuraima Martín, Florinda Amaya, Ana Cristina Vargas, Cheo Carvajal, Gerardo Zavarce, Lorenzo González Casas, Henry Vicente, Henry Rueda, Oscar Rodríguez, Orlando Marín, José Javier Alayón, Odart Graterol, Aliz Mena, Franco Micucci, Ignacio Cardona, Manuel Barrios, Oscar Grauer, David Gouverneur, María Isabel Peña, María Isabel Espinosa, María Gabriela Ochoa, Bernardo Dorbessan, María Mercedes Hernández, Tomás Cervilla, Carlos Ferrer, Lucia Sánchez, Guillermo Frontado, Jorge Villota, Luis Emilio Pacheco, Izaskun Landa, María Eugenia Bacci, Ana Lasala, Isabel Lasala, Alessandro Famiglietti, Juan Castillo, Hernán Zamora, Edgar Aponte, Andrés Makoski, Carolina Izquiel, Ery Marcano, Máximo Sacchini, Luis Enrique Berrizbeitia, Juan Castillo C., Rafael Fuentes, Mikhael Iglesias, thank you for the passionate exchange of ideas about communities and the built environment over the years.

My family has indulged me with endless hours of discussions on these issues. I have enjoyed them, and hope we continue to build on this conversation through future exchanges. To my uncle Juan Silva, I owe the first visit to a *barrio* in Caracas, and the ensuing interest we share to better understand where and how we can contribute. My gratitude to you will always be present. To my aunts and uncles, Marisela Bruzual, Ricardo Silva, Lexa Bustillos de Silva, Maria Inés Silva de Casanova and Rafael Casanova, thank you for your examples of commitment and dedication to significant social causes. I am fortunate to have cousins that are bright and generous of heart, our conversations and experiences together have given me energy along the way and a lot of food for thought: Inés Casanova, Ana Luisa Silva, Juan Pedro Silva, Ricardo Silva, Andrés Casanova, Luis Silva, Rafael Peña, Natalia Brandler, Victor Rivero, María Eugenia Mier y Terán, Clemencia Rivero, María Luisa Rivero, Gabriel Nuñez, Ingrid Nuñez, Jorge Nuñez and Ingrid Perret Gentil. And last but not least, to my parents Victor and Carolyn Silva, and my sister Miriam Silva Preas, thank you for support and help in too many dimensions to count them. We have shared an unrepeatable and immensely rich journey together.

I am tickled when reading the preface to *Privacy and Publicity: Modern Architecture as Mass Media* by Beatriz Colomina, where she candidly discloses her difficulties writing in a different language. This is also a constant struggle for me, even though both English and Spanish are my mother-tongues and first languages. I am deeply grateful to Luis Miguel Isava and Josefina Berrizbeitia who although terribly over qualified for the task, agreed to help me proofread and correct the texts. Language is both a tricky and beautiful affair; I have enjoyed reflecting on examples in the text that illustrate the two.

Elisa Silva, May 2019

PART I

TERRITORIAL INEQUALITY
PUBLIC SPACE
FORMAL, FINANCIAL AND SOCIAL STRATEGIES

INTRODUCTION

May the will to truth mean this to you: that everything should be transformed into the humanly-conceivable, the humanly evident, the humanly palpable! You should follow your senses to the end![1]

Very little has been written about public space in barrios, there has been little research.[2]

Initially, "PURE SPACE: Expanding the public sphere through public space transformations in Latin American barrios," may seem a simple accumulation of twenty-three public space projects in eight Latin American cities. On closer inspection, the presentation of project descriptions, photographs, and annotated drawings reflect a concern to analytically explain the operative aspects at work. As a result, the projects have been systematized and organized according to the strategies and justifications used to develop them.

Yet even this resulting second level of analysis is misleading, as the publication is not intended to serve only as a catalogue, guide, or manual on how to produce public space in spontaneous settlements.[3] Rather, this publication goes beyond the aims of an index of best practices. It is intended, instead, as an empirical base for a critical and theoretical engagement with the problematics of development, social inclusion, public investment, (in)formal settlement, civil society and the public sphere. The publication achieves its final function at this third level, by providing a compelling argument to expand the agency of architects and urban designers and creatively find ways of justifying, financing, and building public spaces in communities – spaces that have a catalytic effectiveness in achieving significant urban and social transformation. By presenting this body of research in a multi-performative fashion, the publication both enriches the current literature on spontaneous settlement improvement and provides a base for its replication in other communities.

The production of public space in spontaneous settlements could be critical for improving the livelihood of their inhabitants. It incorporates them into urban dynamics and thus acknowledges

1 Friedrich Nietzsche, *Thus Spoke Zarathustra* (London: Penguin Books, 1978), 110.

2 Jaime Hernández-García, *Public Space in Informal Settlements* (Cambridge: Cambridge Scholars Publishing, 2013), 4.

3 In Latin American there are different words used to refer to spontaneous settlements or slums. In Argentina they are known as *villas miseria*, Peru and Chile call them *villas* or *campamentos*, in Venezuela and Colombia they are called *barrios* or *barriadas* and in Brazil *favelas*. Over the years these terms have been charged with connotations that are questionably pejorative and condescending. In English, the same criterium applies for the word slum. Rahul Srivastava and Matias Echanove argue in a 2014 article in *The Guardian*, that people who live in slums would never call their own neighborhoods as such. Instead, slums should be called "homegrown neighborhoods" meaning that they emerge from organic processes that do not involve formal planning, and that they could enjoy the same positive connotations as medieval city centers in Europe and the Middle East. Rahul Srivastava and Matias Echanove. "Slum is a loaded term. They are homegrown neighborhoods," *The Guardian* November 28, 2014. https://www.theguardian.com/cities/2014/nov/28/slum-loaded-term-homegrown-neighbourhoods-mumbai-dharavi (accessed June 24, 2018).
It is in this frame that the publication assumes the term "spontaneous settlement", alluding to the non-planned origin of the neighborhood. Avoiding derogatory terminology is an acknowledgement of the power in language to question and educate.

them as part of the city. The case studies in this publication demonstrate that relevant and lasting urban transformation is achieved through interventions that incorporate elements of public space production within their project scope. On a neighborhood scale, such spaces transform a once vague and non-specific place into a distinct and easily recognized one, reflecting a newly visible local identity. As the only spatial variation within spontaneous settlements, public spaces are easily coupled with the plazas and parks that exist in the rest of the city, thereby establishing a more direct urban correlation between formal and informal urban elements. This association generates a significant conceptual mutation in the community's self-awareness and perception as relevant members of civil society.

City making in underdeveloped countries has been notoriously characterized for its simultaneous, although differing modes of operation: a formally planned and legal one that meets the needs and buying power of the wealthier part of the population, and an unplanned, illegal one, caused by the unmet demand of the remaining part whose economic capabilities do not attract the formal sector, neither private nor public. As a result, the second mode consists of self-built homes in spontaneous settlements. The number of people that find themselves in the latter situation is astounding.[4] In the context of Latin America, the frequency increased in the fifties and sixties, when migration to the city became more significant. Today the population living in spontaneous settlements is so substantial that sheer number crunching has led urban designers and city officials to consider self-built homes part of the solution to continued housing deficits. As such they become a permanent part of the city. The imminent environmental risks and social deterioration associated with these unplanned urban areas are notorious –not to mention the evident inequality that threatens the continued prosperity of cities. Designing and implementing effective solutions to improve the living conditions of spontaneous settlement inhabitants is therefore one of the most relevant and imperative assignments cities in Latin America and elsewhere must address in the near to mid future.

To that end, documented studies and programs on housing, community empowerment and participatory design have made valuable contributions. The clarity of their arguments and the fact that they rely on concrete experiences have granted them recognition in academic circles.

On the topic of housing as a way to mitigate the formation of spontaneous settlements, Alejandro Aravena, Andrés Iacobelli and Pablo Allard developed the "Elemental project" in Chile. Ably packaged units, subsidized with public resources, apparently represent a progressive and replicable solution to house people in underprivileged economic circumstances.[5] This strategy has been explained with a simple numeric logic that is both easy to grasp and convincing. However, it relies on the relative wealth of the Chilean state, which does not compare to the finances of most developing countries that cannot afford analogous subsidy programs. Furthermore, the population under the line of poverty in Chile is scarcely 11.7%, significantly lower than in the rest of Latin America, which oscillate between 20% and 40%.[6] Another consideration is that the program is essentially a housing strategy and tacitly aligns more with spontaneous settlement eradication process than with upgrading and transforming existing informal environments.

Alfredo Brillembourg and Hubert Klumpner celebrate informality as a self-empowering action on the part of the underprivileged vis-a-vis an uninterested economically powerful ruling class

4 881,080,000 spontaneous settlement dwellers are estimated to be living in developing countries, and this figure has been calculated considering just four out of the five informal household deprivations included in UN-Habitat´s definition. Therefore, 881 million is considered a global minimum. United Nations, "The Millennium Development Goals Report." UN-Habitat (2015), World Cities Report (2016).

5 Alejandro Aravena and Andrés Iacobelli, *Elemental: Incremental Housing and Participatory Design Manual* (Ostfildern: Hatje Cantz Verlag, 2013).

6 World Bank, "Fewer Chileans living in poverty despite economic slowdown," *Reuters*, 2016. Bolivia is considered to be the poorest country in Latin America. Its poverty rate dropped and was 39% in 2016, while Chile´s poverty rate in 2015 was 11.7%. No official data exists for Venezuela which could have the highest poverty index in 2019.

or, in the Caracas case, a disengaged government.[7] The squatting of Torre David, an unfinished and abandoned structure, is aestheticized and redeemed as an extra legal expression of identity and community power, without regard to the sanitary conditions and the accessibility problems a 45-story building without services represents for the people living there. The resulting analysis is essentially a study on alternative living models accompanied with highly evocative imagery that fascinates urban lovers and design scholars but contributes little if anything to improving spontaneous settlement conditions.[8]

A third approach, endorsed by Marcos L. Rosa, Ricky Burdett and the London School of Economics among others, views community-based urban projects such as those described in the book *Handmade Urbanism* as a sensitive and realistic approach to advance spontaneous settlement conditions from a grassroots perspective. [9] Community involvement in design processes to improve their own living environment is key to any project´s success and sustainability over time. However, such projects tend to remain relatively small and limited in their scope, in stark contrast to the gravity and magnitude of the environmental and urban situations spontaneous settlement dwellers experience.

Each of these examples represents a partial response to the question of spontaneous settlements. The economic conditions of most Latin American countries make Elemental´s example impractical given the cost of assigning subsidies for the number of people in need (sometimes more than half of a city's population). Likewise, the occupation of vacant buildings is neither a replicable model nor a viable alternative to spontaneous settlements. And lastly, despite the unquestionable necessity of community involvement in upgrading initiatives, participatory design processes will only be able to produce the substantial transformations necessary to improve spontaneous settlement conditions with outside technical expertise and substantial economic investment. And another point to consider is that none of them address broader issues of urban integration.

In regard to the core aspects of spontaneous settlement improvement, certain premises appear to be essential to the relevance and usefulness of any given project. First, the interventions must necessarily take place *within* existing spontaneous settlements since a central criterion of the improvement paradigm is to acknowledge that they are part of the developing world´s landscape. Second, interventions should work toward increasing social inclusion, providing tools and frameworks that will allow the population to participate in city dynamics. And third, projects should address issues of personal and environmental risks that both threaten and negatively affect the livelihood of inhabitants.

Since the 1990´s informal settlement rehabilitation projects in Latin America have sustained efforts to better serve *barrio* communities and integrate them into the city. "The Physical Rehabilitation Plan for Barrios" (Plan de Habilitación Física de Barrios) in Venezuela, the "Informal settlement - neighborhood" (Favela Bairro) projects in Rio de Janeiro Brazil, the "Integral Informal Settlement Improvement Program in Medellin" (PRIMED Programa integral de mejoramiento de barrios subnormales en Medellín) and similar programs in other cities and countries have been formulated to improve the quality of life of people living in spontaneous settlements.[10] These efforts tend to focus less on housing and more on integration processes in which the role of local governments and NGO´s centers on resolving larger, complex territorial issues. In

7 Alfredo Brillembourg and Hubert Klumpner, *Torre David: Informal Vertical Communities* (Zurich: Lars Muller Press, 2013). Images by Iwan Baan.

8 The Tower David was first documented by artists Ángela Bonadies and Juan José Olavarría in 2011. Jesús Fuenmayor, "The Tower of David" *Domus*, April 28, 2011. https://www.domusweb.it/en/architecture/2011/04/28/the-tower-of-david.html (accessed March 15, 2019).

9 Marcos L. Rosa and Ute Weiland (Eds.), *Handmade Urbanism: Mumbai, São Paulo, Istanbul, Mexico City, Cape Town: From Community Initiatives to Participatory Models* (Berlin: Jovis Verlag GmbH, 2013).

10 Elisa Silva and Pablo Vaggione, *Políticas Pro Inclusión: Herramientas prácticas para el desarrollo integral de las ciudades en América Latina* (Bogotá: CAF, 2016), 20. The World Bank initially funded these programs.

fact, these approaches acknowledge that housing is the only urban element communities are able to produce on their own, often with sturdy materials and adequate construction methods. Several examples in different parts of the region have effectively generated significant impact on the livelihood of inhabitants by focusing on the complementary aspects to urban living, such as increased access to potable water, public transportation, education, mitigation of natural disaster risks and improved environmental sanitation.[11]

Each of these spontaneous settlement improvement programs has evolved in different directions and been successful in diverse degrees. They represent over two decades of knowledge produced through concrete experiences. For the most part, they remain known only to professionals of related fields and within their local context; seldom, and only in specific cases, have they reached international dissemination.[12] As a body of knowledge, they present an opportunity to review which strategies or approaches were able to generate effective transformations; and which were the key operative elements that most successfully integrated spontaneous settlements into an urban whole.

In a critical review of upgrading interventions, the presence of public space emerges as a key transformative element.[13] Projects in settlements that were able to incorporate some form of public space within their tight urban fabrics, gained much more than square meters of open space. As a place for community interaction, congregation and exchange, newly created public spaces were able to strengthen local identity, elevate the community´s sense of self-worth, improve orientation, provide space for recreation, reduce violence by offering youth more activity options, and, in general, increase social cohesion. A significant transformation in a given location occurred both physically and conceptually, regardless of the specific program.

Open space, however, is scarce in spontaneous settlements due to the very nature of their construction patterns, where homes accumulate in close proximity to each other. Often the ratio of public space per capita is between 10 and 100 times less than in the more established, formally disposed parts of the city.[14] Consequently, creating new public space within already consolidated territories is a challenge. Furthermore, projects to create them may appear trivial when compared to securing basic needs such as potable water, sanitation, and personal security. For this reason, public space initiatives are infrequent in rehabilitation efforts, and seldom considered a priority.

Nevertheless, a case can be made for projects that have been able to generate public space transformations in spontaneous settlements. Documented case studies of projects executed over the past decade in the cities of Valparaiso (Chile), Rio de Janeiro (Brazil), Medellin (Colombia), Guayaquil (Ecuador), Lima (Peru), Mexico City (Mexico), Buenos Aires (Argentina) and Caracas (Venezuela) contain practical knowledge as well as theoretical insights about strategies that have successfully created public space and could be used as models in other communities.[15] The social opportunities associated with such improvements are evident, but there are also concrete political and economic interests that can be channeled toward supporting and significantly increasing public space investments in spontaneous settlements.

11 Such is the case in Medellin with the Comprehensive Urban Project (PUI Proyecto Urbano Integral).

12 Spontaneous settlement upgrading projects in Medellin have been widely published, but they tend to focus only on a few emblematic architectural projects and fail to comment on the social processes that accompanied them. Also, many other valuable interventions remain obscure.

13 The upgrading interventions were known through research and travels that were made possible by the Wheelwright Fellowship, from Harvard University, awarded to Elisa Silva 2011-2012.

14 For example, Petare, the largest *barrio* in Caracas, Venezuela has 0.1 m^2 per inhabitant of public space, while the rest to the city has 1.1 m^2 per capita. These figures are the result of a research by Daniel Belandria, while serving as Director of Public Works in the Sucre Municipality of Caracas in 2012.

15 This research includes 23 projects.

When reviewing those examples, public space making emerges as a pretext to foment and develop social cohesion among community members, but also between citizens of different neighborhoods. Public space serves the specific community it is inserted in but is also able to receive foreign visitors. Its role as an urban integrator extends beyond attenuating physical limits between communities, to work as a potent tool in the construction of cities and citizens. Analytical maps used throughout this study, demonstrate the spatial effects public spaces have on their surroundings and reveal their effectiveness in integrating territories.

Additionally, public space production requires significantly less investment than social housing, which is currently the most prevalent social urban intervention. Hence, local authorities and communities could stand significant gains by recognizing the strategic value public space represents in terms of its viability, low cost and effectiveness in opening arteries that connect diverse segments of the city. To that end, this study collects and analyzes existing public space projects built over the past two decades in spontaneous settlements of Latin America, to identify concrete formal, social and financial strategies that could be used to significantly increase their agency in urban territories.

Among the selected projects, many came up with innovative ways to create public space by building this critical element in larger urban infrastructure, environmental remediation, or sanitation improvement projects. A few were the result of more conventional approaches associated with new buildings or pavement projects. And lastly, some public spaces emerged from the occurrence of an activity or program that altered the way a place was perceived and used. In the selected cases, the primary concern was not design, at least not in the most conventional sense of its role in professional work. Their merit lies instead in the fact that the projects were able to effectively justify an economic and community investment in public space, while responding to the implicit social challenges associated with their implementation. The creative design approaches seen here demonstrate that it is possible to realize projects that appear to go against the grain of social, bureaucratic, logistical, or purely programmatic considerations that tend to obstruct initiatives. As such, they may serve as exemplars for the design of other infrastructure, preservation and sanitation projects in communities throughout Latin America and beyond.[16]

The selection of projects responds to three main criteria. The first is that they represent a variety of conceptual approaches toward public space production and financing, with two or more examples of each strategy.[17] The second is that they illustrate the range of existing financial approaches to fund public space production projects: municipal or state funds, private funding, foundations and public-private partnerships. The third criterium is that they have been applied in a variety of cities and regions in Latin America: the projects proceed from cities in eight countries. In presenting and analyzing them together, our intention is to cover a wide spectrum of approaches to the problem, in the hopes that this might make it easier for interested audiences to find examples that suit their local context both in physical and financial terms.

16 The projects featured in this publication were mostly identified through visits to spontaneous settlement improvement project in five Latin American cities by the author in 2012.

17 The cable car cases in the northeastern hills of Medellin and Complexo do Alemão in Rio de Janeiro, take advantage of a major public works project to build public space, while using different design strategies. The Botero Library and the Moravia Cultural Center, both in Medellin, integrate informal and formal city fabric in different ways.

URBAN INEQUALITY

Although we commonly associate inequity with an uneven distribution of income and economic opportunities, it can also be ascribed to the built environment. This is especially true in the developing world or the Global South, where it is conspicuously visible in the form of spontaneous settlements. The entrepreneurial and creative capabilities of spontaneous settlement inhabitants are often touted as evidence of self-improvement, but such a perspective fails to acknowledge the structural limitations imposed by their surroundings. We should be weary of such impromptu redemptive arguments – they tend to idealize conditions that are very trying and do not offer useful ways to deal with the effects of inequality.[18]

In fact, informal settlements reinforce inequality by perpetuating urban exclusion and difference. Access to public transportation, public services, as well as education, health, and human development opportunities, are radically different for people who live in a spontaneous settlement than for those who live in the planned segments of a city. In Caracas, for example, the population density within *barrios*, as they are called in Venezuela, is between three and four times greater than that of formal neighborhoods.[19] This density however is not compensated with higher endowments of public space and urban services. Furthermore, limited access to opportunities repeats cycles of poverty and creates a fertile ground for young men to choose life projects associated with criminal gangs, as a way to find the companionship they lack at home. Their female counterparts seek early pregnancies to be recognized as mothers and acquire status in their community.

Territorial inequality is widespread and affects a significant portion of the world population. Spontaneous settlements are endemic to city centers in the emerging world, where most of the urban population resides.[20] In some cases, such as Caracas, up to half of citizens live in spontaneous settlements,[21] while the number ascends to 60% in Mumbai, India, and 80% in some African cities.[22] According to the United Nations, since 2003 a sixth of the population,

18 The Tower of David project presented at the 2014 Venice Biennale by Urban Think Tank was awarded the Biennial's highest prize, the Lion Award. The project argued that it was a celebration of the community´s rebellious appropriation of an existing building which in turn, becomes a space to freely express entrepreneurial and cultural capabilities.

19 The population density of formal areas within the Baruta Municipality is 53 inhabitants / hectare. Density in spontaneous settlements is much greater, averaging 375 inhabitants / hectare.

20 World Bank. http://data.worldbank.org (accessed January 7, 2018).

21 Elisa Silva et al., CABA: *Cartografía de los barrios de Caracas 1966-2014* (Caracas, Fundación Espacio, 2015), 181.

22 Aaron Maasho, "Ethiopia 80% of urban population live in slums in Ethiopia." *Sapa-AFP* January 18, 2017. http://nazret.com/blog/index.php/2007/01/18/ethiopia_80_of_urban_population_live_in (accessed January 19, 2019).

one billion people live in informal settlements and they estimate the number will double by 2030.[23] The size of this figure is startling. How has this challenge been approached?

The discourse of modern architecture and urban design has championed social housing to mitigate social inequality and continues to do so.[24] Although a well-intentioned approach, it alone does not help improve urban differences and inequality. Crucial to the reduction of inequality is the degree of integration that can be forged between diverse social segments, and this depends on a set of factors that include geographical proximity, access to amenities and opportunities for citizens. Henri Lefebvre was already prescribing these factors as he observed emerging *bidonvilles* in the Paris banlieues of 1968.[25]

Fortunately, some cities in Latin America, including Rio de Janeiro, Medellín, Bogotá and Guayaquil, have experienced more than two decades of sustained experiences in informal settlement improvement. They have created a concrete spectrum of projects that begin to mitigate and even dissolve territorial differences. Although the approaches among cities and within cities vary, one common denominator is that projects that include components of public space have had very notable effects in advancing urban integration.

SOCIAL HOUSING AND INEQUALITY

After many decades of social housing production, both in Latin America and in the rest of the world, we have not really seen significant progress in reducing urban inequality. Early modern architecture examples include the residential project El Silencio, built in 1943, and the 23 de Enero, built in 1958, both in Caracas and designed by Carlos Raul Villanueva; Mario Pani's Centro Urbano Miguel Alemán, in Mexico City, built in 1948; and Residencia San Felipe in Lima, Peru, designed by Enrique Ciriani and others, built in 1962-69. Later iterations of the social housing agenda evolved toward the progressive urbanism model of *Sites and Services* advanced by John Turner and John Habraken,, and the progressive housing approach of Previ Lima. The *Elemental Chile* project essentially continues this model with a more defined building progression, in some cases enclosing the extent to which the housing unit may grow.[26]

A time line elaborated by Supersudaca for a publication edited by Mariana Leguía is a visible record of all significant social housing projects in Latin America beginning in 1943, with the El Silencio project already mentioned as the first in this series, through 2010, with the Elemental project in Iquique, Chile.[27] Beyond this time line, over the course of the last decade, social housing efforts continue to focus on the unit itself, with little regard for their location, which tends to be in distant peripheral urban areas, where land is less expensive. Furthermore, units are built in mass, without the urban components that make a place livable.[28]

Why and how aren't these examples reducing urban inequality? The first and obvious answer is that they propose housing structures for empty lots, or sites where informal settlements have been razed; they are not conceived to mitigate the limitations of existing settlements. Yet, spontaneous settlements exist and are still growing, so how can such approaches continue

23 United Nations Population, 2015, http://www.unfpa.org/urbanization (accessed January 7, 2018).

24 In 2016, Alejandro Aravena received the Pritzker Prize for his contribution to social housing, and likewise B. J. Doshi was given the award in 2018 for the same reason.

25 Henri Lefebvre, *Writing on Cities* (Oxford: Blackwell Publishers, 1996).

26 Eric Mumford, *The CIAM Discourse on Urbanism, 1928-1960* (Cambridge: MIT Press, 2000); John Turner and R. Fichter (Eds.) *Freedom to build: Dweller control of the housing process*. (New York: Collier-Macmillan, 1972); Alejandro Aravena and Andrés Iacobelli, (2013).

27 Supersudaca, "A timeline of collective housing in Latin America" in Mariana Leguía (Ed.), "Latin America at the Crossroads" *AD Magazine* June 2011, 20-21.

28 This argument is supported by social housing developments visited by the author in Leon (Mexico), Guayaquil (Ecuador), and Caracas (Venezuela) between 2015 and 2018.

to be presented as mitigations of this form of territorial inequality, when they are situated in altogether different settings? Secondly, local authorities tend to simplify the structure of cities and conflate urbanism with housing. In this sense, Jordi Borja, a Catalan urban designer who has been involved in numerous urban renewal processes both in Europe and Latin America, states that from his experience "urban projects and other infrastructure projects tend to focus on a particular sector without maintaining a holistic urban vision. Priority is given to paving streets and building housing."[29] Thirdly, formal housing is not an economically viable response to address the magnitude of people living in spontaneous communities. And this, in and of itself, should be enough to question its appropriateness as an "official" strategy to address social needs.

In 2014, Mexico, despite enormous investments to increase the stock of homes between 2010 and 2014, reported a housing deficit of 9.7 million units, the equivalent of 40 million people, and roughly a third of its population.[30] There are no official reports on the current housing deficit in Venezuela. The Venezuelan Chamber of Construction estimates it was around 2.4 million homes in 2017, which is the equivalent of 9 million people, or 30% of the country's population.[31] Even though in both nations, we are considering roughly a third of the population, housing remains the most championed national strategy to address social inequality.

Mexico continues to be a strong supporter of the housing agenda, with social housing projects partially financed through subsidies from government agencies such as Conavi and Infonafit. This investment is consistently justified as a strategy to address poverty, with housing models designed by top Mexican architects.[32] Recently built social housing projects, partially funded by Conavi on the outskirts of Leon and Cancun, have strived to include "sustainable" strategies and technologies in each housing unit, but have not been conceived with urban integration or inclusion in mind.

In Venezuela, sustained focus on housing is driven by propaganda. The aspiration associated with formal homes has been used for political gains by government systems throughout Latin America and has most recently been practiced by the Venezuelan government with the massive housing initiative Gran Misión Vivienda Venezuela (GMVV) that took place between 2011 and 2016. Multifamily residential structures were built within formally urbanized areas for families displaced by natural disasters and landslides at no cost to them.[33] The aim, however, is not only to create a housing solution for homeless families, but also to project a political message that encourages political affiliation. The program has supposedly served 2 million families, although the Real Estate Chamber of Venezuela has only been able to document less than 8,000 apartments built in and around Caracas between 2011 and 2016.[34] The testimonies regarding the poor construction and faulty structures of buildings are widespread.[35] The choice

29 Jordi Borja, "Ciudades posibles, ciudades resistentes" Barcelona-Quito, September, 2016. The final version of the introduction is part of the publication *Ciudades para cambiar la vida: Una respuesta a Habitat 3*, coordinated by Jordi Borja, Fernando Carrión and Marcelo Corti.

30 SHF Sociedad Hipotecaria Federal, https://www.gob.mx/shf (accessed November 28, 2018).

31 The Venezuelan Chamber of Construction estimates the housing deficit is likely to have diminished due to massive emigration in recent years.

32 *Vivienda Infornavit, Instituto del Fondo Nacional de la Vivienda para los Trabajadores*, Third stage, volume1, number 1 (Mexico: Centro de Investigación para el Desarrollo Sostenible CIDS del Infonavit, 2016).

33 Gran Mision Vivienda Venezuela GMVV is a government program in Venezuela that has built mass housing projects throughout the country. The units are given to families for free. The project has been heavily criticized for its lack of consideration for urban services and public space provisions, threatening to further collapse already under-dimensioned public services.

34 Cámara Inmobiliaria de Venezuela, "Cámara Inmobiliaria de Venezuela: Cifras de viviendas anunciadas por el gobierno son irreales" November 15, 2016. http://www.camarainmobiliaria.org.ve/camara-inmobiliaria-de-venezuela-cifras-de-viviendas-anunciadas-por-el-gobierno-son-irreales/ (accessed January 15, 2019).

35 Both the Mexican and Venezuelan projects have been repeatedly denounced for their scandalous levels of corruption and the poor-quality of construction and services in the apartments.

of sites for projects has also been suspect. A recent GMVV housing project in Playa Grande, about 40 minutes from Caracas and near the coast, was designed and built by a Belarus building company, using mostly imported materials.[36] Ventilation was not considered, even though the climate is hot and humid. Most importantly, work opportunities in close vicinity are scarce and transportation to the capital city is costly and time consuming, making living in these homes inconvenient and expensive.

Both examples show that peripheral housing projects generate greater expenses over time, disproportionately affecting people with lower incomes, and although they operate under very different motivations, both buy into the same positivist discourse, and seem to confirm that the tool, in this case housing, represents the default approach to address underprivileged populations in many parts of the developing world. Nevertheless, when you look at cities through the lens of territorial inequality, such strategies turn out to be counterproductive, as they continue to define territory through internally homogenous, separate and distinct enclaves.

Other motivations have influenced local governments to pursue social housing. One has been to mitigate the further expansion of spontaneous settlements. Another has been to foment economic development by subsidizing a housing market for lower income populations, thereby creating jobs and investment opportunities. In Medellin, government subsidized social housing projects were used to contain the expansion of existing spontaneous settlements. Such was the case of the new neighborhoods at the end of the San Javier - Aurora cable car line, that consists of multistory housing buildings along the upper edge of existing spontaneous settlements. In Chile, the government intends to house the entire population in formal homes, which may seem ambitious but possible given the country´s higher per capita income and relatively lower levels of poverty in comparison to other parts of the region. The Elemental project uses government subsidies to build part of a home with better materials rather than constructing a complete house of lesser quality. Low-income families can access a better home with little upfront investment and benefit from the opportunity to progressively grow in the future according to their income and needs.[37] Chile's private sector plays a key role in making the program viable. Lending institutions are more willing to offer mortgages to future homeowners because of the projected value of the new home.[38] Both the Colombian and Chilean models have made concerted efforts to locate homes within inner city areas or near major transportation infrastructure in order to mitigate the burdens associated with housing in urban peripheries. However, these efforts only meet a small portion of the affordable housing demands and are often above the economic possibility of a sizable part of the population.

Strategies to finance and create affordable housing continue to be relevant for less economically critical segments of the population. However, there are only a few cases in the world where spontaneous settlement eradication through housing has been achieved. The case of Singapore, for example, which has been flaunted as one of the most successful models to follow, is indeed impressive, but also the unique product of an authoritarian regime that imposed financial discipline, practiced inhumane evictions and invested copious state funds in mass housing. These are hardly replicable conditions. Hence, other effective, financially accessible and more democratic approaches to mitigate the social exclusion of spontaneous settlements are warranted.

Ignoring the cost considerations of housing and the purchasing power of the population in demand of homes is essentially allowing spontaneous settlements to continue to grow, maintaining the status quo. It would mean that nothing has been gained from decades of

36 This information was obtained through interviews of workers during the project´s construction phase.

37 In the Chilean case, government public policy regarding housing is focused on providing formal housing for low-income citizens and razing slums. Because poverty levels are below 15% of the population this may be a plausible goal, however it is not a feasible strategy for other Latin American countries where a much larger percentage of the population lives in spontaneous settlements.

38 Fondo Nacional de Vivienda Fonvivienda en Colombia. https://www.fna.gov.co/vivienda

the evident failure in modern city planning to alleviate the flagrant inequality in cities. As new modern cities were being built in the fifties and sixties for the first time, the lack of experience and blind belief in progress had dreadful social and urban consequences. Anthropologist Lisa Peattie notes how modern planning was largely responsible for the propagation of spontaneous settlements, as city plans did not foresee nor accommodate the vast rural migration that new industries and investments were generating. They turned a blind eye to the informal urban phenomenon and naively believed it would disappear as development and economic prosperity continued to increase and spread to the entire population.[39]

RISK MITIGATION

Social housing approaches have also been considered either to relocate families living in high risk situations into new homes within the same community, or to replace precariously built homes with new formal ones. Projects often have to negotiate with tightly built areas, difficult topography and accessibility issues, which translates into smaller scale insertions and higher costs when compared to mass produced housing. The multistory housing structures that were built within the spontaneous settlement of Moravia and the *barrios* along the Juan Bobo Creek, on the northeastern hills of Medellín in the early 2000s, were created for families that needed to be relocated from high risk sites. Each building responds to the specific conditions of its location. The buildings are all the same, but their resolution at the ground level is site specific, which increases overall costs. A very different approach was pursued in the *Rancho por casa* program in Caracas in 2007, where existing homes were replaced with standard housing units distributed as a kit of parts to be assembled on site with skilled labor. The kit structure could not be easily adapted and was difficult to insert on the steep slopes typical of spontaneous settlements in Caracas. The recipients of these homes were required to demolish their existing home, flatten the ground plane and build retaining walls, generating new costs, in addition to paying for workers who could weld steel and erect the structure. Both approaches reveal the expense and challenges of building within existing spontaneous settlements. In the case of Medellin, the extra investment is justified by the need to relocate families and maintain social networks. In Caracas, however, the program is prescriptive and too narrowly focused on the housing unit. It also fails to address the overall environmental or urban conditions surrounding the homes.

IMPROVING EXISTING HOMES

Non-government housing initiatives have focused on helping inhabitants improve their existing homes. Swiss Contact in Bogota,[40] for example, teaches homeowners, builders and hardware store salespeople how to properly build structures that are earthquake resistant. Through a series of courses offered in nearby educational facilities, people become empowered to build safer homes. The initiative is practical and acknowledges that despite government social housing efforts, people continue to build their own homes to fulfill housing demands. In a similar effort, Fudep Venezuela, together with EPA, a hardware store, provided families with microcredits to finance home improvements.[41] These strategies effectively address problems and deficiencies associated with self-built homes. However, they are less attractive for government officials and politicians when compared to the visual impact and propagandistic potential of new social housing projects.

Despite the fact that housing demand continues to increase at a pace far greater than the rate of formal project construction and the availability of economic resources, the housing discourse continues to occupy the center of disciplinary discussions about what to do in the Global South. A new home does not mitigate existing urban exclusion, nor does it represent

39 Lisa Peattie, *The view from the barrio* (Ann Arbor: University of Michigan Press, 1970).

40 Swiss Contact. http://www.swisscontact.org

41 Fudep Venezuela, Fomento para el Desarrollo Popular. http://www.fudep.org

a relevant offer for people who may have a perfectly functional home that just happens to be in a spontaneous settlement. The limitations of such a home are not necessarily associated with the housing structure itself, but have more to do, as we have said, with its exclusion from urban dynamics: access to schools, health centers, jobs and public space. This exclusion is not only physical, it can be detected as well in public policies and urban investments. Funds for public works such as waste management and public services are not equitably allocated, nor are new facilities evenly distributed.

Many architects and urban designers interpret the housing challenge in terms of devising ways to reduce cost and increase access to more economic resources. Much effort is spent on the design and re-design of low-income prototype housing models using prefabricated structures, recycled or economic building materials, under the honest belief that if only the house could be built cheaply enough, demand across the world could be met.[42] This approach disregards the fact that spontaneous settlements are the outcome of a sustained deficit in affordable housing solutions, and that given the extent of their proliferation, the issue now requires mitigating existing conditions, arguably more so than designing formal housing. Innovative low-cost models often do not take the local nature of construction methods, materials and, most importantly, budgets into account. For example, designers presume that modern 3d printing technologies and $30.000 per unit are the fix for housing in the developing world. They fail to consider that such costs are several times greater than what low-income households can afford, that labor is relatively cheap and so prefabrication is actually more expensive than paying for local labor, not to mention the lost benefit to communities of construction jobs, and that the selection of appropriate materials is crucial to address particular climate conditions.[43]

For better or for worse, over the last decades self-built housing has proven to be the most viable and realistic way to mitigate the housing demand. Rapid urban growth in the developing world during the second half of the 20th century and what has advanced of the 21st has mostly occurred in the form of spontaneous settlements. Unfortunately, the theoretical research and practical applications of formal social housing has contributed little if anything toward addressing the real and palpable territorial inequalities of informal urban environments.

Self-built homes represent an option for people who, not having the resources to buy a formal home, can invest their earnings over months and years into a progressively built structure. To be sure, the quality of the construction may be suspect, but it does represent an economically viable solution to their need for shelter. Formal markets have not understood the economic possibilities of this large population segment, nor have they been able to tap into the resources people are able to invest in homes over longer periods of time. The sum of thousands of families in this very same predicament, building their own home over decades, explains how vast territories of spontaneous settlements in cities have emerged.

The social challenges associated with these territories, which include poverty, inadequate access to public services and scant opportunities for self-development, have been identified in critical studies as early as the eighties, for example in the work of Lisa Peattie mentioned previously. This alternative urban story unfolded concurrently with modern urbanization, which did not fully recognize or understand the needs of less affluent segments of society who sought employment in prosperous urban centers. As new modern cities were being designed, such as Ciudad Guayana in Venezuela, the only acknowledgment came in the form of low-income

42 In the aftermath of the Haiti 2000 earthquake, many architects responded with housing proposals. One of them, was put forth by architect Andres Duany, where he proposes using fiberglass and resin to created lightweight modular homes. Such materials are inaccessible in countries like Haiti, nor are they appropriate for the hot and humid climate. Jackie Creaven, "A Low-Cost Housing solution for Haiti Earthquake Victims." *ThroughtCo* June 09, 2018.

43 Rosie Fitzmaurice, "An Italian architect has designed an eco-friendly flat pack home that costs £25,000 and only takes 6 hours to build." *Business Insider UK.* November 23, 2017. This sum of money makes the project too costly for most of the developing world.

housing designed for working class families.[44] Single and multi-family housing, such as the "Minimal Housing Unit for Workers" by Josep Lluis Sert in Tumaco, Colombia (1948), were commendable for their attention to human scale, climate and possible replicability.[45] However, they were neither planned nor funded at the scale and urgency required. Similarly, throughout the following decades, as spontaneous settlements continued to grow, the political and professional response largely negated the phenomenon, and stood firmly by its promotion of infrastructure, housing and "slum-eradication".[46]

No doubt, the vast discord between cost, speed, scale and demand was not internalized as an alert to explore other alternatives. Social housing approaches pursued today, more than a half century later, continue to exhibit remnants of denial. Sheer number crunching reveals that the investment required to relocate the one billion people worldwide living in spontaneous settlements is neither economically nor logistically feasible.[47] Furthermore, housing, as we have mentioned all along, does not address the existing territorial inequality prevalent in cities. If and when we understand that the goal of urban social investment should be oriented to address inequality, we find there is a blatant dearth of adequate and viable strategies.

ALTERNATIVE APPROACHES TO HOUSING

It wasn't until the late seventies and early eighties that alternative approaches to housing started to be considered. *Sites and Services* in the seventies recognized people's capability to build homes for themselves. The approach subsequently focused on demarcating plots and streets and providing access to service infrastructure. For example, the INAVI (National Housing Institute), in Venezuela, led urban strategies that responded to the demands of rapid migration, namely the need to work quickly with scarce resources.

During the eighties, in different cities in Venezuela, several neighborhoods were conceived as part of the Ley Orgánica de Ordenación Urbanistica (Law for structuring neighborhoods).[48] This urbanization method was later denominated "urbanismo progresivo", which translates as urbanism developed over time. Urban planners traced circulation corridors for streets and services that were projected onto sites allocated for new housing. Individuals could begin building their homes while other aspects of the urban plan were simultaneously being constructed. This way the urgency associated with the housing demand was better met and people could contribute to the realization of new neighborhoods with their own work as equity. The understanding was that paved roads, sidewalks, parks and public facilities would also be incorporated in future phases, as resources became available. The strategy produced

44 Ciudad Guayana was officially founded in 1961 by the unification of two preexisting settlements: Puerto Ordaz and San Felix. It was designed by the Harvard MIT Joint Center for Urban Studies to accommodate the professionals and workers who would join the developing iron, steel and aluminum industrial sector. Power was to be supplied locally and nationally by the Guri Dam, a hydroelectric plant that was funded through the World Bank as part of an aid package. Josep Lluis Sert designed some of the housing models for workers.

45 Josep Lluis Sert and the Town and Planning Associates (TPA) designed housing neighborhoods for workers between 1943 and 1953 for several cities In Latin America, including Lima (Peru), Ciudad de los Motores (Brasil), Chimbote, Medellín, Cali, and Bogota (Colombia). CIAM Collection Francis Loeb Library, Harvard University Folder: E003 and Doris Tarchópolus, "La Unidad Vecinal: Objeto de investigación de Josep Lluis Sert." Doctoral Thesis research for the Department of Urbanism and Land Use Planning at the Universidad Polítecnica Cataluña.

46 In Venezuela, the administration of Marcos Pérez Jiménez (1952- 1958) is remembered for its enactment of the "War against the slums" (Guerra contra el barrio), where homes were razed to make way for new multi-family social housing such as 23 de Enero. This approach was maintained as the government´s official stance regarding spontaneous settlements all the way through the end of Carlos Andrés Pérez' administration, in 1993.

47 UN-Habitat, *The challenge of the slums: Global report on human settlements. Nairobi: United Nations Human Settlements Programme* (Nairobi, 2003), quoted by M. Lombard, "Constructing ordinary places: Place-making in urban informal settlements in Mexico." *Progress in Planning* volume 94, November 2014, 94 (2014), 1-53. http://dx.doi.org/10.1016/j.progress.2013.05.003 (accessed September 30 , 2018).

48 Ley Orgánica de Ordenación Urbanistica. *Gaceta Oficial* N. 33.868, December 16, 1987.

well-configured urban structures that were adjusted to the economic possibilities of low-income population segments. The neighborhoods remain thriving and integrated areas of cities.

More recently, David Gouverneur, in his book *Planning and Design for Future Informal Settlements: Shaping the Self-Constructed City* has taken these precedents and synthesized them into a series of instructions that acknowledge the human resource and capability present in the population.[49] Therefore, houses are self-built in previously defined areas, and space for future needs, such as public services, amenities, roadways and public space is reserved and blocked off. One of the model's virtues is that it contemplates a more holistic approach toward building neighborhoods and represents a more economically accessible alternative to building social housing. As a model for urban growth it is premised on the availability of undeveloped land and tacitly endorses the expansion of existing urban footprints, which is negatively associated with urban sprawl.

Other non-housing approaches to consider are interventions and improvements within existing spontaneous settlements. They have mostly focused on new infrastructure and services, implemented in a localized and segmented manner, to provide services such as public transportation, access to potable water, sewage collection, waste management, and/or risk mitigation against natural disasters. In the case of transportation, the challenge has been to connect outlying perimeter areas, where spontaneous settlements are often located, to the inner city, where inhabitants work, go to school, play or enjoy cultural activities. City governments have gradually been able to extend existing transportation networks beyond the formal city edge. However, new roadways for bus routes, bus stops and intermodal stations require space that can sometimes only be secured by restructuring dense conditions, razing homes and relocating families.

Likewise, bringing water to spontaneous settlements, collecting sewage and managing rainwater runoff require considerable investment and alterations in the urban fabric. Because of this complexity and cost, only the most objective and unquestionably necessary projects work their way through the social and economic intricacies of spontaneous settlement projects. In fact, water related services have seen remarkable progress in Latin American, with estimates that indicate 95% of the population has access to running water, and 90% of homes have formal sewage connections.[50] Furthermore, proper sewage collection not only benefits inhabitants, but also helps decontaminate creeks and rainwater drainage channels that in turn contribute to restore urban rivers and lakes. Reaching universal service coverage for water and sewage continues to be a shared goal among most local governments.

Improved waste management and environmental remediation have also been the focus of projects in spontaneous settlements. Conventional garbage trucks cannot enter the narrow roads of settlements, which results in inadequate waste disposal practices such as clandestine dumps and waste burning. There is an opportunity to go beyond conventional waste management practices, and consider waste as a resource for other productive activities, which can even generate employment and income. The NGO Ciudad Saludable, in Peru, has helped municipal governments and communities find creative ways to implement localized waste management and recycling programs. They have been very successful in engaging communities and instilling a greater sense of self-worth among inhabitants as they enjoy healthier and cleaner environments.[51] When necessary, they have introduced motorcycles and vehicles that fit the narrow corridors or climb steep slopes.

Risk management projects in spontaneous settlements are in high demand. Ecologically sensitive land deemed inadequate for building was not considered for development in early

49 David Gouverneur, *Diseño de los nuevos asentamientos informales* (Bogotá: Ediciones Unisalle, 2016).

50 CAF, *Equidad e inclusión social en América Latina: acceso universal al agua y el saneamiento* (Bogotá: CAF, 2013).

51 CAF, *Casos emblemáticos de desarrollo urbano* (Caracas: CAF, 2015), 12. http://scioteca.caf.com/handle/123456789/779). Ciudad Saludable. www.ciudadsaludable.org (accessed January 7, 2018).

land-use plans. However, over time, the absence of enforcement and the proximity of unbuilt sites to existing services, made them susceptible to informal occupation resulting from rapid rural-urban migration and its related housing pressures. Today, numerous settlements have been built on highly vulnerable land, with severe exposure to natural disasters. Risk management measures oriented toward reducing the susceptibility of these populations require structural interventions, such as the relocation of families living in homes subject to floods or landslides, to alternative housing in safer areas of the city. Preventive relocations, however, are often met with resistance on the part of the community and require extensive social support and prolonged transition periods.[52] Unfortunately, in most instances, such projects take place after a disaster has already occurred. Local officials are then compelled to bring solutions to the afflicted, and families face their situation with resignation, even if it entails relocation.

A challenge to overcome is the tendency to formulate isolated interventions for specific services or risk mitigation, which is largely a reflection of sectored organization structures in local and national governments. Different departments manage housing, public works, transportation, water and sanitation, and each has their own budget, director and staff. This structure does not encourage holistic projects that include several urban components and limits the likelihood of formulating comprehensive urban projects. Hence, opportunities are missed to pool resources and achieve more ambitious results.

SPONTANEOUS SETTLEMENT UPGRADING

In Latin America, spontaneous settlement improvement and upgrading began in earnest in the late eighties. The UNDP, UN Habitat and the World Bank advanced the *Programa de Gestión Urbana PGU* (Urban Management Program) in 1986, effectively shifting investment strategies from housing subsidies to transformations of existing spontaneous settlements.[53] The funds were to be used specifically to establish development institutions and promote physical-territorial, environmental and social transformation processes within spontaneous settlements. It was implemented in Brazil, Colombia and Venezuela. In Rio de Janeiro, the program *Favela-Bairro* benefited 73 communities through educational infrastructure investments and social programs.[54] In Venezuela, the initiative took on the form of the *Plan de Habilitación Física de Barrios* (Physical Habilitation Plan for Informal Settlements) in 1996, which created a replicable methodology that prioritized community organization, financial transparency, services and accessibility. In Colombia the *Programa de Mejoramiento de Barrios Sub Normales en Medellin* PRIMED (Sub Normal Settlement Improvement Program in Medellin) developed a comprehensive methodology that benefited 70 peripheral districts. In addition to physical improvements it included a strong social component that evolved into the *Proyectos Urbanos Integrales PUI* (Integral Urban Projects) in the period between 2004 and 2007.[55] Projects and interventions in all three countries and elsewhere have centered on increasing access to water and sanitation, as well as providing, through coordinated efforts, access to legal land tenure, risk management, substitution housing and improved mobility. More than two decades of accumulated practical experiences in these areas have produced valuable knowledge that warrants being analyzed and evaluated to further advance the ideas and procedures of spontaneous settlement improvement.

52 The Juan Bobo Creek project in Medellin relocated families into ten nearby multifamily housing buildings between 2008 and 2011. Alejandro Echeverri and Francisco Orsini, "Informality and Social Urbanism in Medellin" in *Medellin Environment, Urbanism and Society*, 2008, 148. https://pdfs.semanticschoalar.org/0fcb/410c512f443d7455c461bbc-7c560849ef0a5.pdf (accessed January 5, 2018).

53 Silva and Vaggione, 20.

54 Ibid.

55 Ibid., 21.

To that end, between February and December 2012 the author visited over 40 spontaneous settlements in 6 Latin American cities.[56] The documented projects comprised public libraries, cultural institutions, children day care centers, schools, sports facilities, public transportation, waterfront infrastructure, housing and pavement projects. Communities in which the projected intervention included some form of public space gained much more than square meters of open recreation and leisure space: public space projects noticeably created a sense of place. They effectively transformed a once non-defined, non-specific area into a recognized place, identified by inhabitants as a common destination in their community, and present in their daily endeavors. Furthermore, public space in spontaneous settlements motivated changes in the perception of neighbors, who began to see themselves reflected in their own civic spaces as citizens of a complete city.

A PUBLIC SPACE APPROACH TO SPONTANEOUS SETTLEMENT IMPROVEMENT

Jane Jacobs, Christopher Alexander and Jan Gehl have defended the notion that people are the core of cities, and that urban design must consider the human scale as paramount. In the sixties, city planning practices had become overwhelmingly centered on services, traffic flow, market forces and logistical processes, while neglecting people's more quotidian needs. As advocates of a better quality of life for people living in cities, Jacobs and Alexander argued that not enough attention was being given to the human dimension of urban life. Building on that premise, they contributed valuable scholarship toward observing, measuring and justifying the design of cities from the user´s perspective. Gehl noted, for example, how medieval cities grew organically and embedded the human dimension in their scale, in contrast to modern large-scale urban growth which is sized for vehicles and service systems.[57] The resulting body of knowledge consistently pointed to the benefits and value of public space in cities and has served to encourage numerous urban regeneration projects throughout the world. The argument is that public space increases livelihood, economic productivity, and creates more competitive conditions vis-a-vis similar cities.[58] Distinctive attributes ascribed to public space such as flexibility, accessibility, entertainment, recreation and social inclusion, ostensibly make it the most plural dimension of urban space. It contributes to a culture of city enjoyment where citizens and visitors participate and take advantage of their membership in civic life.

By the same token, when public space is produced inside a spontaneous settlement all of the value and connotations of this unique civic expression can be accessed and enjoyed both by the community and the public at large. Public space becomes impregnated with activity, it evokes livelihood, and promotes mutual recognition, which has the fortunate side effects of increasing the perception of safety and discouraging violence. It also acts as a homogenizing agent that equates elements of spontaneous settlements with elements of the rest of the city. Henri Lefebvre, known for his seminal works *The Production of Space* and *The Right to the City*, suggests that the periphery, including spontaneous settlements, could be "homogenized" to increase its degree of inclusion.[59] A visual and phenomenological transference between formal and informal urban areas could be understood as a form of urban integration. Public space is a potential equalizer of conditions that liken a *here* and a *there* in a heterogeneous city. Comparable urban conditions in different spaces may ultimately reduce the tendency to adopt binary definitions of formal and informal areas and enable settlement inhabitants to enjoy equal access to the urban dynamics offered in any other part of the city, including its most well-off, historic and central areas.

56 Travel and research were funded by the Wheelwright Fellowship of Harvard University, 2011.

57 Jahn Gehl and B. Svarre, *How to Study Public Life* (Washington: Island Press, 2013).

58 The city most associated with this urban competitive strategy is Barcelona (Spain), which in 1992, in preparation for the summer Olympics, transformed itself into a popular destination as well as an attractive place to live.

59 Henri Lefebvre, *The Production of Space* (Oxford: Blackwell, 1991), 373 and "The right to the city" in Eleonore Kofman, *Writings on cities* (Cambridge, Massachusetts: Wiley-Blackwell, 1968).

The *Right to the City* has steadily gained ground and become part of the United Nations Habitat III's 2016 New Urban Agenda. Its definition is based on the right to enjoy the economic, social, cultural and productive opportunities cities offer, for all urban inhabitants, both legal and illegal.[60] Inclusion and equality are expressed through access to health, personal development opportunities, personal security and overall well-being. Spontaneous settlements, however, tend to register territorial differences that structure exclusion and inequality. Extending the right to the city to all inhabitants goes beyond previous spontaneous settlement upgrading concepts.[61] In other words, improving existing local conditions is not enough; transformation efforts must also integrate the social and physical dimension of spontaneous settlement into urban dynamics. Weaving together, connecting territories and leveling their differences are strategies that advance integration. Public space is particularly suited to both connect parts of the city and diminish the perception of difference. Empirical evidence shows that the production of public spaces in spontaneous settlements is an effective contributor to increase social inclusion and urban integration.[62] Consequently, public space within all parts of the city should be understood as a human right: the right to enjoy and participate in the positive dynamics urban life offers.

60 New Urban Agenda, United Nations Habitat 2016.

61 CAF and UN-Habitat, *Construcción de ciudades más equitativas* (Bogotá: CAF, 2014), 20.

62 This evidence will be explained in the following chapter.

TERRITORIALLY STRUCTURED INEQUALITY

The fact that spontaneous settlements are the urban manifestation of poverty and inequality has been largely documented by international urban authorities such as UN Habitat, especially since the Istanbul Habitat II conference in 1996. "Increased spread of informal settlements, [...] in low- and middle-income nations of the Global South is nothing less than the physical and spatial manifestations of urban poverty and intra-city inequality."[63] This is especially true in cities of Latin American, one of the most unequal regions in the world.[64] Urban inequality is not solely a matter of income distribution; it is also deeply associated with territorial conditions that structure inequality into everyday life. For example, a person living in a peripheral spontaneous settlement with no access to affordable public transportation, incurs greater expense to move, which reduces potential work opportunities. Another issue is the time invested in moving: a person that spends two hours to go from home to work and back will have lost four hours that could have been spent in more productive and beneficial ways. Likewise, lack of access or difficult access to recreational spaces, inadequate services and insufficient infrastructure limits people´s ability to enjoy the potential advantages city life offers. "The absence of spatial equidistance in terms of access to opportunities, goods and services, hinders human development and the productive capability of society. A context where spatial gaps persist over time generates structural conditions for inequality."[65]

Furthermore, urban inequality has resulted in evident threats to the livelihood of all citizens, as social unease, lack of safety and hindered productivity are direct consequences that affect urban dynamics beyond the territorial confines of spontaneous settlements. Addressing inequality requires a holistic approach that considers not only the physical disparity but also, more importantly, its social implications. Advocacy for social justice and equality is reason enough to support remedial actions. Besides, physical interventions to ameliorate the built environment are also an opportunity to improve the livelihood of all citizens and increase economic prosperity.

Key conditions play a major role in increasing inclusion in urban areas. In that sense, a recent publication by CAF development bank of Latin America argues that public policy should focus on four main areas of investment:[66]

63 UN-Habitat. (2003), quoted by M. Lombard, 11. http://dx.doi.org/10.1016/j.progress.2013.05.003 (accessed September 30, 2018).

64 CAF and UN Habitat, (2014), 30. Income inequality is measured by the Gini Index which was 0.483 for Latin America and the Caribbean in 2008.

65 Silva and Vaggione, 22.

66 Ibid.

1. Improve connectivity and access to public transportation networks,
2. Increase education and training to better prepare individuals for existing jobs,
3. Improve coordination among public services to implement inclusion programs,
4. Guarantee ample access to quality public spaces to improve social cohesion.

This last point addresses the fact that levels of personal safety, civic responsibility and mutual tolerance improve with well-integrated public space. Parks, children playgrounds and plazas are however, notoriously scarce in spontaneous settlements. Creating public spaces in these environments and providing access to them could encourage civic behaviors and activities that blur boundaries and invite participation across all urban sectors.

SCARCE PUBLIC SPACE IN SPONTANEOUS SETTLEMENTS

Spontaneous settlements grow organically; they are the result of numerous individual builders trying to meet the spatial needs of their immediate family. For decades, as settlements grew and became denser, no one was thinking about common areas such as walkways, roads, public space or public amenities, let alone planning for them. Their presence is therefore typically limited, especially in settlements established over complex landforms. The urban fabric they weave is the sum of individually conceived habitable interior spaces that respond to topography and proximity. This means that space outside the home is a remainder: it is not considered as a space in and of itself, and is, therefore susceptible to further appropriations by builders making annexes to existing homes or by new inhabitants looking for their own private space. Only the minimal width for walkways and staircases is left unclaimed as a tacit acknowledgement of the need for communication and access. There is little understanding of what constitutes the public domain. In fact, quotidian urban elements such as sidewalks, roads, gardens, plazas, parks and playgrounds are not part of the urban language of spontaneous settlements.

Exceptions do exist to this short-sighted urban growth pattern: they have been the result of fortuitous relationships with nearby protected territories or the few instances where community organization led to an agreement to reserve spaces for future common needs, such as schools, ambulatories or public spaces. Examples include the ball fields that Pablo Escobar financed and built in the spontaneous settlements of Medellin, during the eighties, when they were less densely populated. Spontaneous settlements, such as the *favela* Maré, in Rio de Janeiro, has a football field inserted within its tight urban fabric: the houses respected the edges, creating a unified line of facades on all four sides of the field.[67] Such examples are of course few and far between. They do prove, however, the unique value and character these communities acquire with the simple presence of an open public space in their midst.

As time passes, spontaneous settlements become denser with fewer opportunities for open unclaimed space to be adapted into public space. Inhabitants invest their earnings in materials for the continued construction of their homes. They build vertically in order to accommodate married children, elderly parents and other relatives. This tendency accounts for the density increase observed in *barrios*, often more than twice that of "formal" areas in the city.[68] As the population grows, the public space per capita ratio decreases. On average spontaneous settlements tend to have less than 0,1 m^2 per inhabitant, which is 100 times less than the amount of public space prescribed by the World Health Organization WHO (10 m^2/ inhabitant).[69] This data not only registers an inherently discriminating condition between formal and

67 "Los estadios de las favelas de Río de Janeiro, la cara b del mundial de Fútbol de Brasil 2014," *Idealista News* June 12, 2014. https://www.idealista.com/news/inmobiliario/internacional/2014/06/12/728995-los-estadios-de-las-favelas-de-rio-de-janeiro-la-cara-b-del-mundial-de-futbol (accessed November 3, 2018).

68 Elisa Silva et al., CABA: *Cartografía de los barrios de Caracas 1966-2014* (Caracas, Fundación Espacio, 2015).

69 Countless publications, articles and presentations use this index and attribute it to the WHO. The WHO however does not have a registered publication with this recommendation; it is in fact an urban myth. However, comparisons can be made with cities considered to have a desirable supply of public space.

informal city segments, but also represents a perceptual limitation since spontaneous settlement inhabitants, who do not have the opportunity to experience and recognize the value of public space in their quotidian lives, are not likely to feel a need for it, much less assume stewardship for the public domain. Unacquainted with the benefits access to quality public spaces could have on their lifestyle, spontaneous settlement inhabitants neither desire nor see the need for such projects.[70]

Public space is a program that is difficult to sell to communities, since its perceived value depends on people´s familiarity and previous experience with it. Government entities and private NGOs are challenged to justify allocating funds to an element that is considered of secondary importance compared to access to potable water, public transportation and risk management. From a physical perspective, it is also very difficult and expensive to build public infrastructure in an established spontaneous settlement. Retroactive interventions necessarily alter the structure of the urban fabric, requiring partial or complete demolitions. This not only entails a monetary cost but may also affect peoples' homes, perhaps even require their relocation, generating a social stress in addition to the cost of a new home. The result is that projects have rarely been formulated with the sole purpose of creating public space. And yet, without its provision, the *barrio* lacks a recognizable neighborhood center. In those cases, the notion of a center is usually supplanted by the amenities and services located along a settlement´s edges, where it meets the formal segments of the city.[71] As we have seen, the absence of public space is an aspect that clearly differentiates the civic dimension of spontaneous settlements from planed areas of the city. Reversing this tendency and decreasing territorial differences implies overcoming financial, physical and social challenges and identifying approaches that allow the production of public space in those settlements to become more commonplace.

PUBLIC SPACE AND URBAN INTEGRATION

The examples presented in this research support arguments for public spaces as urban integrators that attenuate and weaken urban physical boundaries; they even integrate sectors of the city typically considered as opposites. At the same time, they require significantly less financial investment than housing projects. Public space within spontaneous settlements also represents a common ground that can foster social cohesion among different citizens; in other words, among urban inhabitants of different areas. Settlements are typically read as private enclaves where outsiders feel very self-conscious. Open public space allows visitors from the rest of the city as well as community members to share a common space.

The work of architects Flavio Jánchez, Jaime Hernández and Melanie Lombard presents arguments based on examples of public space in spontaneous settlements that stem from their own practices in Buenos Aires (Argentina), Bogota (Colombia) and Xalapa (Mexico), respectively. Their research presents a characterization of each community that includes socio-demographic information, site location maps, project descriptions and production processes. All practitioners coincide on three main ideas regarding public space making: the influence of social space on the construction of local identify; the importance of fostering the community's appropriation of space through participation; and an appreciation for the human scale readily present in the spatial morphology of spontaneous settlements. Moreover, they

70 In the Municipality of Sucre in Caracas, Venezuela, a program named *Espacios Sucre* focused on bringing pocket parks and playgrounds to spontaneous settlements. They successfully built nearly 30 public spaces over a 4-year period. Initially the communities met the program with skepticism. Discussion in meetings to review budget allocation tended to prioritize roads, safety, water access, but never included public space. After a few parks were built and neighbors saw the benefits they brought inhabitants, especially children, plazas and playgrounds began to appear and systematically increased in popularity at budget meetings each year. In other words, once the community had become familiar with the concept of public space, they were interested in petitioning for more of them to be built.

71 *Barrios* and *favelas* on steep slopes rarely have sufficient roads. Their most dynamic urban areas are concentrated along the perimeter access entries.

argue public space is strongly linked to urban integration and offer three conceptual spheres: *meaning*, *methods* and *language*.[72]

The notion of *meaning* associated with public space in spontaneous settlements can be understood from two perspectives: as an effective agent of urban integration, both internally and externally; and as a mirror of society. The first responds to a fundamental condition of spontaneous settlements, which is their inherent difference and segregation from the rest of the city. They are locations largely excluded from common conceptions of what is considered urban and loaded with the tensions produced by difference:

What is "different" is, to begin with, what is excluded: the edges of the city, shanty towns, the spaces of forbidden games, of guerrilla war, or war. Sooner or later, however, the existing center and the forces of homogenization must seek to absorb all such differences, and they will succeed if these retain a defensive posture and no counterattack is mounted from their side. In the latter event, centrality and normality will be tested to the limits of their power to integrate, to recuperate, or to destroy whatever has transgressed.[73]

Lefebvre suggests that the periphery's fate (at the time of his writings, "periphery" was a way of denoting spontaneous settlements outside of Paris,) is to become "homogenized" and that this constitutes a form of inclusion. He also explains that the perception of differences between *this space* and *that space* imbues them with meaning that is dependent on their physical location, since what is here is not the same as what is there. And yet, public spaces, in both inner and outer portions of the city, could potentially homogenize phenomenological and functional conditions that equate a here and a there, and associate similar experiences taking place in formal as well as in informal urban areas. For Jánchez, Hernández and Lombard public space operates as a normalizing force that can directly relate parts of the city: "urban design strategies need to integrate the settlement both internally and externally with the formal context of the city."[74] A public plaza in a spontaneous settlement can denote access to an urban amenity, enable activities and inspire a sense of belonging that correspond to the effects of public spaces in more central and planned areas of the city. Equal operations in contrasting city areas ultimately may serve to reduce long-lasting differences. And it so happens that imitation of formal city elements is already practiced by communities in spontaneous settlements. Hernández believes the formal language spontaneous settlement inhabitants adopt in their homes and on their facades reveals an underlying aspiration to emulate and borrow from dominant groups.[75] The desire to belong could also be capitalized and pursued through the design of parks and plazas. Public spaces within spontaneous settlements could be a way of expressing a community´s interest in being considered equally accessible and equally valuable parts of the city.

The second signifying aspect of public space is how it can function as a mirror of society. Space is not neutral. Unattended, leftover fragments of interstitial space within spontaneous settlements, often filled with traces of waste, are testimony of their unplanned origin, and reveal a disillusioning lack of interest on the part of the community. In contrast, when public spaces are communally invested, well-configured and cared for, they have the potential to

72 Such notions were developed earlier by Henri Lefebvre. Lefebvre, (1991).

73 Ibid.

74 Flavio Jánchez, *Public Space in the Fragmented City: Strategy for Socio-Physical Urban Intervention in Marginalized Communities* (Buenos Aires: Piedra Papel & Tijera, 2012), 5.

75 Jaime Hernández García, *Public Space in Informal Settlements: The Barrios of Bogotá* (Newcastle upon Tyne: Cambridge Scholars Publishing, 2013), 177.

uplift a community's sense of self-worth and dignity. They are part of the language that shapes a community's identity, much in the spirit of Charles Taylor's reflections on "The Politics of Recognition."[76] Art, gestures and love, are modes of expression that allow people to enter into dialogue with others. As the exchange develops in space, it is also determined by it. The effect common spaces have on the interaction between people should not be undervalued. Space is part of the conversation that ultimately defines how people shape their identity and sense of self-worth.

The exchange also adds content onto spaces. Public spaces in particular are containers for quotidian activities that become layered with stories and meaning. "A place is a space invested with meaning,"[77] it is a location where memories are progressively stored. Goodman defines place making as the aggregation of many discourses or stories over time.[78] The accumulation of projections each individual makes of himself in a frequented public space creates a record of reflections and builds a bond between the person and place. The ability of a public space, what Lefebvre calls social space, to stimulate self-recognition can be a mechanism for urban and social transformation: "place making is a process of appropriation of space to create a mirror of self."[79] When the reflection is positive, inhabitants gain a stronger self-image. In other words, the transformation of a once forgotten, unused pocket of space in a spontaneous settlement, into a thriving public space, allows people to see themselves in an improved environment, which ultimately changes their self-perception. What is noteworthy, in terms of urban integration, about this process of reflecting back and forth between space and community, is its potential to attract neighbors in nearby settlements. They too may come to desire and work to implement urban transformations that allow them to feel in dialogue with the city at large.

The second argument scholars use to promote the production of public space in spontaneous settlements has to do with *methods* of implementation and the potential to incorporate participation processes. Sharing a design experience, followed by negotiations associated with the use of a space creates value. The correlation between public space and urban integration should include this participatory dimension, where the contributions of neighbors in the design and construction processes are as important as the physical space itself, since they motivate a sense of appropriation. Participatory design processes have been around since the late eighties with methodologies such as open charrettes and urban design competitions.[80] More recently, they have been applied to public space making projects in Latin American spontaneous settlements. The results have been encouraging for their effectiveness in fomenting an intensified civic use of space.[81]

Lefebvre would argue that the participation of a community is essential for social space to forge a relationship with people. He offers a critical view on the making of social [public] space, in that it "is ultimately much more than a visual ordering of space: it has a mediating role that goes far beyond its formal or geometric character."[82] Social space is where members of a given society see themselves reflected, and this is especially true when they have actively participated in its production. In fact, Lefebvre argues that the potential of a public space to act as a mirror is predicated on the opportunity of neighbors to participate in its making.

76 Charles Taylor, "The Politics of Recognition" in *Multiculturalism: Examining the Politics of Recognition* (Princeton: Princeton University Press, 1994), 32-33.

77 T. Cresswell, *Place a short introduction* (Oxford: Blackwell Publishing, 2004), quoted by Lombard, 12.

78 R. Goodman, *After the planners* (Harmondsworth: Penguin, 1972), quoted by Lombard, 14.

79 J. Friedman, "Reflections on place and place-making in the cities of China," *International Journal of Urban and Regional Research* 31(2), 257-279, quoted by Lombard, 15.

80 The work of Midtown Atlanta Alliance, which conducted several community charrettes between 1996 and 2000 to design future urban transformations along Peachtree Street in Midtown Atlanta, is a good example of this.

81 Examples include the work of Rua Arquitettos in *favela* Maré in Rio de Janeiro, Enlace Arquitectura and Trazando Espacios in Venezuela, and Playspace in Villa Tranquila, Buenos Aires Argentina.

82 Lefebvre, 225.

Can a social group be expected to recognize itself in space merely because that space is held up before it like a mirror? Certainly not. The notion of appropriation implies far more and is far more exigent than the (highly speculative) thesis of a 'mirror-consciousness'.[83]

Lefebvre questions the idea that space alone is enough to motivate urban awareness in people. He prefers to believe it is the process of participation that allows the full potential of an effective social space to be attained. He goes on to state that "the transformation of society presupposes a collective ownership and management of space founded on the permanent participation of the 'interested parties', with their multiple, varied and even contradictory interests."[84]

Participatory methods in designing public space also have the potential to imbed educational processes within them. The opportunity for a community to rethink and formulate an engaged relationship with its surrounding environment stems from the motivation to improve it, and is enabled by newly acquired skills. Through the design process, the community learns how to formulate urban projects and how to resolve conflicting views through negotiation.[85] They also acknowledge their crucial role in motivating urban and social change within their community. The conventional notion that such matters are the sole responsibility of local authorities has caused communities to disengage from addressing pressing spatial and environmental matters. Conversely, increased stewardship for their surroundings and new public spaces has helped diminish the perception of insecurity and violence in communities, which is a key component toward fomenting better integrated cities. In essence, such stewardship is the expression of a *Right to the City,* as advanced by Henri Lefebvre in 1965 and paraphrased later by David Harvey.

The right to the city is far more than the individual liberty to access urban resources: it is a right to change ourselves by changing the city. It is, moreover, a common rather than an individual right since this transformation inevitably depends upon the exercise of a collective power to reshape the processes of urbanization. The freedom to make and remake our cities and ourselves is, I want to argue, one of the most precious yet most neglected of our human rights.[86]

The third argument regarding urban integration has to do with *language*. Words and common phrases used in the discourse of territorial inclusion paradoxically work to cement notions of difference and hierarchy. Language needs to discourage binary distinctions, such as formal-informal and legal-illegal, that reinforce the continued conceptual isolation of spontaneous settlements.[87] The purpose is not to negate the differences, but rather to question the pejorative and discriminating associations attached to those differences. Language has the potential to educate and build definitions on function-based nomenclature. Hence, the use of different words to identify spontaneous settlements, that acknowledges acceptance and a sense of belonging, could begin to shift awareness and motivate a change in the discourse. So, instead

83 Ibid, 417.

84 Ibid, 422.

85 *City Planting* is a program in Venezuela focused on producing public space in spontaneous settlements that is executed by Fudep Venezuela with funding from Citibank. Enlace Arquitectura was hired to design public spaces with the community. Between 2015 and 2018, public space interventions were implemented in 18 communities throughout the country.

86 David Harvey, "The Right to the City," *New Left Review II* (1953), 23–40.

87 M. Lombard, Making a place in the City: *Place-making in urban informal settlements in Mexico* (Unpublished PhD thesis) quoted in Lombard, 2013, 295 and Hernandez, 179.

of being seen as the disorderly, illegitimate, 'other' city, spontaneous settlements could be perceived as places in their own right, and part of the wider city.[88] Lombard believes the urban fabric of spontaneous settlements also reflects positive values, such as "their capacity to be as creative, diverse and distinctive as anywhere else in the city."[89] And yet these associations are not reflected in the words that characterize settlements. New words should be created to better serve contemporary interests in increasing social inclusion and advancing a more open, complete urban integration.

Older cities in Europe are frequently composed of different city fabrics that over time have shed their pejorative characterizations and become valued and even sought out for their distinctive identity. Jewish ghettoes, medieval city centers and modern periphery expansions have, at different moments, been associated with exclusion or class distinctions. Their urban fabrics are notoriously different in scale and morphology and yet they are fully integrated in terms of accessibility, amenities, public transportation and public space. When entering a spontaneous settlement, interruptions would ideally be minimized, allowing visitors to advance along designed corridors and boulevards, reaching common public spaces and accessing public amenities that are unique to the settlement, but inclusive and continuous with the rest of the city. Such urban operations have occurred in Medellin over the past couple of decades, as in the case of the interventions surrounding the San Javier Metro Cable Station, the San Javier Public Library, the San Javier High School, the Barrio Las Independencias escalator and cantilevered walkways along with designed parks, boulevards and playfields. Both tourists and locals are able to enjoy open and welcoming urban spaces with a sense of belonging and comfort. The design operations dilute differences by including recognizable urban elements. The neighborhood thus resists being amalgamated into one simplified notion of informality, and the impulse to linguistically differentiate it from what is seen in the rest of the city also diminishes. Both the impartial language of new urban elements and a renewed vocabulary to address informal urban contexts could have a significant impact on dissolving the pejorative connotations of spontaneous settlements.

The production of public space in spontaneous settlements has therefore been identified through empirical evidence as an effective way to integrate spontaneous settlements into the overall dynamics of a city for several reasons. First, public space in spontaneous settlements functions as a transformed urban context that acquires positive meaning and becomes a reflection of their inhabitant´s sense of self-worth, citizenship and identity. It can also be likened to spaces in more central and consolidated urban areas, which creates a perception of parity and equality. The process of making public space is also instrumental in offering people the opportunity to feel invested in the spaces they help design and build. Participatory design methodologies can incorporate educational activities that motivate inhabitants to become stewards of their surroundings, which in turn empower them to improve their environment in ways that go beyond the passive notions of citizenship practiced in the rest of the city. These advantages are reinforced with another component of urban integration, which is the revision of terminology, steering it away from the derogatory connotations associated with spontaneous settlements. Bringing public space interventions to spontaneous settlements represents an alternative approach that goes beyond improvement and diminishes the perception of borders, increases continuity and potentially creates better-integrated urban territories.

88 Lombard, 17.

89 Lombard, 47.

HOW MUCH PUBLIC SPACE IS NEEDED?

If creating public space in spontaneous settlements were embraced as an effective investment to increase social inclusion and better integrate Latin American cities, how much would have to be built? Quantifying this endeavor and defining a target scope would help optimize resource allocation and public policy. To begin with, public spaces are not as prevalent in Latin American cities as they are in other latitudes of the world. Because of their scarcity, the few that do exist are often heavily overused, and their deterioration exceeds maintenance budgets. Others are almost completely overlooked by people due to their lack of upkeep and poor integration with the surroundings. Urban growth in Latin American cities during the 20th century occurred at an accelerated pace, with little or no regard for planning. Public space was not considered essential and even deemed undesirable since unattended space risked being illegally occupied with informal housing. When compared to economically developable property, public space appeared to be an inefficient use of land.[90] The scarcity of public space means that people have few experiences or memories in them and therefore their relationship to parks and plazas is very tenuous. They are seldom perceived as important urban cultural elements.

Land in the public domain is often public precisely because it could not be used for other purposes, either because it was inappropriate for urbanization or considered too environmentally sensitive. Other undefined remnants of space, such as areas surrounding infrastructure and waterways, sites with adverse topography or residual spaces, are frequently fenced off and rendered "black holes" in the city. Transforming them into well connected, adequate public spaces remains challenging at best and a far cry from the ideal extension of areas for recreation and leisure cities should offer. Over the past two decades, cities in Latin America have gained awareness about the fact that public space is the only urban land use where all social classes are welcome.[91] Furthermore, statistics show that access to well-conditioned public space increases trust among social groups and improves personal safety.[92]

Cities in Latin America, however, are notorious for having low public space indexes: 1.1m^2 per inhabitant in Caracas; 3.64 m^2 in Medellin, and 3.7 m^2 in Santiago de Chile.[93] As a standard, sources will often cite 10 m^2 per inhabitant to reference a desired amount of public space.[94]

90 Silva and Vaggione, 61.

91 Ibid.

92 Julian Spector, "Another Reason to love Urban Green Space: It Fights Crime" *Citylab* April 13, 2016.

93 "Gran Santiago: estudio indica que hay 3,7 metros cuadrados de áreas verdes accesibles por persona" *Fundación Terram*. http://www.terram.cl/2017/05/gran-santiago-estudio-indica-que-hay-37-metros-cuadrados-de-areas-verdes-accesibles-por-persona/ (accessed November 24, 2018).
"Movilidad y espacio público en Medellín," Medellín Como Vamos. https://www.medellincomovamos.org/movilidad-y-espacio-p-blico/ (accessed November 24, 2018).

94 The exact origin of this indicator is unknown, but it is often attributed to the WHO World Health Organization. 10 m^2 of public space / person represents an average of several cities considered to have optimal access to public space.

Very few Latin American cities find themselves in this range, the exceptions being Quito which provides its citizens with 17.8 m^2 per inhabitant and Curitiba, which boasts 64.5 m^2 per person.[95] And yet, even when cities are fortunate enough to count on sufficient public space, it may not be accessible to all parts of the city. We find that the supply of public space is not uniformly distributed: it is often much closer to people living in "formal" areas of the city than to those living in "informal" ones. For example, a study conducted in 2013, revealed that in the entire territory of Petare, which is the largest spontaneous settlement in Caracas, there was scarcely 0.1 m^2 of public space per inhabitant, while the rest to the city has 1.1 m^2 per capita.[96] In other words, the supply of public space in Petare is ten times less than that of the rest of the city and 100 times less than the theoretically ideal amount. With a total population of 218,048 [97] living in a fairly dense informal urban environment, increasing the per capita amount of public space to meet the standard offered in the rest of the city would require approximately 196.243 m^2 or 20 hectares of new conditioned public space, which represents 4.0% of the settlement´s 709 hectares.

Coming to terms with the amount of public space needed is crucial, as it reveals the urgency in developing innovative and unconventional methods of space production that can overcome the challenge of creating open space where none exists. Spontaneous settlements have very different urban conditions which require alternative spatial approaches to the issue of public space. The location, size and distance of a settlement from urban centers also affect how dense it becomes. For example, well located informal communities that enjoy better access to services, and are ostensibly better integrated with the rest of the city, tend to become denser. On the contrary, those located in the periphery, where access to services is poor, tend to remain less dense.

Determining the scale and type of public space making strategy is therefore contingent upon the physical and social conditions of the settlement. Smaller spontaneous settlements, nestled within planned urban areas, benefit from the services and public spaces offered by the rest of the city. In these neighborhoods, smaller insertions of benches, plazas and children playgrounds would already represent a significant contribution to everyday life for their residents and would not require large investments. For activities that require more space such as playing basketball, strolling, or riding bicycles, people would use public facilities and parks in nearby neighborhoods, supporting a healthy exchange of space among communities. When considering larger settlements, however, often located in the city's outskirts and those with areas above 50 hectares, more ambitious and creative strategies are required.

Spontaneous settlement inhabitants tend to have limited experience with public space and see it as an obscure destination in the city or at best as an optional amenity. Hence, identifying the value it could bring to their own community remains part of the challenge to overcome. A starting point could be to identify and upgrade existing common spaces. Such improvements would require modest resources, and would not be met with opposition, since the spaces are already recognized by the community as public. This could help increase people´s interest in public spaces and convince skeptics that they are desirable and beneficial to the community. However, rescuing existing spaces alone is not enough to offset the severe public space deficit. It is not just a matter of doubling or tripling the present amount of public space. As indicated earlier in the statistics from Caracas, the deficit requires a ten fold increase. In the specific case of Petare Sur, the settlement extends over an area of 484 hectares and houses a population of 129.920 inhabitants.[98] The current stock of potential public spaces scarcely amounts to 9,413 m^2 or 9.4 hectares. (Fig. 1) If Petare Sur were to reach the standard of public

95 Matilda van den Bosch (Ed.), *Oxford Textbook of Nature and Public Health: The Role of Nature in Improving the health of a population* (Oxford: Oxford University Press, 2018).

96 Study conducted by architect Daniel Belandria at the Sucre Municipality in Caracas in 2012.

97 Silva (2015), 66.

98 Silva (2015), 92.

space offering of the formally disposed areas of the city, it would have to provide 129.920 m^2 of public space, i.e. one square meter per inhabitant; and 120,507 m^2 or 12.0 hectares of new parks and playgrounds would have to be built. In other words, in the case of Petare Sur, public space should be increased by a factor of twelve. Along the same lines, spontaneous settlements with dense populations of 300.000 or more inhabitants would need to produce 30 hectares of public space in order to offer at least 1 m^2 per person.

One approach that has already been used to produce large new extensions of public space has been to conflate the construction of parks, paths and walkways with the relocation of people living in high risk conditions in order to increase resilience against natural disasters. The removal of structurally unsound homes built over landfills, running creeks, or floodable land along the edges of waterways, can become an opportunity to convert the emptied site into recreational areas. On one hand, it ensures new settlers will not build homes there again, and on the other creates public space. Medellin and Guayaquil for example, have implemented projects along these lines; however, it is important to note those projects are socially complex and costly. Relocating families means covering the expense of new homes, overcoming the emotional hardship of moving, and slowly recovering the environmental conditions of the previously occupied land.

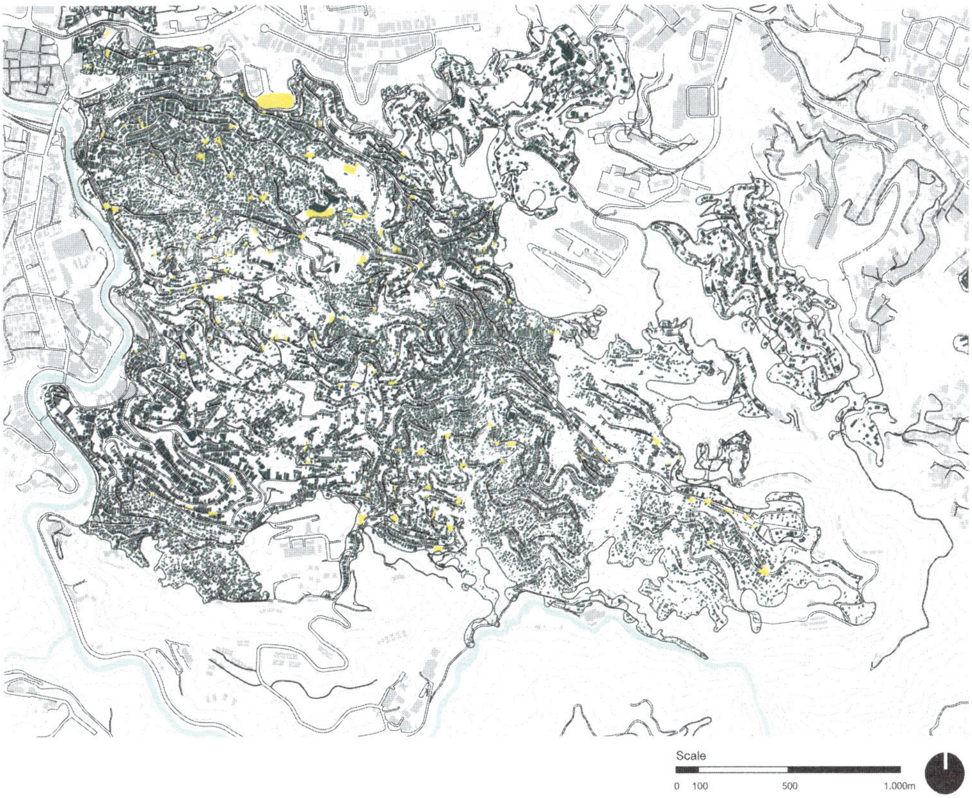

Fig. 1 Plan of Petare Sur, Caracas Venezuela maps existing public spaces or common areas in the barrio. They only add up to 0.94 hectares.

98 Silva (2015), 92.

Since 2000, Guayaquil has been progressively creating a linear park that extends over sev- 72
eral dozen kilometers along the Estero Salado, which is an estuary or saltwater canal. Much of the river´s edges were once invaded with self-built homes over precarious foundations of debris thrown into the estuary to gain land from the water. The mangroves that once lined the *estero* and maintained a lush animal habitat had disappeared and, in their wake, left a forgotten landscape, polluted with sewage and chemical waste, where scarcely any aquatic life remained. Since the risk factor associated with the built homes was high, given their unstable foundations, a municipal project was designed to address their relocation and properly channel sewage water away from the *estero*. The initiative also created an opportunity to restore natural habitat, increase urban resilience and create new public space in the form of a raised walkway along the water edge. The Estero Salado has become progressively cleaner. The linear park allows access to the river which in turn gives neighbors the opportunity to keep watch over what is released into the water, a way of policing themselves for improper waste and sewage disposal. It also helps prevent the construction of future illegal homes. Over time, the segments of linear parks have been connected into a vast network of bicycle paths and walkways that are used not only by neighbors, but also by Guayaquil citizens at large, thereby integrating the city along the river edge. This new park system is also partly responsible for the city´s increase in public space per capita from 1.0 m^2 to 7.9 m^2. Water sports such as rowing, are regularly practiced and the mangroves have returned along with renewed animal life.

The Moravia Ecological Park in Medellin has transformed a landfill into 45.18 hectares of public
park. It was once the city's waste dump. Waste pickers rummaged the open-air dump and 96
lived off of the material they selected and sold to recycling operations. The settlement slowly emerged as the waste-pickers built shacks and homes on site. Over time, it grew and spread across 45 hectares of wasteland, with a population of 37.000.[99] Since waste decomposes and is a very unstable ground for construction, the foundations of homes could collapse at any time. Additionally, gases and bacteria exposed inhabitants to grave health risks. The municipality in conjunction with the community formulated a project to relocate homes away from the landfill into new buildings in nearby sites and neighborhoods. The landfill was closed and a project to transform it into a park with playgrounds, planting and open space was designed. Beginning in 2004, the waste dump was progressively converted into an "ecological park." Approximately 4.000 houses built over the landfill were razed. Negotiations with each family required different agendas and agreements. 140 houses still remain with families that have resisted relocation, but in every other respect, the 9.8 hectares (98,593.95 m^2) of landfill have been converted into a public park over a period of 13 years. Productive vegetable and flower gardens, paths, benches, light posts and pavement have created a lively environment for neighbors. There are also two upcycled structures, a bus and a container, that serve as activity spaces and programmatic extensions of the nearby Moravia Cultural Center. Further east, the park is formally connected to the Cultural Center via the creek that has been transformed into a linear boulevard. This makes the park easily accessible not only to Moravia inhabitants but to visitors and tourists as well. Furthermore, the park is adjacent to the Medellin River, where an ambitious urban renewal project to transform the entire riverside into a linear park has been developed.[100] This will connect Moravia to a metropolitan park system and allow citizens from other areas of Medellin to have direct access to Moravia's public spaces. A network of open and accessible parks weaves its way through the city, allowing people to flow freely from one area to the next.

Another large-scale example of public space creation in spontaneous settlements occurs in Chapéu Mangueira – Babilônia in Rio de Janeiro. The carioca case, however, is not related

99 "Moravia: el barrio que floreció sobre una montaña de basura" *KienYKe*, December 7, 2017. https://www.kienyke.com/historias/moravia-medellin-el-barrio-que-florecio-sobre-una-montana-de-basura (accessed January 26, 2018).

100 Rio Medellin Park Design Competition.
Constanza Cabezas, "Primer Lugar Concurso Público Internacional del Anteproyectos Parque del Río en la Ciudad de Medellín" *Plataforma Arquitectura* December 23, 2013. https://www.plataformaarquitectura.cl/cl/02-320551/primer-lugar-concurso-publico-internacional-de-anteproyectos-parque-del-rio-en-la-ciudad-de-medellin (accessed July 10, 2018).

to risk management, but to environmental preservation. Chapéu Mangueira and Babilônia are nestled on the skirts of a very steep hill or *morro* that defines the northern end of the Copacabana Bay. Once completely deforested, the *morro* is today covered with lush tropical vegetation due to the organized efforts of the community to reforest the land. They created a network of paths between the settlement and the mountaintop in order to survey and tend to the vegetation they planted. The natural reserve´s recovery helps produce cleaner air, generates oxygen and creates a comfortable microclimate for inhabitants. It also serves the community with places for recreation and has become closely associated with its local identity. The forest offers the city 22 hectares (220,909 m^2) of a natural reserve that represents an urban amenity and destination at the metropolitan scale. It not only increases access for locals to public space, but also invites outside visitors to use and enjoy the park. Neighbors of Chapéu Mangueira and Babilônia work as guides and welcome guests through the *favela* into the forest. The communities become integrated with the city through a continuous experience that minimizes the perception of boundaries.

Most spontaneous settlements, however, will need to consider a combination of projects, in order to produce the amount of public space required. Diverse, flexible and practical approaches are needed to take on the challenge of reversing structural differences in urban territories. If we look at Petare Sur as an example, strategies will have to include the recovery of existing spaces, which entails little investment, as well as the addition of large new areas, which involves greater social and financial cost. Both are necessary to reach a more appropriate allocation of public space in spontaneous settlements.

An example of the first approach, intervening existing open spaces, occurred in the neighborhood of La Ceiba in Petare Sur in 2017. A 750 m^2 area, functioning as a *de facto* public space, was the result of a channeled, covered creek, accessible on its lower side from a roadway; along its upper edge two stairways connect to neighborhoods beyond. A provisional basketball court was drawn onto the concrete slab on the upper half of the space, and privately-operated jeeps used for public transportation occupy the lower half of a *de facto* terminal for passengers. The initiative to transform this space into a more active public plaza, was part of an urban program financed by Citibank and coordinated by Fudep Venezuela. Enlace Arquitectura was brought on board to lead the design process together with the community. Between January and June 2018, the space was completely transformed into an operable public space with several programmatic areas geared toward different age groups. Today it is intensively used by the community and has significantly contributed to the livelihood of neighbors.(Fig 2) Furthermore, the project required modest funding and represents a viable method to create new public spaces within existing urban conditions. The map of (Fig. 1) shows available spaces that could also be considered for projects similar to the one in La Ceiba.

A second approach is to take advantage of places currently used to dump waste. Individuals are not claiming them as private property which means that they are implicitly understood as places for common use, albeit for waste. Over the past year, neighbors of various sectors in Petare Sur have initiated campaigns to eliminate waste dumps and convert them into clean, well-kept areas, often painting murals, incorporating basketball hoops or planting vegetation.[101] Small pockets of space are useful and necessary to create a continuous and well-balanced offering of plazas and rest areas. Places such as the covered creak, in La Ceiba, and improvised waste dumps are frequent in Petare. In order to transform them into public spaces, they would need to be systematically subjected to community design processes, where subsequent maintenance plans are also taken into consideration. Approximately 167 public spaces such as the one in La Ceiba would have to be built to satisfy the current public

101 The interview of Katiuska Camargo by Cheo Carvajal, documents the initiative Haciendo Ciudad in Venezuela that has successfully cleared open waste dumps in spontaneous settlements. Cheo Carvajal, "Katiuska Camargo: Entendí que yo era dueña del barrio," *Prodavinci* February 14, 2018. https://prodavinci.com/katiuska-camargo-entendi-que-yo-era-duena-del-barrio/ (accessed July 10, 2018).

space deficit of 12.5 hectares. The reality, however, is that there is not enough open space available for public space; so other approaches are necessary.

For example, the Guaire River, which runs along Petare Sur´s southern border, could potentially be considered an asset instead of a disadvantage, as it is currently perceived since it is an open-sewage channel that runs through the city. The community La Linea is the settlement in Petare that immediately fronts onto the river edge. During the rainy season, it is periodically threatened by floods. Land is not fit for habitation and proper risk management of this informally developed area requires structured, long-term solutions. As both a way of mitigating flood threats and creating new public space for Petare Sur, inhabitants living in portions of this neighborhood would need to be relocated, their homes razed, and the unoccupied land transformed into a floodable linear park. This would allow the terrain to absorb the river´s natural water level changes without harming inhabitants. It would also provide residents with ample open space they could use for leisure and recreation most of the year. Up to 41.159 m^2 or 4 hectares of new public space, the equivalent of 33% of

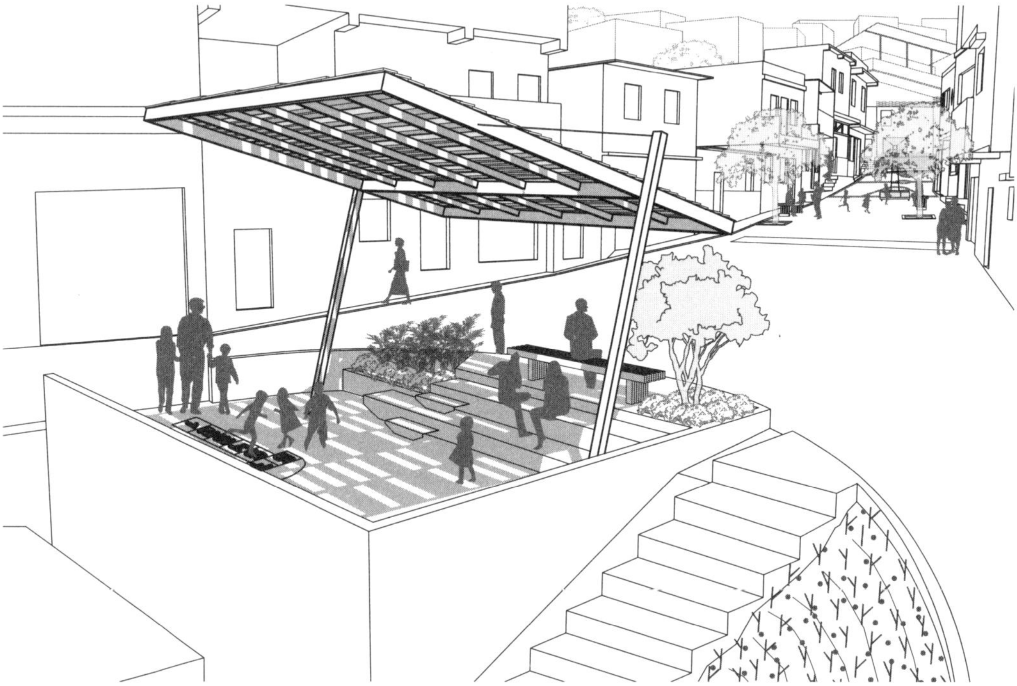

Fig 2. View of the public space Project Plaza Santa Rita in La Ceiba, Barrio Unión, Petare Sur. The project was part of the program City Planting – Fudep, designed by Enlace Arquitectura 2017.

the space needed to level differences between planned and unplanned urban areas, could be created for the benefit of nearby communities along the river edge. Another advantage is that it would represent a segment of a larger public space project along the river, which could potentially traverse the entire city increasing accessibility, facilitating alternative mobility options and connecting several spontaneous settlements, including Petare, with the rest of the city. (Fig 3)

The need for public space in spontaneous settlements requires creative and less obvious approaches, that extend beyond rescuing existing plazas and transforming left over spaces into pocket squares. Communities residing in the city´s periphery, which are particularly underserved by services and amenities, will require multiple, simultaneous and widespread approaches to mitigate their lack of public space. Strategies such as the Moravia Ecological Park, the Estero Salado linear park and the Chapéu Mangueira – Babilônia natural reserve are particularly valuable examples of creative and effective ways to reduce local public space deficits.

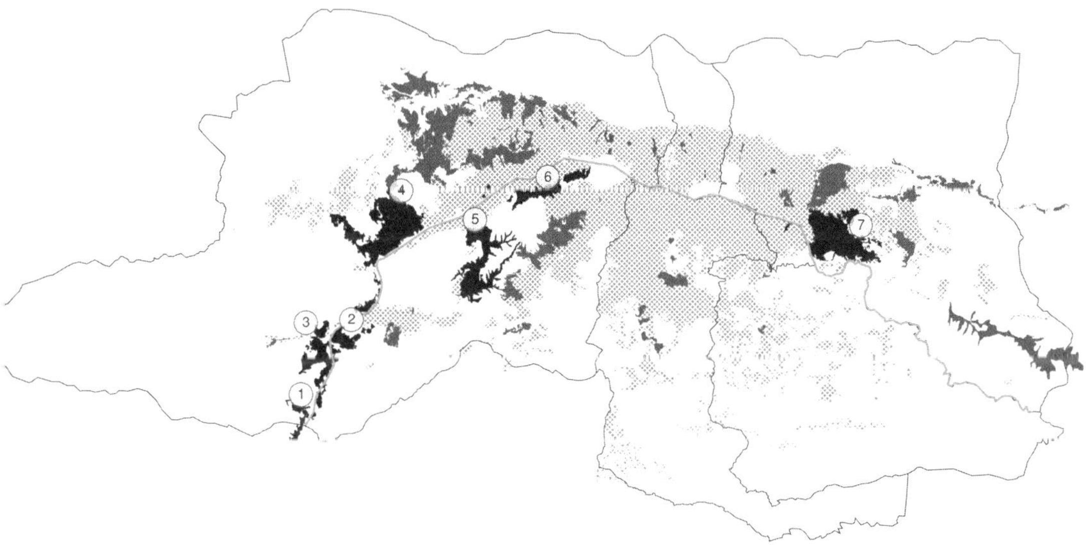

1 Carretera Vieja Los Teques
2 Caricuao
3 Macarao
4 Antímano
5 La Vega
6 San Angustín
7 Petare Sur

Fig. 3. Plan of the Guaire River and the potential linear public space along its edges. It could represent an area of 128 hectares.

FORMAL AND PROGRAMMATIC STRATEGIES TO BUILD PUBLIC SPACES IN SPONTANEOUS SETTLEMENTS

Public space is rarely the focus of projects in spontaneous settlements; rather it tends to complement other driving infrastructure investments. Alone it is not perceived as an element with sufficient merit to motivate urban transformation. Other urban aspects receive greater attention and have less difficulty building consensus and securing funding. Arguments such as scarcity of resources, the indeterminate legal jurisdiction of land, and difficulty gaining approval, are frequent obstacles that frustrate public space projects. Those that do make it through community and municipal processes are few. In response to these limitations and pretexts, this investigation presents successfully completed projects that include public space components and examines the strategies they used. Once known, they can be replicated and adapted to similar conditions in other locations.

The analysis looks at formal urban and architectural approaches, financial mechanisms, participatory design methods and economic sustainability to present a complete picture of key aspects that safeguard the viability of any given project. Many of the case studies included in this publication show innovative ways to leverage and consolidate public space through investments in larger urban infrastructure projects or projects with pressing environmental concerns. A few were the result of more conventional approaches that use new buildings or pavement projects as a ploy to incorporate overlooked in-between spaces. And others sprung from the spatial needs reoccurring activities revealed, activities which were able to coalesce the community into transforming an improvised site into better defined public space. Altogether, this research has identified six approaches to create public space in spontaneous settlements:

1. Environmental and natural resource conservation
2. Waste management and sanitation
3. Risk management
4. Infrastructure
5. Pavement, walkways and the space around buildings
6. Activity

ENVIRONMENTAL AND NATURAL RESOURCE CONSERVATION

Spontaneous settlements are often built on environmentally sensitive land, originally undeveloped due to zoning restrictions that legally forbid formal construction. Their improvised occupation and lack of proper means to manage waste and sewage result in critical ecological damage. Contaminated bodies of water or deforested natural reservations within cities are common byproducts of spontaneous settlement occupation. Remediation efforts to restore these bodies of water and natural forests are costly since the damages affect vast territories. If left unattended, however, the consequences progressively become more severe. Another problem to consider is how to prevent the future occupation of protected land. As discussed earlier, the Guayaquil example along the Estero Salado advocates transforming the improperly inhabited river edges into public space as a way of preserving the waterway's ecology. Consequently, the city has witnessed a substantial increase in its supply of public space.[102] In Rio de Janeiro, the communities of Chapéu Mangueira and Babilônia, coexist with a natural forest reservation at the top of the *morro*, perceived today as a unique resource for the community. The forest is a fully accessible public space that incorporates the *favela* within its sphere of impact. In Lima, near the Rimac River, a community of entrepreneurial women of the settlement El Agustino is engaged in an urban agriculture project along the river edge that protects it from the encroachment of spontaneous settlement, and generates a productive use of public land. In these examples, adequately conditioned public space becomes an effective steward to protect and preserve environmentally sensitive sites.

Guayaquil is located on the delta of the River Guayas as it runs into the Pacific Ocean. Numer-
72 ous natural salt water canals or *esteros* traverse the city on their way toward the river. Once the site of mangroves and coastal fauna, the *esteros* represent an important environmental element in the city, remembered by older generations of Guayaquileños as a place where they swam and played as children. Urban pressures drove economically vulnerable families to build houses along the canal edges by gaining land from the water through improvised landfills. Debris and sewage contaminated the estuary and created severe ecological damage. For nearly two decades the City of Guayaquil and the federal government have sponsored projects to separately collect sewage from homes along the river, and relocate families living in high risk situations. A necklace of parks, playfields, boardwalks, fountains and amphitheaters emerged with each successive intervention. The river's decontamination has allowed birds, fish, reptiles and vegetation to return to what was once their home, and sports such as rowing, fishing and water skiing are practiced as well. The fact that public space has made the river visible allows neighbors and visitors to become guardians and guarantors of its sustainability. As a result, the linear park works as an environmental conservation method that reduces the likelihood of new informal construction and illegal waste dumping.

Chapéu Mangueira and Babilônia are modestly sized spontaneous settlements nestled into
80 the hills north of the Copacabana beach in Rio de Janeiro. They enjoy a privileged location which has made them attractive neighborhoods for youth hostels that cater to foreign college students. The Bar do David, which is a popular restaurant with outdoor tables, is recommended in tourist guide books. An even more compelling attraction for visitors is the natural park reserve just beyond the *favelas*. Once completely deforested in 1995, the slopes of the *morro* were recovered with lush tropical species through a community led planting initiative and the support of a local NGO. Paths lead the way from the settlement through the forest to its rocky crest where a de facto plaza is often used by community youth to fly kites. Since the park reserve is beyond the spontaneous settlement, visitors must traverse it before taking on the ascent. Different city fragments from the beach and its neighborhood bellow, the *favela* and the park, are woven together. The continuous experience dissolves the importance of barriers and advances a certain degree of urban integration. It also creates an opportunity for people from various parts of the city to engage each other and share a common space.

In Lima water is a scarce resource. The land is arid and very challenging to cultivate. The Rimac
88 River traverses the city from east to west and flows contaminated and full of sediment into the Pacific Ocean. Urban development in the city does not acknowledge the presence of the river which remains a secondary element hidden behind urban plots. A community of entrepreneurial women from the nearby settlement El Agustino, near the river, is engaged in an urban agriculture project of vegetable gardens planted along the river edge that is sponsored by the United Nations Development Program UNDP. The irrigation water they use comes from the river and is collected in concrete cylinders built to purify the water through a phytodepuration process. A series of garden plots, irrigated and cared for by the team of women, have been

102 This indicator has been regularly recorded in the "Rendición de cuentas" published each year by the Municipality of Guayaquil.

constructed along the river edge. Production is mostly for self-consumption, but the women also manage to sell excess amounts in local markets. The project´s most touted virtue is its empowerment of women, through organization and insertion in an economically productive enterprise that allows them to provide basic sustenance for their families. However, the garden plots also represent a valid strategy to make the river visible. The communities that tend to them could eventually become stewards of the ecologically sensitive land along the river edge and promote its transformation into a productive public space. The project contributes to local productivity and the social inclusion of underprivileged women and could serve as an environmental recovery strategy that is viable and inexpensive, as well.

WASTE MANAGEMENT - SANITATION

Waste accumulation in spontaneous settlements is a ubiquitous problem. Conventional waste management infrastructure, such as garbage trucks, does not work in the narrow roads and the long steep flights of steps that characterize some settlements. Clandestine waste dumps emerge in corners of unattended land; they contaminate the environment and represent serious health hazards for inhabitants in terms of respiratory diseases and skin allergies. Periodically the dumps are burned, adding air pollution and carbon emissions to the list of damages. Eliminating open-air urban waste has been achieved by spontaneous settlement communities through alternative waste management programs which can be easily replicated in other neighborhoods. Once cleared out, these unclaimed urban remnants of space are valuable potential sites for public use. They represent an opportunity to create new meeting points in the community in addition to improving environmental sanitation.

For example, the community of La Palomera, in southern Caracas, was affected by the pres- 104
ence of an improvised open-air waste dump for over 30 years. The space of this dump became the point of departure to design, in conjunction with the community, a new public space. The first step was clearing waste from the site and devising a new waste management strategy together with the local municipality; the second was to determine possible uses for the newly available space.[103] A modestly sized plaza emerged where several elements were conceived in a way that children could help build them: the pavement included stripes of recycled bottle caps they embedded into the concrete; the children also helped paint a wood bench made of recycled pallets with a colorful scheme of horizontal lines. Ivy was planted along the base of an existing fence, which quickly grew and provided shade over the plaza in the evening hours. This transformation process has been an educational experience for the community and has given them an opportunity to reflect on how access to a new public space has affected their livelihood. Today, La Palomera enjoys a modest, yet effective plaza, with a generous public bench, plenty of shade and a beautiful view, which create the setting of an urban space that enjoys the same characteristics and qualities as public spaces in the planned areas of the city. Despite its small-scale, La Palomera Plaza represents a tactical intervention that does more than solve a waste accumulation problem: it motivates the community, contributes positively to people´s livelihood, and helps advance urban integration.

Another valuable example occurred in the community of Moravia in Medellin mentioned earlier. 96
It was once the site of the city's landfill where waste pickers made a living from the recycled materials they recovered. In time, many built their homes directly over the landfill. Inhabitants were exposed to toxic air pollution. Additionally, the instability of decomposing debris meant the foundations of their homes could collapse at any time. Through a multidisciplinary effort, the municipality devised a project for Moravia that included the relocation of families into nearby multifamily housing and the transformation of the former landfill into a park, considered the only feasible development alternative for unstable, decomposing land. Today, the Moravia Ecological Park is known for its landscape, vegetation, walkways, community gardens and cultural activities. The transformation of a non-place into an effective public park has given

103 The public space was designed by Enlace Arquitectura as part of the *City Planting* program, sponsored by Citibank Venezuela and executed by Fudep Venezuela.

Moravia inhabitants a renewed identity associated with ecological responsibility and improved livelihood. The park has also allowed Moravia to participate in the city´s overall network of public places, linking it through the linear park along the creek to the Moravia Cultural Center and other attractions toward the east on the Avenida Carabobo, and to the future Medellin River park on the west.

RISK MANAGEMENT

Urban resilience has become an increasingly relevant concern for local government officials and communities. Natural disasters can cause cities incalculable economic damage, not to mention personal injuries and the loss of lives. Strategies that help reduce the exposure of people and property to such risks are part of an evolving agenda that cities are looking to assimilate into their urban structures.[104] In Latin America, disasters related to heavy rains, flooding and landslides are far more common than risks associated with earthquakes. This is partly explained by the fact that regional weather conditions for significant parts of the continent are divided into dry and rainy seasons, with tropical rains that can discharge as much as 500 mm in a matter of minutes during peak months.[105] Another significant contributor is the fact that spontaneous settlements often occupy environmentally sensitive land, which puts them at far greater risks than other better planed neighborhoods. For example, houses built over creeks may lose their foundations and get swept downstream when excessive rainfall fills ravines with high volumes of water at significant speed. Excessive rain can also cause landslides; rainwater saturates the ground until its weight overcomes friction with dryer soil beneath, causing it to slide downhill. Massive boulders, segments of earth, trees and debris tumble down slopes destroying homes and any other type of construction they find in their way. Flooding, due to heavy rain, unusual high tides or both conditions combined, also affect homes built too close to the edges of rivers and oceans. Every year news feeds commonly document numerous cases of homes affected by heavy rains. The Juan Bobo Creek in Medellín and the Guasmo Beach in Guayaquil are examples of risk mitigation urban projects along creeks and flood plains that incorporate public space as part as their resilience strategy.

28 The Juan Bobo Creek, which runs along the northeastern hills of Medellin, was once fully occupied by precarious housing structures that were constantly exposed to the risk of flooding and landslides. In an effort to protect people living along the ravine from eminent disaster and ensure that it would not be occupied again in the future, the City of Medellin first relocated families into new multifamily buildings nearby and transformed the banks of the creek into space for recreation and leisure. The intervention also incorporated bridges that effectively brought together communities on opposite sides of the creek. The bridges also diminished the rivalry between youth gangs associated with each side, since the difference between them had essentially been erased. The intervention was able to mitigate the effects of water surges, provide space for recreation and leisure and forge more positive relations between formerly opposed social groups.

112 Guayaquil's Guasmo Floodable Beach is an environmental risk management operation, built on the edge of an *estero*, located south of the city center. Similar to the Malecón Salado example, the edges of these *esteros* have also been occupied with homes built over debris thrown into the water. In addition to the risks posed by their unsound construction, these areas are also exposed to flooding. Furthermore, riverside spontaneous settlements are an eminent ecological threat, since they destroy mangroves and contaminate the river water. A project sponsored by the municipality was undertaken in the Guasmo area to relocate houses and contain the spontaneous urban growth. The Guasmo beach is an urban intervention

104 The 100 Resilient Cities initiative was begun by the Rockefeller Foundation in 2013 to help cities worldwide become more resilient. The 100 chosen cities receive resources to develop roadmaps toward greater resilience. https://www.100resilientcities.org/

105 José Agustín Breña-Naranjo, Adrián Pedrozo-Acuña and Miguel Rico-Ramírez, "World´s greatest rainfall intensities observed by satellite" *Atmospheric Science Letters* 16, December 5. 2014, 420-424.

along the *estero* that consists of several terraces designed to respond to different high tide conditions since each terrace is able to absorb additional volumes of water. At the same time, they function as public spaces apt for recreation activities and at the same time give settlers the chance to engage the *estero*, perhaps for the first time, as an urban amenity and not as a threat. Given the entertainment value of this new public space, it not only serves its immediate neighbors but also attracts visitors from other communities, especially on weekends. The beach also connects to other plazas and playfields nearby, forming an integrated and accessible network of public spaces in the community.

Although less frequent, earthquakes also threaten extended territories in the region along the Andean fault line. Strategies to increase earthquake resilience also create opportunities for public space. Lima is an earthquake prone city where spontaneous settlements are exposed
to greater risk due to the precarious nature of their construction. Santa Maria El Triunfo, is a 120
settlement in the southern part of the city, nestled into a dry and rocky ravine. Safety plazas located along the settlement's main road, and engineered to be seismically resistant, were incorporated into the community´s urban fabric through a project led by the NGO Desco and financed with international grants. People are instructed to take refuge on the safety platforms if and when an earthquake occurs. The platforms were also designed to function as quotidian public space: areas for adults to play chest or dominos and playgrounds for children. Although the design quality of the plazas is suspect, and their lack of shade reduces the hours of the day in which they can be used, they mark spaces that are collectively identified as public, safeguarding them from future private occupations. Neighbors can progressively claim and modify the spaces themselves to better reflect their potential for play, gathering, and leisure. The safety plazas represent a valid natural disaster mitigation strategy that also creates an opportunity to incorporate public space.

TRANSPORTATION INFRASTRUCTURE

Transportation infrastructure is a very effective way to integrate poorly communicated, peripheral spontaneous settlements into the city. Because of the substantial investment they require, financial resources most frequently come from the state or national government. Building infrastructure within already existing communities is challenging. The installation process often requires disruptive excavations and earth movements. The heavy equipment and materials used are difficult to move through the narrow and winding streets, characteristic of dense urban settlements. Another difficulty is that the infrastructure´s technical specifications may require partial or total demolitions of existing structures, which means that families must be relocated to new homes. As discussed previously, housing relocation is met with stark opposition from the community and adds important levels of complexity to already demanding projects. In any given infrastructure project, it is important to embrace these dimensions early on and incorporate strategies that transform necessary demolitions into opportunities to mend, connect and improve the existing urban fabric. The cost associated with remedial work done after an infrastructure intervention to repair the damages would only be slightly augmented if instead of simply repairing surfaces, new public space was built as well. Foresight identifying these opportunities for purposeful public space additions benefits the community and helps offset the discontent produced by the initial demolitions.

The Medellin metrocable, over the northeastern settlements of Santo Domingo Savio, is the 136
first of its kind in Latin America. The system has improved mobility and considerably reduced the time spent on transportation for people that live there. While the metrocable travels above, each column that supports the system, represents an alibi to create public space as it reaches the ground. At a neighborhood scale, the areas adjacent to the column foundations have become new places for gathering and recreation: plazas, playgrounds, or tables for adults to play chess. Furthermore, each cable car station has been designed with generous open spaces in its surrounding areas and are themselves integrated with the urban fabric through renovated streets, vegetation, terraces, reflective pools and walkways that create an extensive network of public space.

160 The cable stations of the Complexo do Alemão system, in Rio de Janeiro, have been configured in a similar way, with open public spaces surrounding the structure and formal roadways servicing the entire community. Complexo do Alemão is a very large and populous spontaneous settlement located north of the city. The metro cable system was installed over the crests of four hills interspersed within this community. Like the Medellin example, the project used public space interventions such as playgrounds, plazas and streets with sidewalks, to restore areas affected by the construction process.[106]

Given the scarcity of open space in spontaneous settlements, infrastructure and service projects including electric cabling, mobility projects, water and sanitation are an important opportunity to create new public space. By simply including an additional cost item in the project for a park or plaza that represents only a small fraction of the overall construction cost, the grounds affected during the installation process can be configured into much-needed public space.

144 In the Barrio Las Independencia of the Comuna 13, in Medellin, local government implemented an innovative mobility project using escalators to access various points in the community, particularly benefiting people with disabilities and senior citizens. The system´s starting point is marked by a new open plaza at the base of the ascent; at the opposite end, the escalators connect to a long walkway that cantilevers over the edge of the hill and receives numerous staircases connected to residences further up. Both, the plaza and the walkway represent important public space contributions for inhabitants. The cantilevered walkway has been appropriated by children as a place to play. Their family members can watch over them from the houses that line the path. A long serpentine banister is also a bench for sitting and gathering. Slides and playground equipment for children has been incorporated into several of the stairs connected to the walkway. The value of this project lies in the fact that the intervention goes beyond the installation of the escalators in creating new public space for the community. Pathways full of children riding bicycles are testimony to the value well-conditioned public spaces have for communities.

152 Similarly, the funicular structure in Dona Marta, Rio de Janeiro, provoked changes in the use of spaces surrounding each stop. Santa Marta is a dense spontaneous settlement situated over a steep hill north of the Botafogo neighborhood, founded nearly a century ago.[107] A funicular lift was installed in 2008 to improve accessibility for the people that live there, since there are no roads within the neighborhood. The funicular allows people to carry bicycles and groceries up the hill and is also a valuable solution for waste to be transported, collected and hauled down to garbage trucks stationed at the bottom of the hill. There are several stops along the ascent, one of which is named Michael Jackson after the famous singer recorded a video there.[108] The last station is the UPP Santa Marta which includes a police station, an Astroturf playfield and a module of the *Sistema* youth orchestra.[109] As passengers wait to board the lift, the area preceding the funicular entrance acts as an urban node and becomes a *de facto* public space. Houses adjacent to each station have taken advantage of the confluence of people and converted their ground levels into convenience stores, lottery kiosks and food

106 This wasn´t always the case, as expressed in the interview with the community leader Alan Brum Pinheiro in Complexo do Alemão. Ava Rose Hoffman, “Knowledge to Create Solutions in Complexo do Alemão: Instituto Raízes em Movimento” *Rio On Watch*, July 11, 2016. http://www.rioonwatch.org/?p=30158 (accessed November 28, 2018).

107 The spontaneous settlement Santa Marta has an area of 53,706 m^2 and around 4,000 residents. Miriane Peregrino, “Tram, Tourism, History and Resistance: ‘Each Brick has its Story’,” *Agência de Notícias das Favelas* July 10, 2018.

108 Michael Jackson filmed the video for “They Don´t Care About Us” in Dona Marta, Rio de Janeiro, in 1994 and the video was released in March 1996.

109 The Sistema is a classical music education program for impoverished children. It was founded in Venezuela in 1975 by the Maestro José Antonio Abreu. Renown musical directors such as Gustavo Dudamel came through Venezuela´s Sistema. Through support from the Inter-American Development Bank IDB and CAF development bank of Latin America, El Sistema was replicated in other parts of Latin America, including Brazil.

joints. The funicular stations have thus imposed a public function on their surrounding areas that, in spite of constrained dimensions, become appropriated by inhabitants as waiting areas and incipient public spaces.

In the case of the Ecotecnia Urbana Miravalle project in Mexico City, water harvesting in- 68
frastructure goes hand in hand with new public space. Through a combination of awards, municipal funds obtained through participatory budget proposals, and community investment, several locations within the neighborhood have been transformed for community uses. The first project was the adaptation of a dome into a rain water catchment device which stores the water in an underground cistern, beneath the amphitheater. Likewise, a second site located a hundred meters away, at a higher elevation on the skirts of an inactive volcano, has been designed to capture rainwater runoff from the hill that is stored in large concrete cisterns. Much like a campus, the site hosts multiple community programs including a dance hall, exhibition and lecture hall, a sports facility, ball courts, exercise equipment, a skate park and a running track. The community´s immediate concern, which is to increase its access to water, has been systematically conflated with opportunities for new open public space.

PAVEMENT, WALKWAYS AND THE SPACE AROUND BUILDINGS

Paved surfaces for walking, vegetation for shade and adornment, outdoor areas for gathering and resting, as well as public buildings and their programs, are common protagonists of the urban experience. Incorporating these elements within spontaneous settlements is an important step toward leveling differences in the city and advancing urban integration. However, identifying opportunities to insert such elements within spontaneous urban communities is complex. What is considered public or private land may not be precisely defined, but rather tacitly agreed upon among settlers over the course of years. Incorporating the community in project planning and implementation is critical in this sense and requires transparent communication between settlers and designers. Built examples of projects in the public domain, in several cities of the region, have generated strategies that could be systematized and pursued by other municipalities and communities.

Designs for formal walkways and plazas implemented in Valparaiso and Guayaquil were particularly successful in achieving a sense of integration and fluidity between informal neighborhoods and their context. Cerro Toro and Cerro Santo Domingo in Valparaiso Chile and Cerro Santa Ana in Guayaquil Ecuador are examples of government funded projects focused on normalizing walkways, stairs and lookout points within the settlement as a way to define the public realm. The first step was to demarcate land not considered private. Through interviews and meetings with the community, the home of each inhabitant was mapped. Unclaimed land, mainly in the form of circulation and remnant spaces, could then be claimed as public and formalized into systems of walkways and plazas. The process allowed inhabitants to gain a renewed appreciation for the public domain and recognize the kinds of activities it enables. The pavement schemes also constructed more fluid and continuous paths between city fragments, as evidenced in the connection between lower parts of Valparaiso and the community of Cerro El Toro above, as well as between the Malecón 2000 River Walkway and the stairs of Cerro Santa Ana.

Other formal public space approaches, include the configuration of space around buildings. Two buildings in Medellín and one in Rio de Janeiro, exemplify design strategies that consider both surrounding areas and accessibility as integral components of the overall intervention. The City of Medellin has invested in spontaneous settlement-upgrading projects for nearly two decades through assertive planning practices focused on education and culture. New urban amenities are constantly built to promote more and better education as well as ample access to cultural institutions. The renowned system of library parks throughout the city, cultural centers and schools are conceived as part of larger interventions that weave themselves into their communities through programmed activities and contiguous public space. The San Cristobal Botero Library and the Moravia Cultural Center are notable examples of how buildings can effectively improve spatial conditions in their surroundings and foster community engagement with the public space they create. In the case of Rio de Janeiro, an abandoned hotel structure has been appropriated and transformed into a vibrant hub of activity.

176 Cerro Toro and Cerro Santo Domingo are part of the informal urban fabric that extends over the hills above the Valparaiso Bay. The municipality issued a request for proposals to define and transform the interstitial areas of the spontaneous settlement into public space. The architecture office Mobil was awarded the project in 2006 and began their work by engaging the community in discussions and mapping exercises to identify the non-private spaces. The process gave way to 18,000 m^2 of public space, including walkways, stairs and small plazas. The architects created a customized design for each corner of the project and a modular prefabricated pavement to ensure better quality in the construction details and finishes. This is a rare case in which the municipality directly instigated a public space transformation through the allocation of public resources to improve accessibility and order in an informal community. It has resulted in a nuanced and sensitive intervention that essentially defines the ground plane, and builds connectivity between the settlement and the rest of the city.

184 Cerro Santa Ana is a historic spontaneous settlement that rests on a hill along the edge of the Guayas River. Its high crime rate once represented a serious threat to citizens and tourist visiting Guayaquil´s River Walkway. The municipality turned this misfortune into an opportunity to transform the settlement into a lively community and a tourist destination. The renovation project brought about the construction of a formal staircase that begins at the base of the hill and culminates over its crest onto an open esplanade with a chapel and a light tower. Along the way, plazas, street lighting, urban furniture, restored facades and storefronts liven the ascent. The development of the Cerro Santa Ana´s transformation came to be considered an extension of the Malecón 2000 River Walkway project and the creation of an intentionally continuous public space.

In addition to serving as an important cultural amenity for the community, the siting of the
192 Botero library affects the way inhabitants navigate their neighborhood. The central atrium provides access to various programs within the library, but also serves as a foyer for the community. Its staircase allows people to ascend up to a level that coincides with the streets and houses located beyond the library´s rear facade. Workshops and practice rooms along the ground floor of this rear façade can be directly accessed from the exterior without having to go through the main library entrance, thereby activating the building's periphery. Wide corridors along the sides of the buildings provide generous space for people to gather, and onlookers to enjoy music or dance rehearsals visible through the façade´s storefront glass. Even though these activities are held within the library's structure the movement they generate resonates in the space between the library and the first line of neighborhood houses. The dynamics of this corridor are similar to those of a vibrant urban street; the inhabitants who live opposite the library have incorporated ice cream shops, cafes and other services on their ground floors to take advantage of the number of people that frequent the site. The atrium is a double story space that connects two levels across the building through an open public staircase that can be used to enter the neighborhood. The library, thus, goes beyond the programmatic functions of its interior spaces and stimulates the urban potential latent in its surroundings.

200 Similar to the library, the Moravia Cultural Center has reconfigured the urban dynamics of its surroundings. Designed by the Colombian architect Rogelio Salmona, it is the place where children and youth in the community go to do their homework, play music, dance, read, use the internet and hang out with friends. The center includes a theatre, practice studios, study rooms and a large central atrium. For youth in the area, it has been a much-appreciated relief to the dysfunctional situations they often experience at home. The center also activates and establishes an urban node within the community together with a significant public space gesture in its immediate surroundings that is part of the project. The space extends toward the west and gives access to a high school built a few years later. To the north it connects with a boulevard built during the same period that runs along the creek and reaches the Moravia

Ecological Park. As a way of extending the center´s sphere of influence, two upcycled structures, a bus and container, have been transformed into satellite workshop spaces situated in the park. Children play tag, jump rope and skateboard in the plaza that surrounds the building. Eventually, this corridor will also connect the center with the future Medellín River Park. Public space and cultural programs allow a lively and dynamic urban environment to emerge and grow into Moravia´s new identity, replacing its historic association with waste and poverty. Furthermore, Moravia´s central location draws people from the nearby urban parks and museums such as the botanical garden and the Explora Park, along the Avenida Carabobo. It enjoys an equal footing with other significant cultural programs in the city and creates an integrated experience for neighbors and visitors that minimizes the need to distinguish whether the urban fabric it belongs to is formal or informal.

The public space produced in Cantagalo, Rio de Janeiro, is less structured than the previous 208
cases. A large abandoned hotel near the top of the favela, has been organically filled with education, culture and sports programs. Espaço Criança, AfroReggae, ball courts, a municipal library and play space for children are the most prominent facilities offering programs and activities for various demographic population segments. As a node for multiple activities that occur simultaneously and in proximity to one another, the entrance, central hallway and areas surrounding the building function as public space and areas for gathering. Furthermore, commercial insertions including a restaurant and cafeteria, add to the mix of programs. The physical structure of the former hotel and its central corridor become extensions of the main roadway that begins in Copacabana and Ipanema, and winds up into the neighborhood. The building can also be accessed through an elevator near the subway station. Improved connectivity has made it easier for Cantagalo to receive visitors and people interested in attending any of the activities offered at the cultural center. In this case, it was the existence of an empty building that created a unique opportunity for Cantagalo to progressively develop and strengthen its local culture, through a distinctive public urban space that welcomes both community members and visitors from the city at large.

A slightly different public space typology was pursued in Villa Tranquila, Buenos Aires. In this 216
case, work with the community through participatory design methods was prepared and financed by an initiative called PlaySpace, in collaboration with the Municipality of Avellaneda. Conversations with neighbors centered on understanding the potential for social and urban integration latent in public space and then putting that understanding into practice. This led to the selection of a strategically located site that became the initiative´s pilot project. The design and construction process yielded a modest park with a playground for children, a reading room, and tables for games. The value of this initiative lies in how inhabitants were included in the design process and the transference of knowledge and skills they received, which enables them to replicate the process and transform other spaces within the community.

ACTIVITY AS PUBLIC SPACE GENERATOR

The reoccurrence of an activity or program in a particular location can alter the way that place is perceived and used; it can even eventually motivate its transformation into a defined public space. In previous examples, infrastructure insertions or environmentally motivated interventions produced public spaces that in turn allowed a myriad of activities to emerge. In this case the relationship is inverted, and the activity precedes the spatial transformation, effectively claiming new areas for public use. Identifying an existing cultural or sports activity that takes place in a particular location can guarantee the success of its transformation into a formal public space for two main reasons. On one hand, the site’s vocation and common interest are acknowledged and accepted by the community; on the other, users have already appropriated the space and therefore their commitment to its upkeep and maintenance is more easily guaranteed. Often the users are young people who are part of a process to reclaim access to the public domain. Projects in Rio de Janeiro, Medellin, Lima and Caracas coincide in using outdoor spaces not only as locations for activities to take place, but as a means to more effectively engage young people in vulnerable situations. Their occupation of public space also helps reduce urban violence.

232 AfroReggae, in Rio de Janeiro, is a cultural institution with several sites in the city. It focuses on engaging youth in cultural activities related to music, dance and visual arts as a vehicle for personal development. The pursuit of healthy lifestyles is encouraged by the institution in response to earlier decades when joining criminal gangs had been the prevalent option. Outdoor spaces are used to rehearse and perform. The courtyard in front of the Vigário General center, located toward the north of the city, was transformed into an amphitheater where children and youth share their talents with the community through performances and concerts. These performers, in turn, become role models for the community´s youth. At the same time, the neighborhood benefits from its association with the arts. The quality of AfroReggae´s performances is well known, which has attracted visitors from the rest of the city and contributed to placing low-income communities on the map for many Rio inhabitants. Most importantly, neighbors enjoy a safer environment, active public spaces and become accustomed to interacting with visitors from the rest of the city.

224 Casa Kolacho, previously known as Pacharte, is another valuable community initiative focused on reducing urban violence in the Comuna 13 of Medellin through a network of artists. They promote activities, including hip-hop, graffiti art, music-mixing and performances, to engage youth and spread a common message against violence. They are very active in social media and produce the content for a community radio station they sponsor. In the public domain they stage music performances, and use graffiti along sidewalks, streets, stairs and pocket plazas to commemorate lives lost to violence, build awareness and deter young children from opting into delinquent lifestyles. Other initiatives include the staging of cultural events and concerts in a local football field on the anniversary of the *Operación Orion*, when the national guard entered the community and killed many youths involved in drug gangs.[110] The group´s focus is to raise awareness regarding the right to live peacefully and without violence in the community, and public space is used as a platform to multiply and carry their message further.

240 Alto Perú is a spontaneous settlement south of Chorrillos, along the pacific edge of Lima. It is also a human development project that teaches underprivileged youth to surf at no cost, as a way of awakening in them a desire to reach goals, live healthy lives and formulate higher aspirations for themselves. The children surf during the warm months, and in the winter, sports activities are substituted with percussion, *batucada* (Brazilian percussion music), and concerts performed in urban centers. For example, one evening in April 2012, the group played at the Miraflores Plaza, in an affluent neighborhood of Lima. The audience was captivated by their performance. This and other gigs became a vehicle for the Alto Perú youth to not only get to know their city, but also to strengthen their self-confidence. Public space is used as a place where youth can receive public recognition for their talent, regardless of their background. The experience allows them to use the city on an equal footing with everyone else, and to benefit from the sense of self-worth that comes from being publicly celebrated.

One last example of public space that results from a recurring activity is the annual event *El*
248 *Calvario Puertas Abiertas* in Caracas, Venezuela. By opening the neighborhood for one day to the entire city through a generous offering of cultural and recreational events, people from outside the community are encouraged to visit and begin to dismiss the prejudices they have about spontaneous settlements as dangerous and uninhabitable places. Both locals and visitors enjoy an urban experience that is novel, entertaining and can potentially reconcile urban city segments previously understood as opposites. The municipality helps promote the event; various organizations participate and contribute to the roster of activities; artists carry out performances or create physical installations; and members of the community open their homes for book readings and concerts. An existing plaza at the top of the settlement, Plaza

110 The *Operación Orión* was a military intervention that occurred in the Comuna 13, San Javier of Medellin, Colombia between October 16 and 17, 2002.

La Cruz, is set up with a stage and sound equipment for several music groups to perform live concerts, while audiences listen and dance with neighbors and visitors. The agenda behind this event is twofold: to place El Calvario definitively on the map of Caracas for all citizens, incorporating it into people´s radius of known places; and also, to discover, through activity and program, the various spaces within the community that could be transformed into permanent public space interventions. In other words, a latent map of potential plazas, park benches and boulevards, becomes visible through the activities planned throughout El Calvario for that day.

Altogether, six strategies have been presented that secure viable scenarios for proposing public space projects in spontaneous settlements. Some have coupled public space with larger agendas such as infrastructure, environmental conservation and urban resilience, to help secure project funding. Moving projects forward that are solely focused on public space making remains a challenge since public authorities, communities and financial entities tend to consider the improvement of other spontaneous settlement aspects more urgent. However, when public space activation is associated with violence and crime mitigation, it has been met with less resistance.[111] These approaches may coincide with the circumstances and available resources of other communities in the region. Extracting the methods, justifications and operative gestures used in the selected projects may encourage and help other urban actors take on similar projects.

111 Tourists and visitors of the newly formed Malecón 2000, had been threatened by youth from the nearby spontaneous settlement Cerro Santa Ana, which motivated its transformation into a picturesque village-like-neighborhood to complement and extend the river walkway in lieu of threatening its safety.
The research of Jota Samper in Colombia is focused on registering the correlation between violence reduction and public space in the urban transformations that have occurred in Medellin Colombia over the past 2 decades. José Samper "Repensando la informalidad: Estrategias de Co-producción del Espacio Urbano" *Issue*, August 31, 2014. https://issuu.com/coproduccion/docs/informe_aug_13_web_version (accessed November 24, 2018).

The United Nations' Sustainable Development Goals (SDGs), established in 2000, focused on the reduction of poverty and had the intention of encouraging more copious and innovative financial strategies to improve the livelihood of less fortunate population segments.[112] The consensus mandate stipulated reducing international levels of poverty in terms of health, nourishment, gender equality and education through the design and approval of new public policy at the national, state and local government levels. It also encouraged multilateral organizations such as the World Bank, Inter-American Development IDB, and CAF development bank of Latin America, to establish special funds that backed projects in developing countries oriented toward achieving the stated goals.[113] The private sector corresponded with a broader commitment to support projects dedicated to advancing the SDGs though social responsibility mechanisms, NGO's worked to implement urban transformation projects by helping communities organize, recognize local talent, and mobilize human resources.

In effect, over the past two decades these investments have generated important advances including better access to potable water, education and decreased levels of infant mortality.[114] 91% of households in Latin America and the Caribbean now have access to potable water, sanitation and sewage collection, with positive effects on public health and productivity. Access to education has gone from 52% coverage to 66% over the past two decades.[115] And life expectancy rates have increased 8.9% to an average of 75 years.[116]

The 2015 revision by the United Nations of its SDGs acknowledged the advances achieved in 15 years, but also highlighted the worrisome increase in levels of inequality. Decreasing inequality became the central focus of the revised goals. Multilateral organizations, foundations and local governments were called upon to increase their advocacy and support for projects that strengthen social inclusion, in addition to reducing poverty. Spontaneous settlement upgrading projects and their associated public investment would need to be evaluated and complemented in order to advance an agenda of inclusion in addition to improvement. This opens an opportunity for public space components to be reconsidered as central and relevant investments in underprivileged communities given their effectiveness in increasing social cohesion and inclusion. There is of yet no clear understanding of how urban invest-

112 The Sustainable Development Goals were established by the United Nations in 2000. They are the following 8: 1.To eradicate extreme poverty and hunger, 2.To achieve universal primary education, 3.To promote gender equality and empower women, 4.To reduce child mortality, 5.To improve maternal health, 6.To combat HIV/AIDS, malaria, and other diseases, 7. To ensure environmental sustainability, 8.To develop a global partnership for development.

113 Ibid.

114 World Bank Data, http://data.worldbank.org (accessed July 10, 2018).

115 UNESCO, "Regional Report about Education for all in Latin America and the Caribbean," April 09, 2014.

116 World Bank Data.

ment can increase equality. Documenting the effects of existing public space projects on reducing territorial inequality is one way to encourage stronger and more frequent advocacy of its relevance. As discussed in chapter 3, a very significant amount of space is needed in spontaneous settlements to balance the availability of public parks and plazas present in the rest of the city. In Latin America alone, the demand of public space to serve the 200 million people living in spontaneous communities is considerable.[117] Increasing available funds for urban public space transformation projects therefore must be addressed.

Urban projects handled by local authorities are often designed and managed through separate departments, such as transportation, public works, economic productivity, social development, to name a few. Public space interventions however do not fall neatly in any of the separate categories that typically structure public entities. They entail multiple aspects that include infrastructure, environmental conditions, social resources and community participation. In many ways, their value stems from the simultaneous considerations of both physical and social urban dimensions. The local government department responsible for their design and implementation may not be readily evident. Sectored organizational structures may even be partly responsible for retarding or even hindering the design of more complex urban projects in the public domain. Likewise, when public space projects are presented to multilateral organizations for financial assistance, they tend to be channeled into one specialized department that only reviews the project from the perspective of its specific areas of competence. To that effect, increased demand for urban development initiatives has generated changes in both public and multilateral organizations in order to better advise, finance and execute multisectoral projects. For example, local governments have reorganized themselves internally and created working groups encompassing several technical and social departments as well as community representatives. Together they formulate, design and implement complex urban interventions through integrated processes.[118] Multilateral institutions have also devised flexible structures to evaluate urban projects that previously would have been difficult to assess under firm department divisions.

Knowledge of existing financial approaches for public space specific to spontaneous settlements in Latin American cities can help designers, communities and local governments identify potential resources to implement new interventions. For example, among the cases included in this investigation a successful approach has been to couple public space initiatives with larger urban projects, since they represent a very discrete percentage of the overall cost. Identifying the potential for public space infrastructure in projects planned for future implementation, early on, is away to create new opportunities for public space and secure necessary funding. On the other hand, civic and community initiatives have been able to achieve important results through organized local labor, donations and community support. In many of these cases organizing and formalizing activities already occurring on site made public space interventions possible.

The financial approaches used by the selected case studies can be classified into three main groups: those that are obtained and managed by local, state or national governments; those administered through private, civic or non-governmental entities; and those that combine public and private resources. Altogether, ten distinctive financial approaches have been pursued in the projects of this body of research.

117 Silva and Vaggione, 2016. Estimates by CAF suggest on average 30% of the urban population in Latin America lives in spontaneous settlements, in other words 191.7 million people. If we are to consider access to 1 m2 per inhabitant, 20.000 hectares of public space would need to be built.

118 EDU Empresa de Desarrollo Urbano in Medellín, and UPP Social in Rio de Janeiro.

I. Local, state or national governments

1. Increased revenues resulting from improved local tax collection and lower administrative costs. This is the case of the City of Guayaquil in Ecuador.
2. Loans or donations from multilateral banks. This is the case of the Favela Bairro and Morar Carioca programs in Rio de Janeiro, funded by the World Bank and IDB.
3. Utility contributions from publicly owned companies, such as state or municipal public services, mining industry and petroleum companies. This is the case of Empresas Públicas Medellín.

II. Private, civic or non-governmental entities

4. Non-refundable donations from private foundations, the United Nations or other non-government entities. This is the case of the project executed by Desco in Lima, Miravalle in Mexico City and Villa Tranquila in Buenos Aires.
5. Funding for social responsibility projects associated with corporations or private companies. This is the case of La Palomera in Caracas, AfroReggae in Rio de Janeiro and Alto Perú in Lima.
6. Self-generated income, such as AfroReggae.
7. Community initiatives, as in the case of Chapéu Mangueira – Babilônia, in Rio de Janeiro.

III. Public-private partnerships

8. Joint collaborations between private sponsors and local government. El Calvario Puertas Abiertas, is an example.
9. Management of public programs by the private sector as part of their social responsibility. The cases of public libraries and cultural centers in Medellin are examples.
10. Local government programs reinforced through collaborations with private NGOs. For example, Alto Perú is working with state sponsored sports associations.

I. LOCAL, STATE OR NATIONAL GOVERNMENTS

1. Municipally funded projects through taxes income and an efficient administration.

When Jaime Nebot became mayor of Guayaquil in 2000, the city was financially broke, crime was rampant, and urban conditions were poor. He continued the incipient renewal agenda his predecessor, Francisco Pérez Febres-Cordero, had started, and further developed it over the course of nearly two decades.[119] Under his leadership, numerous urban projects have been successfully implemented, resulting in better access to public transportation, water, community centers, vocational training and public space, as well as improved sanitary and environmental conditions. At the beginning of his tenure, the City of Guayaquil´s economic situation was precarious. He revised and dramatically changed ways the municipality could increase its income, for example by improving local tax collection through incentives such as providing health examinations and access to social health programs in exchange for a paid tax receipt. With these encouragements, the effectiveness of tax collection increased substantially, which enabled the municipality to finance projects, guarantee loans and provide better services that in turn continued to build tax payer´s confidence and satisfaction. Another important change was the approach toward public administration. Human resources and administrative costs were reduced to less than 10% of the annual budget. The intention was to use nearly all municipal income to directly fund public works projects that could renovate Guayaquil´s collapsed infrastructure and services. Entities outside municipal bureaucracy were created to receive private donations and efficiently finance the execution of projects such as the Fundación Malecón 2000. The foundation also managed and oversaw the construction process. This financial structure helped instill a sense of efficiency and transparency that built confidence and encouraged other investors to make project donations as well. Social inclusion, increased productivity and livelihood have perceivably improved with these and other investments over

119 Jaime Nebot has been the mayor of Guayaquil for 4 continuous administrative periods, 2000, 2004, 2009 and 2014.

the past decades. When asked about the social agenda of his administration, Nebot is often heard replying that in order to advance social inclusion you need money.[120]

2. Multilateral bank loans and non-refundable assistance.
Donations and loans from multilateral banks are also an important source of funding for cities. Previously focused on more regional scales and public works investments, over the past couple of decades multilateral banks have broadened the scope of their funding to include urban projects. One noteworthy example of multilateral financing that ventured into complex city development in Latin America was the *Favela Bairro* program, in Rio de Janeiro; an urban upgrading initiative that focused less on housing subsidies and more on a holistic approach to improve services and accessibility. "It is not a program to meet the housing needs of individual residents but instead addresses the collective needs of the favela as a whole. Upgrading projects for each favela build upon the existing layout of houses, roads and walkways, leaving [...] the basic structure of the settlement [...] unaltered, though upgraded."[121] The IDB was one of the main project sponsors. The project's overall cost was 300 million USD and was distributed in three investment loans between 1995 and 2010.[122] Later in 2010, the World Bank granted Rio de Janeiro the largest award to any municipality to date. The loan was called The Rio de Janeiro Municipality Fiscal Consolidation for Efficiency and Growth Development Program Loan, worth 1.045 billion USD, and supported initiatives aimed at bolstering economic growth and improving the quality and coverage of social services, especially in low income urban areas.[123] In both cases the projects were managed and coordinated at the national level by the Brazilian government.[124]

Many of Jaime Nebot´s projects in Guayaquil were also partially financed with multilateral loans from the World Bank, IDB and CAF. The city´s improved financial capacity allowed it to access loans and guarantee their payment. An important limitation of this investment strategy is that it requires national government approval. When local and state governments are politically aligned this is not an issue. However, when political interests differ, it becomes more challenging for opposition mayors to access multilateral bank loans. Nevertheless, policy shifts are beginning to emerge that allow cities to take on debt independent of central government approval. In Brazil, for example, CAF is financing urban investment projects in cities through negotiations directly with the municipalities.[125]

3. Utilities from publicly owned companies.
A funding strategy that has worked well to finance urban and social projects in Medellin has been its relationship to the Medellin Public Company (Empresa Pública Medellín EPM). EPM provides the city´s public services in a profitable manner and is bound by its corporate bylaws to invest a percentage of its utilities in urban and social projects. These can range from large-scale public transportation interventions to the creation of new childcare centers as well as public space infrastructure. The EPM´s services include electricity, water, sewage, gas and waste management, which are charged to households at different rates depending on their income level. The company has been so successful that it expanded internationally and provides services to other Latin American countries. Its financial strength enables it to access private banking loans in order to fund more ambitious urban projects. Cities in Latin America and worldwide have attempted to replicate the EPM model with different levels of success. It requires fair management, transparency and accountability which make it challenging to

120 New York Conference of Mayors 2015.

121 World Bank, "Slum-upgrading in Rio de Janeiro: Favela Bairro," 2010, 4. (accessed January 5, 2018).

122 The majority of the investment cost (60%) was covered by the IDB, with the remainder covered by municipal sources. Under the *Favela Bairro* program, a maximum of US$ 4,000 could be spent per household.

123 World Bank, (2010), 1.

124 Ibid., 2.

125 Over the past years CAF has entered into agreements to finance urban projects directly with over 16 city governments in Brazil including Fortaleza, Maceio, Salvador, Porto Alegre and Palmas.

adopt for political cultures where corruption is pervasive. Public services in Latin America tend to work completely opposite the EPM model, where services are subsidized and represent a cost for national or local governments, instead of a potential source of income. The fact that a public company generates income and contributes to the city's economy with jobs and investments in social infrastructure, is unique in Latin America. The EPM has financed many of the better-known social projects in communities including the system of public libraries, cultural centers, nurseries, and more recently the Articulated Unit of Life (Unidad de Vida Articulada UVA). It is an innovative and sustainable financial strategy that allows the city to enjoy independence from national government resources.

II. PRIVATE, CIVIC OR NON-GOVERNMENTAL ENTITIES

4. Non-refundable private donations.

Some of the projects discussed in this investigation have been financed through non-refundable donations by private foundations, the United Nations or other non-government entities. NGOs can apply and compete for grants to implement social programs locally. If awarded, they are committed to executing the project according to the guidelines they have stated in
120 their project brief. In the case of Desco, in Lima, the funds came from the European Community. Through an agreement, Desco sets out progressive mile markers to be achieved within a determined amount of time until the project's completion. This financial mechanism is appropriate for more moderately scaled interventions that nonetheless, can have a significant social impact. Typically, projects are designed to address specific United Nations SDGs, such as increasing the empowerment of women in communities, mitigating risk from natural disasters, increasing sanitation and lowering child mortality rates. Increasing resilience was the focus of the Desco project in Lima, where several safety plazas were built throughout the spontaneous settlement of Santa María El Triunfo to provide refuge for people during earthquakes but also to create public space. Resources available for risk mitigation projects in vulnerable communities were coupled with the provision of public space.

In Miravalle, Mexico, a combination of waste management, public space and water harvesting initiatives, advanced over time by an association of local community groups, received the
168 Deutsche Bank Urban Age Award in 2010. The grant money allowed the community to finance a cistern for rainwater collected from a domed roof in a public space. The water is used to serve a nearby soup kitchen for children. The funds also helped develop an educational center with greenhouses, urban agriculture irrigated with water collected from rain, and various productive activities such as using recycled plastic to make planters, benches and household items. Over the course of 7 years, between 2007 and 2014, the Deutsche Bank Award was granted to projects worldwide which, through local partnerships, contributed to improving the quality of life of underprivileged populations using innovative approaches.

88 The urban agriculture project along the Rimac River in Lima was financed by the United Nations Development Program through the Small Grants Project that invites organizations to apply for grants. Proposals are evaluated for their merit, design intention and the social indicators they address. In the Rimac River case, the Central Communal Banks of San Agustino and Santa Anita (Central de Bancos Comunales de Agustino and Santa Anita) presented a project to advance gender inclusion and empower community women through urban agriculture and land remediation. They were awarded a 50,000 USD grant which funded a capacity building workshops for women, the plant-based water filtration infrastructure for irrigation, as well as the vegetable gardens. Women who benefited from the program in turn, became instructors for subsequent cohorts of women farmers.

5. Social responsibility programs in the private sector.

Increasingly, private companies, especially those that work at an international scale, are incorporating social responsibility departments in their operations. The programs they sponsor may coincide with social or environmental issues directly related with their products or services. For example, Procter and Gamble tends to sponsor projects that address water conservation, and Avon funds programs to increase the empowerment of women. In particular cases, such interests extend to urban considerations. This was the case of the Citibank funded program City Planting in Venezuela. The program addressed the built environment of spontaneous 104 settlements by engaging communities in educational processes to renew or build new public spaces. In the Municipality of Baruta in Caracas, a project was chosen and designed by the community to end 30 years of waste dumping on a site and transform it into a public square. It involved the community's buy in and participation, but also the support of the municipality. Together they agreed to uphold a new approach to solid waste management. The municipality also issued an official document recognizing La Palomera Plaza as public space on municipal land.

Financial contributions from private companies are also key components of initiatives such as AfroReggae in Rio de Janeiro and Alto Perú, in Lima. Both receive support and donations from 232 local and international companies on an ongoing basis. Movistar, for example, is a continuous sponsor of AfroReggae; Mapfre, Herbalife and Corona, support Alto Perú. The companies and 240 the initiatives become narrowly associated with one another. As a result, the social initiative gains prestige and recognition through its connection with well-known private companies, while the companies are praised for their support of a worthy cause in addition to benefiting from the marketing and visibility they contractually receive in exchange for sponsorship.

6. Self-generated income.

In addition to the resources AfroReggae receives from the sponsorship of private companies, it also generates income through its own activities. 30% of expenses are covered with funds earned by the institution. AfroReggae hosts events, such as music concerts and dance performances, in which attendance is charged. Fees to participate in courses such as music lessons, dance classes and visual arts programs contribute to the institution´s income as well, although to a lesser degree since the fee are low so that they are accessible to families. Nonetheless, these payments and the ticket sales represent important sources of revenue that have allowed AfroReggae to finance its activates and even grow over the past 20 years.

7. Community initiatives.

Civil society can also organize and contribute human resources toward common goals and create significant urban impact without necessarily relying on financial backing. For example, the *favela* communities of Chapéu Mangueira and Babilônia, took on a reforestation project 80 with the support of a civic organization. Responsible for the deforestation of the natural reserve located on the *morro* immediately above, the community became exposed to increased temperatures and more frequent landslides. They had also lost the recreational and ecological interest this resource once represented for the neighborhood and the city. The community began a process of gradual reforestation, eventually achieving a complete recovery of the forest. They also created paths leading to the crest of the exposed rock, which is a *de facto* public plaza where youth and children fly kites on a regular basis. The project brought important benefits to the community in terms of a cleaner environment, a recovered microclimate and landslide risk mitigation. The initiative also helped recover part of the city´s natural heritage. The new destination increased the frequency and number of guests and sightseers to the *favelas*. This in turn has allowed the inhabitants of Chapéu Mangueira and Babilônia to increase their local productivity through services, restaurants, bars and youth hostels for visitors and foreign students. With nominal financial investment, a very significant urban impact was achieved and the perception of barriers between "formal" and "informal" sectors in the city was weakened.

III. PUBLIC PRIVATE PARTNERSHIPS

8. Joint collaborations between local government and private sponsors.

The "El Calvario Puertas Abiertas" (El Calvario Open Doors) initiative was designed and conceived from the beginning as a joint effort between the Municipality of El Hatillo and a group of private organizations to help integrate El Calvario with its surroundings, especially the historic colonial center of El Hatillo, located only a few meters away. Although the event only lasts a day, there is a great deal of planning involved that creates an excuse for the community, the municipality and various other organizations to work together. The municipality contributes with advertisement on its social media networks. On the day of the event, it also organizes a group of volunteers to guide visitor through the settlement and the various activities taking place. As a result of community advocacy, a pedestrian crosswalk that connects El Calvario with the colonial town center (something that surprisingly did not exist before) was constructed by the municipality in time for the program´s second edition. Private companies participate by funding urban interventions, murals and music concerts; others set up food and drink concessions. Cultural organizations and artists donate their time and creativity to host specific events and interventions within the overall program. The community participates by offering their homes as venues for various activities. The sum of these efforts effectively creates a complete and varied program that rehearses scenarios of collaboration between the community and both private and public entities. These relationships in turn may serve as a base to structure more complex urban initiatives in the future.

The public space project in the Avellaneda District of Buenos Aires has been developed and built through the support of a private foundation. In Villa Tranquila, Buenos Aires, the Plaza Vicente Lopez was the result of collaboration between the community, architects and the Avellaneda Municipality. Funds for the project's development and execution were donated by PlaySpace Foundation, a Dutch-Argentinian entity, expressly created to finance projects that improve the livelihood of children through games and places for play. In addition to the built square, a larger scheme of public spaces for the neighborhood was designed and incorporated into municipal plans for spontaneous settlement rehabilitation.

9. Management of public programs through private sector social responsibility initiatives.

Medellin´s local government has created a very effective collaborative structure between the private and the public sector in which the operation and maintenance of cultural and social programs is often managed by privately funded consortiums, through concession agreements. For example, in the case of the public library parks, the municipality builds the infrastructure and ensures its physical maintenance. Funding to cover operative costs including staff, activities and equipment, however, is shared with private entities known in Colombia as "cajas de compensación" or compensation funds. These are non-for-profit, private entities that redistribute economic resources to improve the quality of life for workers and their families. Confama and Comfenalco are two of the *cajas* that frequently participate in funding cultural programs in Medellin.[126] The municipality organizes, coordinates and unifies the services for each library within the system, including book loan practices and other guidelines. Each library is operated in turn through agreements with an entity from the private sector. The EPM Foundation also plays a key role, especially in the library system, funding cultural activities and programs, as in the case of the Botero Library. The Moravia Cultural Center is somewhat different. It is the result of a very specific community initiative that began as the House for All (Casa para Todos) and later became a cultural center. Still its operation is similarly funded through separate private resources, in this case by Comfenalco Antioquia.[127] The private sector's willingness to share the cost and responsibility for the municipality's social programs has proven a potent and sustainable financial model that engages society at large in championing and sustaining social initiatives.

126 Confama. https://www.comfama.com/webinicio/default.asp, (accessed November 28, 2018).

127 Centro Cultural Moravia. http://www.centroculturalmoravia.org/ (accessed November 28, 2018).

10. Complementary activities of local government programs by private NGOs.

Over the years, Alto Perú in Lima has evolved and grown into a more complex and comprehensive support structure for vulnerable youth. In addition to teaching children how to surf, the organization offers complementary cultural and sports activities in the winter months, and supports children participating in the program with academic activities and homework. Alto Perú has also forged alliances with public entities such as the Instituto Peruano del Deporte (Peruvian Sports Institute), the Federación Nacional de Tabla (National Surf Federation) and the Federación Deportiva Peruana de Muaythay (Peruvian Sports Federation of Muaythay), which are state sponsored sports associations. The benefit of these alliances is that Alto Perú can share its methodology more broadly and reach children in other vulnerable communities of Lima. The intention is to strengthen these existing public institutions that have access to federal resources, with the practical knowledge Alto Perú has generated in youth engagement and create more effective social programs within the public sector.

COMMUNITY ENGAGEMENT STRATEGIES TO STRENGTHEN SPONTANEOUS SETTLEMENT INTERVENTIONS ASSOCIATED WITH PUBLIC SPACE

Urban transformation projects, especially those inserted within spontaneous settlement communities, over time have revealed the critical importance of social processes and the involvement of the community in a project´s success and ultimate sustainability. Projects can be met with resistance if the community feels threatened by an insensitive or aggressive approach, or resents not being considered during the formulation-process. Neighbors know their community well and have observed the land over time, which represents knowledge professionals should consider as projects take shape. Additionally, the community may have ideas and suggestions they should be invited to communicate. The incorporation of these contributions in the design of a particular project represents an important avenue for its assimilation and appropriation by the community. It is also important to identify individuals or social groups that are known to be antagonistic toward community projects. By working closely with neighbors, design teams can find ways to incorporate these groups into the process. It is often the case that antagonists feel excluded or insufficiently acknowledged. Considering their input and opinions helps diminish or even eliminate potential interference with the project down the line. Strategies that create pacific, inclusive and consensual processes may prevent setbacks and ultimately allows resources to be used more efficiently.

In order to formulate projects that respond efficiently to a community´s needs, sensitive observation and a diagnostic phase are crucial. Secondly, projects must be designed as processes that are premised on the participation of communities. Unfortunately, ill-intentioned programs, focused on manipulating people for political support and votes, have created unwelcoming predispositions within spontaneous settlement residents that are challenging to overcome. Communities have good reasons to feel distrust toward new projects, especially if they are generated through initiatives authored by outside individuals or groups. Creating social processes focused on better communication with the community allows them to gain awareness about the issues that threaten their built environment and at the same time recognize the potential for change. This is important since sharing a common language is essential to building consensus on specific aspects of any given urban project. For example, although access to public space could bring many benefits to a community, provide recreation outlets for youth and a perception of greater security, the community may instead associate open space with crime and areas where gangs tend to gather, leading them to reject public space proposals. Other approaches toward strengthening social cohesion and increasing access to opportunities to practice sports, art and culture, are generated through institutionalized programs associated with particular physical infrastructures. Access to these facilities offers youth alternative choices to joining gangs and violent lifestyles.

Two approaches emerge from the case studies included in this research: strategies that facilitate and strengthen the implementation of urban projects, and institutionalized programs associated with physical facilities or public spaces. The first group of social strategies is designed to accompany urban projects implemented in spontaneous settlements. Some of these strategies address the challenges of specific project types. For example, environmentally sensitive projects often require the removal of structures from unsafe land, and must therefore address the social dimension of relocating families and helping then overcome the trauma of leaving a home. Families will tend to see relocation as a tragedy. Acknowledging the emotional stress this creates is essential. Communicating the implications of staying where they are must be explained with sensitivity and compassion for the despair and loss they feel. Housing relocation projects may not even be plausible if proper community mentorship, with the aid of social psychologists and educators, is not considered.

Other strategies are focused on methods. For example, the organization and empowerment of a community is a strategy that convenes neighbors and takes advantage of local human resources to pursue projects of common interest. But building these internal self-governance structures requires the specific skills of professional facilitators. Community members will be served best if they can adopt communication methods that allow them to both listen to each other, converse productively, find common ground, build consensus, and resolve conflicts. The value of an organized and united community is that it can achieve critical projects even with scarce financial resources. Another methodological example is to transform the design and building process of a spontaneous settlement intervention into an inclusive and participatory experience. Participatory design methodologies help neighbors register their desires, build agreements, and ultimately feel connected to a project. Shared urban spaces should enjoy everyone's approval and recognition, including disgruntled neighbors, youth gangs and other disenfranchised individuals. This can be achieved if social processes are specifically designed to be inclusive and respectful. Both, community organization and participatory design processes, foment more fluid and productive forms of communication and help reduce and even avoid potential conflicts that arise during the implementation of an urban transformation project.

The second group of strategies for projects within spontaneous settlements has to do with institutionalized social programs to offset inequalities in terms of economic power, gender and other aspects. They may often be associated with physical structures and urban amenities. For example, access to nurseries for infants is a crucial support for families, because it affords both parents the possibility to work, without compromising their children's upbringing or neglecting them. Nursery programs such as *Buen Comienzo*, in Medellin, guarantee proper attention and nourishment for children, and are a very important step for families to exit the poverty cycle. Children receive proper attention, access to opportunities and education, and mothers can work or complete their schooling, which is necessary to increase a family´s income. Youth are another segment of the population that requires special attention. Programs that encourage them to participate in productive life projects, which offer a sense of belonging and support, are crucial to keep them from falling into the temptation of joining youth gangs. Sports activities, culture and art programs are effective channels to communicate with youth, encourage them to think outside of their immediate context and seek higher goals. Senior citizens are another vulnerable population segment that tends to be overlooked. They need institutionalized care and attention during the day, so as to not compromise the time of productive family members that would otherwise have to leave work to care for them. Social programs that address their needs are, therefore, relevant support structures for families and communities. These and other support programs allow underprivileged population segments opportunities for study and work, which in turn can help them access more productive lifestyles.

The projects presented in this research fall into either one of the two groups mentioned above, and some may even have components of both. At the same time, both groups can be further categorized into three subsets. They will be described in the following order:

I. Social accompaniment
1. Housing relocation social support
2. Participatory design processes
3. Community organization

II. Social programs
4. Programs focused on youth to mitigate violence
5. Empowerment of women
6. Culture and art programs

I. SOCIAL ACCOMPANIMENT

1. Housing relocation social support.

Spontaneous settlements are often established over environmentally sensitive land. Such is the case of structures on the edges of the Estero Salado, in Guayaquil, and the Juan Bobo Creek, in Medellin. A self-built home represents the greatest life investment for families; parting with it is a very traumatic situation. Their attachment is far greater than conventional relationships with houses and apartments. Even though the intention of both the Guayaquil and Medellin examples is to increase resilience and create more sustainable living environments for people, relocating families to safer areas or substitution housing has delicate social implications that require professional assistance to mentor families through the process. To begin with, a diagnostic phase is required and an inventory of the affected homes, including their qualitative conditions and the number of people in each unit, needs to be made. Then conversations begin with the affected families, through which a great deal of trust needs to be built between them and the authorities. This is done through dialogue, but also by showing them possible housing alternatives, discussing what their relocation will entail in terms of cost and time, and explaining in very graphic terms the risks they are exposed to if they continue to live where they are.

Qualified professionals and social psychology experts must be incorporated as part of the project team so that families can receive support and learn to assimilate the changes they will face. Once the first families have been successfully relocated, the process becomes simpler, as others have an easier time believing their relocation can also happen successfully. Community mentorship needs to continue even after the families have been relocated, in order to help neighbors coexist peacefully. Establishing and agreeing on rules for noise, loud music, the use of common spaces and respect for private property, is crucial to guarantee that neighbors will be able to live harmoniously in their new settings. Very often these aspects are left out of project budgets, compromising the success of a costly social investment.[128]

The following step is to raze the original houses, which usually is a difficult event for home owners. Professional assistance is needed for the process to go as smoothly as possible and allow any resistance to be contained or minimized. Even though the safety benefits from relocation are obvious, numerous projects have been frustrated not for financial constraints, but because of the community's resistance. If they are not property taken into consideration during the decision-making phase this is often the result. Coercive measures have been used in the past, but are no longer condoned and ultimately do not ensure success in the long run. They are not only cruel, but also condemned by the most recent United Nations Habitat statutes of the 2016 New Urban Agenda[129]

In the case of the Estero Salado projects in Guayaquil, relocation addressed the risk of families living in unsafe homes over improvised landfills, as well as the ecological damage they were

128 During a visit to the Medellin Juan Bobo housing project, in May 2012, interviews with the community repeatedly highlighted a desire for more social support from the municipality to address issues of coexistence among neighbors.

129 Language in the New Urban Agenda NUA is very firm against unlawful evictions.
UN Habitat, "New Urban Agenda" Habitat III Quito, October, 2016.

creating by discharging sewage and waste into the river. Over the past decade, thousands of families have been relocated into social housing and other alternative options. In their wake several kilometers of linear parks have been created that benefit the population with much needed public space but also discourage future dwellers from building again on the river edges. Access to the Estero Salado through public space ensures that people can appreciate and enjoy the river, and also watch over the continued conservation of this natural resource.

In the case of the relocation associated with the Juan Bobo Creek project, in Medellin, social 128
support was provided by the housing management team of the Empresa de Desarrollo Urbano EDU (Urban Development Company EDU). 300 families were relocated into ten buildings within 100 meters of their original home. Existing homes were evaluated and those with an acceptable construction quality and location were improved and others were adapted to create more regular plot conformations. Slopes along the ravine, where landslides could potentially occur, were reinforced with retaining walls and the entire neighborhood was equipped with public sewage networks to avoid contaminating the creek. These operations also incorporated public space such as walkways, bridges, landscapes and squares to dignify the surrounding area and improve accessibility.[130]

2. Participatory design processes.

The participation and input of neighbors during the initial conception, design development and construction of public space interventions in spontaneous settlements are crucial to ensure a favorable reception of the project by the community. Neighbors who have the opportunity to feel personally invested in the project are more likely to contribute to its maintenances over time. Community participation also makes the project more relevant by tapping into the knowledge of the local population, which can strengthen its content. Participatory processes also help identify potential adversaries early on, allowing the design team and the community sufficient time to devise strategies that incorporate them into the process, before construction begins. The aspiration for any given urban project is for the community to become its champion, and develop a strong sense of identity and pride for what they helped accomplish.

In Cerro Toro and Cerro Santo Domingo, in Valparaiso, the participatory process began during 176
the project´s planning phase. The design team developed a strategy, called *Puerta a puerta cultura local* (door to door local culture), in order to establish a closer, more direct relationship with neighbors. The community was acknowledged and consulted in the project´s decision-making process using this methodology. In the beginning, the dynamic focused on hearing members of the communities share their history and contemporary narratives which were later discussed at large. Then, each individual formulated his/her own ideas for the project and listened to those of their neighbors. They were invited to see themselves as experts on their urban fragment, and voice opinions about the design. The methodology enabled people to participate and contribute toward strengthening the overall project. The shape and materiality of the public space, in the end, was the result of a continuous dialogue, in which trust was built between the community and the design professionals.[131]

3. Community organization.

Communities that count on an organized entity to represent them, whether in the form of a local authority or a group of neighbors, are well prepared to develop and guide the implementation of spontaneous settlement interventions. Community organization doesn't happen spontaneously; it requires sound leadership and key actors who are able to develop communication skills, negotiation skills, and the ability to listen to others and compromise. These capabilities are learned through workshops led by social workers, educators and social psychologists. Proposed urban interventions including public space, and all projects that take

130 Alejandro Echeverri and Francesco Orsini "Informality and Social Urbanism in Medellin" in *Medellin Environment, Urbanism and Society* 2008, 148. https://pdfs.semanticscholar.org/0fcb/410c512f443d7455c461bbc7c560849ef0a5.pdf (accessed January 10, 2018).

131 CAF (2015), p. 40.

place in the common domain within communities, should be consulted with neighbors, represented by their community organizations, for approval. Community organizations also help share project information and effectively disseminate messages among inhabitants. They are able to facilitate the exchange of different opinions with respect and tolerance among neighbors, identifying shared interests and building consensus. The example of Chapéu Mangueira
30 – Babilônia, in Rio de Janeiro, is a case in point. The community decided to recover the forest it had destroyed. A common objective inspired them to join efforts and create a communal organization to direct the project. They ultimately succeeded in reforesting all 42 hectares, by inviting neighbors and friends to plant trees one by one. Through the sheer accumulation of human resources, they were able to reforest the entire natural reserve. Community organizations ultimately can enable significant transformations by creating transparent and inclusive processes that earn people´s trust.

II. SOCIAL PROGRAMS

4. Programs focused on youth to mitigate violence.

Programs that create opportunities for youth to choose more meaningful life projects through sports, arts and culture, can have an important impact on reducing urban violence. Certain sports activities require access to large open spaces in the form of playfields and recreation areas. Cultural and artistic expressions, such as concerts and graffiti art are also directly associated with public space, as well as urban sports such as skate boarding, skating, biking
232 and parkour. AfroReggae, in Rio de Janeiro, represents a cultural institution where youth are invited to practice musical instruments, dance, design, compose and mix music. The initiative operates in several locations and each of their facilities is equipped with state-of-the-art technology. The design of the facilities is inviting and attractive to neighborhood youths who not only see it as an interesting option to occupy their free time but who also want to feel they are part of a socially respected cultural institution in their community. AfroReggae is a vehicle for youth to develop personal talents. Additionally, they learn how to manage their time, in order to meet academic obligations and attend rehearsals and extracurricular courses. Kids also have the opportunity to share their talents with the community and receive public recognition for their efforts. AfroReggae uses public space as a platform for many of its activities, which allows their work to be more visible. It also fills the streets with people which increases the perception of safety. In front of the AfroReggae site, at Vigário Geral, an outdoor amphitheater has been created where performances are held on a regular basis. Their website boasts an ambitious calendar of cultural events directed at the local community as well as visitors and spectators from the city at large.

240 Alto Perú, in Lima, teaches vulnerable youth and children how to surf, through a social program whose deeper, real goal is to help them enter safer, healthier and more productive lives. As the children begin to surf, they understand that in order to become good at it, they need to eat healthily, go to bed early, wake up early and practice. The program encourages them to develop important personal skills, to set goals and work toward achieving them. These skills will be useful to them as they take on future challenges in their continued education and development into adulthood. As the children become talented surfers, the recognition they receive builds a sense of pride and self-confidence. As they adopt healthy lifestyles, the likelihood of falling into violence and gang membership, diminishes. Surfing in this sense is a vehicle for progress toward more productive lives and greater livelihood.

5. Empowerment of women.

Gender inequality is a critical issue in Latin America. It tends to be even more acute in communities of indigenous ancestry. Empowering women to develop personal skills that will grant them access to work opportunities and positions of leadership within their community, is crucial. In that sense, day care facilities are important not only for the children but also for the parents and particularly mothers. Assistance in taking care of their children, enables them to attend courses, finish their education, or gain access to better work opportunities. Women empowerment projects often include education components to strengthen their capabilities and allow them to compete for better quality jobs. Other projects empower women to become social leaders within their communities by teaching and strengthening communication skills and strategies to build consensus and resolve conflicts.

In Lima, the United Nations Development Program (UNDP) and the Food and Agriculture Organization (FAO) of the United Nations implemented an urban agriculture project along the banks of the Rimac River. Families and groups of women created vegetable plots and a 88
phytodepuration water treatment basin to filter the water they used for irrigation. The program, which began with workshops to learn about best practices in agriculture, sought to create food security for families who would be able to feed themselves with fewer resources. This case study is an example of how a project focused on food security, urban agriculture and environmental issues, can be successfully coupled with a social strategy to empower women and address gender inequality. It is also a successful example of how public space can include agriculture.

6. Culture and art programs.

The cultural centers and public library parks inserted within Medellin´s spontaneous settlements are allowing people of all demographic sectors (children, youth, adults and the elderly) to easily access forms of expression and communication such as visual arts, movies, theatre, dance, poetry, urban dance, and more. In the case of the Moravia Cultural Center, although 20
the building is many times larger than the self-made residential structures that surround it, its disposition is not monumental. The inner atrium is used by youth to rehearse choreographed dances, read or recite poetry. The auditorium is constantly in use for rehearsals by musicians, orchestras and bands, as well as the drama groups that have emerged precisely because of the newly acquired access they have to a first-rate facility. Likewise, practice rooms allow children and people of all ages to rehearse their instruments in a state-of-the-art facility. In other words, the existence of a physical structure, especially with the design integrity of this particular building, encourages the community to take advantage of it and increases demand for cultural activities. The director of the cultural center maintains a busy calendar of movie series, foreign films, theatre productions and musical concerts, as a way to further engage the community. The cultural center resists territorial distinctions based on wealth, since numerous forms of culture are accessible to neighbors of less privilege, with the same quality as those offered by other cultural institution, both locally and internationally.

The Botero library, also in Medellin, has been designed to offer communities, especially youth, the opportunity to engage art and culture. The library's western façade faces the community and is lined at the ground floor with practice rooms that youth reserve to choreograph dances. Glass storefronts along these rooms make them visible from the outside, encouraging people passing by to linger and look on. Younger children can see their older peers dancing, and may aspire to imitate them. The presence of the library has allowed a new urban dynamic to develop within the spontaneous settlement; one that offers alternative lifestyles for youth. The library also stages movie series and theatrical performances which take place in the auditorium. Bringing cultural programs and art to spontaneous settlement inhabitants gives them the opportunity to engage with alternative forms of discourse. Furthermore, the library's program of activities is disseminated beyond the community, incorporating San Cristobal into Medellín´s map of urban destinations.

Recognition is the most critical factor in advancing social inclusion and increased equality in urban territories. A crucial step in that direction is for all of society, including municipal institutions and the national government, to admit that in fact disparity exists in the way spontaneous settlements are perceived and treated. Recognition does not mean creating ad hoc programs for spontaneous settlement improvement, or specific initiatives to address particular social needs. It means a systematic look at how resources and time are spent within a city and acknowledging how the attention given to formal and informal sectors continues to be categorically different. For example, waste management is often resolved with garbage trucks that are dimensioned for the conventional roads of formal neighborhoods. These trucks do not work on the narrow streets, walkways and staircases of spontaneous settlements. And yet a parallel or equivalent solution is not adopted to serve these neighbors, even though adequate models are already being used in other parts of Latin America.[132] Just because conventional waste management solutions do not work in informal territories does not mean a municipality is exempt from serving them. For one, they are residents of the municipality. Secondly, other cities have already resolved the logistical nuances of working in a different urban typology (as in the case of waste collection). And most importantly, people living in spontaneous settlements often account for a very large percentage of a municipality's population. Therefore, they too should receive attention and resources to address their needs in terms of services, security and improvements.

Another example of how different consideration between formal and informal parts of the city are maintained by local government is street signage. As you approach Baruta or El Hatillo in Caracas, street signs indicate many neighborhoods. Even though La Palomera in Baruta or El Calvario in El Hatillo (both are spontaneous settlements) might be located a few meters away from these signs, they are not mentioned. It is as though two cities were superimposed, never meeting and never acknowledging one another. One presumption could be that previous administrations had not included these settlements on signage, and so by inertia the trend continued. And yet when new "formal" neighborhoods appear, they are incorporated into signs almost immediately, sometimes even before their construction is complete. From the perspective of civic society, no one seems to complain about this discrimination either, perhaps because they assume people that circulate by car are not going to spontaneous settlements anyways and so why would they need a street sign? Another reason could be a lingering desire for these settlements to be eradicated and replaced with formal neighborhoods, or for their inhabitants to be relocated to a "formal" neighborhood at another location. Either way, the supposition is that what exists is somehow reproachable and warrants being excluded. These examples reveal an entrenched pathology in the way cities are perceived, and furthermore in the messages that continue to be repeated and enforced.

132 *Ciudad Saludable* in Lima Peru has developed strategies for spontaneous settlements in Lima, and has been a consultant to municipalities in numerous other cities of the Global South.

One way to encourage the recognition of spontaneous settlements by fellow citizens is to create more occasions for public space within them, because it is the setting or platform that can allow people of different social groups to share a common space. One of the earliest advocates for public spaces as a spatial manifestation of inclusion was Frederick Law Olmstead in the mid 19th century. When writing *Parks and the expansion of towns* he was keen to emphasize this point.[133] Olmsted was fascinated by how people of lesser economic standing would frequent parks, wear their best clothes and behave in the most "genteel" and correct manner. He noted how gentlemen too, and families of well-to-do backgrounds visited the park. He felt it was important for different people to share the grounds of Central Park in New York or Prospect Park in Brooklyn, as a way of acknowledging and celebrating what city life had brought to people in terms of opportunities for work and self-improvement. The park could appeal to all social classes for reasons centered on personal wellbeing, health and entertainment. The trees in the park, Olmsted explained, provide clean air, and the open space allows more sunlight to enter the city. He also stressed how parks provide an outlet for recreation and contact with nature which he argued helped city dwellers recover inner peace in an otherwise hostile urban environment. He noted how the number of men in parks had increased on weekends, often in the company of their families, while those seated in "grogshops" had decreased. Furthermore, Olmstead calls on local authorities and cities as well as the private sector to reserve as much space for parks as possible, since parks not only safeguard the possibility for citizens to enjoy the outdoors, but they also help ameliorate crime levels, reduce diseases, increase life expectancy, and mitigate stress and other urban ills. He even documented how properties around Central Park had increased in value and how other private property owners had reserved open space as a strategy to increase the value of their land. Nearly two centuries later, public space continues to bring these environmental and social benefits to cities. In comparison to other urban land uses, it is the only one that preserves a common ground for all citizens and offers the possibility for social integration.

When contemplating smaller scales of public spaces, such as those one may find in a spontaneous settlement, they are still the only places within a neighborhood that welcome all segments of society, without regard to economic status, race or color. Making such spaces accessible and more frequent in spontaneous settlements gives outsiders a destination where they can arrive that is accepted by locals as public. Once these small plazas and playgrounds becomes commonplace, they create opportunities for dissimilar people to share the same moment in space and time. Incorporating these places more and more into the informal fabric, in turn, communicates acknowledgement. It is in this sense that public space becomes a platform for recognition and a way to edge cities toward greater urban integration.

Another consideration regarding spontaneous settlements is that their existing urban morphology offers spaces that already function as public space, although in ways that are different from the codes practiced in "formal" public spaces. As we become more familiar and accustomed with the particular nature of spontaneous settlement communities, appreciating the existing value in those spaces, just as they are, with renewed eyes, without prejudice and less preconceptions, is also a gesture of inclusion and recognition. The dimensions and morphologies of walkways, staircases and their intersections do not fit the typical definitions of plazas, playgrounds and boulevards. Instead, they have their own inherent quality and offer opportunities for social exchanges equal or perhaps even more nuanced than those associated with conventional public spaces. Learning to appreciate and ultimately recognize the very rich spatial qualities of spontaneous settlement urban fabric could ultimately be the single most important conceptual shift that can allow a city to be understood as "complete."[134]

133 Frederick Law Olmsted, "Public Parks and the expansion of towns." In Charles Beveridge (Ed.), *Frederick Law Olmsted: Writings on Landscape, Culture and Society* (Baltimore: John Hopkins University Press, 2015).

134 Enlace Arquitectura and Ciudad Laboratorio worked together on a program in Caracas called Integration Process Caracas that created a Manifesto to the Complete City as part of its activities. The Manifesto also addressed several of the discriminatory practices by municipalities mentioned in this text and the importance of recognition.

Appreciating the uniqueness of spontaneous settlement public space and creating new plazas and parks, however, is not enough. Efforts need to be made to create motives and premises for people to begin to visit and use the services of spontaneous settlements within their urban routines. Lack of personal safety is often used as an excuse to explain why spontaneous settlements are not included in peoples´ mental city maps. In some select cases this may be true, but there are also numerous communities that are no more or less dangerous than the rest of the city. Many settlements have been around now for nearly a century, enabling generations of families to access the benefits of city life, and improve their livelihood to the point where most have become well-educated working-class citizens. The inner dynamics of these settlements in many cases is even safer than those of more dispersed areas in the city simply because neighbors know each other, their families are intertwined and they enjoy a strong sense of community. *Barrios* have a lot to offer the city in terms of culinary culture, music, festivities and celebrations. Getting to know them, and allowing them to share their spaces with the rest of the city is key to building bridges and avenues for sincere recognition. Initiatives such as AfroReggae, Casa Kolacho and El Calvario Puertas Abiertas are instrumental in creating such opportunities. They open spaces for culture, music and celebration that appeal to the city at large and build foundations for integration.

Both the public and private sector have developed a segregated, discontinuous and fragmented fabric in cities of Latin America, over the last decades. This reality is not innocuous; it seriously threatens the continued prosperity and social stability of cities. We cannot deny that inequality has deteriorated the quality of cities and the livelihood of its inhabitants. For national governments to continue to focus solely on housing, knowing it can only benefit a small percentage of the people excluded from urban dynamics is irresponsible and even reproachable. For municipalities to continuing serving their inhabitants differently based on the typology of their neighborhood is blatant discrimination. For civil society to continue to be an indifferent spectator of these occurrences, makes it an accomplice to the persistence of inequality. However, taking steps to at least restore a basic level of inclusion and belonging, can go a long way toward improving the social, environmental and social prognosis of cities. In that sense, public space investments offer a promising strategy to begin a process of recognition of all territories, inhabitants and histories within a city. Achieving a "complete city" where everyone participates in the delivery and defense of recognition as a basic human right, is more than a good intention. It is a timely and effective strategy for cities to continue to be the vehicle of modernity par excellence, that allows people to access opportunities and pursue their aspirations.

PART II

CASE STUDIES:

– CONSERVATION
– WASTE MANAGEMENT
– RISK MANAGEMENT
– INFRASTRUCTURE
– PAVEMENTS & BUILDINGS
– ACTIVITY

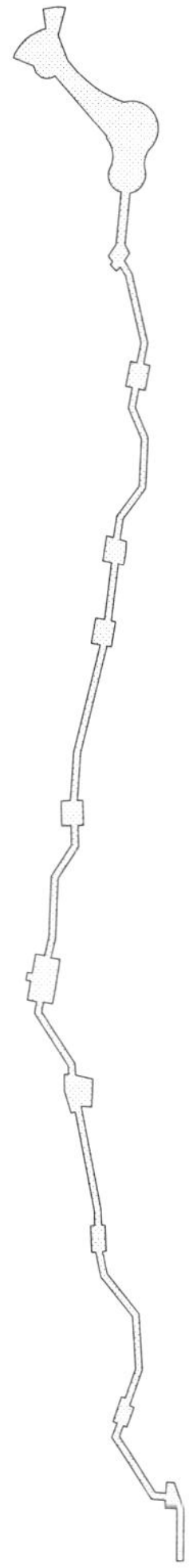

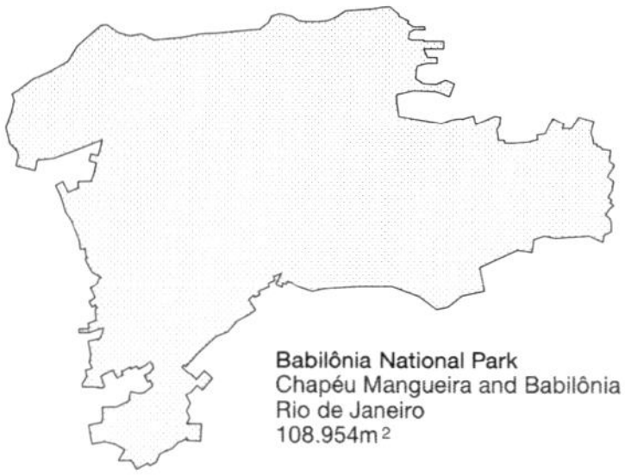

Babilônia National Park
Chapéu Mangueira and Babilônia
Rio de Janeiro
108.954m²

Urban agriculture along the Rimac River
Rimac River
Lima
3.521m²

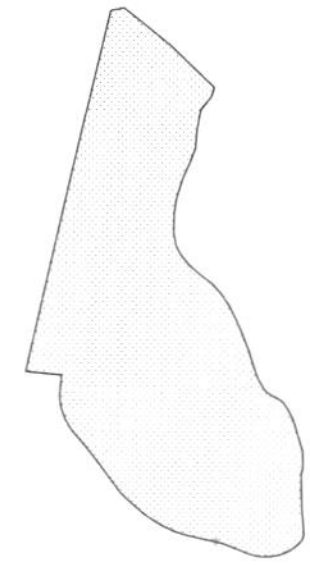

Moravia Ecological Park
Moravia
Medellin
32.766m²

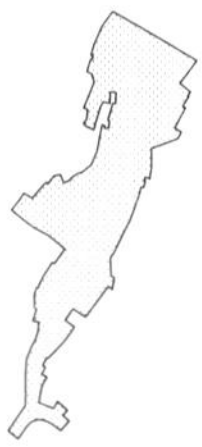

Recovery of the Juan Bobo Creek
Comuna 2 Santa Cruz
Medellin
16.850m²

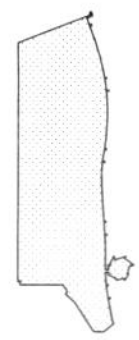

El Guasmo Beach floodable park
Estero Salado
Guayaquil
11.016m²

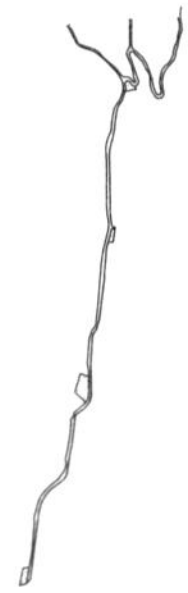

Safety Plazas
Santa María El Triunfo
Villa María del Triunfo
Lima
12.088m²

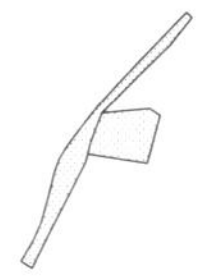

Plaza La Cruz La Palomera
La Palomera
Caracas
225m²

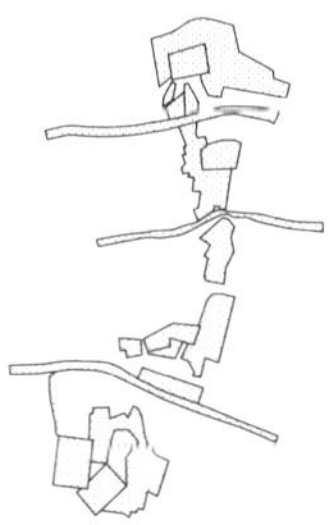

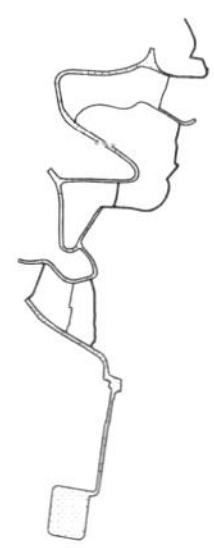

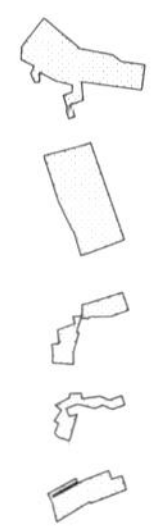

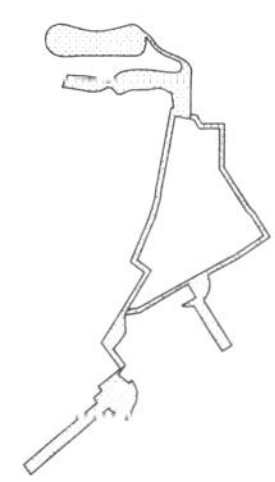

Linear parks along the Estero Salado
Estero Salado
Guayaquil
194.446m²

Northeast cable car parks
Comuna 1 La Popular
Medellin
19.491m²

El Calvario Puertas Abiertas
El Calvario
Caracas
9.092m²

Funicular in Dona Marta
Dona Marta
Rio de Janeiro
3.214m²

Cerro Santa Ana urban rehabilitation
Santa Ana
Guayaquil
31.492m²

Complexo Alemão
Complexo Alemão
Rio de Janeiro
36.926m²

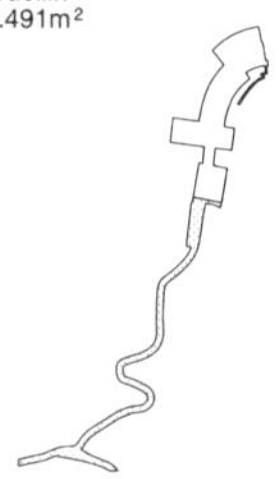

Espaço Criança and community programs
Cantagalo
Rio de Janeiro
3.122m²

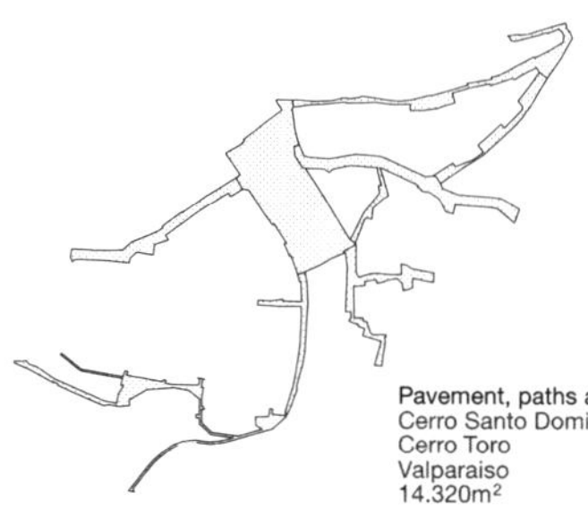

Pavement, paths and stairs
Cerro Santo Domingo and Cerro Toro
Valparaiso
14.320m²

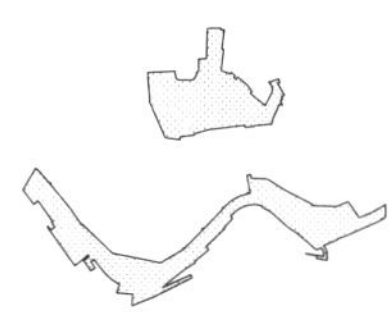

Barrio Las Independencias escalators and walkways
Comuna 13 San Javier
Medellin
13.784m²

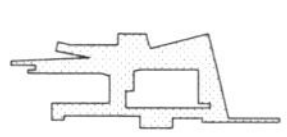

Fernando Botero Library
San Cristóbal
Medellin
1.073m²

Alto Perú
Alto Perú
Lima
3.258m²

Moravia Cultural Center
Moravia
Medellin
1.187m²

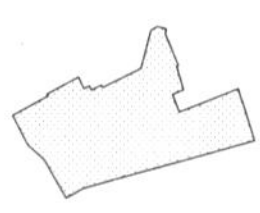

Plaza in Villa Tranquila
Villa Tranquila
Buenos Aires
5.167m²

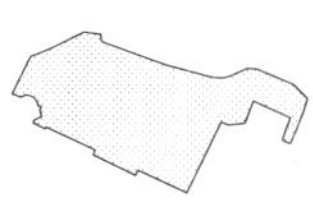

Casa Kolacho
Comuna 13 San Javier
Medellin
4.674m²

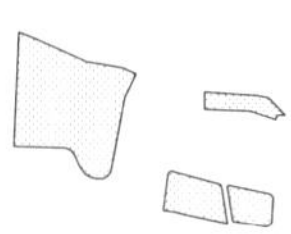

Ecotecnia Urbana Miravalle
Miravalle
Mexico City
9.082m²

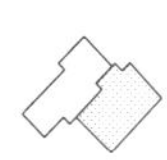

AfroReggae Cultural Center
Vigario Geral
Rio de Janeiro
850m²

LINEAR PARKS ALONG THE EDGES OF THE ESTERO SALADO GUAYAQUIL

Guayaquil is located on the delta of the River Guayas as it runs into the Pacific Ocean. The urban fabric shares space with water canals, known as *esteros*, that traverse the city. Once lined with mangroves, the encroachment of spontaneous settlements along the water edges caused severe ecological damage. Self- built homes were constructed over debris and waste, used to gain land from the river. Their sewage was dumped directly into the river. Furthermore, because of their precarious foundations, these homes were constantly exposed to the risk of collapsing. Over the course of the last decade, the City of Guayaquil has progressively relocated families living in the most vulnerable areas and subsequently transformed the banks of the *estero* into linear parks with play fields, ball courts and boardwalks. Access to public space has consequently increased, from 1 m^2 per capita to 7 m^2.[1] These measures have also helped decontaminate the water allowing fauna to return and sports, such as rowing, to flourish. The Malecón Salado is a segment of the park system located in the Urdaneta Parish that borders the southern edge of the *estero* over a linear distance of 1.9 km.

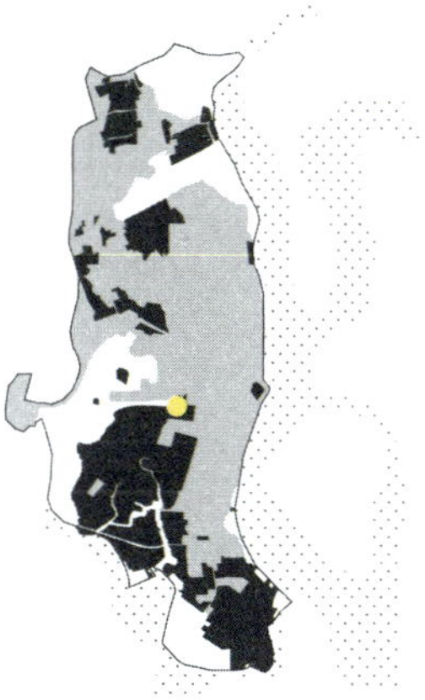

Location
Estero Salado, Guayaquil, Ecuador

Project team:
Municipality of Guayaquil and Malecón 2000 Foundation

Date
2009 - 2012

Coordinates
2 °11'24.85 "S79°54'06.25" O

Investment
40 million USD

Public space area
12,000 m²

Urban density
115.36 hab / ha

Population benefited
33,769 hab

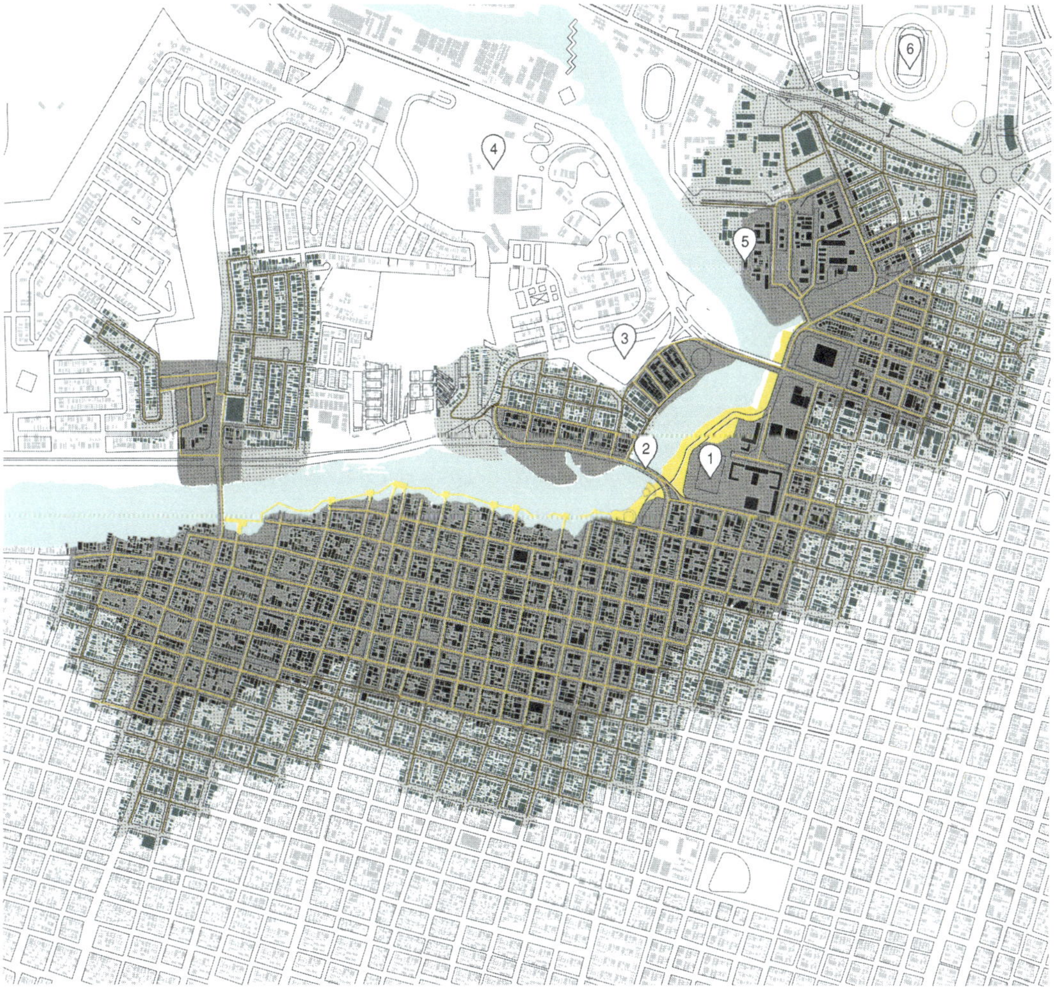

PUBLIC SPACE

Ecologically sensitive areas, declared natural reservations within cities, are at risk of becoming spontaneous settlements if left unattended. They can be effectively protected and preserved by providing access to them and allowing the edges to function as public space. The Estero Salado's linear park system is progressively restoring the ecological balance of the river network and preventing further urban encroachments by making the space visible and accessible.

HISTORY

Guayaquil is an international port city and represents an important commercial and economic center for Ecuador. During the eighties and early nineties, a weak local government administration allowed public services to deteriorate and passively witnessed an increase in informal urban development. In 1992, in response to this situation, the municipality began a comprehensive program called Urban Regeneration, which among other improvements addressed public services and building a network of public space along the Guayas river and the *esteros* that flow into it.[2]

SOCIAL AND POLITICAL CONTEXT

In 1992, León Febres-Cordero, former president of Ecuador, became the mayor of Guayaquil and introduced greater transparency and efficiency to the way public administration was handled. Then, in 2000, Jaime Nebot continued his predecessor's impetus through urban improvements focused on activating the private sector, increasing tourism and strengthening social cohesion. The Malecón 2000 was an emblematic project of the Urban Regeneration program. A public policy framework was established to ensure the maintenance and sustainability of these investments.[3]

ENVIRONMENTAL SITUATION

Even though the river edges were protected by zoning laws, they became urbanized with spontaneous settlements as rural-urban migration increased. Self-built homes along the *estero*, on precariously constructed landfill made of waste and debris, represented an imminent threat for the families living in them. Furthermore, residents disposed of their sewage water and waste in the river. High levels of contamination devastated the *estero*´s native flora and fauna. The Urban Regeneration program mitigated many of these urban ills, and produced new parks, as mentioned earlier.[4] This increased the city´s supply of public space and helped prevent future constructions and the improper disposal of sewage by making the river visible. The park network is continuous between informal and formal urban areas, thereby contributing to the city´s physical integration.

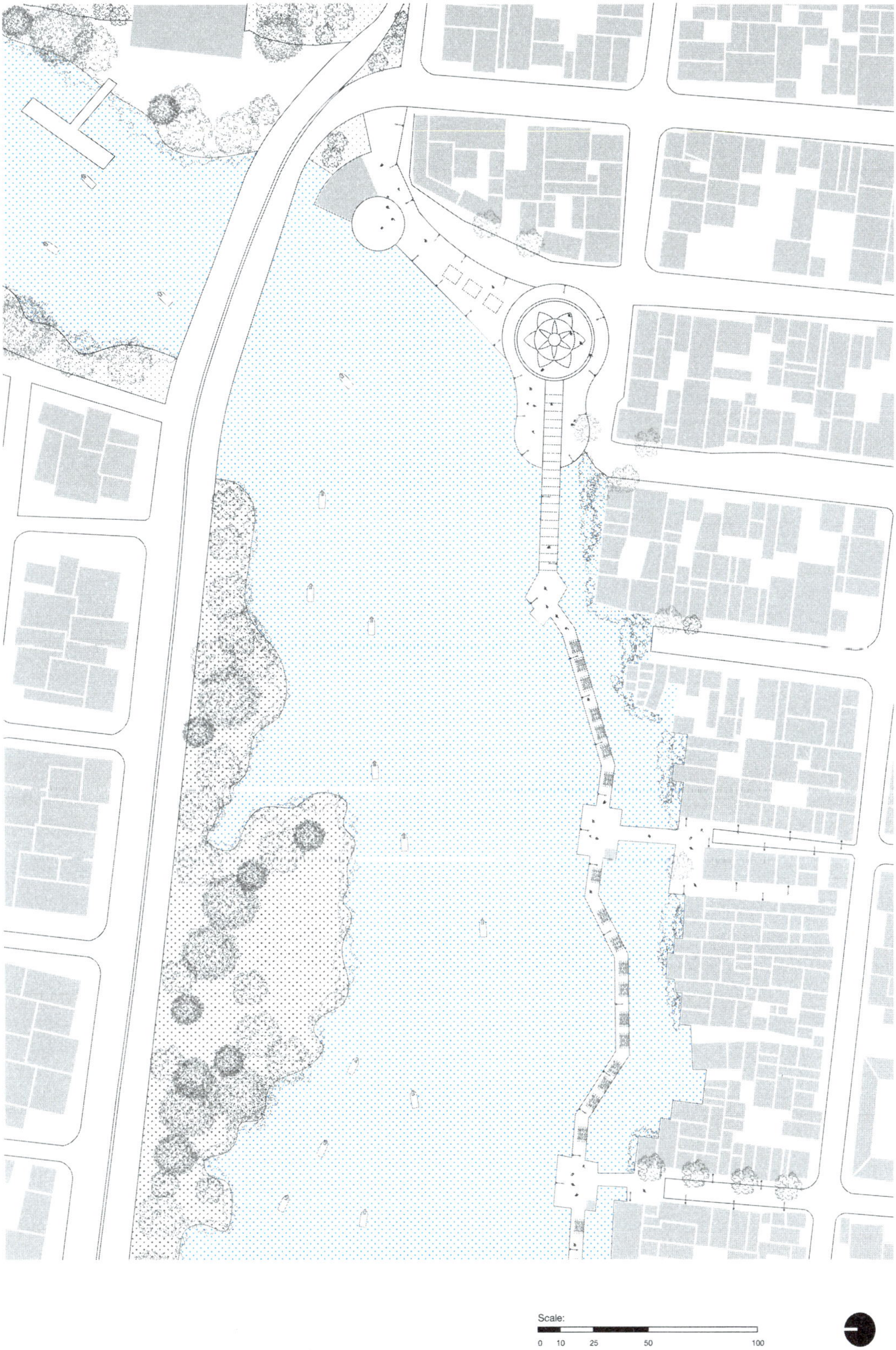
Scale:
0 10 25 50 100

URBAN SITUATION

The commercial and economic activity associated with Guayaquil's port attracted migrants from the countryside as well as from other countries in search for better employment opportunities. The city's existing housing infrastructure could not accommodate the vast new population, which led to the proliferation of spontaneous settlements. In some instances, these settlements occupied the edges of the *esteros* that run through the city, until then protected for environmental reasons. Since the *esteros* could not be accessed nor seen from urban centers, it was fairly easy to build on their banks unobserved.

The river linear park system is part of the Urban Regeneration program that began after 2000. This new network of public space has created a more direct relationship between the river and the city. Separate sewage collection and better control of growth along the river edge, has helped recover animal life as well as the mangroves. Water sports are also practiced.

PROJECT FUNDING

The project was funded and executed by the Municipality of Guayaquil. Resources for the construction of the river walk were administered by the Malecón 2000 Foundation. In 1997, a law was passed allowing individual contributors and companies to donate up to 25% of their income taxes toward the *Malecón's* construction.

RELATED PROGRAMS

The federal government, the Municipality of Guayaquil, as well as independent civic groups have worked on several parallel projects to increase awareness and the commitment from citizens in the recovery process of the *estero*'s water quality. Movilización Cívica (Civic Mobilization) is a municipal program that raises awareness and organizes periodic cleaning initiatives in the estuary. Agreements are forged with the surrounding communities, in which they commit to maintaining public spaces and green areas clear of waste.[5] The municipality has also contributed with larger city-wide programs to eliminate floating waste from the *estero*. In July 2011, 482,532 bags of solid waste were collected in the northern and southern segments of the Estero Salado.[6] Civic groups, such as Friends of the Estero, work to raise awareness regarding the importance of preserving the water ways through the program Become active for the Estero.[7]

The federal government, through the Environmental Ministry and the Ministry of Urban Development and Housing, have promoted a program called Ecological Recovery of the Estero Salado since 2010. It has an educational component, but also helps relocate families living in risk on environmentally sensitive sites. This has helped advance the decontamination of the *estero* and created opportunities to build parks and recover the natural landscape along the water edge.[8]

ACTIVITIES

The recovery of the Estero Salado through linear parks has offered marginalized segments of the population better access to services and public space. The municipality regularly plans activities for the esplanade of the Malecón Salado, Plaza de la Música (Music Square), including concerts and fairs. Locals use the Malecón Salado to stroll or to reach other areas of the settlement. It also serves as an alternative mobility route to connect with the rest of the city. Other segments of the park system include ball courts, playgrounds, lookout points, restrooms and fountains. Paddle and rowing boat rentals are available through private initiatives, and individuals bring their equipment to practice water sports. The park system has contributed to the livelihood of citizens and represents a destination for tourists as well.

URBAN INTEGRATION

The Estero Salado´s linear parks help control the negative impact of spontaneous settlements built along the edges. They have also improved the quality of life of inhabitants who previously suffered the consequences of living alongside a polluted river. The parks offer new space for recreation and leisure but also improve mobility and have created opportunities for businesses and tourism.

The parks also attract people from outside the community, which has helped include the river settlements into the dynamics of the entire city. These interactions were very unlikely prior to the public space intervention. By making the river edge accessible, and facilitating communication between distant parts of the city, boundaries and distinctions in people´s mental maps have diminished.

1 Alcaldía de Guayaquil, *Rendición de cuentas del Alcalde 2010 - 2011* (Guayaquil: Wong & Wong, 2011).

2 Silva and Vaggione (2015), 117.

3 D. W. Chauvet, *Del caos al orden. Guayaquil y su desarrollo urbano actual* (Guayaquil: Ciudades, 2005), 186.

4 Silva and Vaggione (2015), 119.

5 "Un parque lineal termina con la insalubridad del estero Las Ranas," *El Telégrafo* October 11, 2013. https://www.eltelegrafo.com.ec/noticias/guayaquil/10/el-cuidado-de-parques-esta-bajo-la-responsabilidad-de-los-vecinos (accessed May 7, 2018).

6 "Arrancó la limpieza del Estero Salado en etapas," *El Universo* July 6, 2003.

7 "Con jornada ecológica se motiva cuidado de estero," *De Estero Salado a Estero Salvado,* March 22, 2015. http://esterosalado.blogspot.com/ (accessed April 07, 2018).

8 Ministerio de Desarrollo Urbano y Vivienda, "Generación de áreas verdes y espacios recreativos públicos para provincia de Guayas," *Hábitat y Vivienda* 2015, 3. https://www.habitatyvivienda.gob.ec/wp-content/uploads/downloads/2015/06/PROYECTO-GUAYAS-ECOLOGICO-FINAL29-ENERO-V3-en-formulacion.pdf (accessed January 10, 2019).

LINEAR PARKS ALONG THE EDGES OF THE ESTERO SALADO GUAYAQUIL

ESTERO SALADO, GUAYAQUIL, ECUADOR

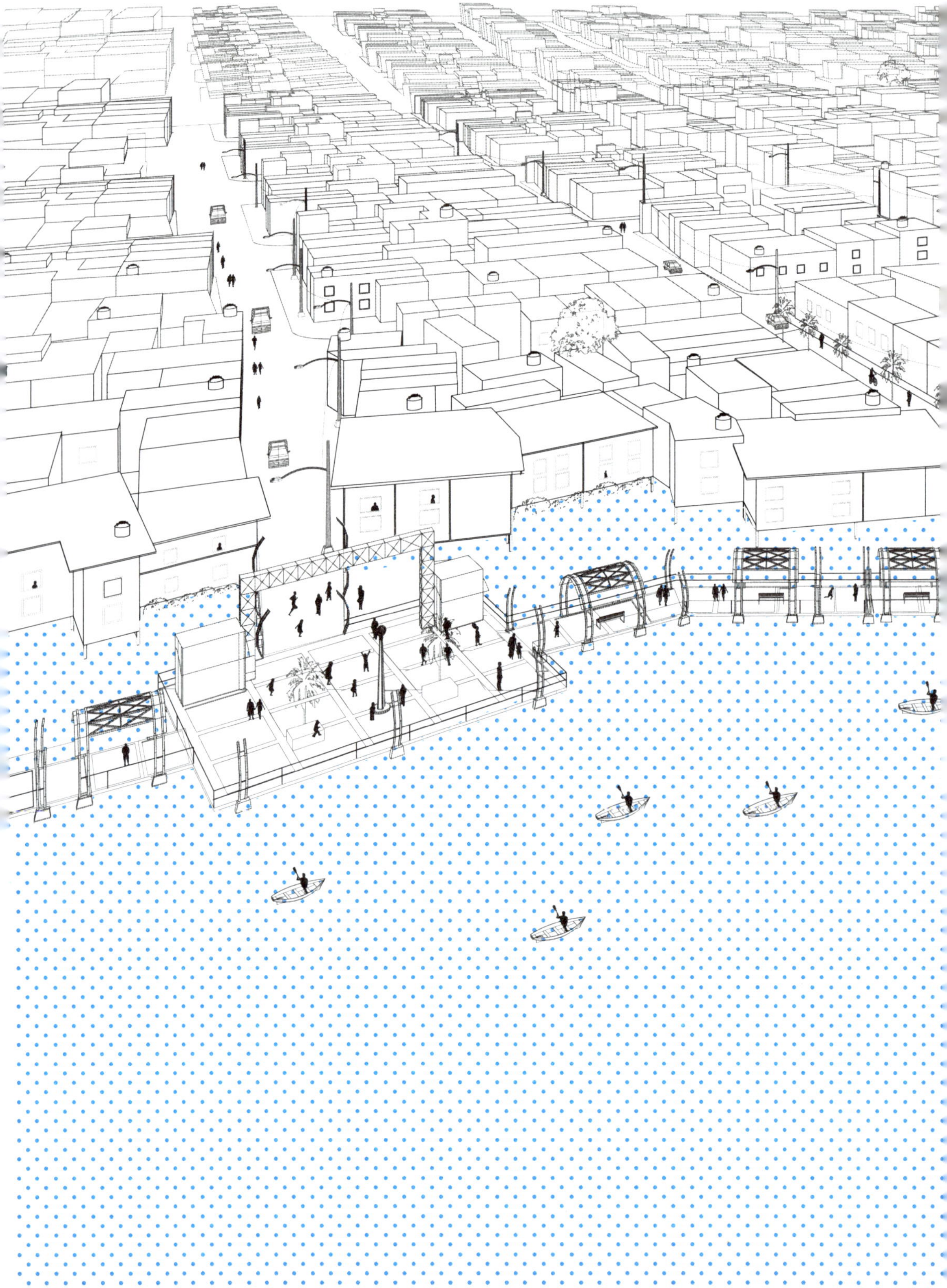

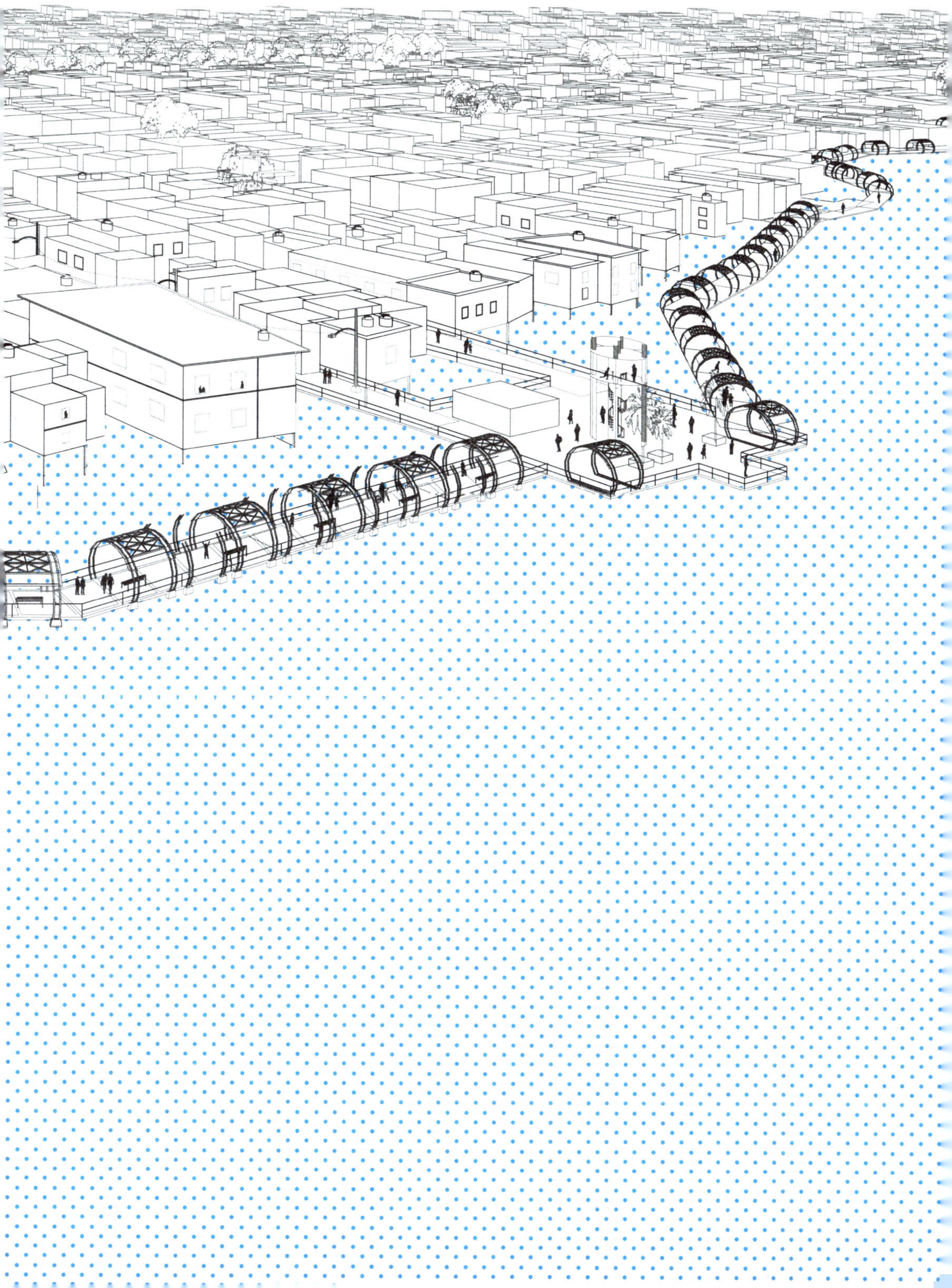

CHAPÉU MANGUEIRA AND BABILÔNIA - NATIONAL PARK

Chapéu Mangheira and Babilônia are *favelas* located over the morro Babilônia, just north of the Copacabana beach. Given their privileged location, they are fairly well integrated with the rest of the city through shared destinations such as the Bar do David, frequented by people from the entire city for lunch, or the youth hostels often used by foreign students. However, the natural reserve just above the settlements, is their most compelling attraction. Once completely deforested, in 1995, the slopes of the *morro* were replanted with lush tropical forests by the community. It can be visited through guided tours offered by *favela* neighbors. The rocky surface of the crest serves as a de facto plaza, often used by kids and adolescents to fly kites.

Location
Morro de Babilônia, Leme, Rio de Janeiro, Brazil

Project team:
Dwellers Association of Chapéu Mangueira (Associação de Moradores do Chapéu Mangueira) and the Municipal Department for the Environment (Secretaria Municipal de Meio Ambiente)

Date 2008

Coordinates
22°57'37.28"S 43°10'09.95"O

Investment n / a

Public space area
600,000 m²

Urban density 162.33 hab / ha

Population benefited 3,586 hab

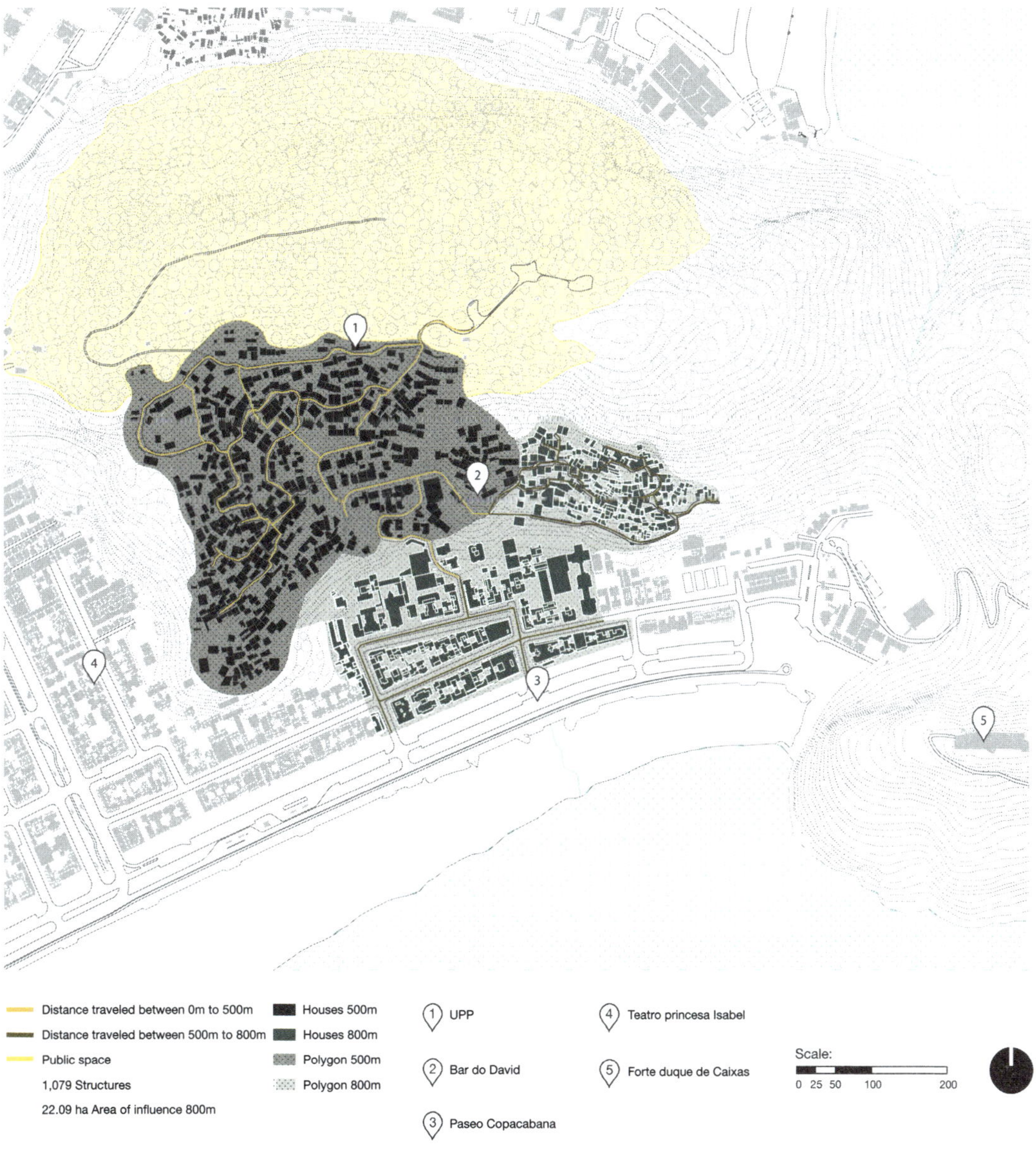

PUBLIC SPACE

The natural reserve is located beyond the *favelas*. In order to arrive at the forest and enjoy the views from the *morro's* crest, visitors first have to walk through the *favela*. This gives them a chance to engage with the community, and learn that they had a key role in preserving the natural reserve. The passage from the *asfalto*, as locals call the lower planned areas of the city, through the *favela* and into the forest park is fused into a single experience. The barriers and differences between locals and visitors are seemingly reduced.

HISTORY

The name Chapéu Mangueira is said to have come from the fact that this was an area that produced mangos. Babilônia, on the other hand, acquired its name from the nearby train station. Since many of the *morros* along the coast, including Babilônia, had been considered strategic for military purposes, fortifications were built during colonial times and, more recently, in WWII to keep watch over the Bahia de Guanabara. Soldiers working at these fortifications began to occupy nearby areas with housing.[1] In 1908, a group of houses in Quinta Boa Vista, a city center neighborhood, were demolished and their inhabitants moved to Mangueira. 10 years later, families affected by a fire in Morro do Santo Antonio were moved as well to Chapéu Mangueira. This created a heterogenous population formed of people displaced from other communities. Wood from the forest over the *morro* was used for construction, which over time destroyed its natural ecology.[2]

SOCIAL AND POLITICAL CONTEXT

In 2008, the Police Pacification Units (UPP Unidade de Polícia Pacificadora), a government initiative to purportedly establish order and peace by controlling drug trade and violence through the permanent presence of police forces, were incorporated into many *favelas* including Chapéu Mangueira and Babilônia. It successfully reduced levels of crime and homicides in the neighborhood and displaced the drug activity to other parts of Rio de Janeiro. The initiative has been heavily criticized for its use of excessive force and for undermining more socially oriented and sustainable approaches to mitigate crime.

On the other hand, the increased security perceived among neighbors and people from the rest of the city has transformed the community, evident in greater amounts of pedestrian traffic, even at night. This has allowed tourism to emerge as one of the productive forces within the *favela*, particularly in the form of restaurants, youth hostels and bars.

Scale:
0 2.5 5 10 25

ENVIRONMENTAL SITUATION

The Brazilian Government declared the *morro* an Environmental Protection Area and converted it into the Carioca Municipal Park in the eighties. The Babilônia Morro is connected to other *morros* in the Selva Atlantica ecosystem that begins in Tijuca and extends all the way to the Corcovado. Its biodiversity consists of a jungle biosphere with indigenous species and plants such as the Mata Atlantica[3]

Chapéu Mangueira is an example of how a deteriorated ecosystem can be recovered through community initiatives. In 2001, with the support of a civic organization, Bairrinho and Morar Carioca Verde, the community engaged in tree planting activities. They successfully recovered the forest and continue to reforest and watch over the park´s preservation.

URBAN SITUATION

Copacabana beach is among the most popular tourist destinations in Rio de Janeiro. It is lined by several blocks of high-end formal neighborhoods with buildings up to 12 stories high. As the topography rises toward the *morro* Babilônia, the urban fabric changes into self-built homes, one to three stories high, that make up the two *favelas*. The road zig zags its way through the constructed landscape in order to mitigate the steep slope. The highest point on the hill is 200 meters above sea level and offers 360 degree views of the city including Sugar Loaf Mountain, the Copacabana and Flamengo bays as well as the Corcovado, in the distance.

The recovery of the forest ecology and the *favela*´s increased level of personal security through the UPP, have allowed a modest, but growing tourism to emerge. Hotels, bars, cafes, and youth hostels are also part of the urban landscape in Chapéu Mangueira and Babilônia.

PROJECT FUNDING

Three key entities made the reforestation of the Babilônia Moro Park possible: the federal government, by declaring the area a natural reserve, the community, who planted trees and built the paths through the forest, and a local NGO, that supported the community with knowledge, expertise and modest resources.[4] Outside investment was negligible. The human capital of the neighbors that participated in the initiative was the project´s main resource.

RELATED PROGRAMS

The identity of Chapéu Mangueira and Babilônia has been partly formed by its traditions, but it is also closely tied to the presence of the forest above. Samba is an important cultural activity associated with many communities in Brazil. Local institutions prepare presentations for Rio´s famous carnival festival, as well as concerts, often visited by outside guests interested in *carioca* musical culture. Sports programs can be accessed through the Villa Olimpica Mangueira sports facility, which was built in the eighties and is frequented by youths and adults. Tourism is also a significant activity in the *favelas*. Coop Babilônia is a group of residents that offers guided tours of the park reserve to visitors. They are also committed to the maintenance and continued recovery of the forest.

ACTIVITIES

The park system offers several possibilities for residents and visitors. The ascent through the *favela* and park is considered by many an urban stroll; others use it to exercise. Along the paths, tags include the name of vegetation species and create a didactic experience for those interested in botany. Various platforms or lookout points throughout the park open onto deep views over Rio´s singular landscape. At the top of the *morro*, on the bald rock surface, kids from the *favela* fly kites and mirror the youth flying kites in neighboring hills such as Cantagalo and Santa Marta.

URBAN INTEGRATION

The experience of walking through a *favela* to reach a park that operates at the metropolitan scale incorporates the neighborhood into a broader urban dynamic by making it visible, acknowledged and enjoyed by all. For visitors, the *favela* is part of the urban experience, while at the same time local residents benefit from productive opportunities associated with hospitality and food, or as tour guides to the park. Key to the project´s success is the community´s sense of responsibility toward maintaining and preserving the natural forest. They have become stewards and defenders of its continued preservation.

1 Q. Gomes, "Historia do Morro da Mangueira," *Diario Do Río Do Janeiro* February 21, 2016.

2 "Morro de Babilônia, un lugar lleno de historias que regala una imagen diferente de Río de Janeiro," *Imaginario de Janeiro*. https://imaginariodejaneiro.com/morro-de-babilonia/ (accessed January 22, 2019).

3 Ibid.

4 Ibid., 42-56.

CHAPÉU MANGUEIRA AND BABILÔNIA - NATIONAL PARK
RIO DE JANEIRO, BRAZIL

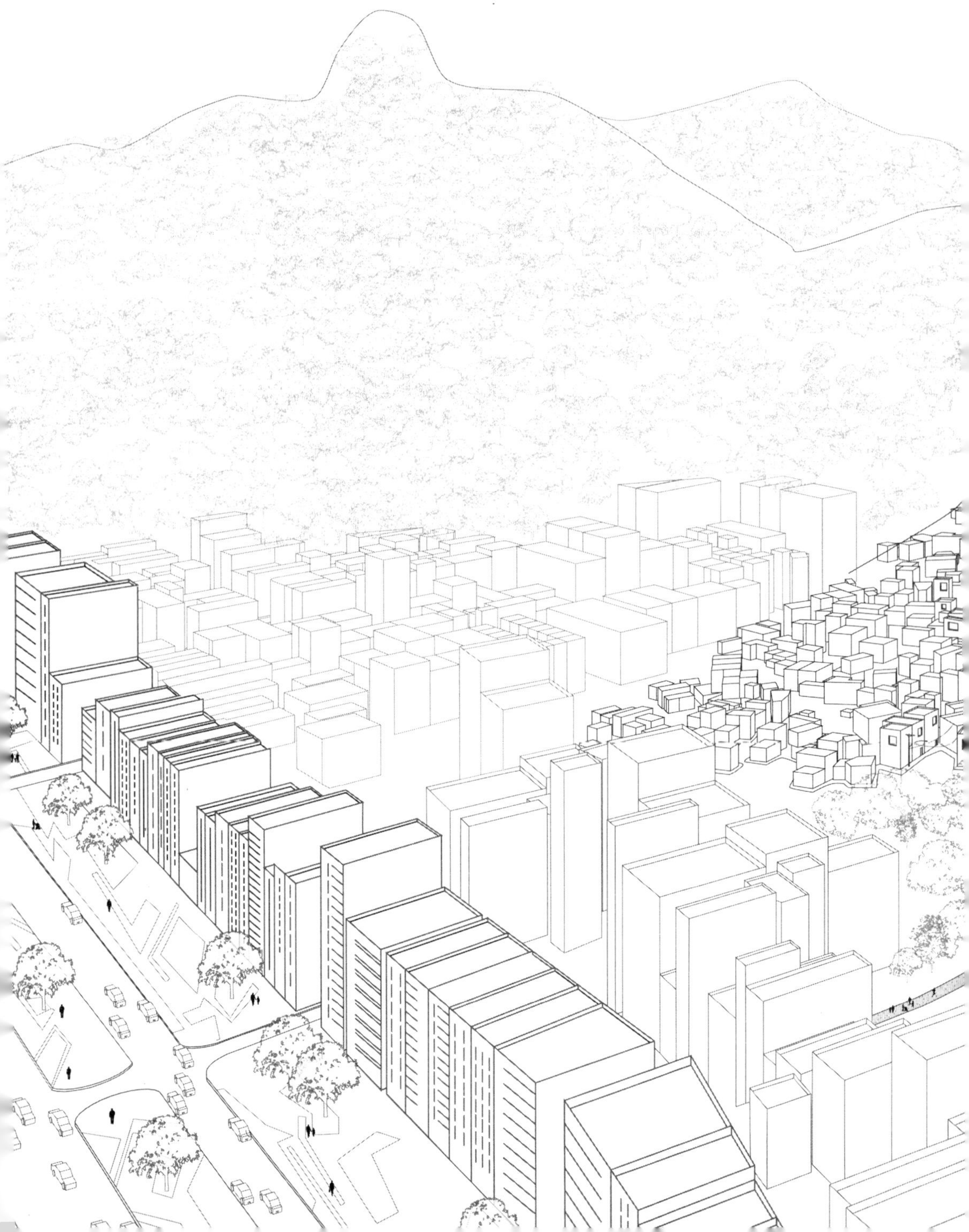

BAR DO DAVID

URBAN AGRICULTURE ALONG THE RIMAC RIVER

Lima is a city in a desert. Access to water varies according to the relative wealth of the district, hence it tends to be scarcer in spontaneous settlements. And yet the Rimac River runs through the city with a watershed that begins a distance 160 km. into the highlands of the Hiarochirí Province. Along the edges of the river, a community of entrepreneurial women from the spontaneous settlement El Agustino is engaged in an urban agriculture project and a capacity building program sponsored by the United Nations Development Program (UNDP). Women in the community work together and learn how to manage vegetable plots for self-sustenance and to sell produce in local markets. The gardens are irrigated with water from the river that has been treated through a phytodepuration process, using aquatic plants.

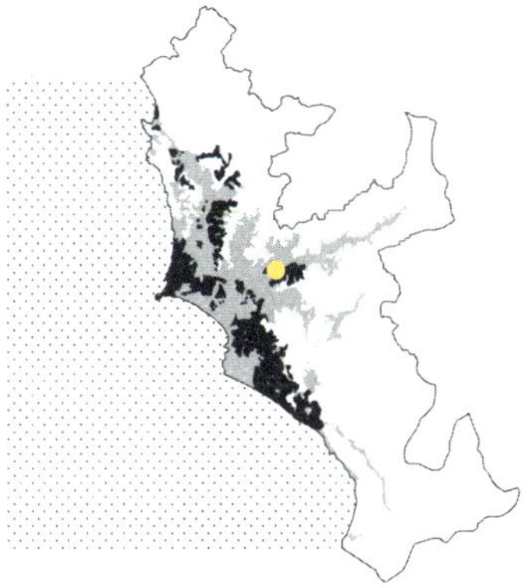

Location
San Agustino District, Lima, Peru

Project team:
Center for Comunal Banks of El Agustino and Santa Anita (Central de Bancos Comunales de El Agustino y Santa Anita), Small Grants Project UNDP

Date 2008

Coordinantes
12°01'50.18"S 77°00'27.12"O

Investment **50,000 USD**

Public space area
7,865,62 m²

Urban density
147.30 hab / ha

Population benefited
8,384 hab

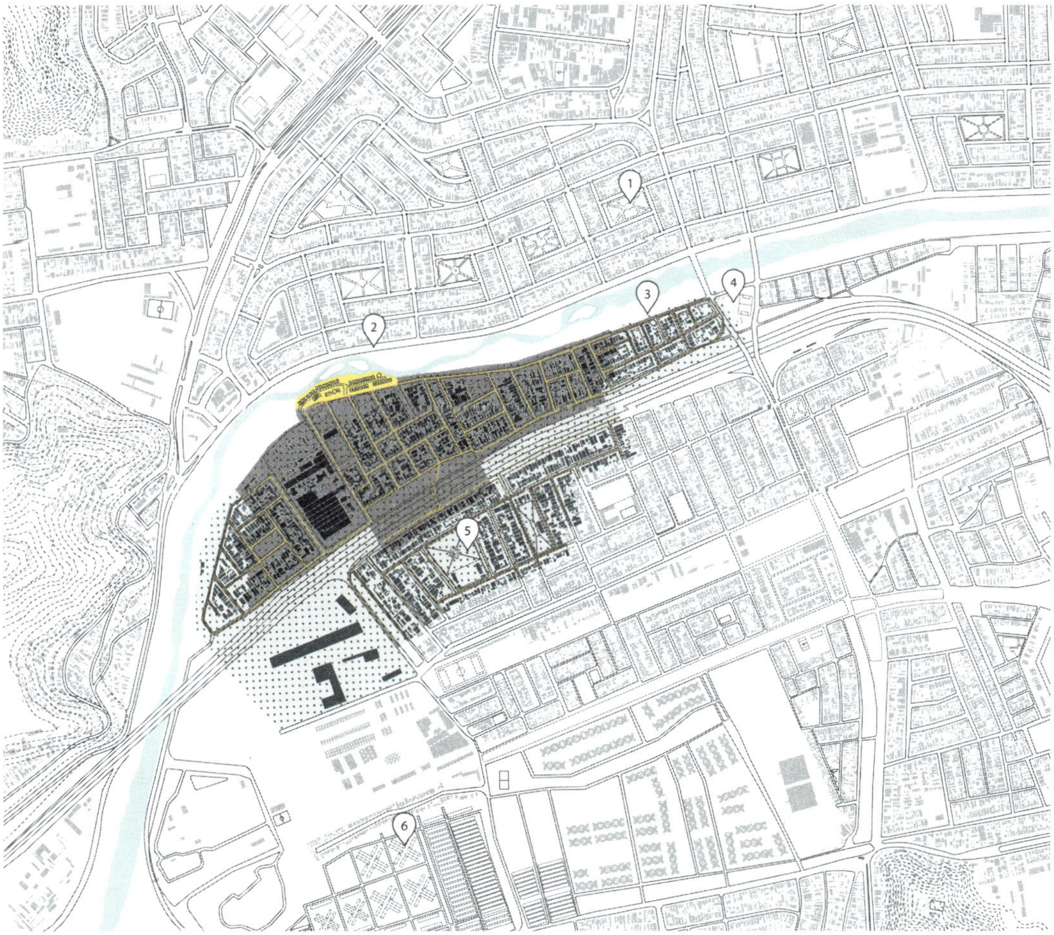

Distance traveled between 0m to 500m
Distance traveled between 500m to 800m
Public space
1,945 Structures
56.92 Ha area of influence 800m

Houses 500m
Houses 800m
Polygon 500m
Polygon 800m

1. Parque Tupac Amaru
2. Malecón Checa Eguiguren
3. Malecón de la Amistad
4. Complejo Deportivo Pedro Huillca
5. Parque Primavera
6. Museo Cementerio Presbítero Maestro

Escala:
0 2.5 5 10 25

PUBLIC SPACE

Urban agriculture is an activity that could be replicated along the entire length of the river as a way to contribute toward local productivity and the social inclusion of underprivileged women. It also increases the river´s presence in the city and allows people to see it as a resource and not a means to dispose of sewage and waste.

HISTORY

Lima´s location on the Pacific Coast is largely defined by the presence of three rivers, Chillón, Rimac, and Lurín, in a valley enclosed by hills that are part of the Andes Mountains. Prior to colonial occupation, the Inca population constructed channels to irrigate the land and cultivate food.[1] Since these early times, the rivers had an important relationship with agriculture. However, the urban footprint's expansion and the river´s progressive contamination forced these uses to disappear, especially along the Rimac River, which traverses the city from east to west. Furthermore, the city´s relationship with the river is very weak, with few opportunities to visually engage it, further contributing to its state of abandonment.

The San Agustino district was once a *hacienda* that produced fruits and vegetables. It was later subdivided into lots. Rural urban migration, in the mid forties, created new demand for housing and settlers built their homes along the Agustino hills. By the sixties, they had grown to occupy the lower and flatter areas of the district.

SOCIAL AND POLITICAL CONTEXT

UNDP assessments consider El Agustino a community with a medium level of development. However, it ranks among the lowest within the city of Lima due to low levels of education and per capita income.[2] Over the last decade poverty has diminished with the country´s general economic prosperity and increased access to employment opportunities in construction and the commercial sector. At the scale of the community, a dense urban environment has emerged that lacks access to public space, services and community facilities.

ENVIRONMENTAL SITUATION

Lima´s annual precipitation is very low because of its desert condition. The city has historically depended on rivers for access to water, but increased urbanization and contamination have made water management one of the city´s most pressing issues. Expensive investments in water treatment plants contribute only marginally to offset unmet demand. One such plant is located in the El Agustino district: the Atarjea Water Treatment Plant. Even though it has the capacity to process 18 m^3 of water a second, this is not enough to serve the 10 million people living in Lima, a fact that begs the question of whether such strategies should continue to be considered given their cost and limited effectiveness.[3]

1

Other environmental risks are the diminished vegetation and the increased erosion and degradation of soil quality due to urban encroachment along the Rimac River edges. Some agricultural activity continues to exist along the Chillón and Lurín Rivers, although continued urban expansion also threatens these territories and in consequence, the city´s provision of locally grown produce.

URBAN SITUATION

The urban fabric of Lima largely negates the presence of its rivers; walls and fences often enclose its 25-kilometer course through the city. It went from celebrating its rivers to denying their existence and instead, uses them to transport sewage. The community of El Agustino is located south of the Rimac River, and east of the Zurco Canal. In the 1950s, its urban fabric developed within a regular urban grid of streets and parceled lots that were sold illegally. The interior of each block grew irregularly: some have been completely built-up while others have maintained inner courtyards. This urban growth pattern did not provide areas for public space and community facilities. Likewise, the river´s presence is not acknowledged. Streets dead-end onto the river edge and urban lots back onto it, allowing debris to be dumped unobserved.

PROJECT FUNDING

The project's funds came from the UNDP´s Small Grants Program GEF that promotes local projects with large scale impact on environmental restoration and community empowerment.[4] The project is run locally by the Bancos Comunales de El Agustino and Santa Anita (Communal Banks of El Agustino and Santa Anita), a social organization responsible for the management of projects to improve the quality of life of community inhabitants and create opportunities to strengthen their capacities. 130 women leading entrepreneurial projects in their communities are members of the organization.

The project "Tara (vetch) cultivation to reforest degraded and risk prone areas in El Agustino Lima" received a grant for 50,000 USD to create an initiative where women would lead the reforestation and productive use of the Rimac River's banks through a cooperative system.[5] The funds were used to build vegetable gardens and greenhouses, produce agricultural products, organize educational workshops and forge the cooperative´s management structure, including a business plan for the sale of the products the women grew. The project allowed a group of women to emerge with experience in produce cultivation and micro farming management, and access to a new source of income. Those benefited also helped educate new groups of women.

RELATED PROGRAMS

The Rio Verde plan for the Rimac River, which began in the eighties, is an initiative that includes playgrounds, public pools, sports facilities, ball courts and pedestrian bridges to connect both sides of the river. After the implementation of the UNDP project, the Municipality of Lima showed interest in its methodology and considered incorporating it in the Rio Verde project. This would allow groups of vulnerable women to engage in productive activities all along the river, while recovering green spaces and encouraging a new relationship between the city and the river. It would also represent a sustainable strategy for park maintenance, in which the women of the Central de Bancos de El Agustino and Santa Anita would essentially act as stewards of the reclaimed landscape.

ACTIVITIES

The program´s main focus was the capacity building workshops for women in terms of both technical expertise regarding cultivation, horticulture and natural water treatment methods, as well as knowledge of how to manage, process and commercialize produce through markets and distribution networks. As the women implemented the productive aspects of the project, they also reforested the river banks and helped begin the soil´s recovery process.

URBAN INTEGRATION

Forging a more honest relationship with the Rimac River would be a very effective way to integrate the city. Strategic bridges along its course could connect the northern and southern river banks and their neighborhoods. The edges of its 25 km course through the city offer an enormous potential for much needed public space. Making the river accessible would, at the same time, help pressure and motivate local authorities to prioritize its recovery and sanitation. The river axis could incorporate paths for alternative mobility and help connect distant areas of the city.

Urban agriculture and the stewardship of women producers could be a strategy to guarantee the maintenance and upkeep of the park system. As a mutually beneficial relationship, the use of a public good to generate income for vulnerable population segments allows the communities along the river and the city at large, to enjoy an accessible park system, while reducing maintenance costs for the municipality.

1 Autoridad Nacional de Lima, *Rimac: Historia del Río Hablador* (Lima: Perúcuadros Eirl., 2016), 13-14.

2 United Nations Food and Agriculture Organization. http://www.fao.org/ag/agp/greenercities/es/cmvalc/lima.html (accessed January 22, 2019).

3 G. Merzthal, “Agua y agricultura urbana,” *Agricultura Urbana* 2018, 7-9.

4 The GEF Small Grants Programme, “Mission and History.” https://sgp.undp.org/index.php?option=com_content&view=article&id=98&Itemid=223#.WsuKAi5ublU (accessed January 22, 2019).

5 Ibid.

URBAN AGRICULTURE ALONG THE RIMAC RIVER
LIMA, PERU

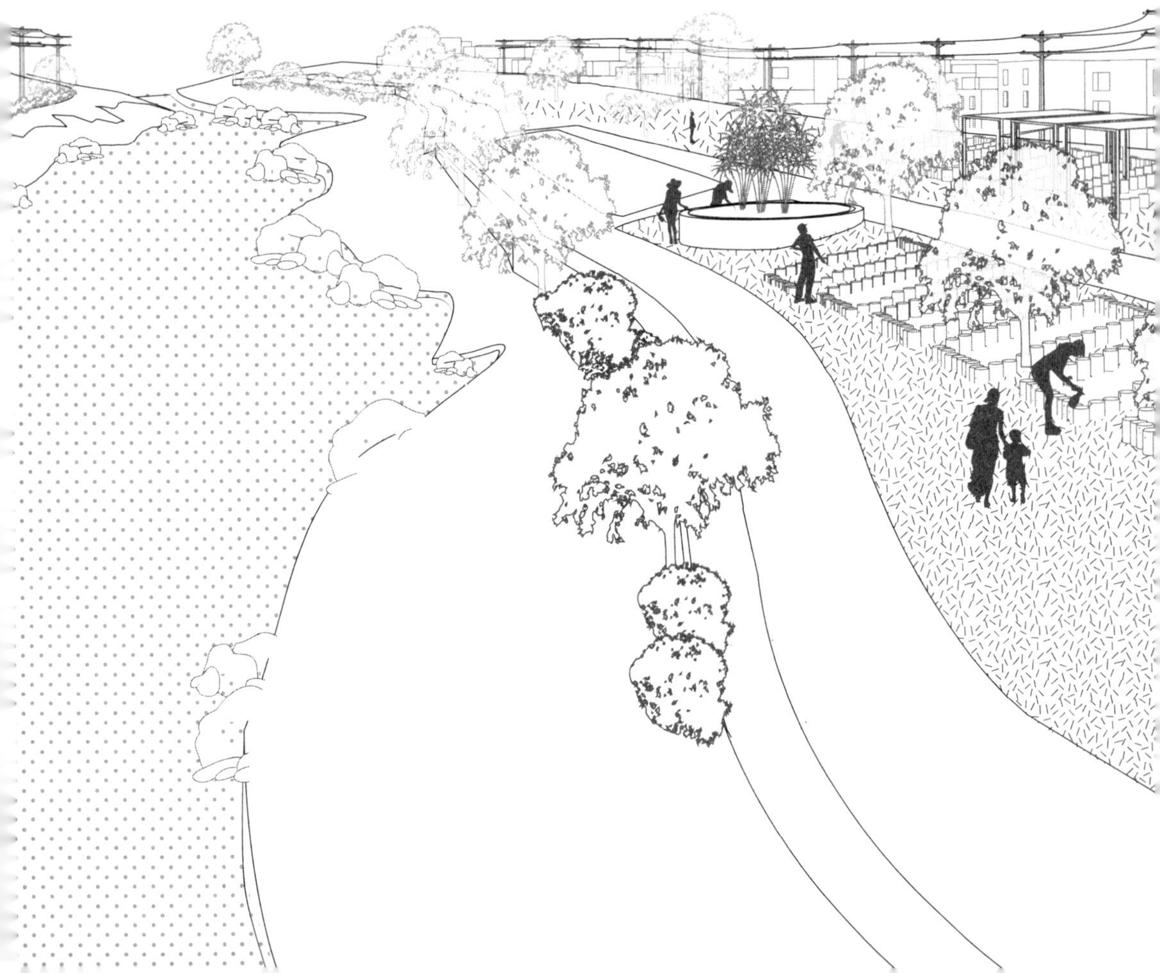

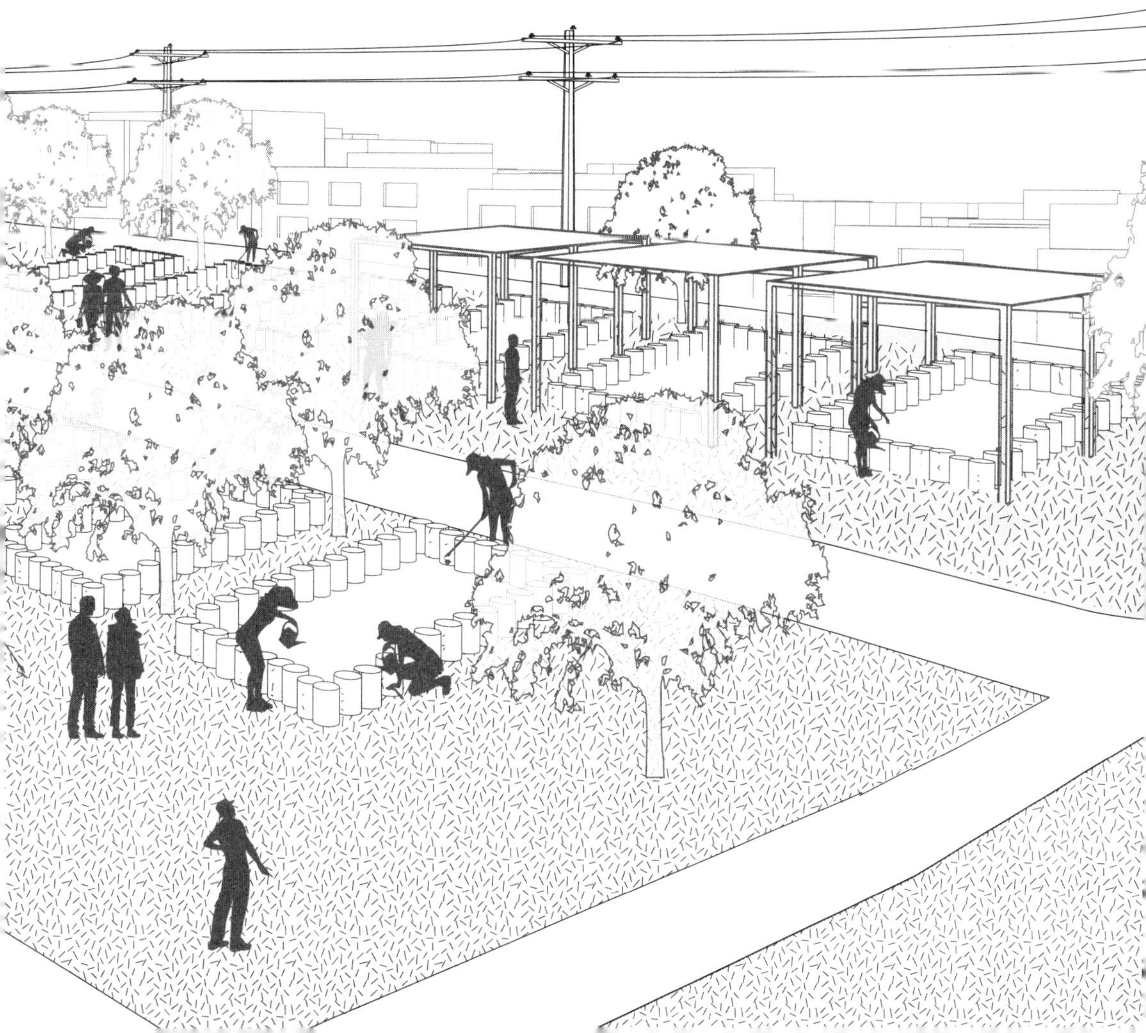

MORAVIA ECOLOGICAL PARK

Part of what is known today as the neighborhood of Moravia was once Medellin´s landfill, where some people lived off of the materials they recycled from the waste. When the landfill was closed, this growing community and new migrants began building their homes over the mountain of waste. The conditions were insanitary and the decomposing waste beneath structures meant they could collapse at any time. Consequently, the municipality transformed this sector by relocating families into multifamily housing nearby and converting the grounds of the decomposing landfill into a public park. Today the Moravia Ecological Park is known for its landscape, vegetation, walkways, community gardens and cultural activities for all ages.

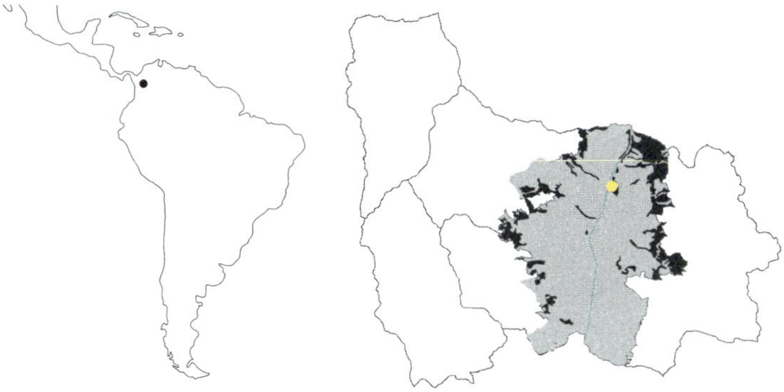

Location
Moravia, Comuna 4 Aranjuez, Medellin, Colombia

Project team:
Antioquia University, UNESCO Department of Sustainability Cataluña Politechnic University (Cátedra UNESCO de Sostenibilidad de la Universidad Politécnica de Cataluña), Municipality of Medellin

Date 2009

Coordinates
6°17'47.92"N 75°34'05.28"O

Investment 100,000 USD

Public space area 11,475,11 m²

Urban density 334.64 hab / ha

Population benefited 6,639 hab

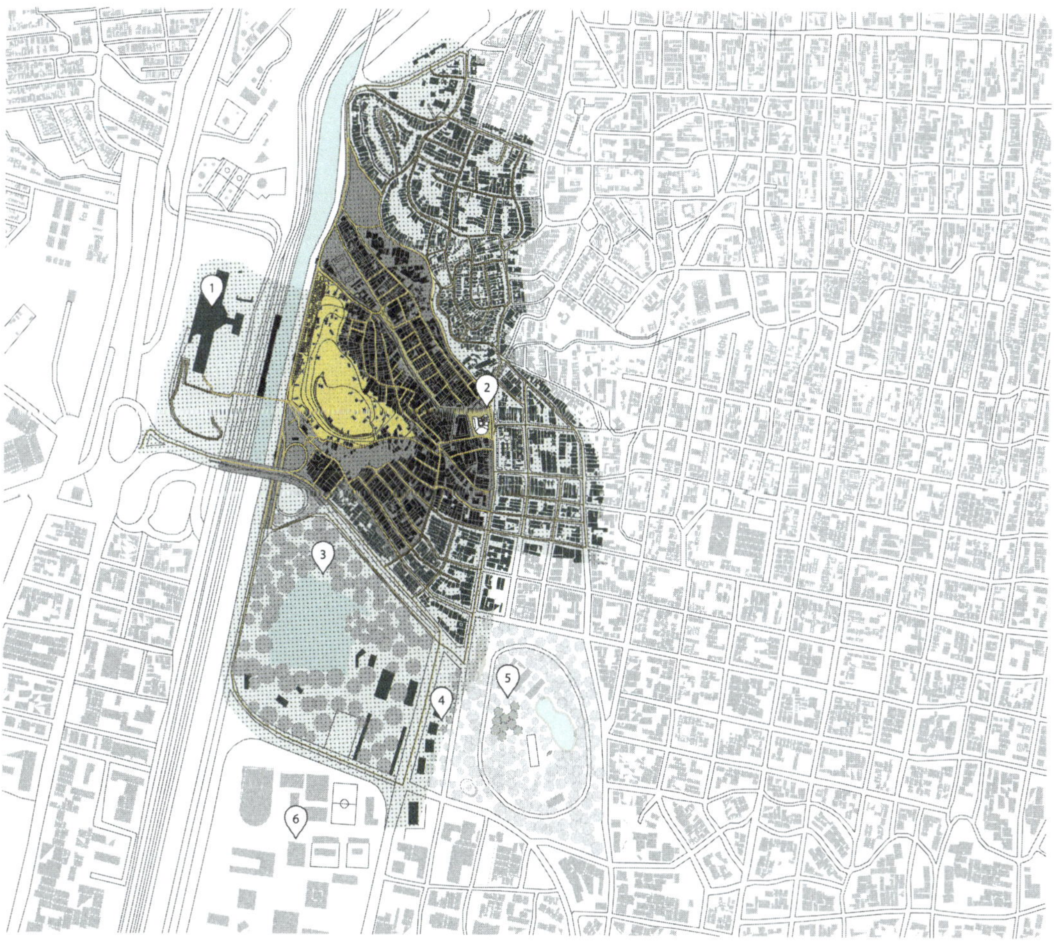

Distance traveled between 0m to 500m
Distance traveled between 500m to 800m
Public space

2,367 Structures

19.84 ha Area of influence 800m

Houses 500m
Houses 800m
Polygon 500m
Polygon 800m

1 Terminal del Norte Medellín
2 Centro de Desarrollo Cultural Moravia
3 Parque Norte J. Emilio Valderrama
4 Parque Explora
5 Orquideorama Jardín Botánico
6 Universidad de Antioquia

Scale:
0 50 100 200 400

PUBLIC SPACE

The transformation of a non-place into an effective public space has renovated the identity of the Moravia community from a settlement of squalor and waste to a dignified, ecologically responsible, productive and culturally stimulating neighborhood. Furthermore, the park is connected through a network of public spaces to facilities and cultural destinations that operate at a metropolitan scale making the community feel integrated with the city.

HISTORY

Moravia is located in the Comuna 4 Aranjuez of Medellin. Up until the fifties, it had been a landscape of cattle, fruit trees and a place for recreation and leisure among Medellin´s elite. The Comuna received its earliest rural migration settlers in the forties. Later, in the seventies, new areas were urbanized along the edge of the Medellin River, among them Moravia.[1] 10-hectares of flat land near the river bank were originally reserved for a public space that would further extend the existing Parque Norte. However, in 1976 the municipality decided to provisionally use it for waste collection and over the course of the following 10 years it grew into a 35-meter-high mountain with 1.5 million tons of waste.[2] In 1983 the landfill was closed. New migrants with few economic resources found a place to make their home here, in areas surrounding the landfill and slowly began building over the mound of waste.

Over the course of these years, the municipality´s presence was limited, while organized crime associated with the drug cartels controlled the neighborhood. Military interventions in 1991reduced Moravia's levels of violence and a new Territorial Zoning Plan (Plan de Ordenamiento Territorial) was created for the Comuna, designating Moravia as a special intervention area. In 2004 the site was publicly declared a health emergency, after the University of Antioquia released a study documenting the negative effects gases and toxic liquids released by the decomposing waste had on Moravia settlers.[3] In 2006, the municipality began relocating families and the urban fabric was reorganized to improve environmental conditions and opportunities for human development.[4]

SOCIAL AND POLITICAL CONTEXT

Moravia has historically been the poorest segment of the Comuna 4, associated with extreme poverty, waste and foul odors.[5] Inhabitants were stigmatized for their work as waste pickers and for their substandard living conditions. During the eighties, criminal drug gangs overtook the neighborhood and the desperation of poverty and lack of opportunities pushed young men into illegal armed groups.

The neighborhood´s transformation process was largely motivated by community leaders and mothers desperate to end the violence. An unsustainable environmental situation also required urban interventions. The community´s tight network of relations after decades of living in Moravia had created a strong connection with the site. For that reason, inhabitants met the prospect of relocation away from their community with resistance. Nevertheless, the municipality was able to relocate many families nearby and maintain their social connections. Those that had to be relocated in further away neighborhoods were able to remain linked to Moravia by having access to a small piece of land where they could produce urban agriculture.[6]

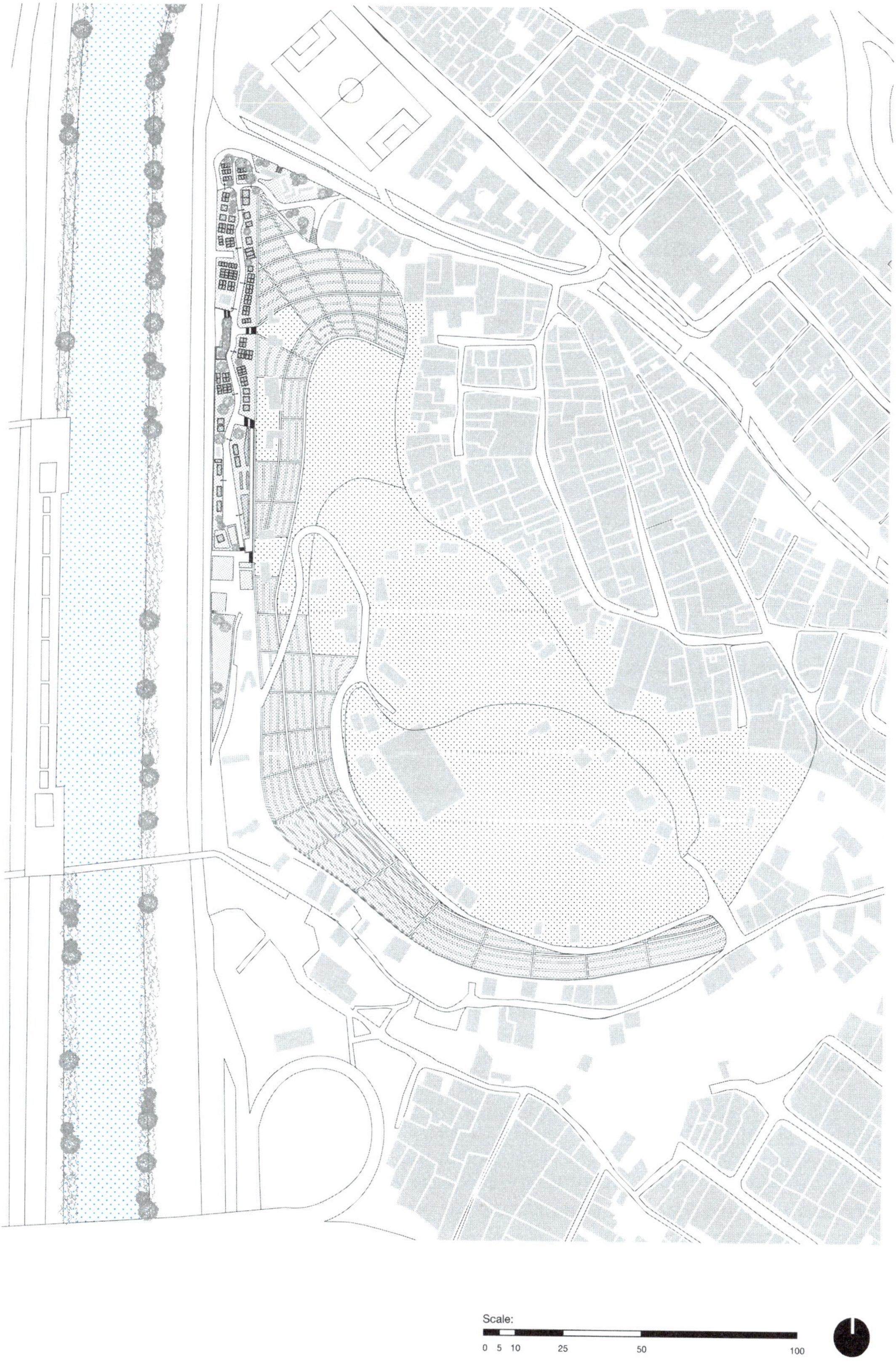
Scale:
0 5 10 25 50 100

ENVIRONMENTAL SITUATION

Moravia´s environmental problems stemmed from the landfill and the proximity of homes to the toxic gases and liquids it released. Furthermore, as settlers built their homes over the waste mound, the compacted ground they prepared for foundations was very unstable and could collapse at any time due to the waste´s progressive decomposition.

URBAN SITUATION

Moravia is strategically located between the Regional Highway and the Carabobo Avenue, making it very attractive for real estate developers. Inhabitants of the landfill justifiably felt threatened by the intentions of developers. Typical of spontaneous settlements, streets are irregularly defined by the edges of self-constructed homes, which tend to be two and three stories high. Since Moravia is near the Medelin River, land is flat except for the hill of accumulated waste. The community enjoys good access to public transportation and mobility along nearby major roadways that serve the city at the metropolitan scale. It is also within walking distance of the Caribe metro station.

PROJECT FUNDING

Several departments in the City of Medellin worked together to finance and execute Moravia´s landfill transformation. They addressed the relocation of families and the demolition of evacuated homes, provided social programs to assist families and ultimately transformed the waste mound into a park. Research regarding the levels of contamination experienced in Moravia, carried out by the University of Antioquia, was critical to justify the project´s urgency and the allocation of resources.[7]

RELATED PROGRAMS

Several social and environmental programs supported Moravia's urban transformation project. The first was the environmental recovery program, supervised by the city´s social development department, which implemented phyto and bioremediation processes, the planting of ornamental species and the creation of artificial wetlands to help the soil´s decomposition process. Secondly, a capacity building program offered the community the opportunity to learn about agriculture and soil management. Lastly, the Institute of Social Housing and Habitat in Medellin led efforts to build substitution housing for relocated families in places that would allow them to remain close to their existing social and community networks.

ACTIVITIES

The park provides opportunities for inhabitants to cultivate plants and vegetables. Ornamental plants and flowers are grown for commercial purposes. The Moravia Cultural Center offers children and adult workshops within two recycled structures, a bus and a container, on the park´s grounds. Local guides offer tours and share the history of how Moravia converted the landfill into a public park.

URBAN INTEGRATION

The Ecoparque Moravia transformed the neighborhood into a pleasant destination in the city through agricultural landscapes and public space. Urban agriculture is tended to by both locals and displaced families that remain connected to the site through its farming. Tourists, neighbors, locals and visitors are aware of Moravia´s significance in the city. The transformation effectively rid Moravia of the negative associations it previously carried tied to poverty and waste. Once the linear park projected along the Medellin River is built, the Ecoparque will connect to it, increasing access opportunities to Moravia via a citywide public space corridor.

1 Alcaldía de Medellín, *Plan de desarrollo local Comuna 4 Aranjuez.* (Medellín: Alcaldía de Medellín, 2015), 31.

2 G. Arango, "Moravia, una historia de mejoramiento urbano," *Procesos Urbanos Informales* 2012, 1.

3 J.I.Montoya, O. Cuesta, O. Flecha, D. Viadé, A. Gallegos, and J. Morató, "Moravia como ejemplo de transformación de áreas urbanas degradadas: tecnologías apropiadas para la restauración integral de cuencas degradadas," *Publicación Científica en Ciencias Biomédicas*, 2011, 42.

4 "Memoria Territorial, extensión de Moravia a la ciudad," *Historia de Moravia* May 2, 2017. http://g4moravia.blogspot.com/2007/05/historia-moravia.html (accessed January 19, 2019).

5 G. Arango (2012).

6 *Moravia, la ruta de la esperanza* Dir. Matías Boero Lutz. YouTube, Moravia UAB-Unesco. December 3, 2013. https://www.imdb.com/title/tt5097092/ (accessed January 22, 2019).

7 Montoya (2011).

MORAVIA ECOLOGICAL PARK
MEDELLIN, COLOMBIA

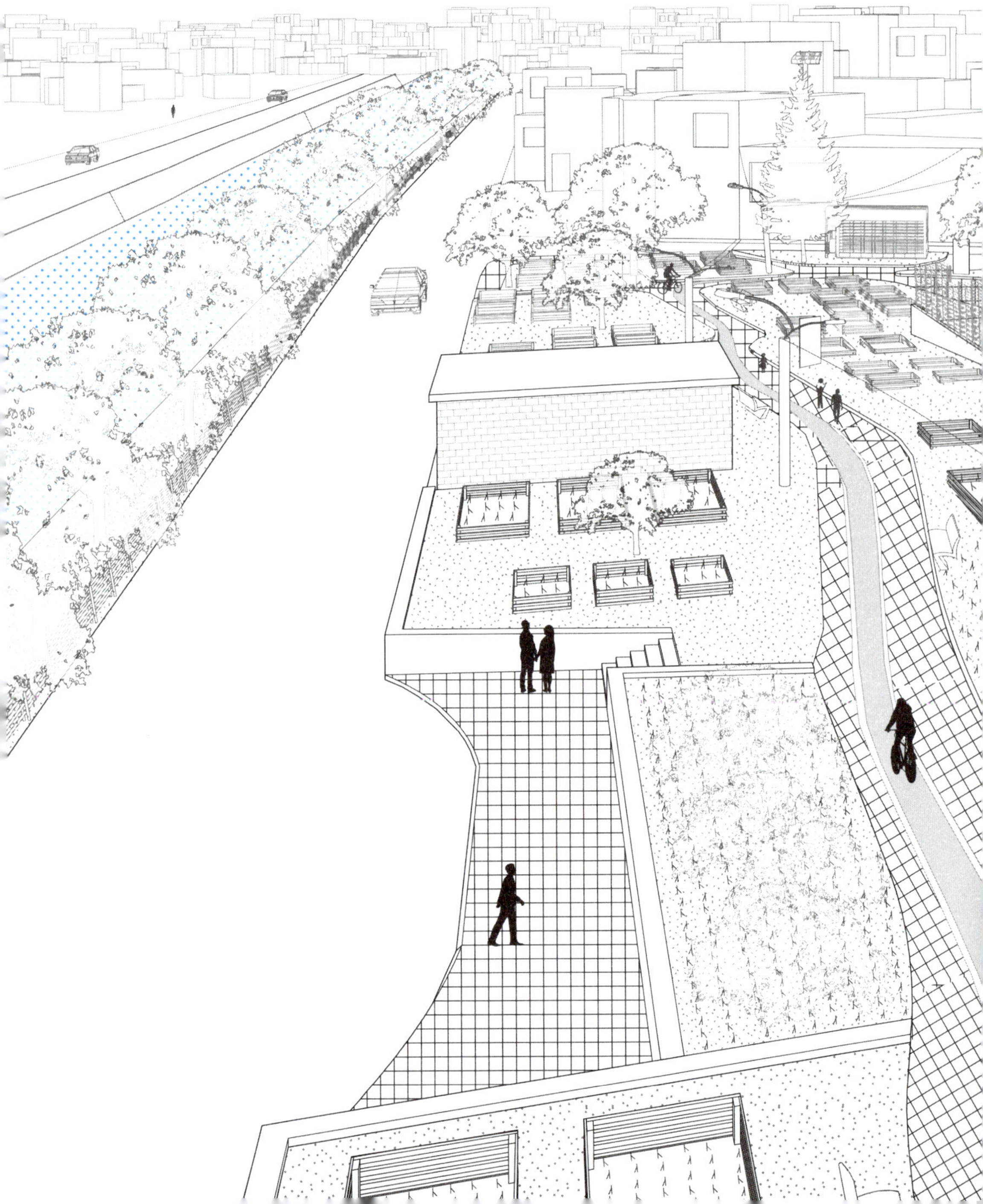

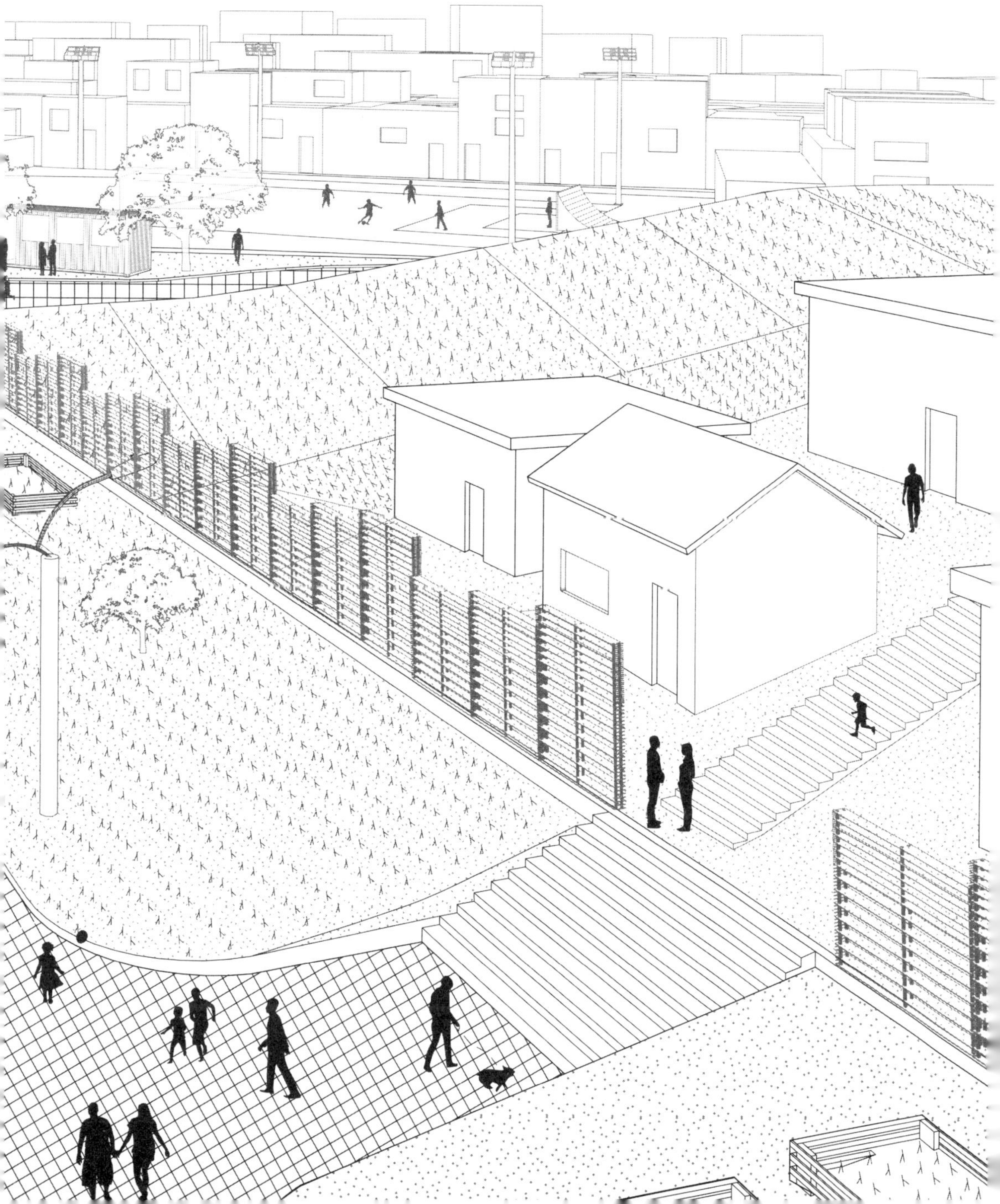

PLAZA LA CRUZ LA PALOMERA

A new public plaza in La Palomera was created through an educational program called City Planting, sponsored by Citibank and Fudep. The program encourages neighbors to reflect on their surroundings and envision ways in which they could generate change. Educational workshops take place over the course of several months and include people of all ages, where the discussions are centered on the role of public space in the community. What had been an open-air waste dump for over 30 years was chosen by the community as the site for a new public space. First it was cleared of all debris and waste with the support of the community and the municipality. Neighbors adopted a new waste management practice using existing containers located at the settlement´s entrances from the town of Baruta. The space was designed jointly between Enlace Arquitectura and the community. The design incorporated interventions in which the children of a nearby school could participate. Other contributions came from university student volunteers, a local carpenter and local construction workers. The plaza has been embraced by neighbors as a place that positively contributes to their livelihood.

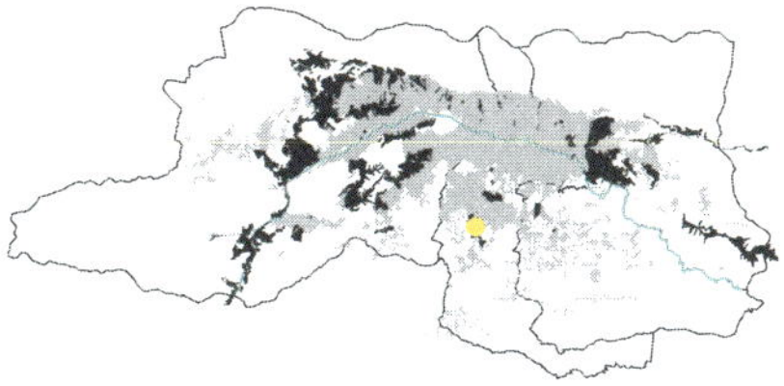

Location
La Palomera, Municipio Baruta, Distrito Capital, Venezuela

Project team:
FUDEP, Citibank Venezuela and Enlace Arquitectura

Date
2017

Coordinates
10°25’53.41”N 66°52’35.67”O

Investment
9,000 USD

Public space area
137.04 m²

Urban density
436.78 hab / ha

Population benefited
9,710 hab

Distance traveled from 0m to 500m
Distance traveled from 700m to 800m
Public space

1.459 Builds

9.710 Inhabitants benefited

39,68 Ha area of influence 800m

Houses 500m
Houses 800m
Polygon 500m
Polygon 800m

1 Plaza Bolívar de Baruta
2 Alcaldía de Baruta
3 Cementerio Municipal de Baruta
4 Colegio Miguel José Sanz

Scale:
0 25 50 100 200

PUBLIC SPACE

Despite the small-scale of this public space intervention, Plaza La Cruz represents a tactical intervention that reflects the motivation of neighbors to transform their surroundings. The new plaza is a place where people can comfortably engage one another, by providing opportunities for congregation and casual meetings. It also represents a place where outside visitors can arrive and feel welcome since the plaza´s vocation is public, unlike the rest of the tight urban fabric, which is perceived to be more private.

HISTORY

La Palomera is a spontaneous settlement located on a hill directly south of the colonial town of Baruta, which dates back to the Spanish presence in Venezuela. Founded in 1637, Baruta's urban fabric is gridded, following the guidelines stipulated in the Law of the Indies, and includes the Plaza Bolívar and the Church of Our Lady of the Rosary. Baruta was a separate town from Caracas, but over the course of the 20th century, as the capital grew in territory, Baruta became part of Caracas´ continuous urban sprawl. The land currently occupied by La Palomera was once owned by the Catholic Church. The community´s foundation year is officially recorded as 1937, which is when the settlement's earliest homes were built.[1] It grew and extended over 16 hectares of land. Houses progressively gained heights of between 2 and 4 stories, making La Palomera a dense urban area in the city.

SOCIAL AND POLITICAL CONTEXT

Many inhabitants of La Palomera are direct descendants of the community´s founders. Settlers, often from the same family, created groups of housing structures that evolved into the nine sectors that compose La Palomera today: La Acequia, Barrialito, Las Brisas, La Ceiba, Copacabana, La Cruz, Santo Domingo, Fundadores and Piedra Pintada.[2] According to the nomenclature established in 1966 by the Physical Habilitation Program for Informal Settlements (Plan de Habilitación Física de Barrios), La Palomera is considered an Isolated Design Unit (Unidad de Diseño Aislado)[3] due to its smaller size and the fact that it is not part of a larger extension of spontaneous settlements as in the case of Petare and Catia. It is, however, near other isolated spontaneous settlement units such as El Placer de María toward the north, and Picapiedras, Monterrey and Ojo de Agua, toward the south. La Palomera's culture is closely associated with the religious and historical traditions of Baruta, including festivities to celebrate the Paradura del Niño, and the Cruz de Mayo.

ENVIRONMENTAL SITUATION

Risk in La Palomera is primarily associated with the poor construction quality of the houses and the fact that they have been built over unstable, steep slopes, often without proper foundations. Improvised sewage collection is faulty and allows water to infiltrate the ground, which can provoke landslides in the rainy season. Waste management is problematic due to the settlement´s limited road system which precludes waste collection trucks from entering the community. This has re-

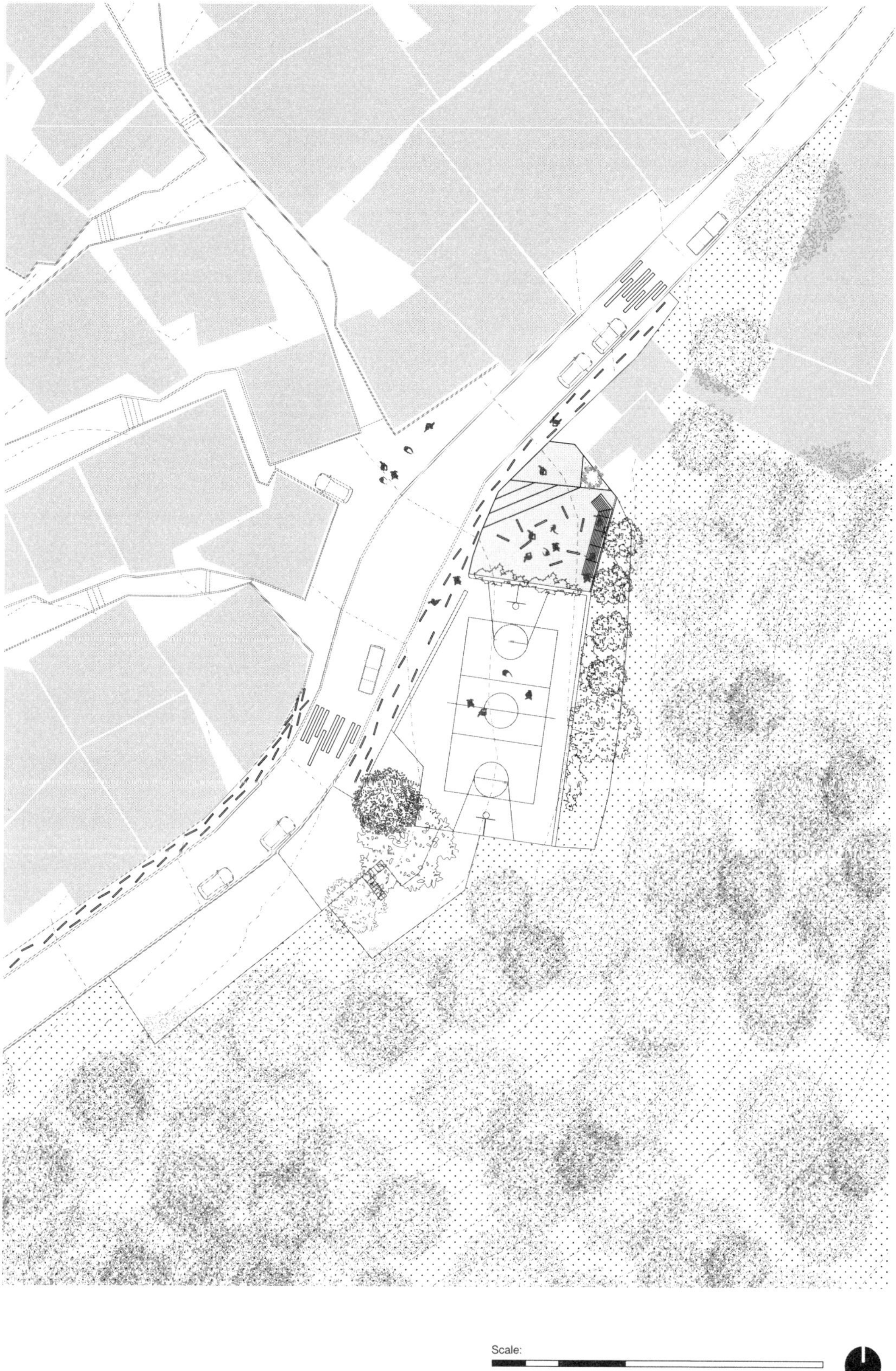
Scale:
0 2.5 5 10 25

sulted in the appearance of clandestine open waste dumps along the upper edge of the *barrio*, which is the sector furthest away from Baruta. Some neighbors dispose of waste by throwing it over the edge of the cliff that separates La Palomera from the Piedra Azul neighborhood bellow. These practices expose La Palomera to spontaneous fires ignited by glass or other debris. Part of the reasoning behind the public space transformation of the ridge is to encourage neighbors to value open space differently and change their current attitude about waste.

URBAN SITUATION

La Palomera is a predominantly residential urban settlement just south of Baruta. The community has four access points from the town where streets running north-south become staircases as they rise into the *barrio*. Paez Street is the only one that extends from the town grid and ascends around La Palomera´s western edge to the top of the hill. Plaza La Cruz is located at the end of this street, just before it narrows into a pedestrian walkway. The population density is 436 persons per hectare,[4] among the highest in the city, and reflects the neighborhoods´ compact nature and lack of open space. Nevertheless, the upper ridge of the neighborhood hosts several incipient public spaces including two bocce ball courts, a seating area, a basketball court and the La Palomera Plaza. This ridge has the potential of becoming a fully articulated park that links several spaces, once the open waste dumps are cleared and a new approach to waste management is definitively assumed. Also, spaces occupied for parking and abandoned cars can be emptied and made available. Combining these opportunities along the ridge could contribute 250 linear meters of public space to neighbors and the city at large.

PROJECT FUNDING

Funds for the project were administered through the City Planting program sponsored by Citibank Venezuela, that consists of small public space interventions designed through educational workshops with communities as part of a capacity building experience. Every year, six communities participate and compete against each other for seed capital to build a larger public space. The winning project is carried forward.[5] La Palomera unfortunately did not win the competition. The modest plaza that stands today was part of the program´s intervention during the educational workshops.

RELATED PROGRAMS

The new public space forms part of a daily routine for the children that attend a nearby pre-school, Concentración 094. They used to have to walk across the open waste dump as they went to play in an existing basketball court located just beyond, exposing themselves to the contamination and diseases associated with decomposing organic waste. The children participated in the design and construction of the new plaza and regard it as their own. They use it regularly to play and visit with friends. Other programs nearby, such as the Punto Solidario soup kitchen, could become more closely linked to the plaza and use it for outdoor activities. Likewise, children from other schools and nurseries are encouraged to use the plaza for events that require open space.

ACTIVITIES

The plaza's design process incorporated several activities that sought to encourage the community's participation. During the initial phase, games such as trivia and memory with content about parks and playgrounds were played with children and neighbors as a ploy to talk about the value and opportunities access to public space could create for them. A new waste management structure was devised with the municipality and the community to ensure the space would no longer be used to deposit waste. Then, during the construction process, elements of the design were specifically conceived so that children from the nearby school could help make patterns in the pavement with recycled plastic bottle caps. Several areas of the plaza were set aside for neighbors to plant vegetation.

URBAN INTEGRATION

La Palomera and Baruta share numerous daily dynamics. Children from La Palomera attend schools in Baruta; neighbors depend on services and goods they purchase in the town and must go there to access transportation routes toward other parts of Caracas. The relationship mostly occurs in one direction with few reasons for people from Baruta or other parts of the city to ascend into La Palomera. Public spaces may represent a strategy to create destinations within La Palomera that can interest outside visitors. For example, the bocce courts could hold tournaments among people of various neighborhoods and a playground might attract children from nearby communities. Plaza La Cruz is in many respects a catalyst to begin envisioning the entire southern ridge of La Palomera as a potential public park that operates at a broader metropolitan scale.

1 G. R. Flamerich, "Baruta: Un pueblo con su propio ritmo," *Cátedra de periodismo UCAB* May 12, 2012. https://periodismo001.wordpress.com/2012/05/16/baruta-un-pueblo-de-ciudad/ (accessed January 19, 2019).

2 Instituto de Estudios Regionales y Urbanos, *Proyecto de Habilitación Integral de La Palomera* (Caracas: Universidad Simón Bolívar, 2002).

3 Josefina Baldó and Federico Villanueva, *Un plan para los barrios de Caracas* (Caracas: Consejo Nacional de la Vivienda, 1997).

4 Silva (2015).

5 *Sembrando Ciudad La Palomera*. YouTube, Enlace Arquitectura, 2017 http://www.enlacearquitectura.net/projects/2017/08/citi-planting-la-palomera/

PLAZA LA CRUZ LA PALOMERA
CARACAS, VENEZUELA

EL GUASMO BEACH

El Guasmo Beach is a constructed landscape on the edge of a saltwater canal or *estero*, south of the city of Guayaquil. It is an area where people began building their homes over land gained from the river. This exposed them to the effects of periodic flooding, but because foundations were constructed over debris and waste, families could also suffer structural collapse. The settlements have also damaged the ecology of the site by destroying mangroves and contaminating the water. The Recreation Center Guasmo Beach is simultaneously a risk management solution and a strategy to mitigate environmental degradation. Several terrace levels proposed in the project respond to changing tide levels and at the same time offer people space for recreation. Behind the beach, a populous informal community gains a new perspective of the *estero* and sees it as a benefit to their livelihood.

Project team:
Douglas Dreher, architect.
Municipality of Guayaquil

Location
Guasmo Sur, Ximena Parish,
Guayaquil, Ecuador

Date 2004

Coordinates
2°17'08.09"S 79°53'00.72"O

Investment
1.1 million USD

Public space area
9,609.14 m²

Urban density
115.36 hab / ha

Population benefited
8,248 hab

PUBLIC SPACE

The size and dimensions of the Guasmo Beach project respond to the water´s behavior and create a threshold of protection for local residents. Additionally, the facilities provide ample space for recreation, leisure and sports activities that improve the quality of life for residents living in the surrounding spontaneous settlements.

HISTORY

The earliest settlers of El Guasmo arrived in 1973 and built on property that had been part of an agriculture farm, later expropriated by the government for public use.[1] Since then, the population and the extension of the settlement have grown at rates of 5.000 inhabitants and 140 hectares a year. As the settlement expanded, land eventually ran out and the newest houses were built directly on the edge of the *estero*.[2] For many years, El Guasmo remained a spontaneous settlement comprised of unpaved streets submerged in sewage water, deficient public services, scarce urban amenities and precarious homes. Over the course of the past two decades, through interventions sponsored by the Municipality of Guayaquil, new infrastructure, public services, access to public transportation, community engagement programs, and the construction of new public spaces have improved the formal and social conditions of El Guasmo.

SOCIAL AND POLITICAL CONTEXT

500.000 inhabitants reside in El Guasmo. They are represented by six neighborhood organizations. The population extends over an area of 2.000 hectares, with a medium density of 250 people per hectare. Settlers are mostly migrants and their descendants. They came to Guayaquil in search of better paying jobs associated with industrial production and port activity. The housing demand this migration generated, resulted in the occupation of undeveloped territories along the edges of the *estero*, over a significant portion of the city´s water edge. Poor waste management and untreated sewage released into the *esteros* affect both the health of inhabitants and the environment.

ENVIRONMENTAL SITUATION

El Guasmo´s urban setting is defined by its proximity to the Estero Salado. Flooding occurs periodically; a very severe one occurred in 2015 when sixteen neighborhoods in Guayaquil were flooded due to the coincidence of heavy rains and a high tide.[3] Self-built informal homes along the edges of the water are the most frequently affected since they occupy environmentally sensitive land not apt for residential purposes. In addition, homes are exposed to seismic risk due to the low quality of their construction. Procuring their relocation becomes a necessity.

URBAN SITUATION

El Guasmo is a predominantly residential neighborhood of self-built homes, between one and three stories high. The existing network of streets is insufficient to access each of the urban sectors.[4] As in the case of most spontaneous settlements, El Guasmo´s urban territory was formed without provision for public services, public amenities or public space. In regard to urban transportation,

Scale:
0 5 10 25 50

the Metrovia, a bus system with dedicated lanes managed by the Municipality of Guayaquil, has two stations in El Guasmo's most consolidated and historic areas,[5] but the less formal southern portions of the neighborhood are serviced by private, non-municipal transportation operators.

Urban areas, both formal and informal, developed in El Guasmo without acknowledging the behavior of the Estero Salado, which was mostly seen as a threat. Consequently, the Recreation Center Guasmo Beach represents a fundamental change in the city's perception of the *estero.* It faces the river with a terraced topography that can absorb higher water levels without threatening inhabitants nor exposing expensive infrastructure to flood damage. The terraces include a platform for bathing, recreation areas, kiosks, concessions and markets. The beach is also connected to other public spaces and playfields within the community.

PROJECT FUNDING

The Guasmo Beach Recreation Center was financed by the Municipality of Guayaquil for 1.1 million USD. It is considered part of the city´s Urban Regeneration plan that began in 2001 and was planned with the intention of advancing greater economic, social and environmental sustainability in the city.[6] The project in El Guasmo sought to alleviate urban pressures through the creation of public space and a tourist attraction that would, at the same time, value the environmental and landscape qualities of the Estero Salado and increase awareness regarding the importance of its conservation and care.

ACTIVITIES

The Recreational Center Guasmo Beach has become a very successful amenity for neighbors and for people from the entire city who use it as a recreation place on weekends and holidays. The space is flexible and can host a myriad of uses, not only related to water activities, such as rowing, bathing and swimming, but also as a playfield for soccer and other ball games. An area for concessions with kiosks and shaded seating is used by families for meals and snacks. Other interventions within the residential fabric, further inland, including a child nursery, a municipal primary school and a basketball court are connected to one another through pedestrian walkways, benches and other urban furniture. Public transportation networks link these areas to the rest of the city.

URBAN INTEGRATION

Interventions such as the Recreational Center Guasmo Beach have created a local tourist economy through urban renewal and the adaptation of recreation areas that serve both neighbors and people from the rest of Guayaquil. Access to public space manifests the right of inhabitants to urban amenities, recreation and play within the city. Prior to the intervention, this part of Guayaquil had an index of 0.4 m^2 of public space per inhabitant. The progressive addition of public space throughout the city of Guayaquil has increased per capita access to 7 m^2 per inhabitant.[7] Public spaces located along the Estero Salado, such as El Guasmo Beach, also help mitigate risks associated with flooding and the continued contamination of rivers.

The distinction between spontaneous and formal areas of the city, i.e., between the center and the periphery, is common in Latin American cities such as Guayaquil. For many years inhabitants of spontaneous settlements depended on the city center for employment, services and other necessities. Through progressive urban interventions, service improvements and public transportation, El Guasmo has evolved into a new urban center in its own right.

1 "El Guasmo, la hacienda que se convirtió en micro ciudad," *El Telégrafo* January 29, 2017.

2 J. V. Buchwald, "Guayaquil, una ciudad de cemento que desplazó al bosque tropical," *El Universo* September 24, 2012.

3 "16 zonas de Guayaquil se inundan cada vez que hay precipitaciones," *El Telégrafo* April 13, 2015.

4 "El Guasmo, la hacienda que se convirtió en micro ciudad," (2017).

5 "Proyecto de desarrollo de las zonas urbano marginales de Guayaquil," *Programas de desarrollo social* (Guayaquil: Unidad de gestión, ZUMAR, 2006).

6 D. Dreher, "La regeneración urbana de la ciudad de Guayaquil," Douglas Dreher Arquitectos, June 2007. http://www.douglasdreher.com/noticias/noticia.asp?id=271&sc=9 (accessed January 19, 2019).

7 "Plan Masa del Guasmo Sur elevará los índices de acceso a espacios verdes en Guayaquil," *El Ciudadano* May 10, 2014.

EL GUASMO BEACH
GUAYAQUIL, ECUADOR

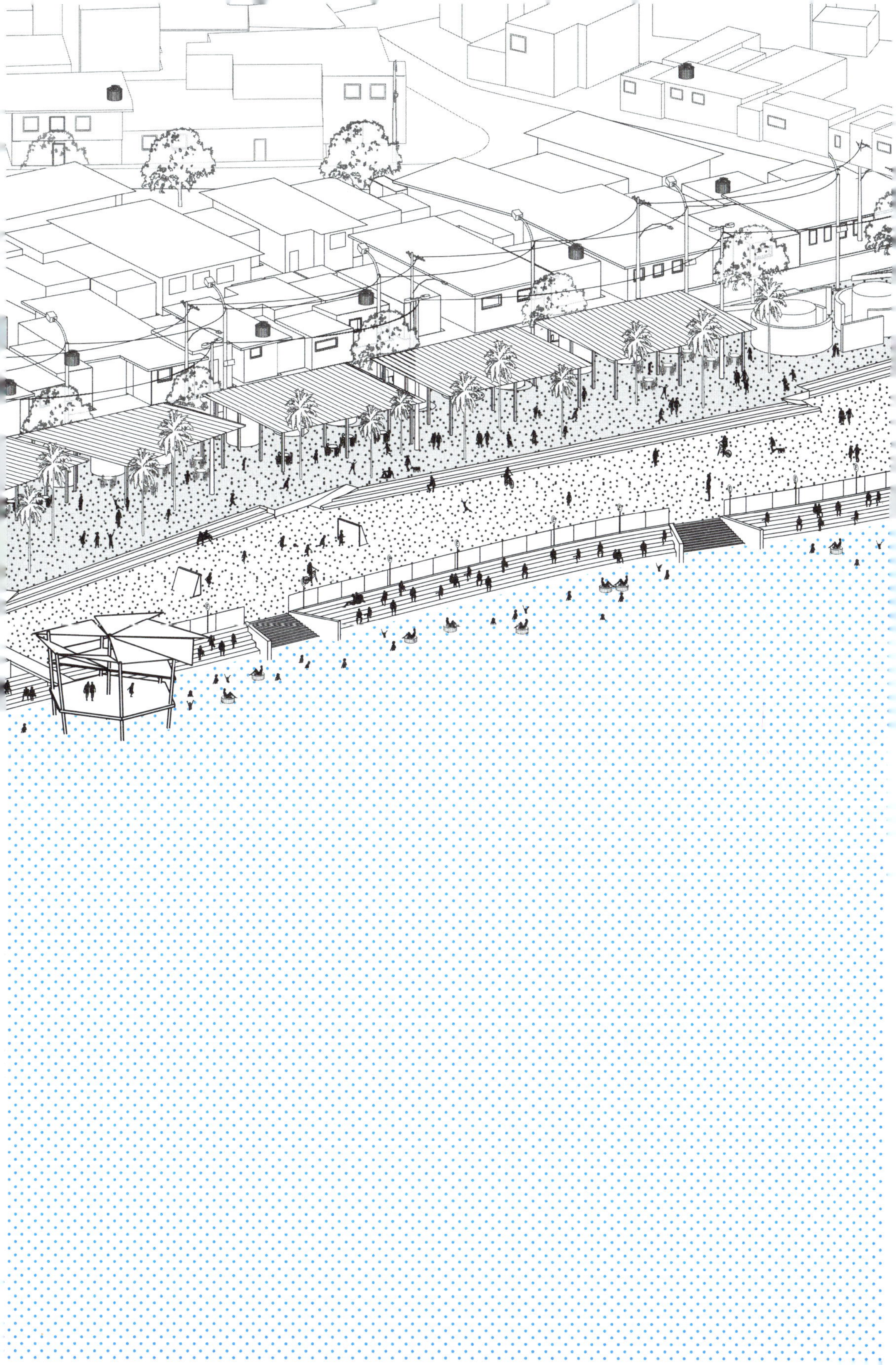

SANTA MARÍA EL TRIUNFO

Santa María El Triunfo, in Nueva Esperanza, is a spontaneous settlement located south of Lima, in the district of Villa María del Triunfo. Houses occupy the sides of a ravine, on dry and rocky soil. The community is vulnerable to earthquakes due to the precarious construction of their homes and the eroded surface of the sloped landscape they occupy. A partial mitigation strategy for these risks was implemented by the NGO Desco (Center for Studies and the Promotion of Development), through seismically engineered platforms that offer safety spaces at several locations along the community´s main road, the Asentamientos Humanos Amor y Paz Street. In the case of an earthquake, settlers are instructed to take refuge on these platforms. On a daily basis, however, the plazas benefit the community as places for meetings, recreation and play.

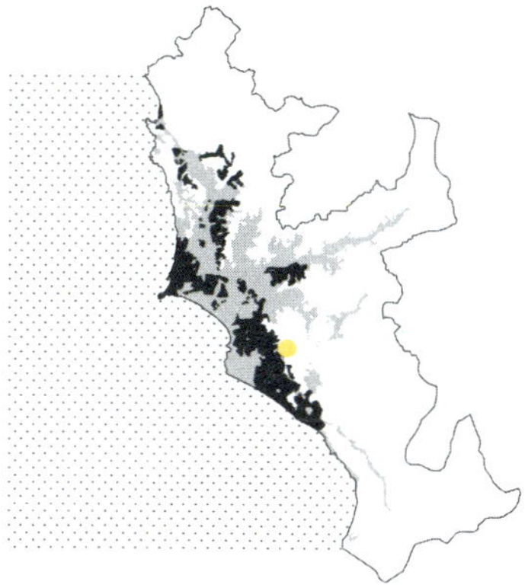

Location
Santa María, Sector Nueva Esperanza, Distrito Santa María del Triunfo, Lima, Peru

Project team:
Desco, GIZ Deutsche Gesellschaft für Internationale Zusammenarbeit, MISEROR Municipalidad de Villa María del Triunfo

Date 2006

Coordinates
12°09'25.79"S 76°54'43.40"O

Investment 85,000 USD

Public space area
2,494 m²

Urban density
58.97 hab / ha

Population benefited
7,014 hab

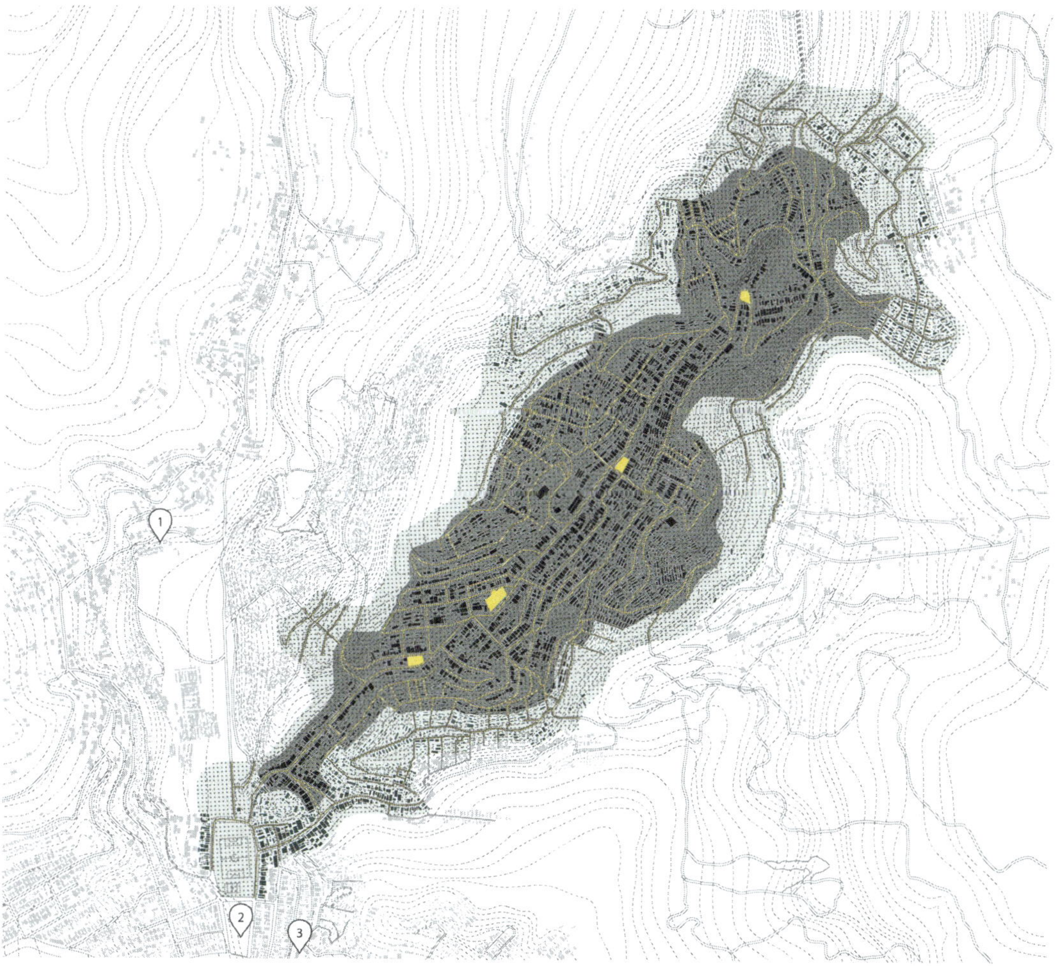

PUBLIC SPACE

The plazas are a valuable addition to the neighborhood, despite shortcomings such as insufficient shade. Their value also lies in the fact that funds available for resilience and risk mitigation projects were used to create much needed public space within settlements as a byproduct.

HISTORY

The district of Villa María del Triunfo, once mostly land used for agriculture, constitutes part of Lima´s urban periphery. It is a working-class settlement that resulted from organized movements such as the Society of Workers Sacred Heart of Jesus Surquillo and the Housing Association Nueva Esperanza in the 1940s.[1] The population grew with the increase of rural- urban migration, since spontaneous settlements represented an affordable housing option for migrants. In 1961, Villa María del Triunfo was formally recognized as a district and the settlers occupying the territory were given amnesty and secure land tenure.[2] Basic services were built through public investment and over the next 20 years the settlements continued to grow in population and territory. Since the 1990s new homes have increasingly encroached on higher risk areas along the pronounced slopes of ravines.[3]

SOCIAL AND POLITICAL CONTEXT

The invasion process of Lima´s southern periphery was led by workers associations who searched for land to build their homes. Land occupation through divided plots was organized by community leaders, whose efforts eventually earned the settlement's legal recognition as a district, and access to public services through public investment.

More than half of Villa María del Triunfo´s inhabitants are considered poor. A substantial percentage of homes do not have access to water, drainage or electricity and residents have limited access to health and education.[4] Within the district, Santa María del Triunfo is a new *barrio* or spontaneous settlement that is infamous for its unstable ground and the precarious quality of its constructions. Desco worked with the community to develop urban renewal plans through a participatory model. Neighbors first learned to diagnose their community´s problems and subsequently designed and built urban interventions, such as the safety plazas.[5]

ENVIRONMENTAL SITUATION

All of Peru is exposed to earthquake risk. Its Pacific coast line is especially vulnerable, Pisco, Lima, and Huacho being considered the most susceptible areas. Within Lima, the District of Villa María del Triunfo is one of the highest risk areas due to its sandy soil and the low construction quality of its self-built houses. Desco's work with the community revealed a desire to create open public spaces within the neighborhood, which were coupled with risk mitigation strategies. As seismically engineered platforms, the safety plazas are earthquake refuge areas that offer the community public space throughout the year.

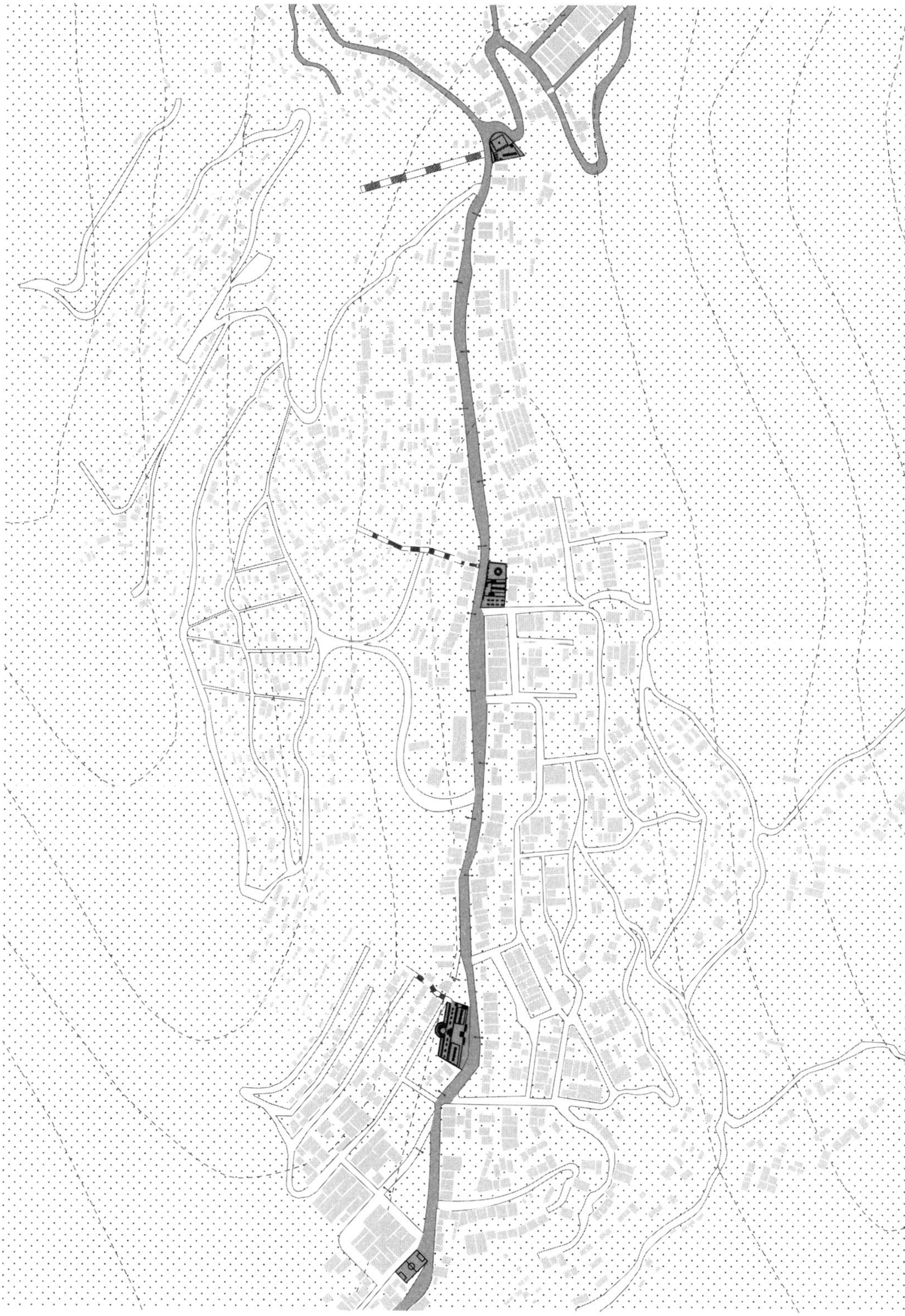

Scale:

0 10 25 50 100

URBAN SITUATION

The district of Villa María del Triunfo is the result of several waves of peripheral expansion, each of which created a different urban configuration.[6] The flatter and older parts of the settlement are comprised of orthogonal blocks with large residential plots. Continued urban growth required new settlers to build on increasingly smaller lots, located on less stable land. Finally, the least favorable conditions are found along the higher parts of ravines with limited road access. The spontaneous settlement Nueva Esperanza, in Santa María El Triunfo, where the safety plazas are located, is nestled within a narrow ravine. The Asentamientos Humanos de Unión y Paz Street runs along the lowest part of the land formation and remains unpaved. Houses are arranged along the slopes of the hills without a regular alignment. Homes beyond the street edge are accessed through steep steps.

PROJECT FUNDING

"Nueva Esperanza: Improvement of Villa María del Triunfo and Villa El Salvador informal settlements through participation in urban management" was the name given to the neighborhood improvement program. The specific project for Santa María El Triunfo was formulated through Desco´s "participatory project competitions" methodology.[7] The project was evaluated and selected by the European Community for implementation. Funding was secured through the Misereor International Agency GIZ fund, in partnership with the Municipality of Villa María del Triunfo and the community, who contributed with labor.

ACTIVITIES

The plazas and safety spaces of Santa María El Triunfo serve as places for recreational activities, entertainment, concerts, fairs and markets, as well as artistic presentations. Children from the community use these spaces to play after school. Adults use them to meet friends and play chess or dominos.

The Desco competition motivated the community to organize and participate in its transformation. The enthusiasm has persisted as neighbors continue to care for the maintenance of the plazas. Another positive result from the competition has been the implementation of a parallel program of nurseries for small children linked to an existing network of mother caregivers, supported by the Ministry of Women and Social Development.[8]

URBAN INTEGRATION

As Villa María del Triunfo developed, it did not reserve land for community amenities or public space. The community acknowledged the need for public space in the diagnostic exercise of the Desco Participatory Project Competition, as mentioned before. Space for gathering and recreation within the community helps strengthen ties among settlers, but also creates a place that can receive visitors from the rest of the city. By creating a network of public spaces along the community´s main access road, the settlement begins to project a more continuous urban experience that links it perceptually to other public spaces throughout the city.

1 "Historia Villa María Lima." http://villamarialima.galeon.com/productos1689543.html (accessed, January 19, 2019).

2 INDECI, PNUD, ECHO, MDVMT, *Escenario de riesgo sísmico y medidas de mitigación en Villa María del Triunfo* (Lima: INDECI, 2011), 12.

3 "Nueva Esperanza: Mejoramiento de nuevos barrios en Villa María del Triunfo a través de la participación en la gestión urbana," *DESCO Programa Urbano*, 2006. http://urbano.org.pe/project/nueva-esperanza-mejoramiento-de-nuevos-barrios-de-villa-maria-del-triunfo-a-traves-de-la-participacion-en-la-gestion-urbana/ (accessed January 19, 2019).

4 Ibid.

5 Programa Urbano DESCO, *Concurso Participativo de Proyectos: gestión participativa del territorio y movilización social en la mejor del barrio* (Lima: DESCO, 2008).

6 Municipalidad de Villa María del Triunfo.

7 Programa Urbano DESCO, *Concursos Participativos de Proyectos Sociales: fortaleciendo capacidades de desarrollo para una gestión participative* (Lima: DESCO, 2009).

8 Ibid.

SANTA MARÍA EL TRIUNFO
LIMA, PERU

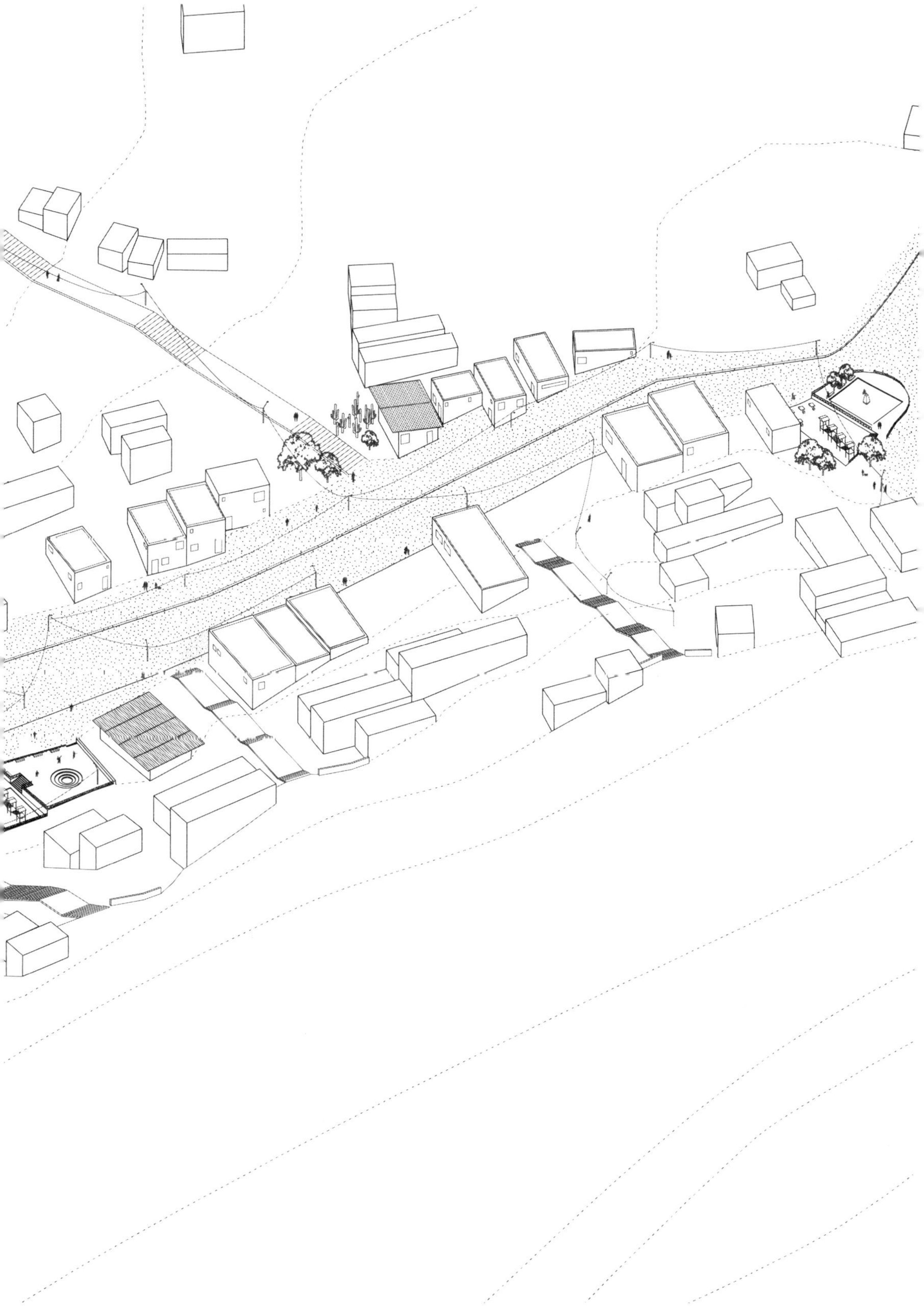

JUAN BOBO CREEK

The Juan Bobo creek is part of Comuna 2, a densely populated urban district on the northeastern slopes of Medellin. As space for new homes ran out and demand for housing continued to increase, people built precarious structures directly over the creek, exposing themselves to the risk of floods and landslides. The City of Medellin relocated these families into new multifamily buildings nearby and transformed the banks of the creek into space for recreation and leisure. The intervention also incorporated bridges over the creek, bringing community youth together that had previously maintained antagonistic relationships.

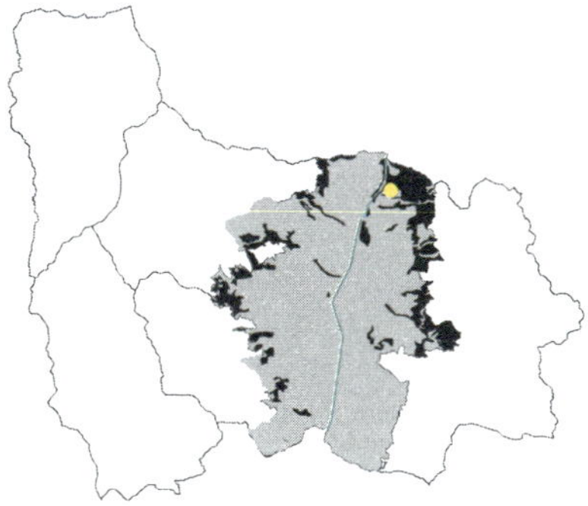

Location
Barrios Andalucía, Villa Niza and Villa del Socorro, Comuna 2 Santa Cruz, Zona Nororiental, Medellin, Colombia

Project team:
Taller de Vivienda, Empresa de Desarrollo Urbano EDU, Empresa Pública de Medellin (EPM), Municipality of Medellin

Date 2005

Coordinates
°17'39.58"N 75°32'47.19"O

Investment 5.5 million USD

Public space area
6,831 m²

Urban density
349 hab / ha

Population benefited
45,841 hab

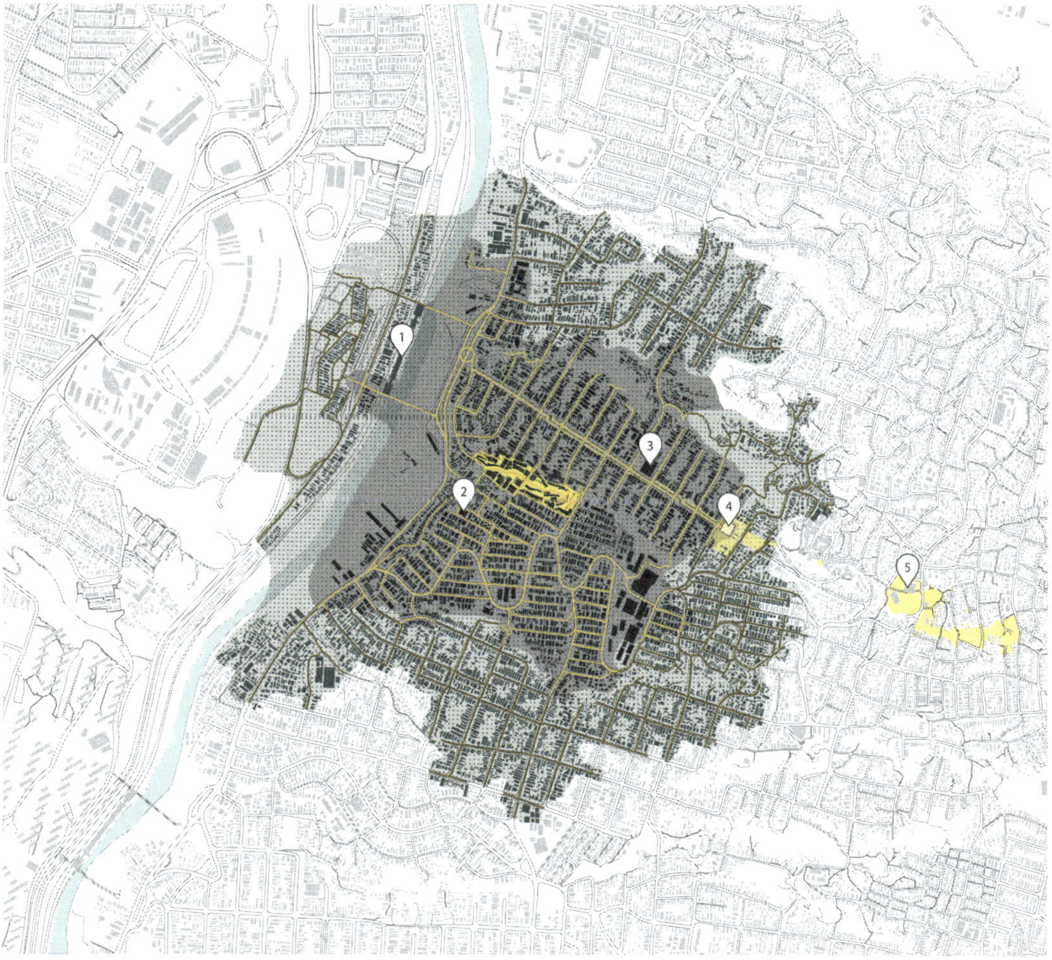

Distance traveled between 0m to 500m
Distance traveled between 500m to 800m
Public space
7,172 Structures
131.35 ha Area of influence 800m

Houses 500m
Houses 800m
Polygon 500m
Polygon 800m

1 Metro Estación Acevedo
2 Parque Primaveral Nuestra Señora del Camino
3 Parque Recreativo Andalucía
4 Metro Estación Andalucía
5 Estación La Popular

Scale:
0 50 100 200 400

PUBLIC SPACE

In an effort to protect people living along the creek from imminent disaster and ensure newcomers did not continue building homes on inadequate land, high risk areas along the Juan Bobo Creek were evacuated and converted into public space. The freed areas correspond to the space affected by changes in the creek´s volume of water. When the water level is low, this space is used for leisure and recreation. The site´s transformation also increased inhabitants´ sense of personal safety in their community.

HISTORY

Medellin received a heavy flow of migration from the countryside in the mid 20th century, as people fled the violence of armed militia. The city was not prepared to accommodate such numbers nor did it have a sufficiently large economy to employ them. As a result, spontaneous settlements make up 25% of the urban territory in Medellin.[1] They emerged early on over the northeastern hills of the city, between the Oriental Tramway and the Andalucia River. In the 1960s, public housing initiatives urbanized land to satisfy the housing deficit, and extra-legal constructions amplified the urban footprint in areas considered inadequate for development, such as the Juan Bobo creek. At first, the government´s intention was to raze all informally built urban areas,[2] but as demand continued to increase, they came to realize that spontaneous communities were needed to meet the need for housing. The municipality began accommodating services in the northeastern settlements, which progressively became denser. Popular, Santa Cruz, Manríquez and Aranjuez are the 4 *comunas* that structure this territory, which are themselves subdivided in 54 neighborhoods or barrios that reflect the different housing initiatives built over time.

In the 1990s, popular sectors in Medellin became the stage of gang violence associated with drug cartels. In many respects, the urban transformation projects designed for the northeastern hills, including the Integral Urban Project (PUI Plan Urbano Integral) and the Juan Bobo creek housing interventions, were conceived as social processes to empower neighbors.[3] Transforming neighborhoods through the incorporation of public space, schools, cultural institutions and other facilities was meant to mitigate the structural causes of violence.

SOCIAL AND POLITICAL CONTEXT

Urban Development Plans and the Territorial Zoning Plans (POT Plan de Ordenamiento Territorial) developed by the Municipality of Medellin in the late 1990s came with changes in the Colombian constitution which decentralized many government functions.[4] Municipalities gained jurisdiction over urban planning and the administration of local finances. Mayors were no longer assigned but elected. New legal planning instruments were adopted to guide the development of cities over an extended time, beyond the tenure period of local government.[5]

Implementation strategies for projects, such as the Juan Bobo Creek, relied on a team of specialized social workers to interact with the communities and document their economic and social situation. They also facilitated citizen participation in the definition of projects and were able to strengthen the community´s trust in local government institutions, which had been eroded during the years of violent confrontations in the 1990s. These initiatives also created community organization structures that have endured over time.

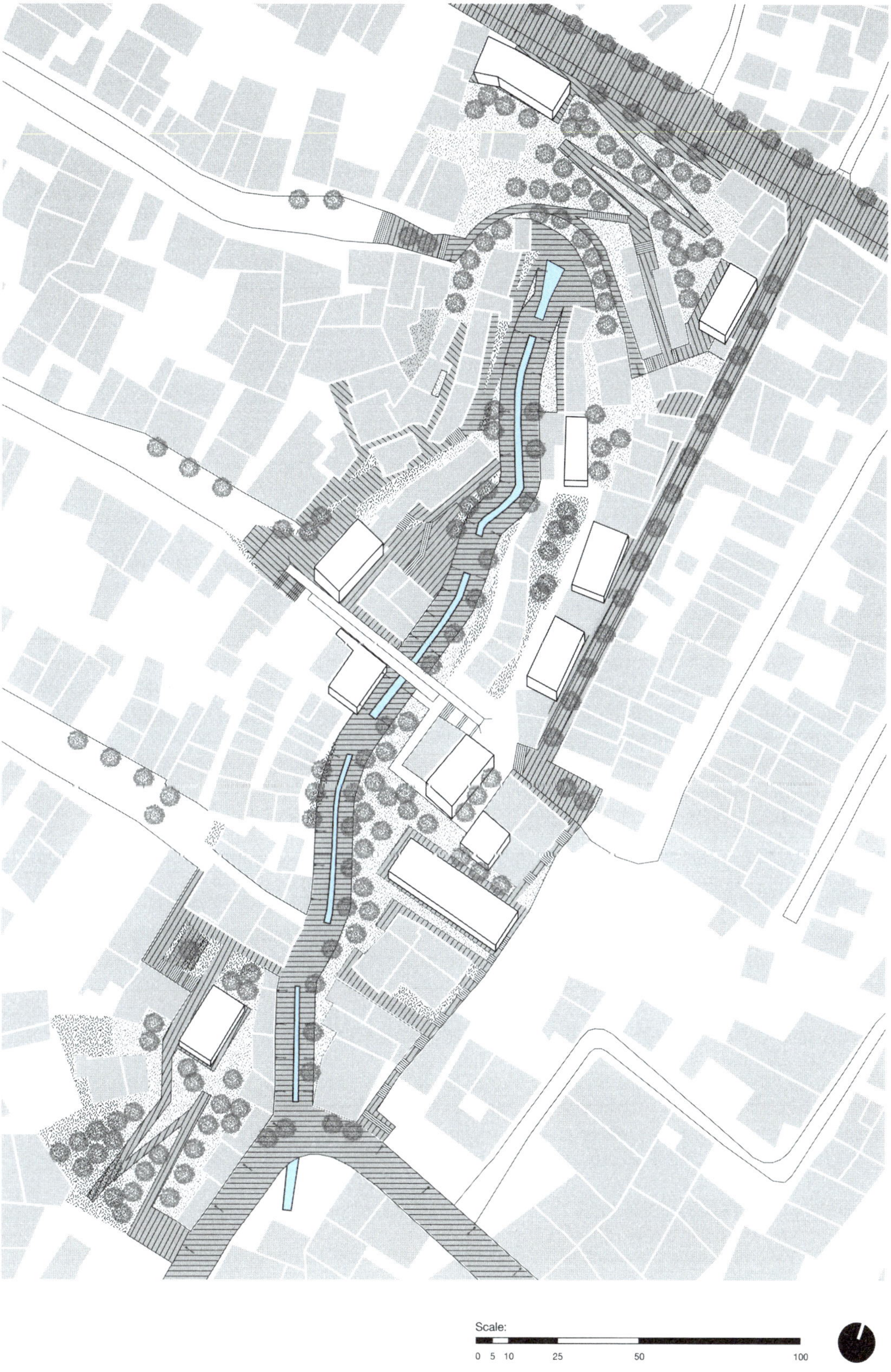
Scale:
0 5 10 25 50 100

ENVIRONMENTAL SITUATION

The presence of informal housing built directly over a creek and the unstable ground along its edges was deemed highly problematic by environmental and social assessments prepared for the northeastern hills of Medellin.[6] The direct disposal of sewage water into the creek also made it a dangerous health hazard. The municipality surveyed the location of houses releasing sewage waste into the creek and those affected by running water infiltrations in the ground, which made them more prone to potential landslides.

The housing project for Juan Bobo Creek relocated families living in high risk homes to new multifamily structures built in the vicinity. Other homes in less precarious conditions were improved through access to services and better physical communication with surrounding areas.[7]

URBAN SITUATION

Juan Bobo creek runs for 800 meters before it reaches the Medellin River. Initially, in 1960, more regular neighborhoods had been traced on either side of the creek, prudently distanced from the water to respect the fluctuating volumes during the high rainy season. Later, these buffer areas and the creek itself became occupied with spontaneous settlements. Road access to these areas was difficult; most homes were reached through narrow walkways and stairs.

The Housing Consolidation and Environmental Sanitation project generated a relocation process that gave way to 5.000 m^2 of new public space. 107 new housing units in multifamily structures were built to accommodate the relocated families.[8] These buildings take advantage of the site´s topography by allowing the lower levels to be accessed from the ground, while walkways at a higher ground elevation coincide with the fourth level, providing access to the top four floors. This way an 8-story building can function without an elevator, reducing construction and maintenance costs.

PROJECT FUNDING

The Juan Bobo Creek project was formulated by the Municipality of Medellin and executed by the Urban Development Company (EDU Empresa de Desarrollo Urbano). They were responsible, jointly with the Municipality´s Social Development Department, for all of the project phases including diagnostics, community engagement and participation as well as for the construction phase. Funds were pooled from resources assigned to various departments within the municipality: Public Works, the Department of Health; EPM, Planning and Administration, and the Department of Social Development.[9] 90% of the new relocation housing was paid through subsidies from the municipal government. The remaining 10% was the responsibility of each beneficiary family. Payment was structured according to the possibilities and means of each recipient.

RELATED PROGRAMS

Several other programs were designed and implemented by the municipality concurrently with the transformation of the Juan Bobo Creek. The environmental agency installed a waste recycling and management program. They also taught the community how to produce agriculture locally. Another initiative was to create risk prevention committees to teach people what to do during natural disasters, as part of the Municipality´s Disaster Prevention and First Aid System. The Department of Citizen Culture organized community gatherings to strengthen inhabitant's sense of ownership and responsibility for the preservation of public spaces.

The Center for Zonal Entrepreneurial Development (CEDEZO Centro de Desarrollo Embresarial Zonal)) is a city-wide program with venues located in many of Medellin´s spontaneous settlements. It provides logistical support and educational programs for community members to better manage family businesses or build new income generating activities. Other municipal programs include the library parks and the program Buen Comienzo (Good Beginning), which supports nurseries for infants and small children.

ACTIVITIES

The new public spaces along the Juan Bobo Creek are mostly walkways and paths that follow the water´s course. There are also spaces large enough to program small theatre performances, concerts, exercise sessions for senior citizens, ball games and religious rituals. Sometimes urban artists paint murals in commemoration of specific community celebrations and the municipality lends support with maintenance and cleaning.

URBAN INTEGRATION

The community of Juan Bobo remained isolated and disconnected from its surroundings for many years due to its complex topography, ineffective means of circulation and high density. Furthermore, negative social stigmas and violence discouraged people in the vicinity from going there. Common space was scarce. The municipality´s housing and relocation project freed land along the creek and converted it into public space. The interventions also addressed accessibility by clarifying circulation through a network of walkways, bridges and public squares. Connections with the neighboring communities of Andalucía and Villa Niza were also strengthened. These urban improvements completely transformed the face of this urban area and made it visible to the rest of the city.

1 M. Hermelin et al., *Medellín Medio-Ambiente Urbanismo Sociedad*. (Medellín: Fondo Editorial Universidad EAFIT, 2010), 135.

2 Empresa de Desarrollo Urbano, *Medellín: Modelo de transformación urbana* (Medellín, 2015), 24.

3 C. A. Correa, "Proyecto Urbano Integral en la zona nororiental de Medellín," I Congreso Internacional sobre Desarrollo Humano, 2006.

4 Francesco Orsini and Alejandro Echeverri, "Informalidad y urbanismo social en Medellín," *Sensible* 2009. https://upcommons.upc.edu/bitstream/handle/2099/11900/111103_RS3_AEcheverri_%20P%2011-24.pdf (accessed January 10, 2019).

5 Ibid.

6 Correa, (2006).

7 C. P. Cano, "Viviendas con corazón en la quebrada Juan Bobo Medellín, Colombia," *Ciudades para un Futuro más Sostenible* November 13, 2018. http://habitat.aq.upm.es/dubai/08/bp1982.html (accessed January 19, 2019).

8 Ibid., 150, 153.

9 Ibid.

JUAN BOBO CREEK
MEDELLIN, COLOMBIA

MEDELLIN NORTHEAST CABLE CAR PUBLIC SPACES

The cable car over the spontaneous settlements along the northeastern slopes of Medellin is the first of its kind in Latin America. The system has improved transportation for inhabitants and configured new public space at the ground level in areas affected by the cable car´s construction. Each station has been designed with generous open space, which the community uses for activities. The stations are connected with the rest of the neighborhoods through an extensive network of public space in the form of renovated streets, plazas and playgrounds, circuits of terraces, pools and walkways.

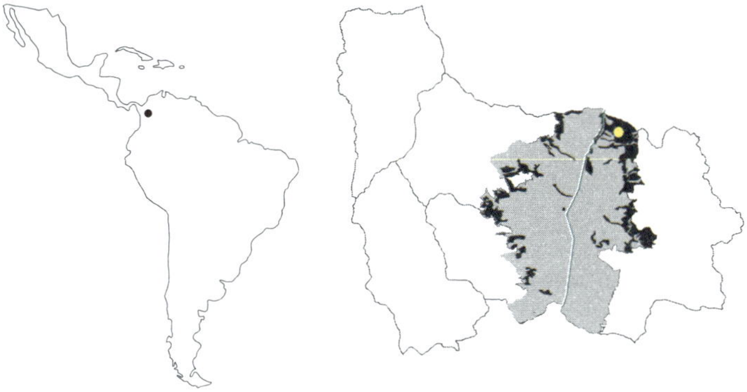

Location
Barrios Andalucía and Santo Domingo, Comuna 1 La Popular and Comuna 2 Santa Cruz

Project team:
Empresa de Desarrollo Urbano EDU, Municipality of Medellin

Date 2004 - 2007

Coordinates
6°17'44.55"N 75°33'03.46"O

Investment
4.2 million USD[1]

Public space area
37,738 m2

Urban density
514 hab / ha

Population benefited
169,727 hab

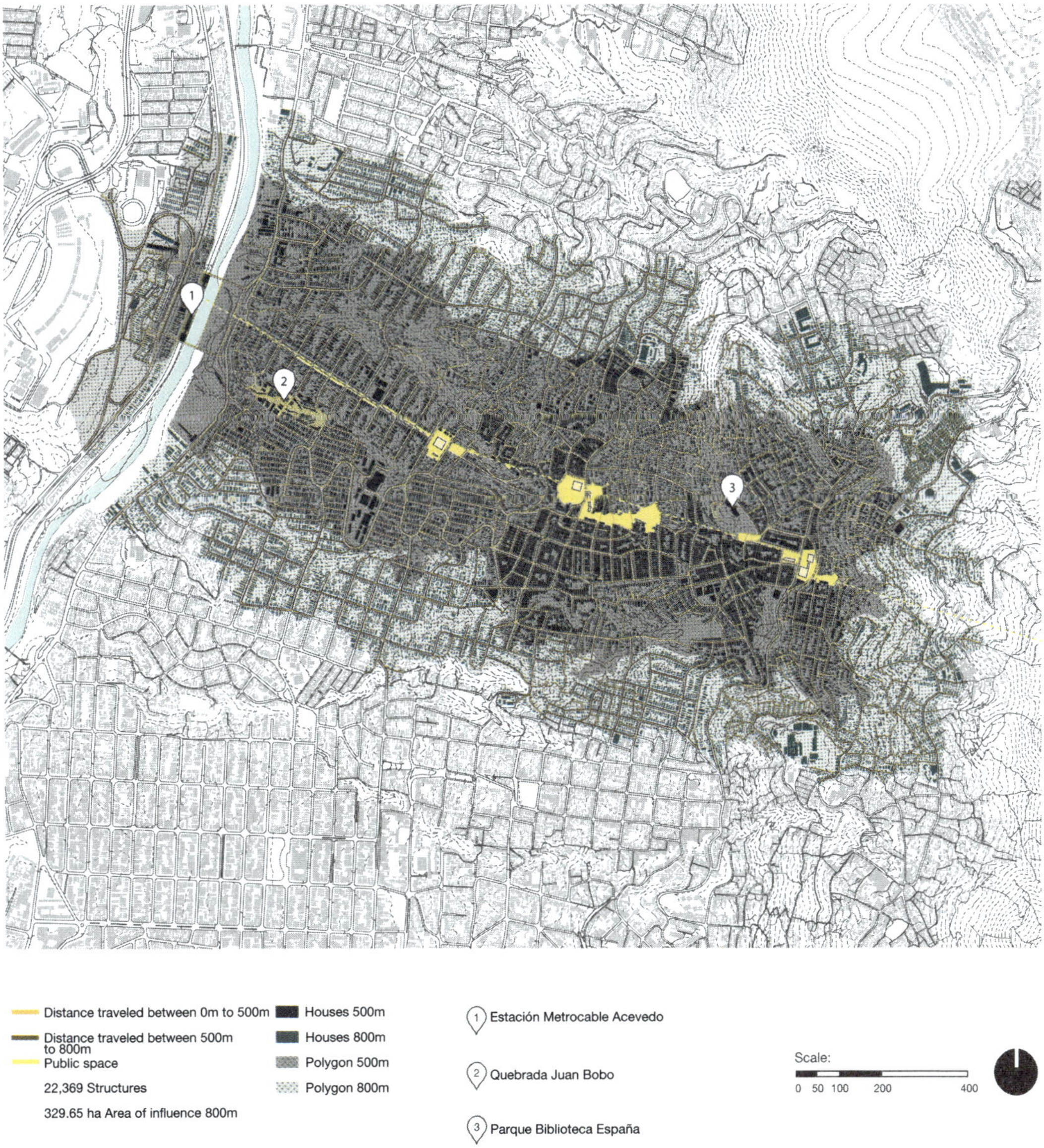

PUBLIC SPACE

The construction of each column supporting the cable car was a pretext to create a plaza, a playground or tables for adults to play chess. While the gondolas travel above, bellow the supporting structure is resolved on the ground to benefit neighbors with new places for gathering and recreation.[1]

HISTORY

The Comunas 1 and 2 on the northeastern hills of Medellin are conglomerations of working-class settlements built as early as 1932, on what had previously been private farmland. Streets and blocks were laid out orthogonally. As the urban areas grew upward toward the steeper parts of the mountain, self-built homes adapted to the site´s topography. This more elevated and informal urban area is known as Santo Domingo Savio and dates back to 1963. Successive migration waves of farmers displaced by violence increased demand for housing, and the urban fabric kept encroaching higher up on land less apt for construction. These occupations were illegal and land tenure disputes persisted for many years.[2]

Over the course of the following decades the community witnessed several transformations. Basic services, access to potable water and street lights were installed by the municipality in the sixties. Then, in the seventies, the community set aside land for schools and ball courts. Personal security was greatly affected in the eighties and nintiess by drug gangs that took control of streets and open areas, sequestering families within the confines of their homes for fear of being caught in cross fires. More recent changes include the implementation of the Integral Urban Project (PUI Plan Urban Integral), through which public transportation was improved. A series of new public spaces, cultural institutions and educational facilities were built and managed by various departments in the Municipality of Medellin.[3]

SOCIAL AND POLITICAL CONTEXT

Prior to the implementation of the PUI project, surveys and analyses of Comunas 1 and 2 revealed that the main challenges were poverty, lack of trust in public institutions, insufficient public space, health risks, and the structural vulnerability of homes due to landslides and poor construction quality.[4] During the decade of 1990, drug related violence and street gangs were prevalent; furthermore, Santo Domingo barrio served as an important base of operations for the drug cartel.

The settlements of the northeastern hills are among the earliest non-planned communities in Medellin.[5] They extend over a territory of 383 hectares and have a population of 125,000 which translates to 349 inhabitants/hectare,[6] considerably more than the population density of Manhattan.[7]

ENVIRONMENTAL SITUATION

Landslides are the most pressing risk in the area. In 1974 and 1979, strong rain and sewage water filtrations in the subsoil, due to inefficient drainage systems, caused landslides that resulted in

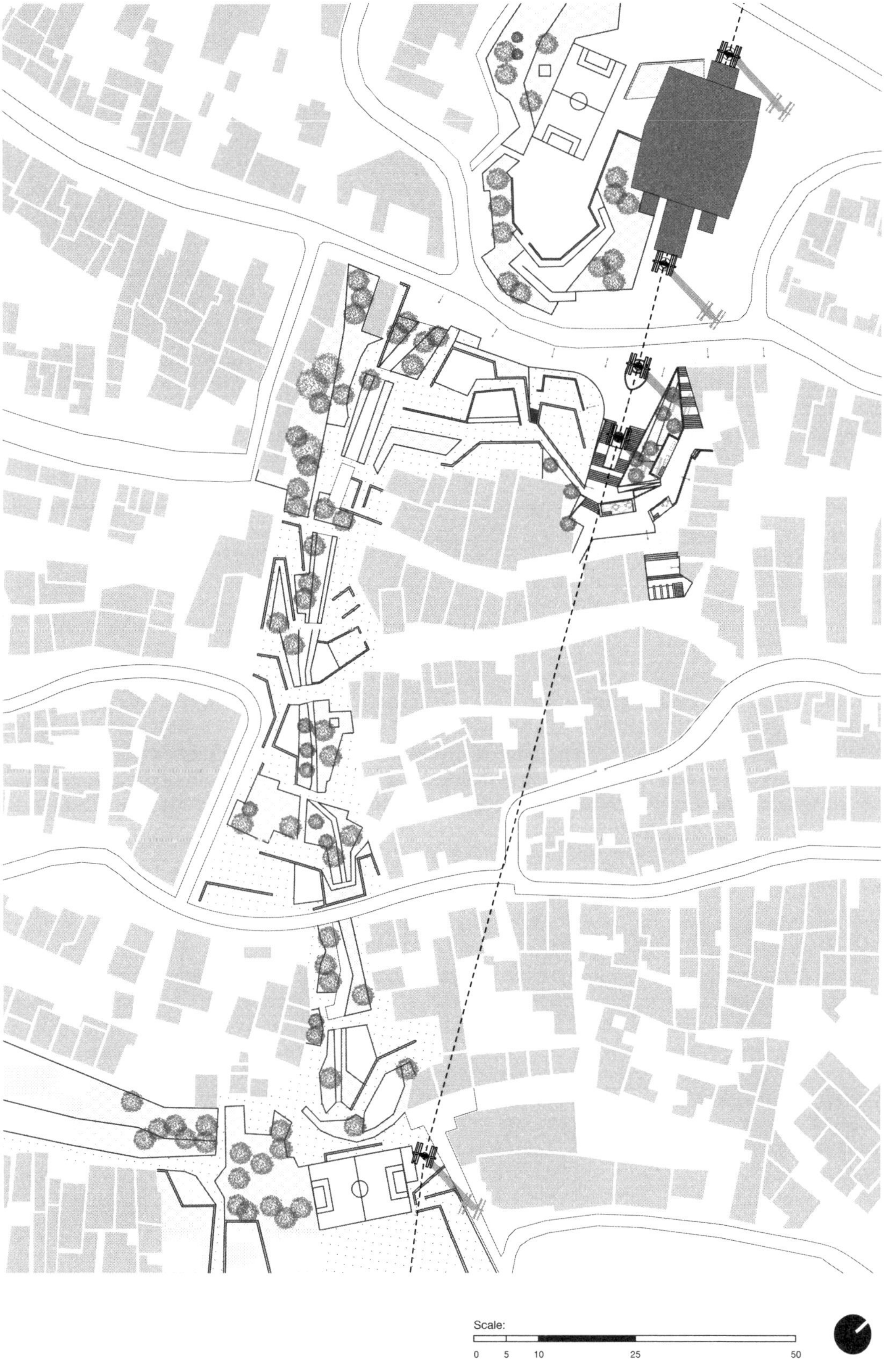
Scale:
0 5 10 25 50

fatalities and an important loss of homes. Structures of poor construction quality located on steep slopes above a 50% incline, were the most affected.8 Families that lost their homes or still lived in high-risk conditions were relocated after the 1979 events to safer areas in the neighborhood. In addition, neighbors also had to contend with public health threats associated with poor waste and sewage management.

URBAN SITUATION

The Comunas 1 and 2 are connected to the city's public transportation system through the cable car which feeds into the elevated metro system at the Acevedo station. The cable car, known as the K-line, reaches three stations along its ascent: Andalucia, Popular, and Santo Domingo. It was inaugurated in 2004 and its trajectory is 2.07 km long. The posts of the cable system coincide with the 107th Street for the first part of the trajectory. The sidewalks were widened in order to receive each column, creating ample new public space in addition to resolving infrastructure requirements.[9] Further up the ascent, the cable system posts fall within residential fabric, and become opportunities to incorporate playgrounds, plazas and reflective pools, such as the ones in the Herrera Linear Park. The necklace of public spaces in the urban fabric mirrors the path of the cable car above. The public spaces improve connectivity within the community and offers neighbors places to gather and children spaces to play.

PROJECT FUNDING

The cable car is part of Medellin´s public transportation system together with the elevated metro line, BRTs, tramways and neighborhood buses. The cable car was financed in part by the municipality, which covered 55% of the cost; the remaining 45% was financed by the Metro Company.[10] Resources for the construction of the Herrera Park were pooled together by the Metropolitan Area of the Aburra Valley and the Municipal Environmental Agency. All construction aspects were managed by the Urban Development Company (EDU).

RELATED PROGRAMS

The cable car system is one of many municipal projects built in the northeastern communities to improve the livelihood of neighbors and increase their access to opportunities. A network of library parks in Medellin has one of its most prominent buildings in Santo Domingo Savio: the Spain Library (Biblioteca España). A high school building and a nursery that is part of the Good Beginning (Buen Comienzo) program have also been built nearby. A CEDEZO educational center helps adults learn skills to support their productive activities through computer training, accounting and finance courses as well as social media advertisement. Recycling programs have been implemented to improve waste management. Public spaces are regularly maintained by a dedicated municipal staff. Overall, these programs and facilities create a dynamic urban environment that engages inhabitants and summons visitors from the rest of the city.

ACTIVITIES

The construction of the cable system and the various public spaces that complement it have created scenarios for new activities within the settlement: playgrounds for children; places for adults and senior citizens to gather and play board games; and areas for exercise classes, music concerts and theatre. The Herrera Park´s reflective pools are frequently used by children for play. Increased accessibility, generated by improved walkways and staircases, has allowed neighbors to develop street side businesses and kiosks that improve the perception of personal safety.

URBAN INTEGRATION

Medellin´s periphery was stigmatized as poor, violent and illegal for more than 60 years. Inhabitants of the Comunas 1 and 2, on the northeastern hills, were considered second class citizens and excluded from urban dynamics.[11] The PUI, the construction of the cable car system and related public spaces as well as the various implemented programs have contributed to a broader acknowledgement of this part of the city. The Comunas 1 and 2 are now well connected to the rest of the city through public transportation and offer generous access to public space. Violence related to gangs has been quelled and to a certain degree replaced by numerous youth programs. New commercial areas with small bars and restaurants on the main Santo Domingo square are an attractive option for university students looking for a safe place to gather that is also less expensive. Singular views over Medellin from the square are part of its allure. The flow of people from across the city into these areas is no doubt proof of this spontaneous settlement's successful urban integration.

1 Investment to build the Andalucía Boulevard and La Herrera Linear Park.

2 Proyecto BAQ, "Archivo BAQ Arquitectura Panamericana," Proyecto Urbano Integral (PUI) Nororiental, Comunas 1 y 2 - Áreas de influencia sistema metrocable de Medellín, September 27 2018. http://www.arquitecturapanamericana.com/proyecto-urbano-integral-pui-nororiental-comunas-1-y-2-areas-de-influencia-sistema-metrocable-medellin/ (accessed January 10, 2019).

3 M. Hermelin, A. Echeverri and J. Giraldo, *Medellín Medio Ambiente y Sociedad* (Medellín: Fondo Editorial Universidad de EAFIT, 2010), 140-141.

4 Empresa de Desarrollo Urbano. "Medellín: Modelo de transformación urbana," 2015.

5 "Las comunas de Medellín," *Insumisos*. https://www.insumisos.com/lecturasinsumisas/MEDELLIN%20FRONTERAS%20INVISIBLES%20III.pdf (accessed January 19, 2019).

6 Ministerio de Tecnologías de la Información y las Comunicaciones de Colombia,"Población de Medellín 2018-2020," 2019. https://www.datos.gov.co/Estad-sticas-Nacionales/Poblacion-Medellin-2018-2020/j8ze-v9z6 (accessed December 9, 2019)

7 The population density of Manhattan is 254 persons / hectare.

8 Alcaldía de Medellín, *Plan de Desarrollo Local Comuna 1 La Popular* (Medellín: Alcaldía de Medellín, 2015), 39.

9 Empresa de Desarrollo Urbano. (2015), 80-81.

10 Silva y Vaggione (2016).

11 Empresa de Desarrollo Urbano. "Proyectos Urbanos Integrales," 2010. http://proyectosurbanosintegrales.blogspot.com/p/que-es-el-pui.html (accessed January 19, 2019).

NORTHEASTERN CABLE CAR PUBLIC SPACES
MEDELLIN, COLOMBIA

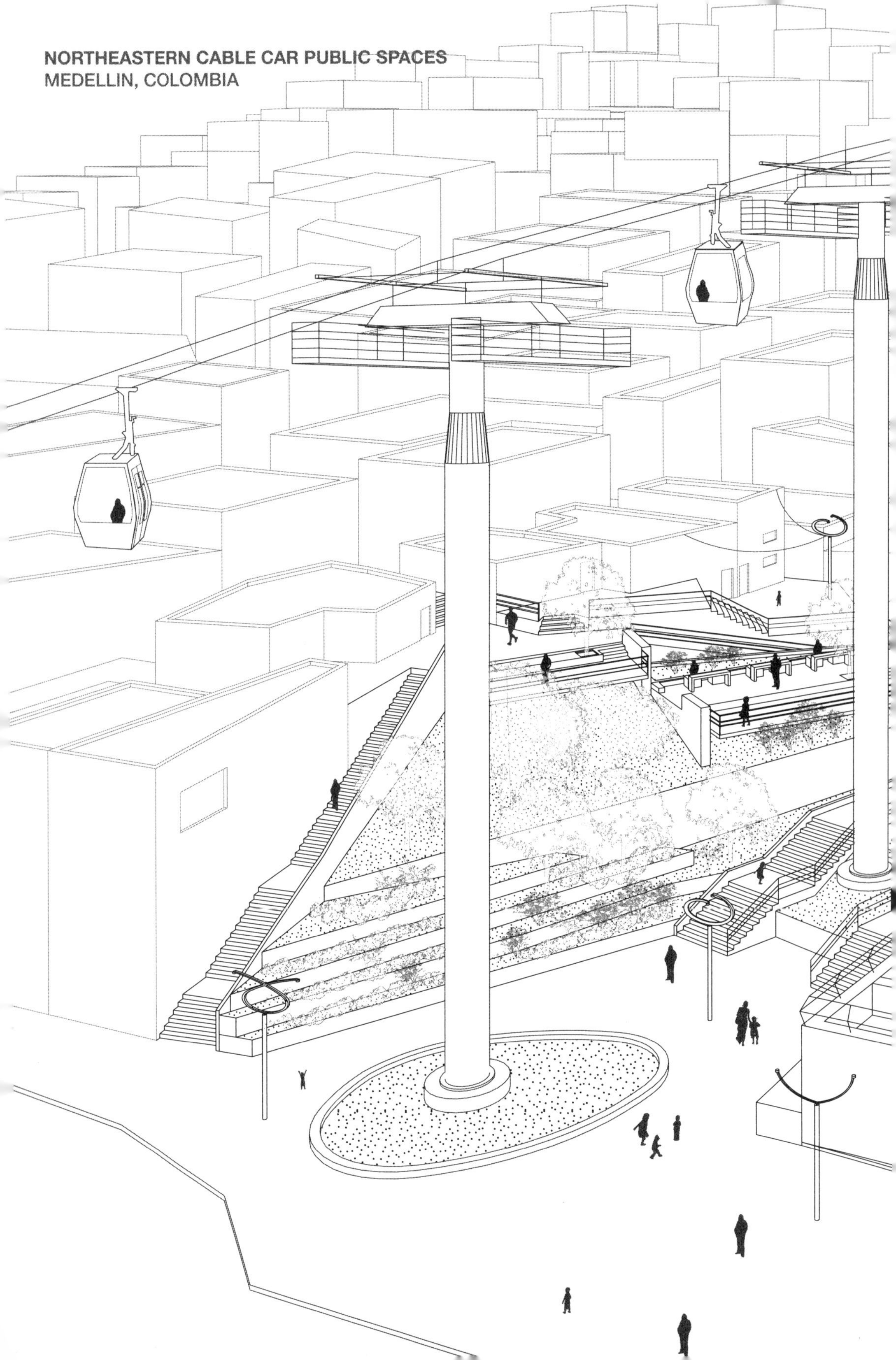

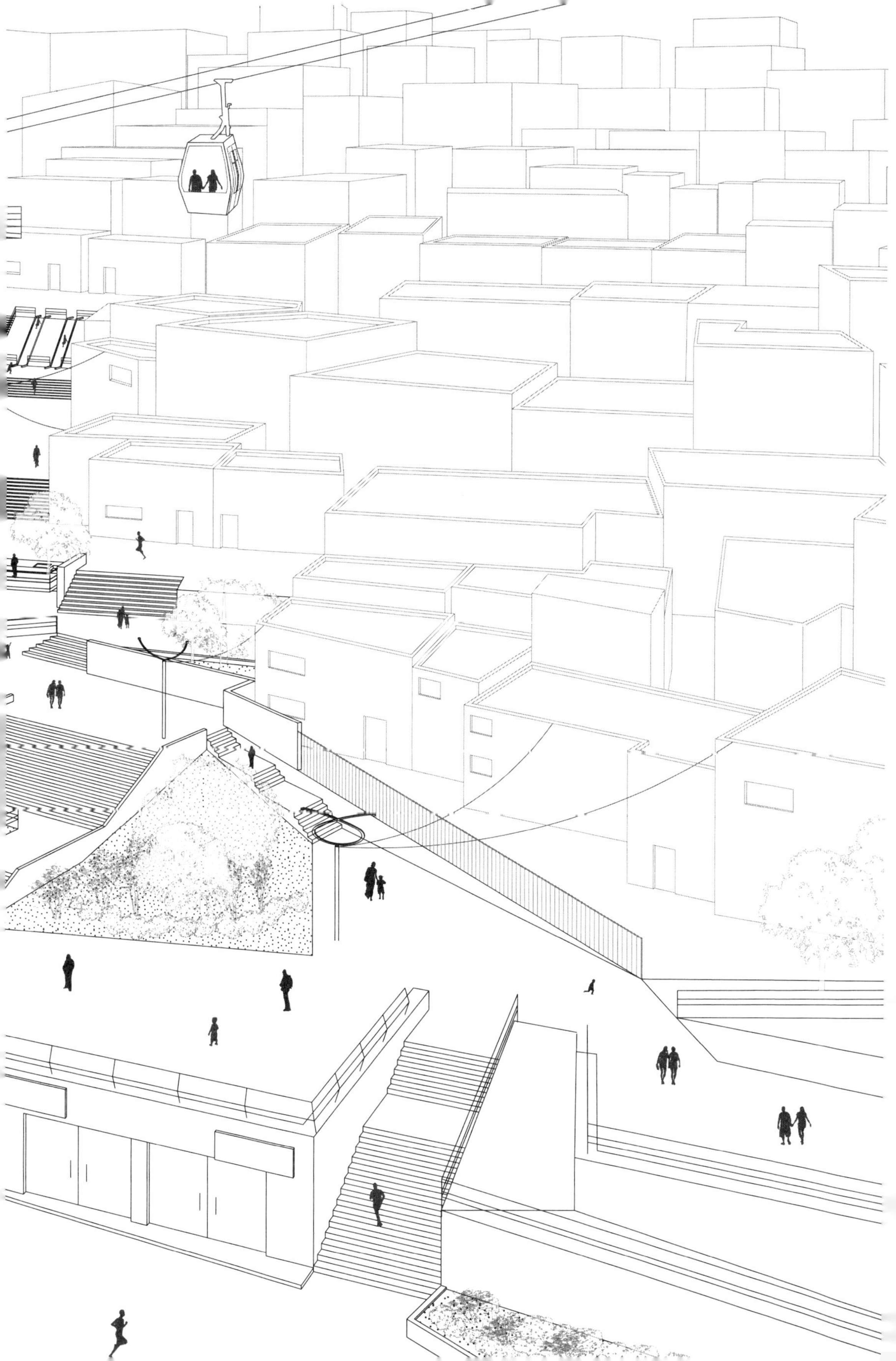

BARRIO LAS INDEPENDENCIAS ESCALATORS AND WALKWAYS

In the Comuna 13, the City of Medellin implemented a mobility project using escalators to access various elevations in the community. Below, the escalators can be reached through a new open plaza, and, at the opposite end, they connect to a long walkway that cantilevers over the edge of the hill. The escalators have benefited the population, especially senior citizens and people with disabilities. But the project´s public space contributions have been equally impacting. They represent new areas where children can play close to home, neighbors can gather, and new commercial activity can flourish.

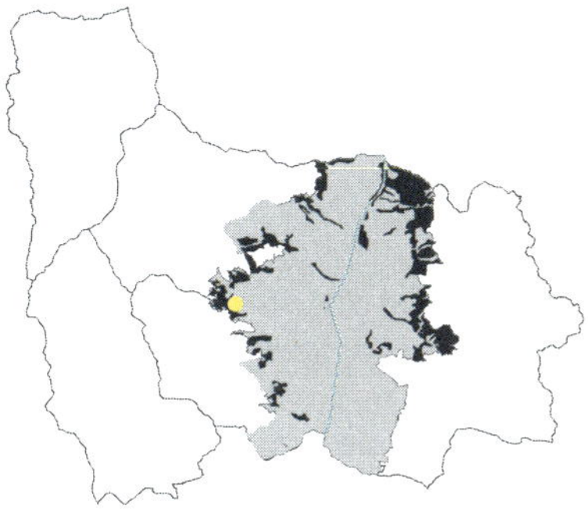

Location
Barrio La Independencia, Comuna 13 San Javier, Medellin, Colombia

Project team:
Empresa de Desarrollo Urbano EDU, Municipality of Medellin

Date **2011**

Coordinates
6°14´53.73"N 75°37'19.26"O

Investment
35 million USD for the entire project, and 3.5 million USD for the public space component[1]

Public space area
1,978 m²

Urban density
199 hab / ha

Population benefited
5,207 hab

PUBLIC SPACE

The value of this project lies in the fact that the intervention goes beyond the installation of escalators and creates new public space in the community. Walkways full of children riding bicycles are testimony to the close relationship between quality public spaces and the wellbeing of the community.

HISTORY

San Javier, in Medellin, also known as the Comuna 13, is located in the western-central part to the city, and dates back to 1910, when it was a *hacienda* called La Granja. Gradually, self-built homes began occupying the land, and in 1946 the city zoned it for residential use.[2] Heavy migration in the fifties and sixties, provoked by violent armed conflicts in the countryside, triggered unplanned urban growth in illegally occupied plots built by the displaced farmers.[3] Public services and access to employment remained scarce in these community for many years.

In the eighties, urban armed groups controlled the streets of the Comuna 13.[4] Prolonged efforts by the Colombian Military and the Air Force were considered necessary to control and mitigate the violence of the drug cartels. Once the situation improved, the municipality introduced multiple infrastructure development projects over the course of the following decade.[5]

The PUI methodology, designed and implemented in Medellín in 2004, contemplated 30 specific urban projects for Comuna 13 that included public space, cultural and educational facilities as well as infrastructure. The escalators and public spaces of Barrio Las Independencias were part of this initiative.

SOCIAL AND POLITICAL CONTEXT

Early settlers in the Comuna 13 were migrants from the countryside as well as the Caribbean and Pacific coast lines; they were poor, illiterate and mal nourished. Local culture in the community is the result of mixing together the traditions and the artistic expressions each of these groups brought from their homeland.

During the eighties, drug cartels converted the Comuna 13 into one of the most dangerous areas in Medellin.[6] In 2002, a military intervention, called the "Operation Orion", targeted urban militias associated with the Revolutionary Armed Forces of Colombia (FARC Fuerzas Armadas Revolucionarias de Colombia) and the National Liberation Army (ELN Ejército de Liberación Nacional).[7] It took nearly a year for the government to successfully regain control of the territory, leaving scars of death within the community. Even though armed groups continue to operate in these neighborhoods, [8] the focus of investments thereafter has sought to engage youth and reinsert people who had been involved in gangs into productive lives. To that end, access to education, culture, public space and mobility has been improved.

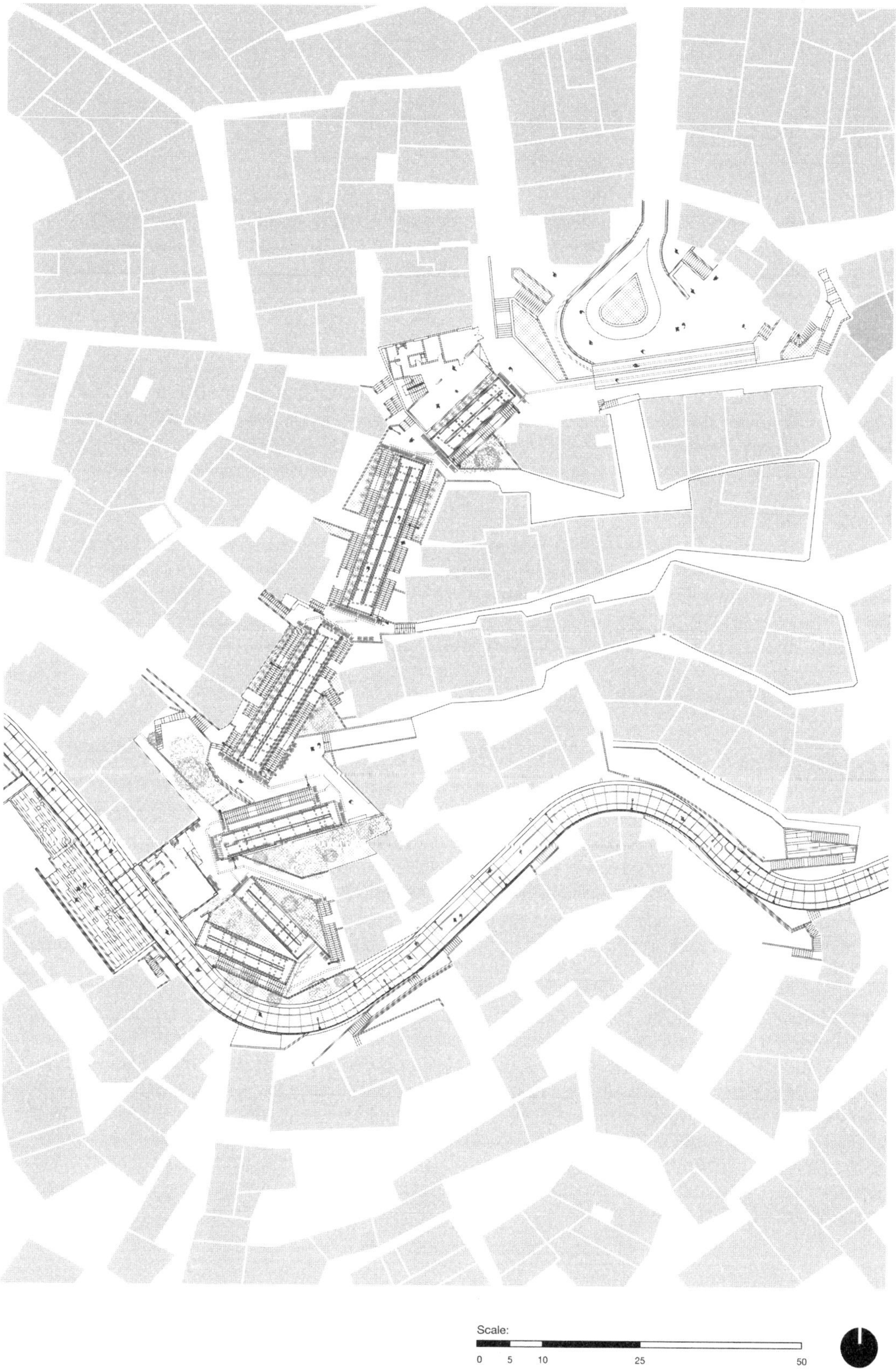
Scale:
0 5 10 25 50

ENVIRONMENTAL SITUATION

Environmental risk in the Comuna 13 is associated with the precarious nature of constructions and the geological instability of sloped territories prone to erosion. 46.4 of the Comuna 13´s 275 hectares are considered high risk areas where construction should not be permitted.[9] Other issues that require attention are the contaminated creeks.

URBAN SITUATION

The urban fabric of the Comuna 13 is not uniform. Early settlers occupied land along the lower segments of the hill with orthogonally laid out blocks. As the settlement grew uphill toward steeper slopes, the fabric became more organic and less accessible. The population density is 199 persons per hectare,[10] which is high compared to the rest of the city.[11]

The PUI for Comuna 13 successfully implemented 10 projects that represent 110,000 m^2 of constructed space.[12] One of the projects is the Barrio Las Independencias mechanical steps, which has benefited inhabitants with improved accessibility. Five groups of escalators climb the equivalent of twenty-three stories.[13] Between stairs, each intermediate platform has given way to a small urban space with commercial stores and services. The public spaces at each end of the circulation system have facilitated new urban dynamics: children play and spend time visiting with their neighbors on their way to and from the escalators.

PROJECT FUNDING

The Barrio Las Independencias project was financed by the municipality with funds from income tax and the Medellin Public Company (EPM). The project´s execution and management are the responsibility of the Urban Development Company (EDU) and part of an ongoing effort to invest in disenfranchised neighborhoods in order to mitigate historic territorial inequalities. Six continuous local government administrations have maintained similar public policies, restoring people´s trust in the municipality.[14]

RELATED PROGRAMS

The Comuna 13´s PUI included the San Javier library, near the San Javier metro station; a new high school facility, near an existing soccer field, that has shaped the western area of the Comuna; the Good Beginning nursery; and the CEDEZO capacity building center for adults. More recently a local development plan for 2010-2020, designed together with the community, places social inclusion, economic development and livelihood at the center of subsequent initiatives.[15]

ACTIVITIES

The spaces associated with the escalators have created new social dynamics within the community. The walkway that leads to the top of the escalators is lined with a public bench along its entire length and pockets of space with play equipment for children are built into the hill. The paved walkway is wide enough for children to ride bicycles and offers new gathering space for the community. Homes along the escalators have incorporated shops, cafes and stores in their facades to take advantage of pedestrian circulation through the site. Murals have also been painted by urban artists and youths, as acknowledgement of what has become an important focal point for the community.

INTEGRATION

Moving in cities and having access to basic services are human rights.[16] Projects such as the Barrio Las Independencias escalators improve accessibility for families living on the steeper areas of the neighborhood. They also contribute to diminish differences in the quality of urban services between these communities and the rest of the city. The new infrastructure has made it easier for outside visitors, previously reluctant to do so, to visit this part of the city and learn about its local culture.

The public spaces associated with the escalators are the project´s most critical elements. They function as a network of common areas fully integrated with the daily routine of inhabitants. These interventions have changed the dynamics of the settlement so that gathering, playing and enjoying the neighborhood are now part of a shared social culture.

1 "Investment in public space according to Urban Development Company. Independence 1 Connection Path", Social Planning: VII Inter-American Biennial of Architecture and Urbanism (Medellín: Urban Development Company, 2010).

2 "Historia Comuna 13," 2010. https://es.slideshare.net/adrima0204/historia-comuna-13 (accessed January 19, 2019).

3 "Las comunas de Medellín." https://www.insumisos.com/lecturasinsumisas/MEDELLIN%20FRONTERAS%20INVISIBLES%20III.pdf (accessed January 19, 2019).

4 Arturo Bullard, "Comuna 13 de Medellín: Cuando la Violencia se Arrodilla ante la Cultura," Arturo Bullard: travel photography, March 28, 2015. https://arturobullard.com/comuna-13-de-medellin-cuando-la-violencia-se-arrodilla-ante-la-cultura/ (accessed January 19, 2019).

5 "Historia Comuna 13" (2010).

6 Bullard (2015).

7 "Operación Orión: 10 años de impunidad," *Verdad Abierta* October 16, 2012. http://www.verdadabierta.com/victimas-seccion/desaparecidos/4264-operacion-orion-la-verdad-diez-anos-despues (accessed January 19, 2019).

8 José Jaime Samper has worked in the Comuna 13 mapping organized armed groups and manifestations of conflict that reveal a parallel story to the discourse of successful violence mitigation promoted by the Municipality.

9 Alcaldía de Medellín, "*Plan de desarrollo local Comuna 13, San Javier* (Medellín, 2012).

10 Ministerio de Tecnologías de la Información y las Comunicaciones de Colombia (2019).

11 Medellin´s population density is 58.2 persons / hectare. Alcaldía de Medellín, "Proyecciones de población 2016 a 2020." https://www.medellin.gov.co/irj/portal/medellin?NavigationTarget=navurl://06bdb-4d911e35cb-9d3de717115deedc3 (accessed August 19, 2019).

12 D. Arenas, and M. Arenas, "El Proyecto Urbano Integral Comuna 13 como modelo de transformación urbana. Antioquía," 2015, 61.

13 Silva and Vaggione (2016), 142.

14 Ibid., 135.

15 Alcaldía de Medellín (2012).

16 Right to the City is a notion first expressed by Henri Lefebvre and developed by David Harvey, who explains that fluid and free movement in a city is a human right. David Harvey, "The right to the city," *New Left Review* 53, 2008, 23-40.

BARRIO LAS INDEPENDENCIAS ESCALATORS AND WALKWAYS
MEDELLIN, COLOMBIA

SANTA MARTA FUNICULAR

Santa Marta is a spontaneous settlement in Rio de Janeiro that dates to the 1920s. Situated on the south facing side of a hill north of Botafogo, it is considered one of the steepest *favelas* that exist. A funicular lift was installed in 2008 to improve accessibility for inhabitants, since there are no roads within the *favela.* The funicular allows people to carry bicycles and groceries up the hill, and is also used to transport waste to the bottom of the *morro*, where it is collected and carried away by municipal garbage trucks. There are several stops along the ascent, one of which is named Michael Jackson after a famous video recorded there by the artist in 1966. The last station is the UPP Santa Marta which includes a police station, an artificial turf playfield and a module of the "Sistema" youth orchestra.

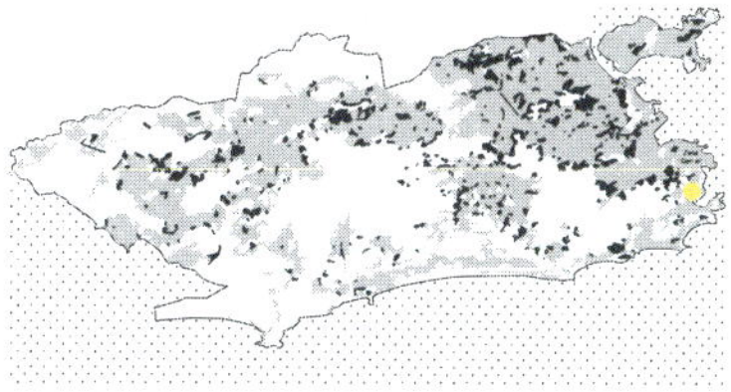

Location
Morro Santa Marta, Botafogo, Zona Sul, Rio de Janeiro, Brazil

Project team:
State Government of Rio de Janeiro (Governo do Estado do Río de Janeiro)

Date
2008

Coordinates
22°56'51.07"S 43°11'35.57"O

Investment
6.4 million USD

Public space area
1,368,55 m2

Urban density
172.72 hab / ha

Population benefited
14,787 hab

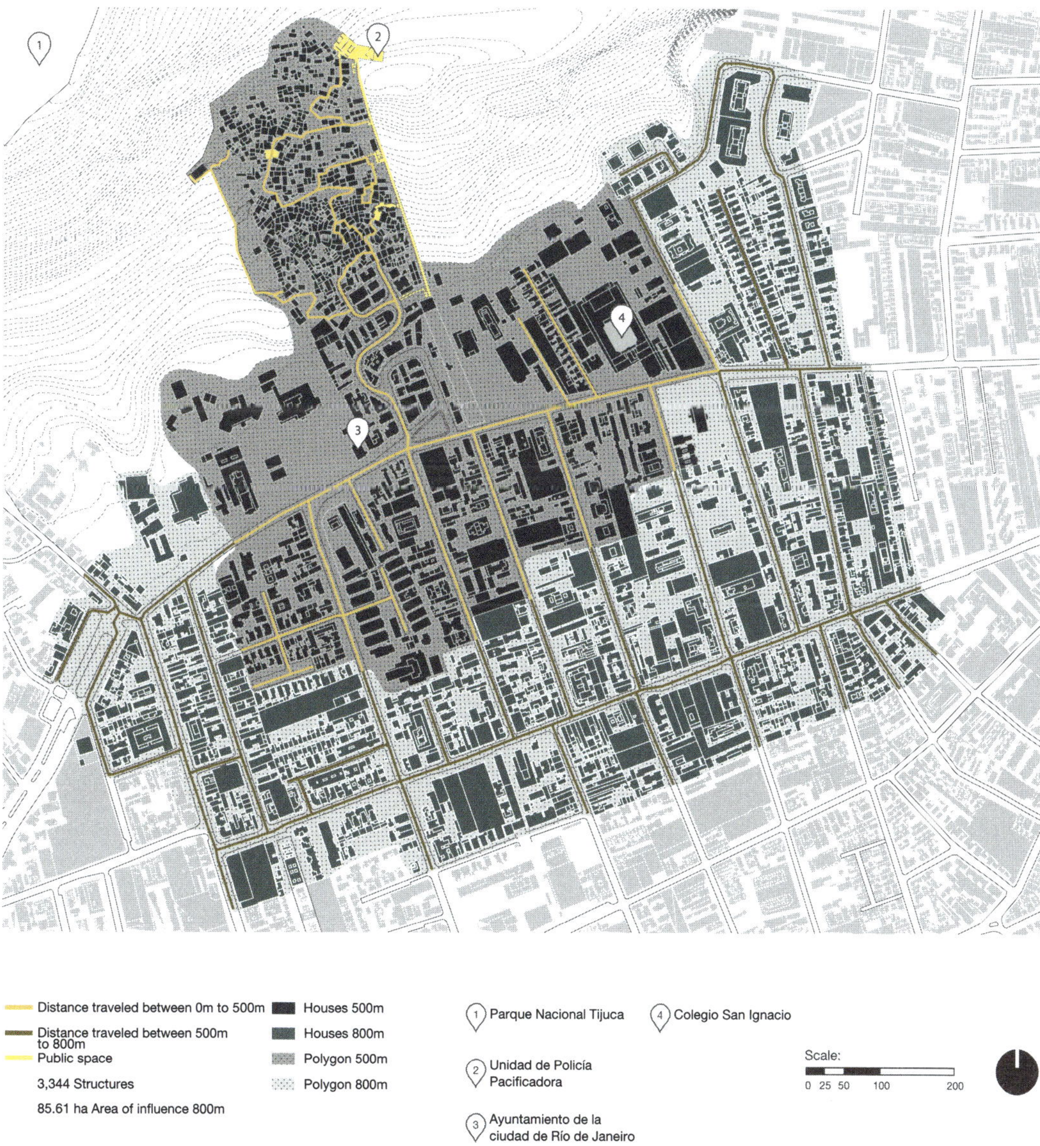

PUBLIC SPACE

The five funicular stations have added a public dimension to their surrounding areas, which did not exist before. As passengers arrive and wait to board the lift, the space around the station becomes a new urban node.

HISTORY

Santa Marta, also known as Dona Marta, was initially a *hacienda* on the skirts of the Corcovado mountain. During the first half of the 19th century, it was owned by the Baron de Vassouras and later by the Baron of Maoaubas. In 1902, a Jesuit congregation built the Saint Ignatius School, on San Clemente Street, just across from the Santa Marta forest. The school´s construction and other activities attracted workers who began building homes in the forest with the consent of the religious order. It soon became a focal point for new migrants to the city and a spontaneous settlement emerged. At the beginning, all services, potable water and food, had to be carried by inhabitants from the bottom of the hill to their homes. In 1959, a water tank was built at the top of the hill allowing water to be distributed by gravity and significantly improving the living conditions of inhabitants. But sewage collection, street lighting, public transportation, urban amenities and access to commercial areas were still lacking.[1] During the sixties, while Brazil was under the rule of a dictatorship, urban public policy focused on the eradication of *favelas*, which was implemented in many instances. The high density and degree of consolidation of the Santa Marta community made it very challenging to evict residents and raze their homes, so the *favela* remained intact.

Then in the eighties, drug gangs took over the streets, as they fought for control of the territory. Similar dynamics ensued once again in the 2000s.[2] The government's response to quell violence and criminal activity in 2008 was the notorious implementation of the Police Pacification Unit (UPP). Additionally, the community of Santa Marta founded a neighborhood association to seek improvements for their built environment. Over the course of the last three decades they have gained access to electricity, sewage water collection and drainage. Retention walls, play fields and housing improvements have also been built.

SOCIAL AND POLITICAL CONTEXT

Spontaneous settlements were first acknowledged in Brazil´s history in 1927, with the Renovation Plan for the City of Rio de Janeiro. *Favelas* were considered a social and aesthetic problem that needed to be eradicated.[3] In the 1960s and 1970s, during the country´s military dictatorship, many of them were razed and families were transferred to the city´s periphery. In 1992, Rio´s spontaneous settlements were mapped in the city´s Master Plan, a fact that demonstrated a change in the regard of *favelas*. Initial projects to improve the conditions of existing *favelas* were articulated through the Favela- Bairro program, partially funded by the World Bank and IDB.[4] These programs had several editions and evolved into the Morar Carioca projects of 2010.[5]

The presence of drug operations in Rio´s *favelas* has been recurrent and persists in many communities. In 2008, the Police Pacification Units (UPP) were installed in several *favelas*. They were essentially a military occupation of the communities to maintain peace, and have been widely contested as a nearsighted approach to the mitigation of urban violence.

Scale:
0 5 10 25 50 100

ENVIRONMENTAL SITUATION

Rio de Janeiro´s geography is unique in that it is defined by a ridge of rounded mountains, many of which are protected under environmental laws for their singular geology and ecology.[6] Paradoxically, *favelas* have emerged precisely in many of these areas. Dona Marta is inserted into a tropical forest of native rainforest vegetation, locally known as Mata Atlántica, at the base of the Corcovado Mountain.[7] The settlement destroyed part of this ecosystem, although its extension is fortunately contained by the funicular to the north and a retention wall and steep level change to the south. The exposure of Dona Marta inhabitants to risk is unclear. Geological studies by the local government argue the upper areas of the *favela* are vulnerable to landslides; the Santa Marta Neighborhood Association sustains that since it is a rock formation, the ground is stable.

URBAN SITUATION

Dona Marta can be accessed from the Botafogo neighborhood through the San Clemente Street, which defines the division between formal and informal urban fabrics. Botafogo is a well-established community with institutional buildings, Rio de Janeiro´s City Hall, schools, –including the San Ignacio School–, cultural centers and consulates. The Dona Marta side is made of dense informal constructions, two and four stories high. Before the funicular was built, inhabitants had to climb an average of 800 steps to reach their homes; now it only takes 10 minutes to reach any part of the settlement. Interspersed among existing houses along the northeaster edge of the *favela,* near the funicular, the state government has built a few recent social housing constructions.

The funicular ascends 160 meters, the equivalent of 55 stories. 5 stations allow inhabitants to reach various levels of the *favela*. The lowest station is located on the Marechal Francisco de Moura Street. The highest station reaches the uppermost part of the *favela* at the Dona Marta lookout point where an AstroTurf soccer field, a cultural center and the UPP police quarters are located. This upper part of the *favela* also has vehicular access from the Osvaldo Seabra Street. Each station constitutes a busy urban node in the community, where a few houses have decided to convert their ground floors into services and stores to take advantage of the confluence of people. They function as *de facto* public spaces even though they do not present the conventional formal characteristics normally associated with public plazas.

PROJECT FUNDING

Funds for the project were initially the responsibility of both the City of Rio de Janeiro and the national government, but in the end, they came solely from the latter.[8] The project began in 2000 and was ultimately executed in 2008 for a cost equivalent to 6.4 million USD at the time.[9] The funicular system only represents part of the overall project cost.

RELATED PROGRAMS

The funicular system was part of a larger investment program that included a playfield, cultural facilities and the UPP quarters located at the top of Dona Marta. Another important municipal program the funicular facilitated, in addition to public transportation, was waste collection. The funicular cabin is divided into two compartments: one for passengers and the other for carrying larger objects and provisions. This second compartment is also used to transport collected waste down the hill where it is gathered in a container and taken away with conventional garbage trucks.

ACTIVITIES

Dona Marta has been the site of movie films and famous music videos such as Michael Jackson´s song "They don´t care about us," which was filmed at the Cantao Plaza in 1996, with the Cristo Corcovado as its backdrop. Today this plaza has a statue of the artist and is often visited by tourists who ascend using the funicular and stop at the station that now carries his name.[10] The community also provides guided tours of the *favela*, centered on the funicular and the views of the city from its highest point. These tourist activities are an important contribution to Santa Marta´s local economy.

URBAN INTEGRATION

The funicular has improved the quality of life for Dona Marta inhabitants, by reducing travel time and enabling people with disabilities and older generations to move more comfortably. The fluid movement of people to and from Dona Marta, including tourists, acknowledges that the *favela* is a part of Rio de Janeiro, experienced by both locals and visitors. The stations along the ascent have created new nodes of activity in the community generated by the confluence of people descending from or waiting for the lift. Commercial activity and services reinforce these nodes and consequently, the space is perceived as public even though it has not been designed specifically for public use. It constitutes a different public space morphology that is unique to spontaneous settlements, although equally functional and vibrant.

1 Livia Minoja, *Favelascape: tools of integration for the favela Santa Marta in Rio de Janeiro.* Thesis Politecnico di Milano, 2011, 27-51.

2 "Ciudad Maravillosa: Una guía para conocer Río de Janeiro," *Una favela por dentro* April 6, 2012. https://ciudadmaravillosa.wordpress.com/2012/04/06/una-favela-por-dentro/ (accessed January 19. 2019).

3 F. Caixeta, and F. Damásio, "Tourism and slums: A study about Favela," *Cuadernos Proarq* 19, 255.

4 V. Andreatta, "Favela-Bairro, un nuevo paradigma de urbanización para asentamientos informales," *UPCommons Portal del cneixement obert de la UPC* July 24, 2005, 3, 4. https://upcommons.upc.edu/bitstream/handle/2099/1586/01_Favela-Bairro.pdf. (accessed January 10, 2019).

5 K. Steiker-Ginzberg, "Morar Carioca: The Dismantling of a Dream Favela Upgrading Program," *Rio On Watch* September 10, 2014.

6 Ibid.

7 R. Souza, "Plano inclinado do Morro Santa Marta, Estación 1," *TGBR Ferrovías Brasil* 2009. http://www.tgvbr.org/viewtopic.php?t=2843 (accessed January 10, 2019).

8 "Ciudad Maravillosa: Una guía para conocer Río de Janeiro," 6 de abril, 2012.

9 "Reurbanização do Dona Marta sai do papel e esta em fase de licitação," *Licitacao.net* April 22, 2004. https://www.licitacao.net/noticias_mostra.asp?p_cd_notc=704# (accessed January 10, 2019).

10 Caixeta, 259-262.

SANTA MARTA FUNICULAR
RIO DE JANEIRO, BRAZIL

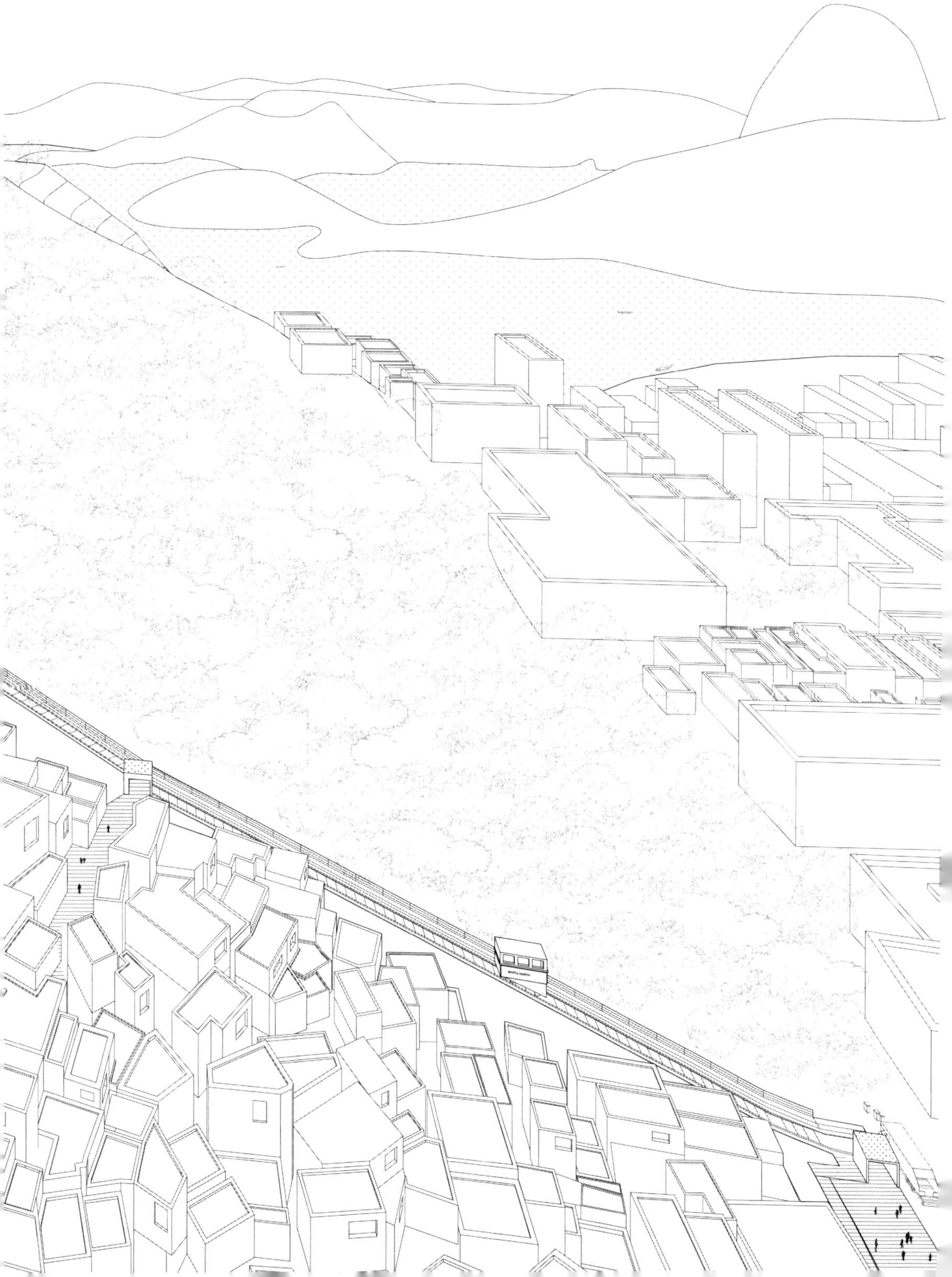
SANTA MARTA

COMPLEXO DO ALEMÃO CABLE CAR AND PUBLIC SPACES

Complexo do Alemão is a large and populous *favela* located on the northern side of Rio de Janeiro. A cable car was installed along the crest of the hills in this community that is directly connected to the Bonsucesso station and its various transportation systems. In addition to shortening travel time to the city for inhabitants, the project comprised public space interventions such as playgrounds, plazas and streets with sidewalks. Several of these improvements occurred along roads and locations used to transport materials and prefabricated elements during the cable car´s construction process.

Location	**Complexo do Alemão, Rio de Janeiro, Brazil**
Project team:	**Jorge Mario Jáuregui, Growth Acceleration Program PAC and State Government of Rio de Janeiro (Governo do Estado de Rio de Janeiro), Instituto Raízes em Movimento**
Date	**2011**
Coordinates	**22°51'29.21"S 43°16'15.53"O**
Investment	**133 million USD**
Public space area	**56,848,92 m2**
Urban density	**447.02 hab / ha**
Population benefited	**130,501 hab**

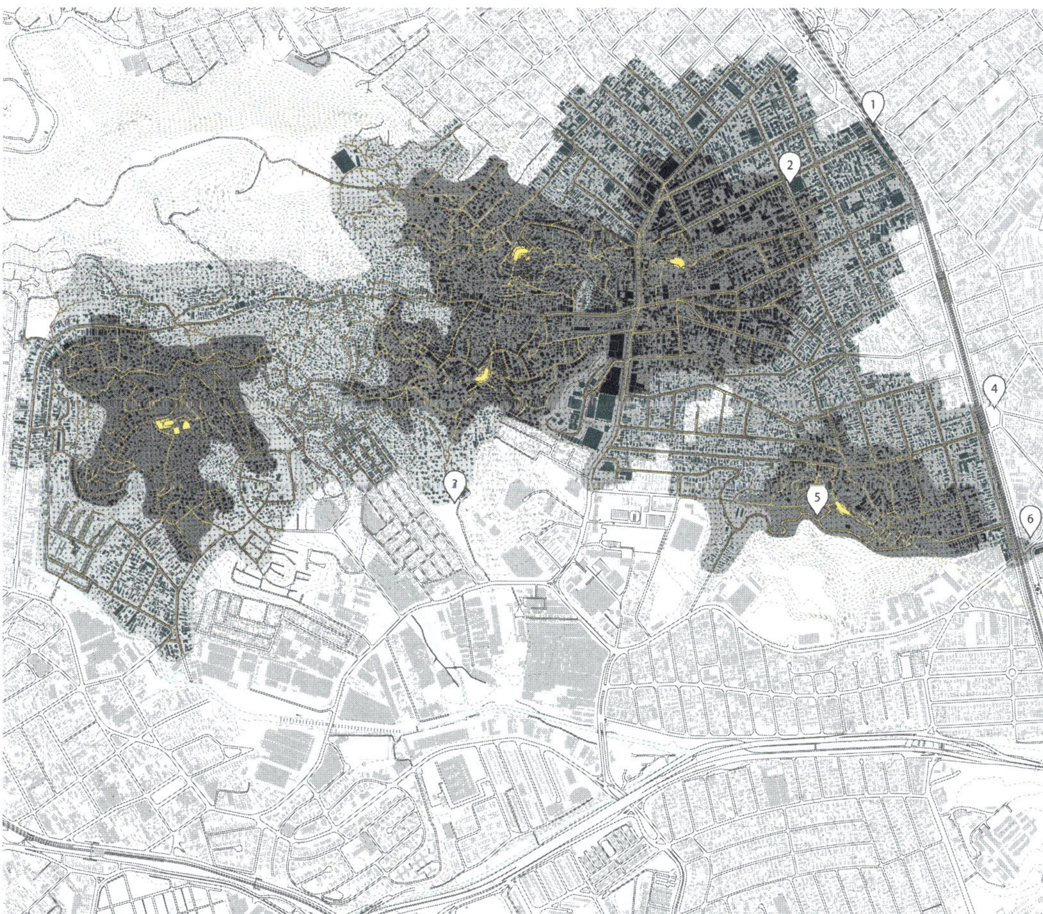

Distance traveled between 0m to 500m
Distance traveled between 500m to 800m
Public space
16,697 Structures
291.93 ha Area of influence 800m

Houses 500m
Houses 800m
Polygon 500m
Polygon 800m

1 Estación de tren Ramos
2 Escuela de Samba Imperatriz Leopoldinense
3 Plaza Do Conhecimento
4 Plaza Lopes Ribeiro
5 Plaza-mirador Morro do Adeus
6 Estación de tren y metrocable Bonsucceso

Scale:
0 50 100 200 400

PUBLIC SPACE

Given the scarcity of open space in spontaneous settlements, infrastructure and service projects including transportation, electric cabling, mobility, water and sanitation, represent opportunities to create new public space. A small percentage of construction costs can be used to transform ground affected by the infrastructure installation into plazas and parks.

HISTORY

The Complexo do Alemão is a group of 15 *favelas* along the Sierra de la Misericordia.[1] The area was previously used for agriculture but with the construction of the rail line toward the north of Rio de Janeiro in 1950, areas adjacent to it were zoned for industrial use.[2] The Sierra´s proximity to the industrial sites made it attractive for workers as a place to live and subsequently, spontaneous settlements began to emerge.[3]

The *favelas* lacked basic services and infrastructure for several decades; drug related violence was prevalent. During the nineties, Complexo do Alemão arguably had the highest homicide rate of Rio de Janeiro.[4] In 1995, it was included in the Favela Bairro program, which addressed access to infrastructure and basic services, as well as the relocation of families in vulnerable housing situations. In 2008, the Growth Acceleration Program (PAC Programa de Aceleração do Crescimento) was a joint effort between the federal and state government to continue improving urban conditions in the *favelas*.[5] The cable car, modeled after examples in Medellin, was designed and implemented through the PAC initiative and was meant to reduce travel time to the city for inhabitants. The project, however, has been criticized for the fact that its design and development did not contemplate the community's participation.

SOCIAL AND POLITICAL CONTEXT

The implementation of the PAC program in Complexo do Alemão was met with resistance from the community, since they were not considered in the design process. Although improvements to their infrastructure were welcomed, the community´s main concerns were not addressed by the projected investments. Construction of the cable car was deemed by inhabitants to serve more as a tourist attraction than the transportation needs of neighbors.[6] In its wake, many empty spaces were left after houses and buildings were razed to make way for wider roads. The Roots in Movement Institute, (Instituto Raízes em Movimento), a community-based NGO in Complexo do Alemão, began repurposing these affected areas into public spaces through collective projects. They built a public plaza opposite the organization's headquarters on Avenida Central, Morro do Alemão.[7] Raizes has continued to collaborate with other groups and Rio's Culture Secretariat to transform abandoned sites into public spaces.

ENVIRONMENTAL SITUATION

According to the Department of Public Works, Complexo do Alemão is included in the map of areas subject to high landslide risk. Water infiltrations into the soil caused by inadequate drain-

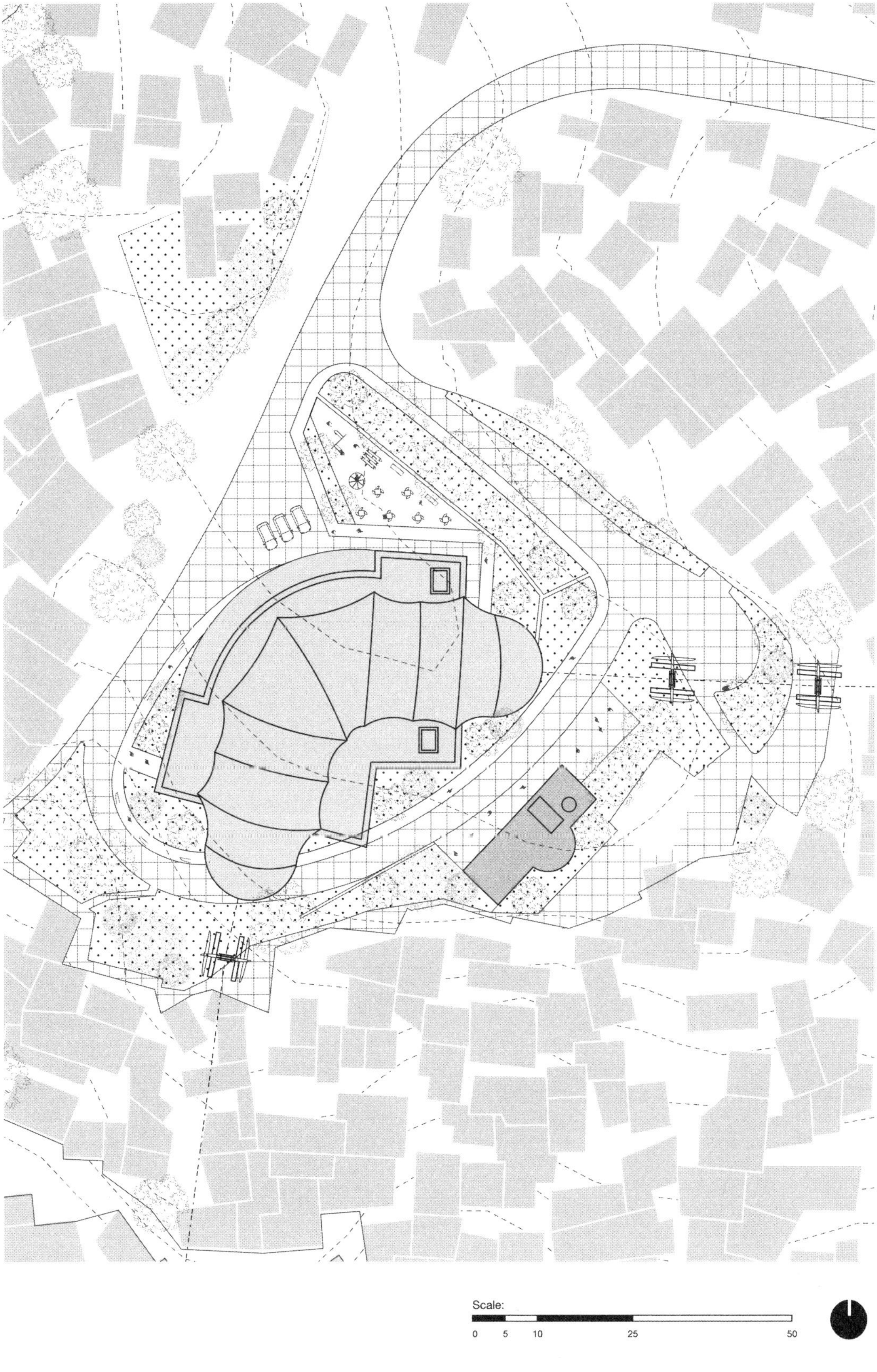
Scale:
0 5 10 25 50

age and sewage systems further increase risk.[8] The PAC initiative funded efforts to stabilize land affected by heavy rains in 2010 and provided new housing for families that had lost their homes.[9] Despite these interventions, heavy rain in 2013 produced new landslides and many families took refuge in the Palmeiras cable car station.

URBAN SITUATION

The cable car system extends over 3.5 kilometers. It connects the hills Baiana, del Adiós, del Alemán, Itararé, Cruziero, Fazendinha and Palmeiras, to the Bonsucesso railway station bellow. Travel time from Palmeiras, the last station, to Bonsucesso, is 16 minutes as opposed to the 50 minutes it takes to travel by land. Bonsuccesso station is an important intermodal hub that connects the cable car with trains, buses, *combis*, motorcycle taxis and bicycles.

The *favela's* morphology is complex, marked by a steep topography. Roads tend to be narrow, windy and long, which means inhabitants have to invest a lot of time to reach the city center. Despite the cable car's presence, inhabitants continue to rely heavily on motorcycle taxis, which reveals that the stations were not strategically placed to meet the population´s movement patterns.[10] The new stations, however, have created new centralities within the community since they also incorporate communal facilities and public space. The cable car has made it possible to reach previously inaccessible areas and the aerial trajectory of the gondolas has increased security as passengers observe people from above.

PROJECT FUNDING

The cable car and associated projects were financed through the federal government's Growth Acceleration Program (PAC) initiative for a sum of 133 million USD. These funds also covered the cost of sewage collection in areas around the stations and housing for families that had to be relocated due to the project´s construction.[11]

RELATED PROGRAMS

The PAC for Complexo do Alemão also addressed investments in new community and social facilities, libraries, and legal assistance.[12] The areas around the stations were adapted into public spaces such as ball courts and parks; other areas were reforested. Baiana, Aleman and Itararé stations also include municipal entities such as Pouso, an urban and social orientation agency; CRJ youth reference center; INSS health system; CRAS social reference center; and FIRJAN class rooms, where capacity-building courses are given free of charge for inhabitants.[13] Furthermore, commercial spaces, banks, a dance academy and an e-library have emmerged around the new urban centers. Unfortunately, the cable car´s operation was stopped in 2015 due to its high maintenance cost. While this situation is resolved, the programs that are housed in the stations and the public spaces that surround them continue to be a positive contribution to the community.

URBAN INTEGRATION

The Complexo do Alemão cable car in and of itself could be considered an agent of urban integration since it connects the *favela* to the rest of the city with an efficient transportation alternative. But in actuality, it seems to benefit outside visitors more than the local population given the fact that inhabitants continue to prefer other transportation methods. This proves that community participation is not only desirable but necessary for projects to succeed. Community organizations, such as Raízes em Movimento, contrast with the way the government´s PAC projects operate, by offering avenues for productive community participation that produce successful urban transformations. The organization not only promotes the physical construction of public spaces, but also opens platforms for discussion and debate regarding the disparity that persist in the perception of formal and informal city segments in Rio de Janeiro. Alan Brum Pinheiro, the NGO´s founder, explains that the organization´s name includes the word "in movement" to address the imaginary walls that separate the *favela* from the rest of the city. He argues people must engage with diverse spaces and places in the city in order to dissolve these walls: "It is the insertion of Complexo do Alemão in the city, and the city in Complexo do Alemão" that builds urban bridges. [14]

1 Portal Geo, 2018. http://portalgeo.rio.rj.gov.br (accessed June 11, 2018)

2 L. De Souza Pereira, "Pacificação do Complexo do Alemão em tempos de megaeventos esportivos na cidade do Rio de Janeiro – Brasil," *Revista Geográfica de Amérca Central* special number EGAL, 201, 3-4.

3 Fernanda Pontes, "Pesquisadoras traçam a história da ocupação do Complexo do Alemão. Pioneiro da região veio da Polônia," *O Globo* October 4, 2014. https://oglobo.globo.com/rio/pesquisadoras-tracam-historia-da-ocupacao-do-complexo-do-alemao-10247995 (accessed June 14, 2018).

4 De Souza Pereira (2011), 4.

5 Ibid.

6 Ava Rose Hoffman. "Knowledge to Create Solutions in Complexo do Alemão: Instituto Raízes em Movimento." *Rio on watch*, June 11, 2016. http://www.rioonwatch.org/?p=30158 (accessed January 10, 2019).

7 Ibid.

8 C. Freitas, "Comissária da ONU vai ao Alemão ver estragos da chuva," *Jornal Do Brasil* 2013.

9 Governo do Rio de Janeiro, "Estado recupera áreas de risco dentro do Complexo do Alemão. Rio de Janeiro," 2011.

10 F. Izaga, and M. da Silva Pereira, "A mobilidade urbana na urbanização das favelas no Rio de Janeiro," *Cadernos do Desenvolvimento Fluminense* 2014, 100-101.

11 "Gondola in Complexo do Alemão Favelas," *The Rio Times* July 12, 2011. http://riotimesonline.com/brazil-news/rio-politics/gondola-in-complexo-do-alemao-favelas/ (accessed June 8, 2018).

12 Ibid.

13 Governo do Rio de Janeiro, "Transportes Teleférico do Alemão," 2018. http://www.rj.gov.br/web/setrans/exibeconteudo?article-id=1400154 (accessed June 12, 2018).

14 Hoffman (2016).

COMPLEXO DO ALEMÃO CABLE CAR AND PUBLIC SPACES
RIO DE JANEIRO, BRAZIL

ECOTECNIA URBANA MIRAVALLE

The community of Miravalle has transformed its surroundings through participatory projects that have been funded through competitions and grants. In 2006, Miravalle received funding and technical support from the UrbanXChangers award, sponsored by the Alfred Herrhausen Gesellschaft (AHG) - Deutsche Bank and later, in 2010, the community received the Deutsche Bank Urban Age Award.[1] These funds enabled the transformation of a number of previously abandoned spaces into a variety of facilities and programs, including a library, a digital center, a soup kitchen, an amphitheatre, a health center, a recycling center, ball courts and playgrounds. Public spaces were adapted to collect rainwater that benefits a local soup kitchen. The community is also striving to adopt more sustainable practices in terms of urban agriculture, collection and use of harvested water, recycled waste and stewardship of their adjacent natural reserve.

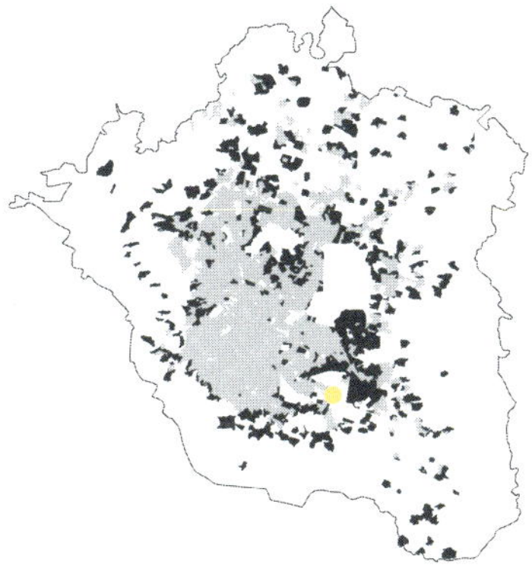

Location
Delegación Iztapalapa, Mexico DF, Mexico

Project team:
Miravalle Community Council, GDF Cultural Department, Human Rights Commission of Mexico City, Hannes Meyer Studio, Rozana Montiel Estudio de Arquitectura and the LAHAS Laboratory of the National University of Mexico School of Architecture

Date **2011**

Coordinates
19°20'6.17"N 98°59'47.34"O

Investment **100,000 USD**

Public space area **4,269,55 m2**

Urban density **157.39 hab / ha**

Habitantes beneficiados **11,828 hab**

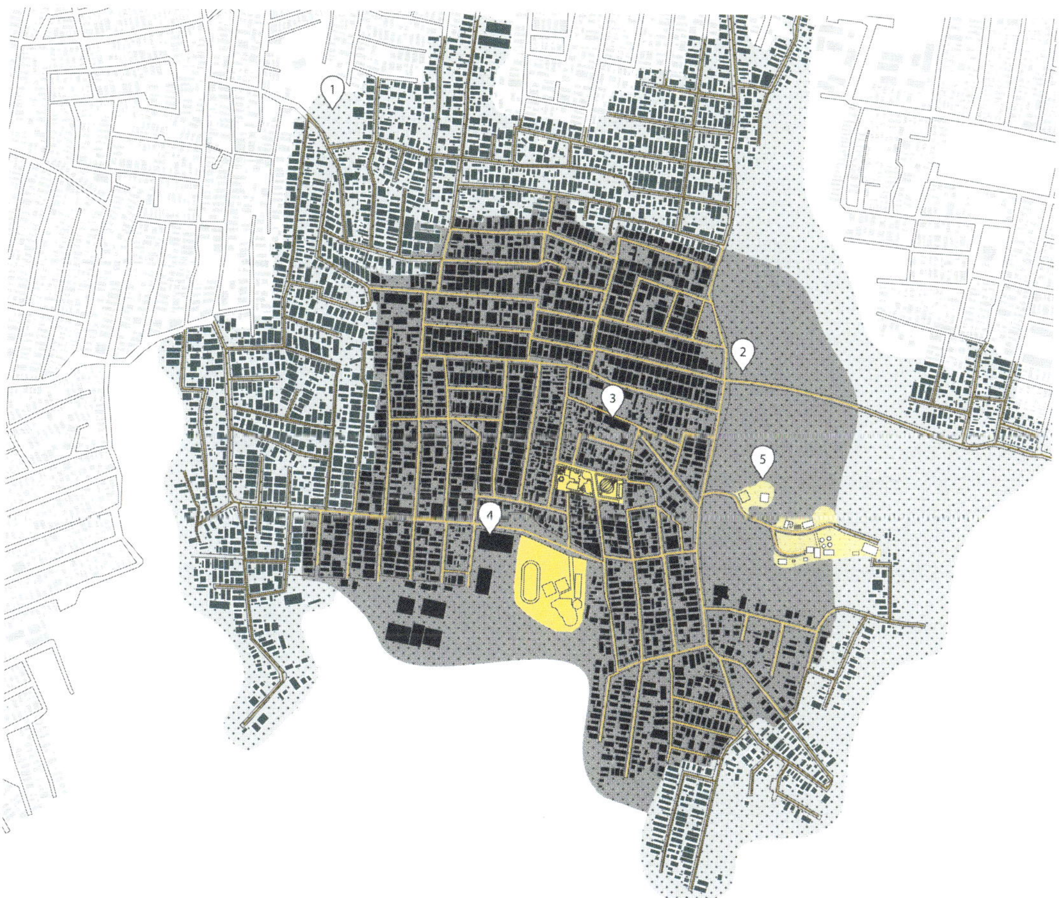

PUBLIC SPACE

Various interventions over the course of years have recovered and created public spaces for recreation and gathering in the community. They are also being used to collect and store rainwater, in order to mitigate ongoing difficulties in the community with respect to water through more sustainable practices.

HISTORY

Mexico City is divided into 16 sectors or "delegations." Ecotecnia Miravalle is located in the delegation of Iztapalapa, east of the city center. The land has historical significance due to vestiges of the Culhuas indigenous population that inhabited the valley between La Estrella Mountain and the edges of the Texcoco Lake. What remains are traces of the agricultural culture they practiced before colonial times. Agricultural use of the land continued until urban growth, fueled by massive rural-urban migration, reached this area. Residential neighborhoods of self-built houses, known as *colonias* in Mexico, emerged since the periphery´s lower land value was the only option for people with scarce resources. By the seventies, spontaneous settlements began to spread toward the base of inactive volcanoes of the Sierra Santa Catarina.[2]

Within these mountains, the settlers of Miravalle occupied the lower segment of the Guadalupe Volcano in 1983.[3] Neighbors created the Miravalle Community Council in the 1990s, to lobby for services from the municipality.

SOCIAL AND POLITICAL CONTEXT

Miravalle's population is approximately 15.000 people. Inhabitants come from Oaxaca, Puebla, Veracruz, and other areas of Mexico City who arrived through successive waves of migration. For a number of years, the community lacked access to potable water, electricity and public transportation. Unemployment, drug and alcohol addiction, violence related to youth gangs and poverty has also prevailed.[4] The Miravalle Community Council created a robust network of local stakeholders interested in improving the community´s living conditions that includes specialists and civil organizations. Together, they have been able to lobby for government support and improve access to services. The Council´s objective is to motivate more socially and economically sustainable urban dynamics in terms of water management, education and food production. The organization represents a model for other marginalized urban communities.[5]

ENVIRONMENTAL SITUATION

The ecosystem of the Sierra Santa Catarina plays an important role in mitigating Mexico City´s flood risk. The permeable rock formation of the volcanoes and mountains absorbs water and allows it to filter into the aquifers. Current basalt and sand extraction processes, as well as the continued encroachment of spontaneous settlements, have diminished the land´s ability to absorb water, increasing runoff and the risk of flooding.[6] Ironically, communities in this area are affected by water shortages, which is why recent interventions in public spaces collect and store rain water for community uses. Furthermore, a didactic urban agriculture facility shows inhabitants how to take advantage of rainwater for productive uses.

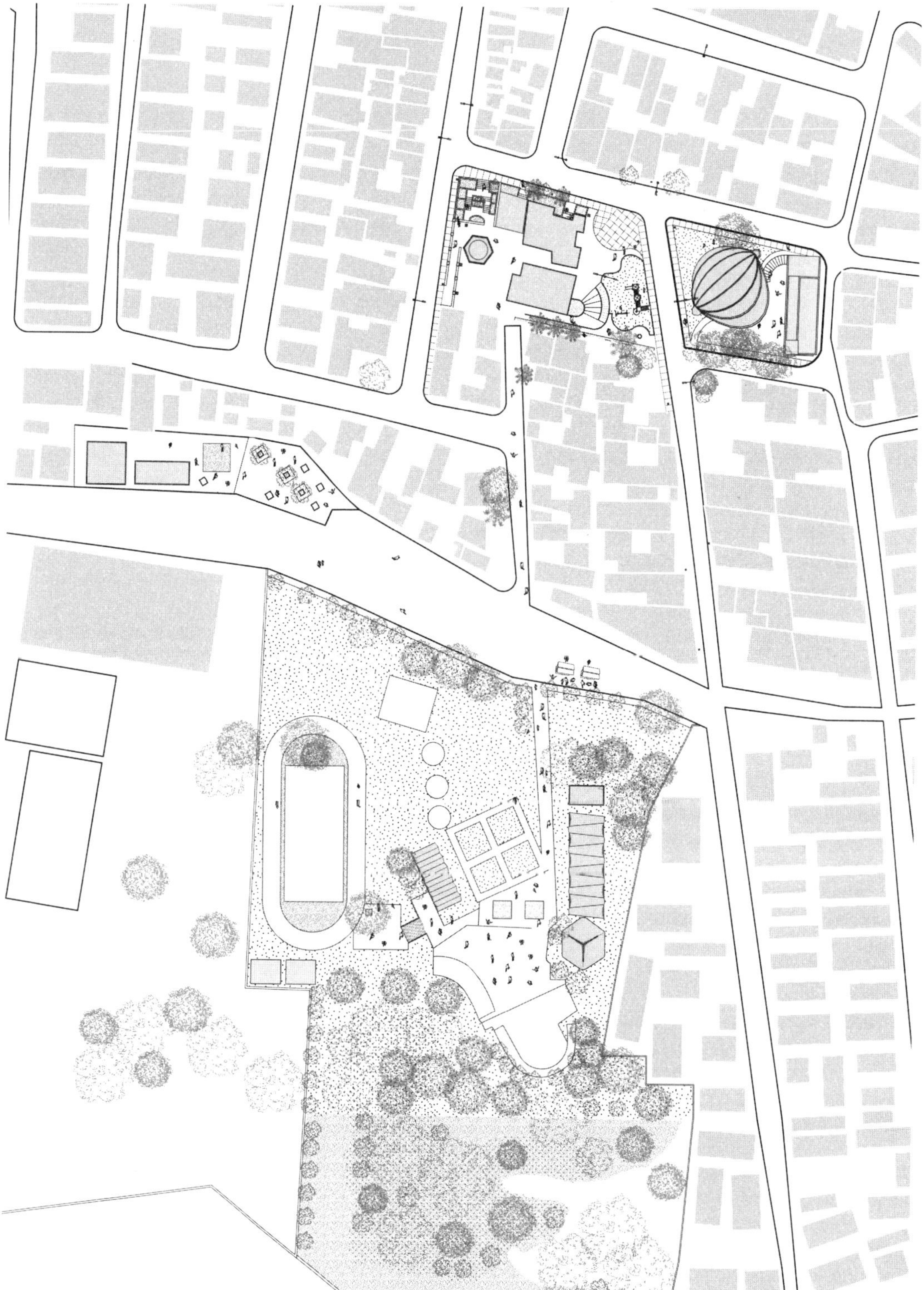
Scale:
0 5 10 25 50

URBAN SITUATION

Miravalle´s urban fabric consists for self-built homes that were initially of poor quality. Over time, as families were able to prosper, houses were gradually upgraded with better materials. The irregular grid of streets reflects the site's steep topography. Lack of planning resulted in limited possibilities for open space and community facilities, which is why the Miravalle Community Council´s efforts have focused on transforming underutilized or abandoned land into productive and lively public spaces. Currently, a dome collects water and provides shade over an open amphitheater in a town square. At a different location, cisterns collect and store water at the base of the Guadalupe Volcano and provide space for recreation, culture and sports.

PROJECT FUNDING

Miravalle received the UrbanXchangers award from the Alfred Herrhausen Society-Deutsche Bank in 2006 which allowed them to convert an existing dome into a means for collecting rain water, with the support of German professionals.[7] Later in 2010, Ecotecnia Miravalle won the Deutsche Bank Urban Age Award for 100.000 USD in recognition of the community´s efforts to improve surrounding areas and people´s quality of life.[8] The money was used to recover an existing health center, create a new library and digital center, a medicinal garden, a soup kitchen and public spaces. Since then, the Miravalle Community Council, with the support of students and professors from the National Autonomous University of Mexico (UNAM) School of Architecture, have designed and built new projects such as public space, a cultural facility, a dance hall and a multipurpose sports facility with funds awarded through the City of Mexico´s participatory budget competition.[9]

RELATED PROGRAMS

The Miravalle Community Council is responsible for organizing and fashioning spaces for education, recreation, recycling and health. The soup kitchen is a low-cost source of nourishment for the community. The library, digital center and toy library are managed and maintained by the Municipal Government of Iztapalapa, and represent valuable resources for children and youth.[10] The PET Recovery Program designs and creates objects made of recycled plastic with the support of the Goethe Mexico Institute, the UNAM and the Thermal Fusion Studio of the Miravalle Community Council.[11] The Miravalle Marinista Elementary School is an important stakeholder in the community and organizes many of the Council´s initiatives. Capacity building courses in carpentry, masonry and cooking are also offered by the Council. Environmental education and community awareness campaigns promote a more responsible use of water, and stewardship for the rainwater collection systems.

The didactic ecological center Ecotecnia Miravalle is another community initiative. It is on a site that collects rainwater and runoff from the slopes of the volcano, stores and uses it for urban agriculture. Didactic displays in greenhouses help the community learn how and what to plant. Stationary bicycles are used to pump water for irrigation.[12]

ACTIVITIES

The public spaces in Miravalle are coupled with cultural amenities, such as the library and the amphitheater. Recently, the community created a new public space at the foot of the volcano on a 5,000 m^2 site, where three new community structures have been built. The *Calmeca* center is used for gatherings and courses taught by the community through voluntary contributions. The *A Escena* building is a space often used by local schools for dance and choreography courses. *Encuentro* is a multipurpose sports center where martial arts and other forms of exercise are taught to children and adults.[13] A skate park, a running track, a basketball court and outdoor exercise equipment for adults complete the park.

URBAN INTEGRATION

Miravalle is an important model of how community organization can effectively transform and improve the livelihood of spontaneous settlement inhabitants. Through the program UrbanXChangers, the community became more aware of the potential their environment and geographical location could represent for them. In successive urban projects to further transform their surroundings, the community has maintained its focus on recovering and transforming public spaces through sustainable practices. Furthermore, the parks and plazas represent a space for outside visitors to gather and feel welcome in a part of the city that has been generally understood as marginal.

1 UrbanXChangers, "Mexico City: Miravalle Community Council." http://www.urbanxchanger.com/eng/conteudos/visualizar/Miravalle-Community-Council (accessed January 10, 2019).

2 Ibid.

3 Ibid.

4 CAF, "Casos emblemáticos de desarrollo urbano: temas," *StudyLIb, 47.* https://studylib.es/doc/6899666/casos-emblem%C3%A1ticos-de-desarrollo-urbano--temas.---inicio (accessed January 7, 2018).

5 Interview of Jorge Carvajal, teacher at the Miravalle Marinist School and member of the Miravalle Community Council, by Elisa Silva. Mexico City, Mexico. September. 22, 2018.

6 Ibid.

7 Marcos Rosa, Ute E. Weiland, (Eds). *Handmade Urbanism: From Community Initiatives to Participatory Models.* (Berlin: Jovis Verlag GmbH, 2013).

8 The award is granted by the London School of Economics and Political Science and the Alfred Herrhausen Society – Deutsche Bank.

9 Jorge Carvajal, (2018).

10 Ibid.

11 Rosa (2013).

12 Jorge Carvajal, (2018).

13 Interview of Edgar Pichardo, director of Calmaca community center by Elisa Silva. Mexico City, Mexico. September 22, 2018.

ECOTECNIA URBANA MIRAVALLE
MEXICO CITY, MEXICO

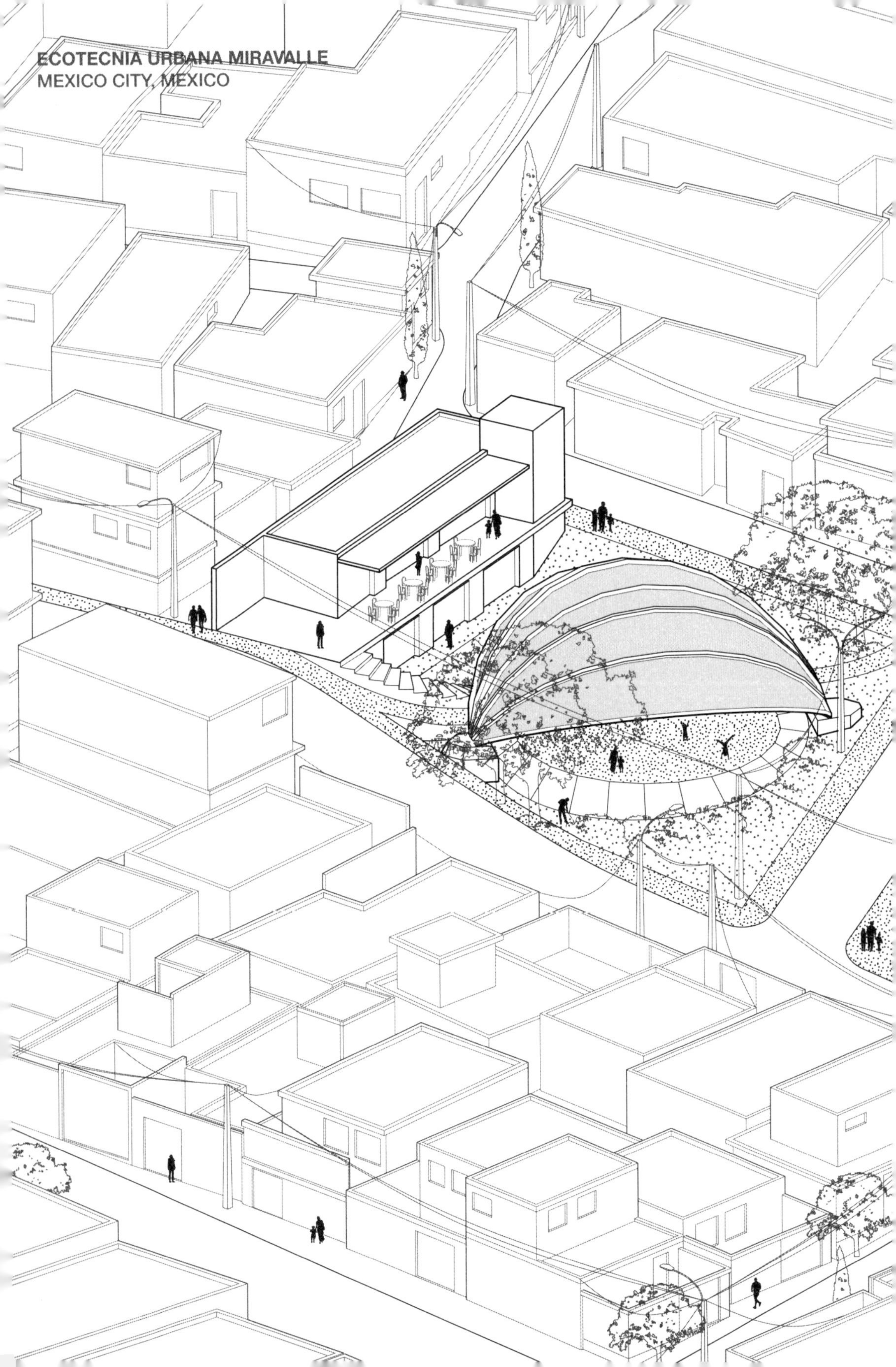

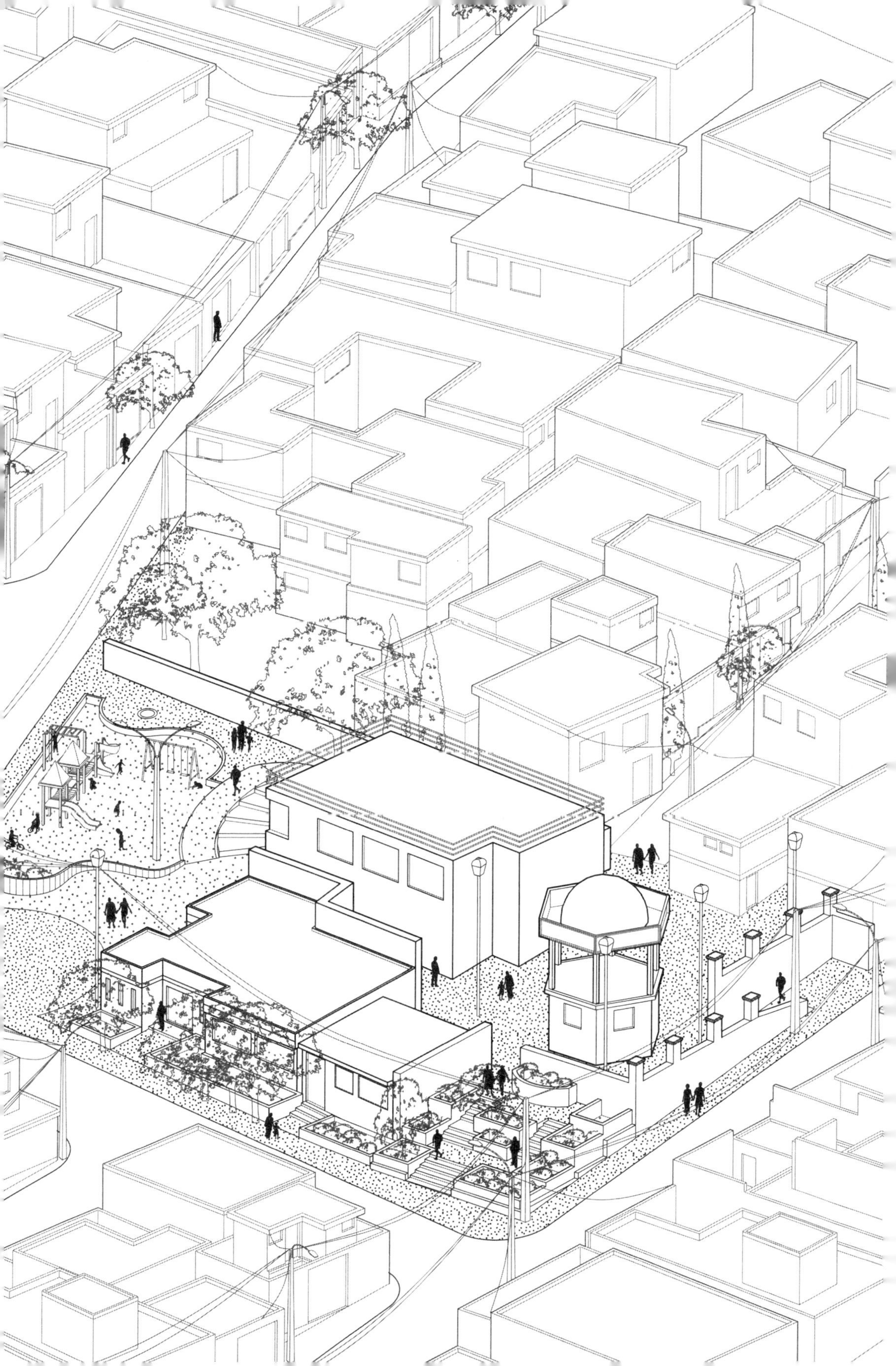

PAVEMENT AND PUBLIC SPACES IN CERRO SANTO DOMINGO AND TORO

Cerro El Toro and Santo Domingo are part of the informal urban fabric that lines the hills of Valparaiso. The municipality issued a request for proposals to consolidate the interstitial spaces of the spontaneous settlements as public space. It was titled "Design for the Improvement of Neighborhood Public Spaces- Recovery and Urban Development Program of Valparaiso."[1] The selected architects were commissioned to discuss and design the nature of the non-private spaces with the community and subsequently build a network of walkways, stairs and gathering areas, incorporating existing open spaces. Additionally, a modular prefabricated pavement was designed that would simplify construction and guarantee better-quality details and finishes. The project gave way to 9.000 m² of well-defined public spaces.

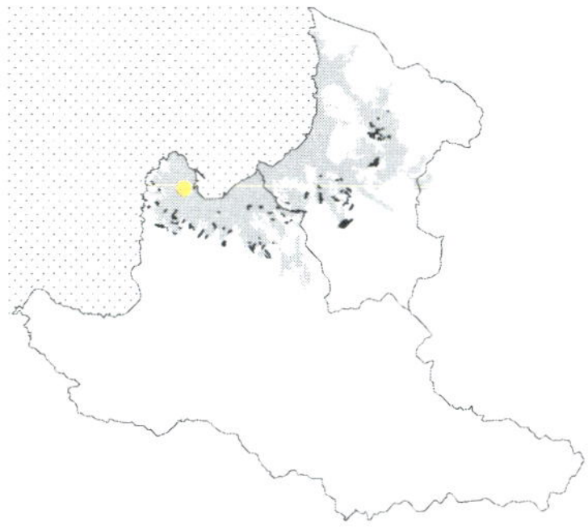

Location
Cerro Santo Domingo and Cerro Toro, Valparaiso, Chile

Project team:
Mobil Arquitectos, Antonio Lipthay, Cecilia Puga, Guillermo Jullian, Ilustre Municipalidad de Valparaíso

Date 2009

Coordinates
33°02'16.89"S 71°38'11.79"O

Investment 3.2 million USD

Public space area
17,980,60 m2

Urban density
96.21 hab / ha

Population benefited
5,005 hab

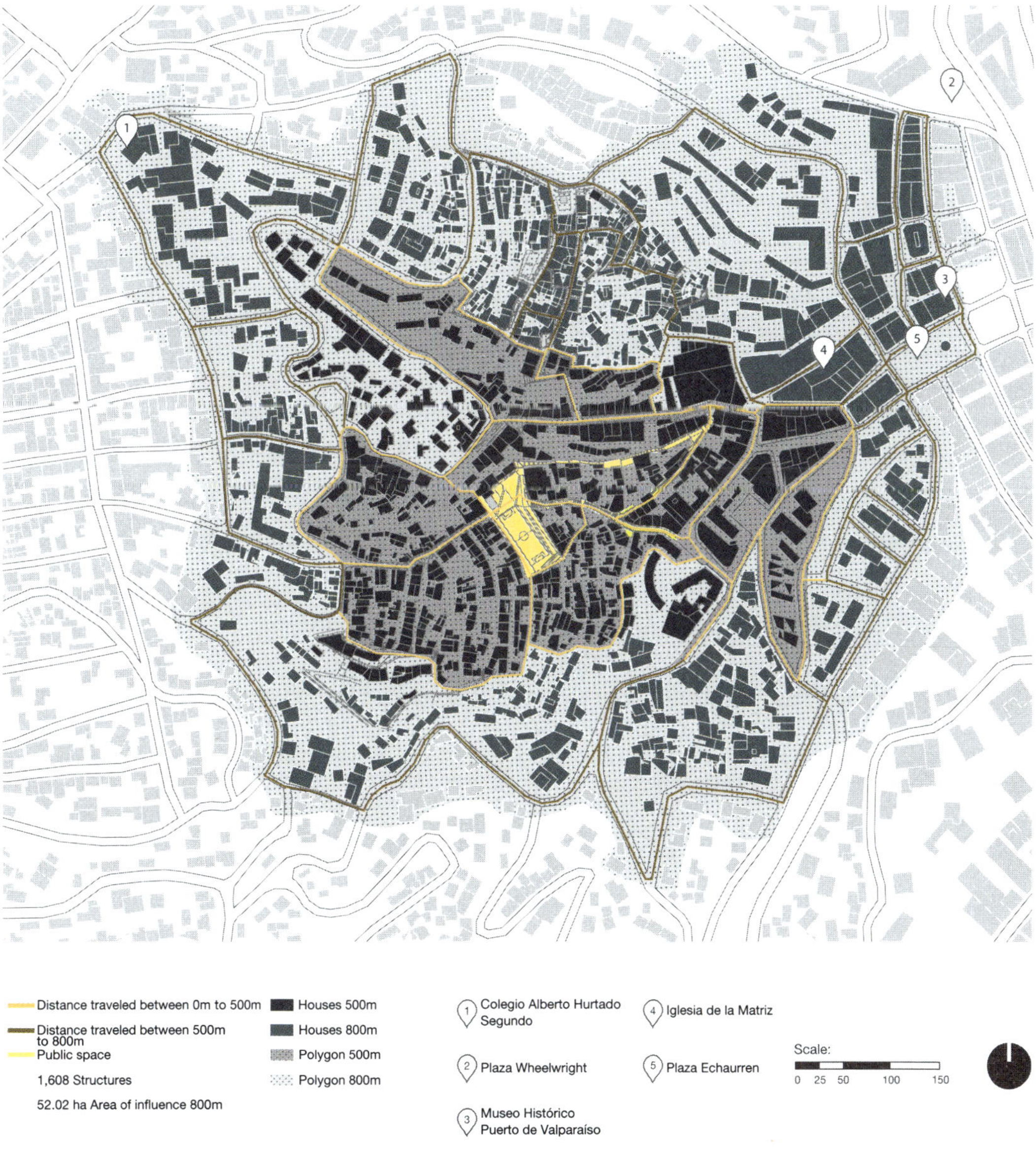

PUBLIC SPACE

Unlike previous examples, the Valparaiso project is the result of a municipal request for proposals to specifically create public space. The Municipality of Valparaiso allocated public resources to improve accessibility and establish a continuous pedestrian network from the flatter, formal areas of the city bellow, toward more impoverished communities at higher elevations.

HISTORY

Valparaiso is Chile´s main port onto the Pacific Ocean. The city was built in 1541, on the flat part of the territory near the port.[2] As the space was filled, later urban growth spread to the hills known for their rugged topography and steep slopes. The *plan*, as locals call the sector of the city closest to the coast, houses the administrative, historical, commercial and economic functions of the city. The area between the Prat Pier and the Church of the Matrix was declared a World Heritage Site by UNESCO in 2003.[3] What most distinguishes Valparaiso from other cities is the chain of forty-two hills that were occupied over time for residential use. Winding paths intermittently afford impressive views over the port and bay. The housing stock that still exists includes military buildings used to control the colonial territory and large mansions that belonged to European immigrants. The geographical peculiarity of Valparaiso represents a historic challenge for urban connections between the hills and the port. The colonial roads that originate in the *plan* and rise towards the hills, as well as the elevators and funiculars, reflect the early date in which the slopes were urbanized.

The communities of Cerro Santo Domingo and Cerro Toro are among the first settlements to emerge on the hills of Valparaiso and fall within the World Heritage area of the city.[4] The neighborhoods have a close relationship with the *plan* since they depend on its commercial and cultural facilities. They also share a common history. The paving project in Cerro Santo Domingo and Cerro Torocreates a more formal continuity between the two, through the definition of the ground plane and public space.

SOCIAL AND POLITICAL CONTEXT

Valparaiso´s prominence as a port city goes back to the early 19th century, when capitalist trade was financed by the British and a significant commercial movement flourished between Europe and Chile.[5] The city´s hills were mostly populated by English, German and Spanish immigrants. Today, Valparaiso is known for its cultural and social traditions. The participatory design process used by the design team was called "door to door local culture." It revealed the connection felt by the communities of Cerro el Toro and Cerro Santo Domingo to their neighborhoods. The dynamics enabled the design team to gain expert knowledge from the community on specific fragments of the territory. The process also allowed neighbors to interpret and modify the design, so that in the end the resulting project was produced through a dialogue with the community. [6] Both Cerro el Toro and Cerro Santo Domingo have community neighborhood associations that were started several decades ago.[7]

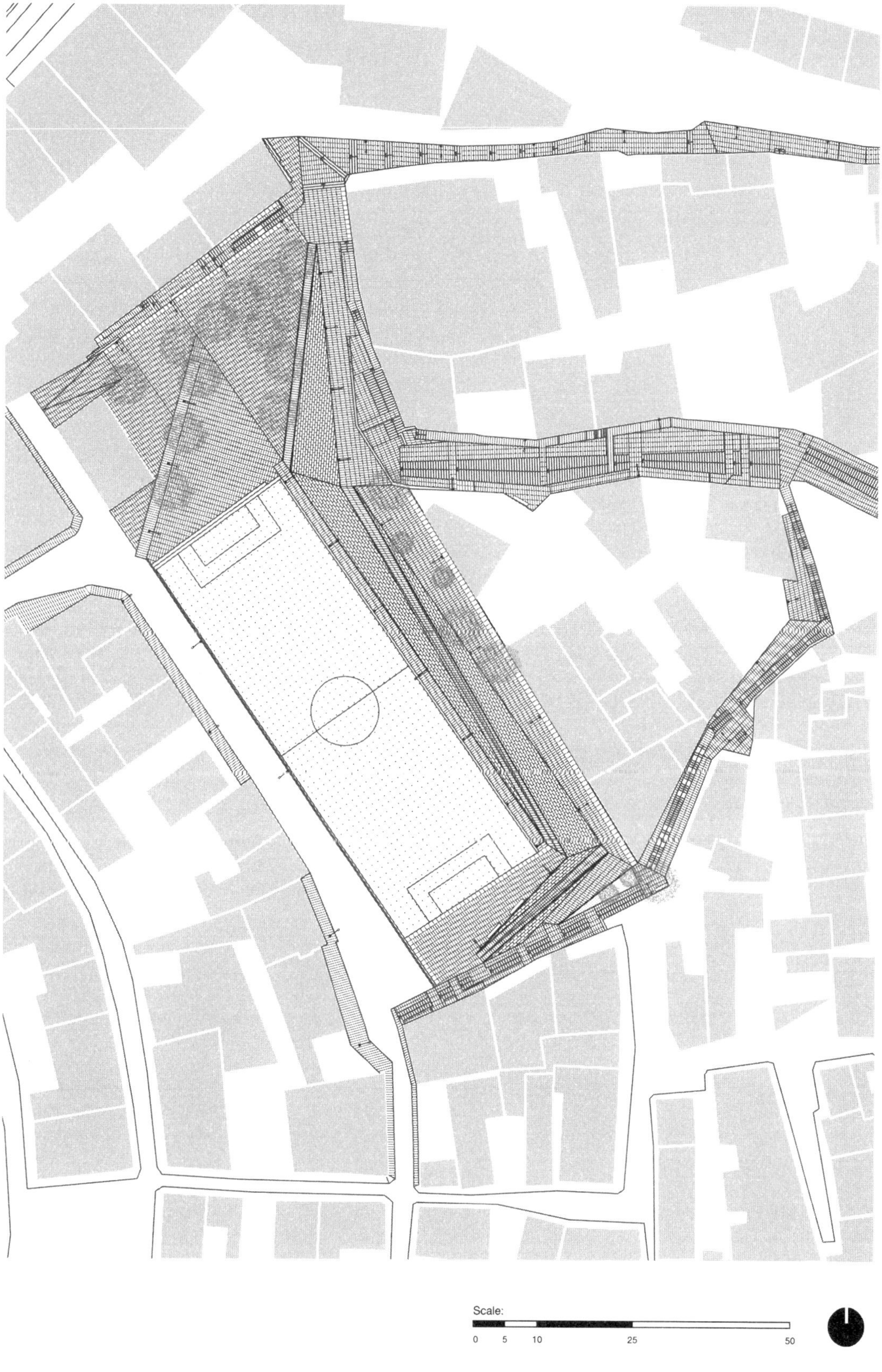
Scale:
0 5 10 25 50

ENVIRONMENTAL SITUATION

Valparaiso is particularly vulnerable to fires due to its topographic condition and the strong northern winds that meet the slopes of the hills and enhance the effect of fires. Many of the creeks that run down the hills once represented natural firebreaks of humidity and vegetation. However, most have been channeled or covered, thereby eliminating their ability to contain fires.[8] Another eminent risk is exposure to landslides due to erosion. Superficial water runoff over the inclined slopes can cause the substrate to detach and slide.[9] Roads and streets on the hills reveal the erosion effects caused by rain. The paving project decreases these effects and increases humidity through the implementation of a porous prefabricated tile pavement, which allows water to percolate into the subsoil. The increased humidity helps mitigate fires and the infiltration process decreases surface runoff and erosion.

URBAN SITUATION

The City of Valparaiso's urban fabric is composed of the bay, the *plan* and the hills.[10] Cerro Santo Domingo is its oldest hillside settlement, dating back to colonial times, and the closest to the historic city center. Cobble stone paths bellow, become stairs as they enter the neighborhood and old-fashioned funicular trains connect the *plan* and the hill. Towards the interior of the settlement, winding roads and irregular paths access each house and offer impressive views over the bay of Valparaiso. Housing typologies vary from traditional British style structures with stone foundations to houses built with modest resources. Together, they create Valparaiso´s praised picturesque landscape.

The project´s paved walkways and plazas in Cerro Santo Domingo and Cerro Toro, enhance the community's connection to the city center and create small meeting spaces. They also recall the aesthetic value of the colonial cobble stone streets, through a contemporary language of concrete pavers.[11]

PROJECT FUNDING

Funds for the project came from the Recovery and Development Program of Valparaiso, a governmental initiative to both preserve and improve the city´s UNESCO World Heritage area. The program´s total budget was 76 million USD financed through a loan from the Inter-American Development Bank (IDB) and municipal funds. 3.2 million USD were used for the paving project. The Municipality of Valparaiso and the Division of Regional Development shared responsibility for the plan´s implementation.[12] The project's design and execution were assigned to the firm Mobil Arquitectos through a public bidding process in 2006.[13]

RELATED PROGRAMS

The "Recovery and Development of Valparaiso" program, in which the Cerro Santo Domingo and Cerro Toro pavement project is inscribed, promotes economic, sociocultural and institutional development as well as communication and civic participation.[14] The pavement effectively creates a more amenable pedestrian situation for inhabitants, with urban spaces next to shops and stores. It also successfully connects the *plan* bellow with the hills above, generating opportunities for tourism. Finally, the project facilitates community gatherings and recreation for neighbors.

URBAN INTEGRATION

Valparaiso is the only Latin American city with spontaneous settlements that date back to the times of the Spanish colony. The distinction between planned and spontaneous territories in Valparaiso is less pronounced because the city was mostly made of self-built homes adapted to the hill's geography. The marginalization of the Valparaiso hills is more a consequence of a deterioration process than of segregation or social exclusion. The pedestrian network of walkways built for Cerro Santo Domingo and Cerro Toro, highlights community gathering spaces, nestled within the organic urban fabric, and strengthens spatial continuity. On a neighborhood scale, the pavement project improves access to each house, it regularizes the ground plane, makes it easier for people with limited mobility to walk, and decreases rainwater runoff. At the metropolitan scale, the project helps suture the urban fabric between the *plan* and the hills.

1 Antonio Lipthay, "Reparación del tejido urbano Cerro Toro y Cerro Santo Domingo," *ARQ* n. 7, December, 2009, 28.

2 Alfredo Sánchez, Joaquín Bosque and Cecilia Jiménez, "Valparaíso: su geografía, su historia y su identidad como Patrimonio de la Humanidad." *Estudios Geográficos* June, 2009, 269.

3 Ibid.

4 Ricardo Verdejo, "Valparaíso: miradas a un proceso de construcción socio-urbano e identitario," *Revista austral de ciencias sociales* n. 28, 2015, 186.

5 bid.

6 Antonio Lipthay (2009), 28-35.

7 Verdejo (2015).

8 Claudio Magrini, Presentation at Limapolis 2017, Facultad de Arquitectura y Urbanismo de la Pontificia Universidad Católica del Perú. March 5, 2017.

9 Gobierno de Chile, *Plan de inversiones. Reconstrucción y rehabilitación urbana*, Valparaíso, 2014, 20.

10 Alfredo Sánchez, Joaquín Bosque and Cecilia Jiménez, "Valparaíso: su geografía, su historia y su identidad como Patrimonio de la Humanidad," *Estudios Geográficos* June 2009, 269.

11 Empresa Constructora Pukara. "Síntesis diagnóstico: Memoria proyecto cerro Santo Domingo," Valparaíso, 2010. 3-4

12 Ibid.

13 Lipthay, 30.

14 Ibid

PAVEMENT AND PUBLIC SPACES IN CERRO SANTO DOMINGO AND TORO
VALPARAISO, CHILE

CERRO SANTA ANA REHABILITATION

Cerro Santa Ana is a spontaneous settlement situated on a hill along the edge of the Guayas River. Its high crime rate represented a threat to citizens and tourists visiting the Malecón 2000 river walk, adjacent to the southern edge of the settlement. In order to mitigate the negative effects of this proximity to the then recently inaugurated urban renewal project, the municipality worked with the community to transform and incorporate Cerro Santa Ana into the tourist experience along the water front. An improved, formal staircase was built that begins at the base of the settlement and culminates at an open esplanade with a chapel and a light tower over the hill´s crest. Along the way are plazas, lighting, urban furniture, renovated facades and storefronts.

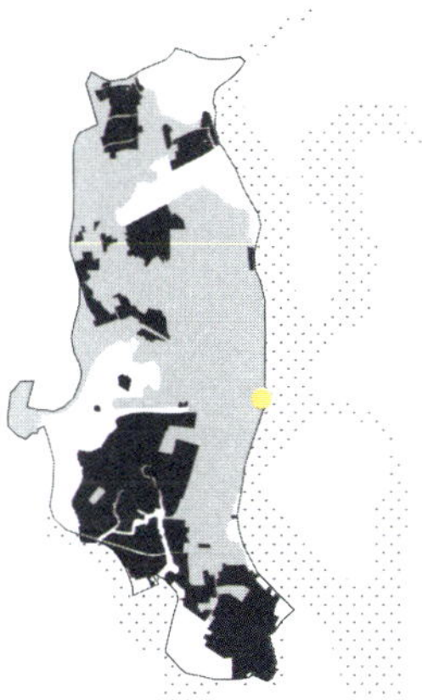

Location
Cerro Santa Ana, Guayaquil, Ecuador

Project team:
The Municipality of Guayaquil,
Fundación Guayaquil Siglo XXI,
Fundación Malecón 2000

Date 2009

Coordinates
2°10'53.59"S 79°54'06.25"O

Investment
20 million USD

Public space area
5,115 m2

Urban density
115.36 hab / ha

Population benefited
13,831 hab

Distance traveled between 0m to 500m
Distance traveled between 500m to 800m
Public space
2,198 Structures
119.89 ha Area of influence 800m

Houses 500m
Houses 800m
Polygon 500m
Polygon 800m

1. Museo Antropológico y de Arte Contemporáneo
2. Escuela Superior Politécnica del Litoral
3. Hospital Luis Vernaza
4. Hospital Neumonológico Alfedo Valenzuela
5. Cementerio General

Scale:
0 50 100 200 400

PUBLIC SPACE

The success of the river walk required the transformation of a contiguous spontaneous settlement; this transformation also became the premise for an intentionally continuous public space design that would blur the barriers between formal and informal fragments of the city.

HISTORY

Cerro Santa Ana is closely linked to the foundation of Guayaquil. Considered one of the city´s oldest urban areas, dating back to the XVI century. It is located on a hill just northwest of the city center, overlooking the Guayas River, strategically located to defend the city.[1] Cerro Santa Ana is geographically linked to the historic Las Peñas neighborhood and the *Malecón* boardwalk, along the river. Over the course of the 17th century, commercial activity developed and the *Malecón*, originally known as the "Calle de la Orilla", was used to anchor fishing boats and ships carrying produce.[2] Numa Pompillo Street, at the base of the hill, became a fashionable address with large houses built for privileged families. During the following century much of the Barrio Las Peñas burned in fires, and was later rebuilt according to its original scheme.[3]

In time, intense economic activity related to the port began transforming the area. In 1931, street lighting and public spaces were introduced.[4] In 1963, a maritime port was built, effectively ending the city´s relationship with the water front which progressively caused the abandonment of the adjacent historic center. The area became associated with violence and drug trafficking.[5] By then, Las Peñas and Santa Ana were already populated with impoverished communities and were deemed responsible for the lack of personal safety perceived downtown.

After numerous attempts to rebuild the *Malecón* in order to reverse the trend of deteriorarion in the downtown area, in 1996 work began in earnest on the boardwalk´s recovery which culminated in the Malecón 2000 project. The plan emphasized the historic city center´s restoration, the boardwalk and the creation of a tourist route linking the *Malecón* and Cerro Santa Ana. Las Peñas neighborhood underwent an important transformation through the Urban Regeneration Plan of Guayaquil.[6]

SOCIAL AND POLITICAL CONTEXT

The combined area and population of Cerro Santa Ana and Las Peñas neighborhoods is 13.5 hectares and 4,834 inhabitants respectively.[7] Population density is 358 inhabitants per hectare, which is high compared to the rest of the city. The urban renewal project in Cerro Santa Ana improved walkways, stairs, and helped restore the facades of many homes.[8] Before the renovation project, there were only five legally established stores in Cerro Santa Ana. Currently, there are more than 75 and 70% of the people in the neighborhood have acquired or started a small business of their own. Businesses serve nearly 20,000 people a week.[9] In other words, the Cerro Santa Ana´s urban renewal project did not only help upgrade the neighborhood's infrastructure, but also generated new employment opportunities through tourism and services.

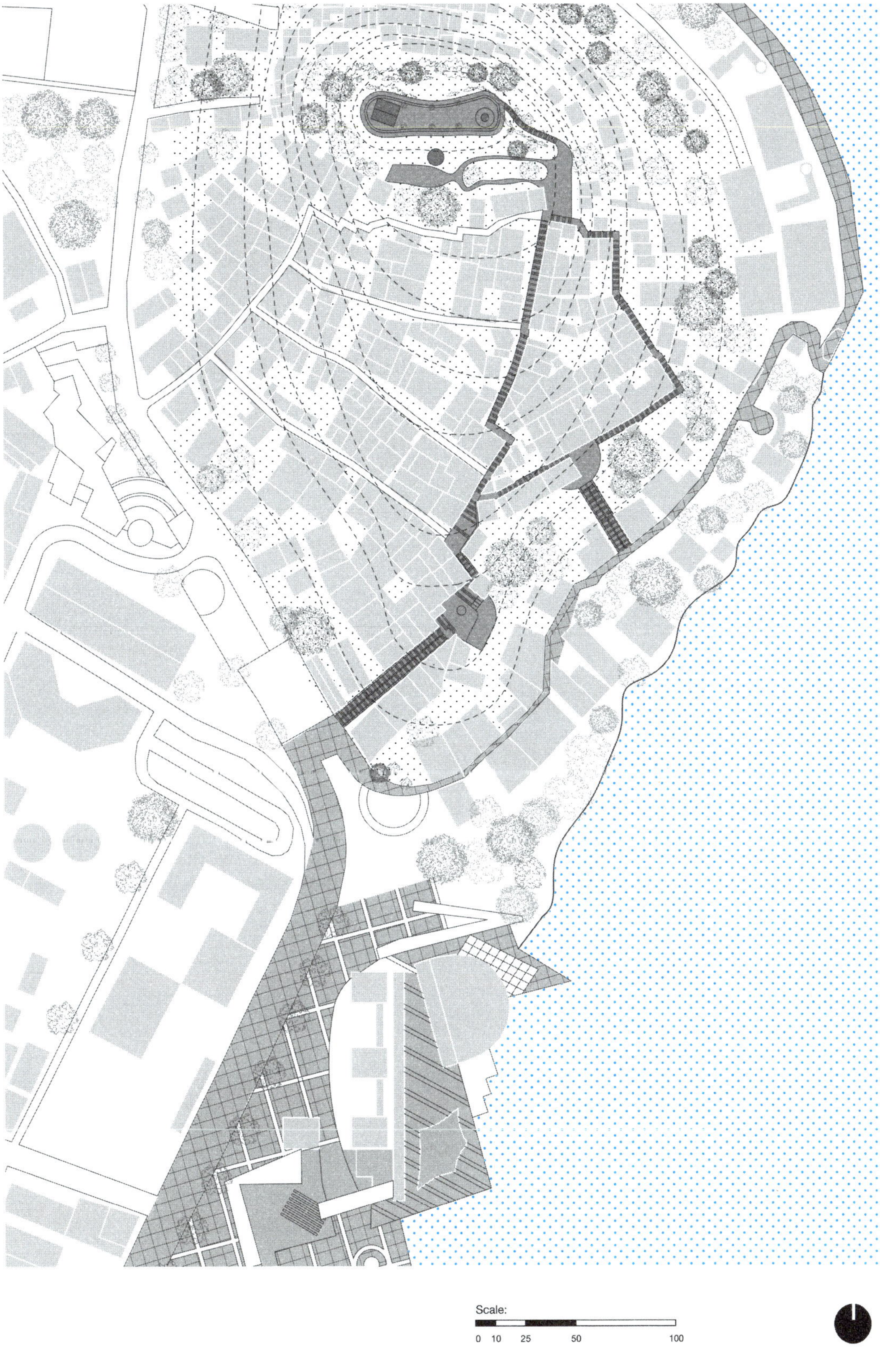
Scale:
0 10 25 50 100

ENVIRONMENTAL SITUATION

Cerro Santa Ana is prone to landslides due to the combination of its steep topography and the filtration of improperly channeled sewage water into the subsoil. Heavy deforestation further aggravates the ground's lack of stability.

URBAN SITUATION

Even though Cerro Santa Ana is a historic neighborhood in Guayaquil, its housing structure is mostly informal. Plots follow the contours of the topography and contrast starkly with the rest of the city´s orthogonal grid. The transformation of the river walk, through the Malecón 2000 program, was extended to include the rehabilitation of Cerro Santa Ana. This initiative created a powerful message of continuity and integration between the formal and informal urban fabric. The Diego Noboa steps guide the ascent from the base of Cerro Santa Ana to a lookout platform at the top the hill. Along the way, visitors encounter a completely renovated streetscape. The historic character of buildings, the pedestrian walkways and public spaces contribute to Cerro Santa Ana´s attractiveness for tourism.

PROJECT FUNDING

The Urban Renewal project for Cerro Santa Ana was executed by the Municipality of Guayaquil with support from the Fundación Guayaquil Siglo XXI, the Fundación Malecón 2000, the community of Cerro Santa Ana, the Guayaquil Chamber of Commerce, the Casa Grande University, the Pacific University Business School, the Polytechnic Higher Education of Ecuador and Oxfam-Ecuador.[10]

Funding for the Cerro Santa Ana regeneration project was channeled through the Fundación Guayaquil Siglo XXI, an independent NGO, specifically created for the execution of large urban renewal projects.[11] The foundation allowed the City to raise funds from the private sector and channel resources from the municipality. Altogether, 20 million USD were invested in the Cerro Santa Ana and Las Peñas recovery project.[12] The foundation´s independence from city government makes it more agile, since it doesn't involve the same levels of bureaucracy, and additionally allows donors to feel more confident about the efficient use of funds.

RELATED PROGRAMS

The Urban Renewal Plan was supported by a social program called the Municipal Program for the Social and Productive Improvement of Cerro Santa Ana and Carmen. It was established by the Department of Social Action and Education (DASE Departamento de Acción Social y Educación) through the Municipality´s Integral Development Office, which provides social services for children, youth and adults.[13]

In 2009, an alliance was forged between the municipality and an NGO specialized in social initiatives anad together they implemented two programs: "Comprehensive cultural development for children" and "Development of productive skills". The first program creates playful and recreational spaces for children and adolescents, to stimulate the development of civic values and environmental stewardship. Activities include *capoeira,* chess, puppets, painting, *tae kwon do*, ballet, dance, film and theater workshops.[14] The second program aims to generate opportunities for women and men from 18 to 65 years of age to develop productive skills and increase their family income. Some of the courses include serigraphy, painting children's faces and developing cacao products. Other courses are offered on entrepreneurship and how to run a small business.[15]

ACTIVITIES

Cerro Santa Ana´s transformation included initiatives to help increase economic opportunities for the community. In 2001, the Municipality´s Department of Social Action and Education was able to assist 230 low-income families with access to entrepreneurship courses. 55 micro entrepreneurs emerged from the experience working on food, entertainment and handicrafts. Many of them are located in homes along the Diego Noboa stairs.

As a result of the Urban Renewal Plan, tourism has developed in Cerro Santa Ana. The community has responded by creating new cultural and commercial services including art galleries, craft shops, cybercafes, bars and restaurants. Many of these were developed as part of the municipality´s program "Development of Productive Skills".

URBAN INTEGRATION

One of the key contributions of the Cerro Santa Ana Urban Renewal project was its connection to and extension of the public space axis along the river. The views of Guayaquil from Cerro Santa Ana, along with its shops and cafes, attract tourists and visitors from other parts of the city, blurring the distinction between the formal city and Cerro Santa Ana.

1 Marie Sophie Bock, "Estudio macro-espacial de la arquitectura y de la sociedad guayaquileñas (1900-1940)," *Guayaquil: Arquitectura, espacio y sociedad, 1900-1940* (Lima: Institut français d'études andines, 1992).

2 Ibid.

3 Ibid.

4 G. N. Perrone, *Malecón 2000 El inicio de la regeneración urbana de Guayaquil: un enfoque proyectual* (Quito: Flacso, 2012).

5 D.W. Chauvet, *Del caos al orden. Guayaquil y su desarrollo urbano actual* (Guayaquil: Ciudades, 2005), 184.

6 Fundación Malecón 2000. http://malecon.org.ec/quienes-somos (accessed June 4, 2018)

7 Silva and Vaggione (2016), 109.

8 Ibid.

9 D.E. Delgado, *Estudio del impacto del plan de regeneración urbana en la calidad de vida de los habitantes del cerro Santa Ana, escalinatas Diego Noboa y Arteta* (Guayaquil: Universidad Católica de Santiago de Guayaquil, 2012), 86

10 DASE. Dirección de Acción Social y Educación. (Guayaquil, 2014).

11 Alcaldía de Guayaquil, "Guayaquil es mi destino," 2018. http://www.guayaquilesmidestino.com/es/historia-arte-y-cultura/cerro-santa-ana (accessed May 9, 2018).

12 Silva and Vaggione (2016), 120.

13 DASE (2014).

14 *Municipalidad de Guayaquil. Rendición de cuentas 2009 - 2010* (Guayaquil: Wong y Wong Consultores Asociados, 2010), 44, 45.

15 Ibid.

CERRO SANTA ANA REHABILITATION
GUAYAQUIL, ECUADOR

FERNANDO BOTERO LIBRARY

The Fernando Botero Library is located on the slope of the San Cristobal neighborhood, in Medellin. It serves as an important cultural amenity for the community and represents an entrance threshold to the spontaneous settlement. The outdoor central atrium gives access to various programs inside the library, while its interior staircase allows people to ascend one level and reach the streets and houses that face the library´s rear façade. In turn, practice rooms along this back side activate urban space, since they can be accessed directly from the outside without having to go through the main library entrance.

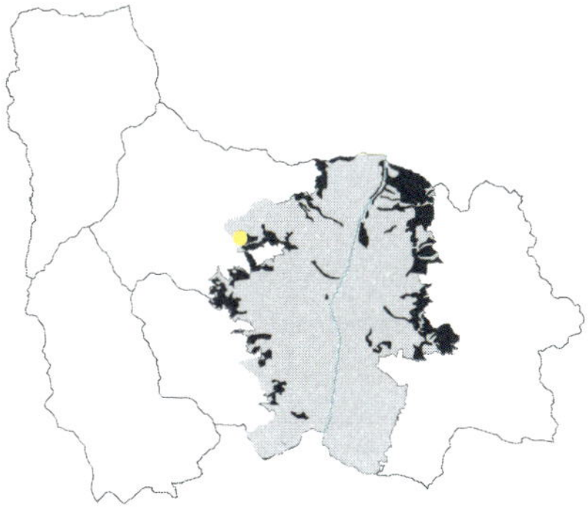

Location
San Cristóbal, Medellin, Colombia

Project team:
G Ateliers Architecture, Orlando García, EDU Empresa de Desarrollo Urbano de Medellin

Date 2009

Coordinates
66°16'40.47"N 75°38'12.44"O

Investment
5.2 million USD

Public space area
2,412 m²

Urban density 704 hab / ha

Population benefited 18,621 hab

- Distance traveled between 0m to 500m
- Distance traveled between 500m to 800m
- Public space
- 1,925 Structures
- 26.45 ha Area of influence 800m

- Houses 500m
- Houses 800m
- Polygon 500m
- Polygon 800m

1. Institución Educativa San Cristobal
2. UVA Mirador de San Cristobal
3. Unidad Hospitalaria San Cristobal
4. Parque principal de San Cristobal
5. Quebrada La Iguana

Scale: 0 25 50 100 150

PUBLIC SPACE

The library does not only fulfill programmatic requirements but also contributes to the urban logic of its surroundings. Public space is activated by the cellular rooms for activities that open directly onto the neighborhood. The atrium functions as a prolonged entrance threshold to the community.

HISTORY

San Cristobal is a settlement in Medellin´s urban periphery founded in 1752.[1] Community members are descendants of an ethnically mixed population of farmers. They built irrigation channels through the fields fed by the Iguaná Creek. In 1770, San Cristobal was declared the first parish independent from Medellin. Since colonial times, however, it has been defined by its proximity to the city as a place of passage linked to commercial exchanges between Medellin and the rest of Antioquia. Among its various productive activities, the extraction of construction materials such as sand and gravel are well known. San Cristobal is also a common entry point to the city for migrants traveling from the west, although this phenomenon diminished after a highway between Medellin and the Pacific coast was built in 1998.[2]

San Cristobal is a unique urban center: it is considered part of the Antioquia Metropolitan and Regional Strategic Corridor and acts as an edge to contain urban expansion and protect natural resources, including the watershed basin and its ecology. The Fernando Botero Library is part of San Cristobal´s Local Development Plan which determines the town´s urban, environmental and productive investments. The library´s location allows it to operate at the metropolitan scale with programs that appeal to the city at large, while serving the immediate community with educational, cultural, and recreational opportunities. The library´s objective is to help consolidate the social fabric, better incorporate marginalized sectors through access to culture, and increase the municipality´s institutional presence.[3]

SOCIAL AND POLITICAL CONTEXT

San Cristobal was originally a rural settlement of farmers. More than half of its current population has always lived there. There are also many recent migrants from the countryside, who have fled the violence of guerilla groups. The community´s identity is largely defined by its agricultural activity, and yet urban expansion and newer neighborhoods of social housing threaten the continuity of the rural landscape.[4] Illegal activities associated with gangs, drugs and violence occur on a regular basis. Low literacy levels and insufficient access to education are among the community´s greatest social problems.

ENVIRONMENTAL SITUATION

The territory of San Cristobal, once a mix of agriculture and forest areas, has been transformed into a hybrid rural-urban landscape with both formal and spontaneous settlements. The area is traversed by creeks and water systems that flow into the Medellin River hence, the conservation of its watershed is considered very important for the preservation of the Aburrá Valley´s ecology.[5] However, La Iguaná Creek, at the top of the watershed, is contaminated by sewage water and

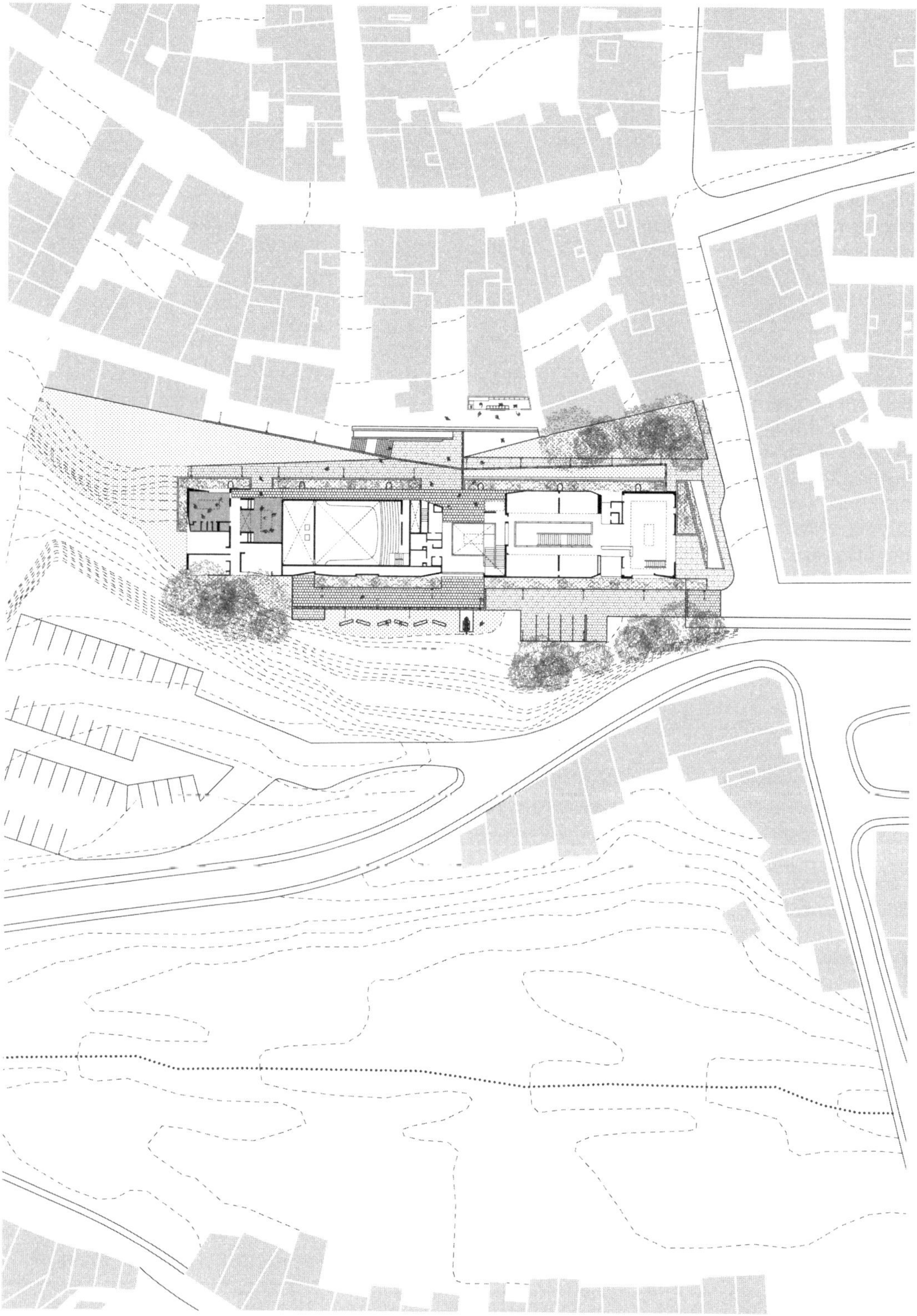

Scale:
0 5 10 25 50

waste. Deforestation, illegal mining, and housing constructed within preservation corridors, near the source of the creek, further contribute to its contamination.[6] The extraction of sand and gravel by construction industries degrades the quality of soil and depletes its nutrients, threatening the preservation of native flora and fauna.[7] San Cristobal is part of the Las Baldías mountain range and the only plateau ecosystem in the Aburra Valley. In order to increase environmental awareness, the Fernando Botero Library offers educational programs for youth, community neighbors and visitors.[8]

URBAN SITUATION

San Cristobal´s territory is a mix of agricultural, residential, and industrial land uses. The San Jerónimo Road, which runs parallel to La Iguaná Creek, is the town´s main access corridor. The northeastern areas are agricultural fields with structures interspersed in the landscape. Toward the south, the informal urban fabric extends uniformly from the Comuna 13 up to San Cristobal. New social housing developments have been built in the town center; however, access to services and urban conditions are insufficient.[9] San Cristobal is connected to Medellin through the Comuna 13 San Javier cable car system, which includes transfers to public transportation at the Aurora Station. San Jeronimo Road also leads to the city center.

PROJECT FUNDING

The project was financed with resources from the municipal and regional government. The project´s design was the result of an international architecture competition won by the Spanish office G Ateliers Architecture and Orlando García.[10] The project´s design development and construction were handled by the Urban Development Company (EDU).

RELATED PROGRAMS

The Fernando Botero Library is part of the municipality´s Public Library Parks and offers a series of cultural and educational programs pertaining to the overall library system. "Let's Walk San Cristobal," for example, is led by a community organization and consists of walks through the district to become familiar with its landscape and learn about local agriculture practices.[11] "Future planting" is a program that teaches agriculture techniques and environmental responsibility. "Grandparents tell stories" attempts to preserve local history through stories for children, enacted by community senior citizens.[12] Additionally, the library staff disseminates its cultural agenda and programs through door-to-door visits to the community.[13]

ACTIVITIES

The Fernando Botero Library has a reading room, a computer room, a toy library, visual art studios, dance and music halls, multipurpose rooms and exhibition spaces. It is open to all inhabitants of San Cristobal as well as everyone in the city.[14] Dance and multipurpose rooms can be accessed directly from the library´s rear façade which faces the settlement. The public space surrounding the rooms are enlivened by youth dancing, choreographing and mingling.

URBAN INTEGRATION

Public space reinforces the cultural and artistic vocations of the library and helps connect it to the settlement´s network of walkways and steps, integrating the building with the urban fabric. In San Cristobal, the settlement is located at a slightly higher elevation than the library, where roads lead to an open public space adjacent to the library. Programmatic spaces along the rear facade, accessible from the outside, much like storefronts, have been appropriated by young people to choreograph dances, as mentioned earlier. These activities create an intense and lively environment. As a result, the houses facing the library have opened shops and stores to serve the people that frequent the site.

The library also represents a threshold between more formal parts of San Cristobal and the spontaneous settlement. The atrium acts as an exchange volume where residents can enter, ascend using the stairs, and continue on toward their homes as part of a single journey. This opportunity not only creates a more enjoyable trajectory, but also integrates the library with people´s everyday experiences and makes it part of the community´s public sphere. It is also a celebrated piece of contemporary architecture visited by architects worldwide.

1 R. Velásquez, "El páramo más pequeño del país está en el Aburrá," *El Colombiano* 2017.

2 Ibid.

3 María Victoria Alcaraz, "Latinoamérica: reflexiones sobre las infraestructuras y equipamientos culturales." In S. Catalán Romero and A. J. González Rueda, "Manual Atalaya de apoyo a la gestión cultural" 2014, 3. http://atalayagestioncultural.es/capitulos/gestion-cultural/1 (accessed January 19, 2019)

4 Alcaldía de Medellín, *Plan de Desarrollo Local Corregimiento San Cristóbal*. (Medellín: Alcaldía de Medellín, 2015), 60.

5 Velásquez (2017).

6 Alcaldía de Medellín (2015).

7 Ibid., 67.

8 J. Cuadros, J.Valencia and A. Valencia, "Las bibliotecas públicas como escenario de participación ciudadana e inclusión socia," *Rastros y rostros*, 2013, 81.

9 Ibid., 27, 28.

10 C. Escobar, C. Borja and L. M. Arredondo, "Informe especial construcción de la Biblioteca San Cristóbal de la Empresa de Desarrollo Urbano," 2011.

11 Elena Maldonado, "Parque Biblioteca Fernando Botero San Cristóbal," *Caminos y Memorias* No. 1 August, 2017, 17.

12 Ibid.

13 Ibid., 16-19.

14 "El Parque Biblioteca Fernando Botero partió la historia de los corregimientos." *Periódico de la Alcaldía de Medellín* October 14, 2011, 8-9.

FERNANDO BOTERO LIBRARY
MEDELLIN, COLOMBIA

MORAVIA CULTURAL CENTER

The Moravia Cultural Center, designed by the Colombian architect Rogelio Salmona, is a dynamic urban node. Children and teenagers spend time there on a daily base to do their homework, play music, dance, read, use internet and hang out with friends. Given the precarious conditions some of these young people experience at home, the center is a much-appreciated alternative. The surrounding areas are equally dynamic and include a plaza, a boulevard along the creek and a school. The boulevard connects with the Moravia Ecological Park along a path parallel to the creek. Two satellite modules in the park complement the center´s program with activities such as art workshops and book readings.

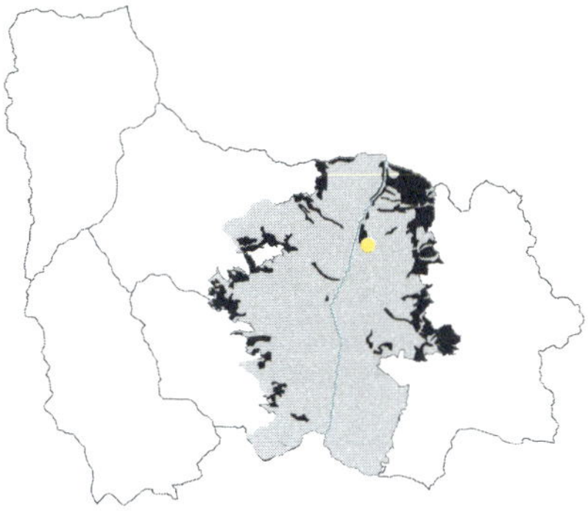

Location
Moravia, Comuna 4 Aranjuez, Medellin, Colombia

Project team:
Rogelio Salmona, Comfenalco Antioquia, Municipality of Medellin

Date 2004 - 2007

Coordinates
6°17'34.99"N 75°33'52.31"O

Investment
2.6 million USD

Public space area 615.37m^2

Urban density 277 hab / ha

Benefited inhabitants
6,847 hab

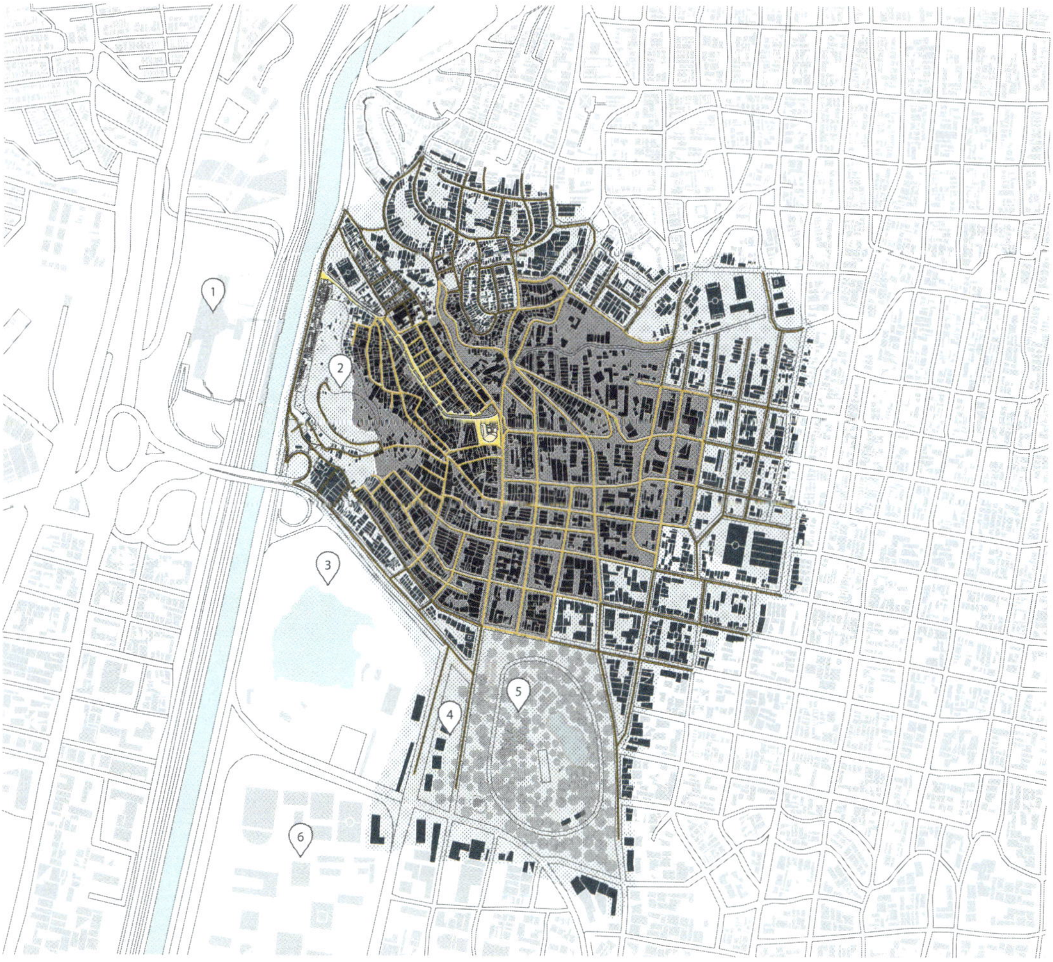

Distance traveled between 0m to 500m
Distance traveled between 500m to 800m
Public space
2,902 Structures
24.72 ha Area of influence 800m

Houses 500m
Houses 800m
Polygon 500m
Polygon 800m

1. Terminal del Norte Medellín
2. Parque Ecológico Moravia
3. Parque Norte J. Emilio Valderrama
4. Parque Explora
5. Orquideorama Jardín Botánico
6. Universidad de Antioquia

Scale:
0 25 50 100 150

PUBLIC SPACE

The Moravia Cultural Center both activates and defines an urban node with generous allotments of public space in its surroundings. It represents the heart of the Moravia community, but also attracts people from the nearby Explora Park and the botanical garden.

HISTORY

Moravia is a spontaneous settlement within the Comuna 4 Aranjuez. It developed between the forties and sixties on illegally sold plots of land in which rural migrants, displaced by guerilla violence, built their homes. Later during the seventies, a site reserved for the construction of a park between Moravia and the Medellin River, was used instead by the municipality for an open-air waste dump.[1] Moravia residents began rummaging the waste for recyclable materials. Since space in Moravia became increasingly scarce, new immigrants began building their homes directly on top of the waste dump. At the same time, the weak presence of local authorities, high levels of poverty among the population, and scarce access to work opportunities led to the proliferation of crime and armed gangs.[2]

In 1983 the municipality began a series of conversations with the community and a year later a mutual agreement was reached to close the waste dump.[3] In order to counteract the scarcity of cultural and recreational spaces, as well as insufficient institutional presence, a comprehensive plan for Moravia considered three key projects: the environmental remediation of the waste dump, new substitution housing for people living on the waste hill, and the construction of the Moravia Cultural Center, also known as La Casa de Todos (Everyone´s House).[4]

SOCIAL AND POLITICAL CONTEXT

Moravia comprises two sectors: one that extends along the eastern edge, close to the Avenida Carabobo, and one that grew over the waste hill. Inhabitants of both segments lived in precarious self-built homes with deficient access to services. Real estate pressures and public policy favored formal development in this well-located piece of land in the city, which would require razing existing houses and relocating families. The community responded with opposition and leaders organized resistance movements.[5] People´s skepticism and distrust in local authorities increased as a result and made it easier for drug cartel leaders and armed groups to fill the vacuum.

Moravia´s transformation process started in 2004[6] with a diagnosis of the community´s most pressing issues: illiteracy, lack of cultural spaces, low engagement of youth in higher education, low levels of employment, and dysfunctional families.[7] Conversations in town hall meetings further clarified the community´s needs and expectations. These encounters led to the municipality´s commitment to increase its presence in the community and support civic education and cultural programs.

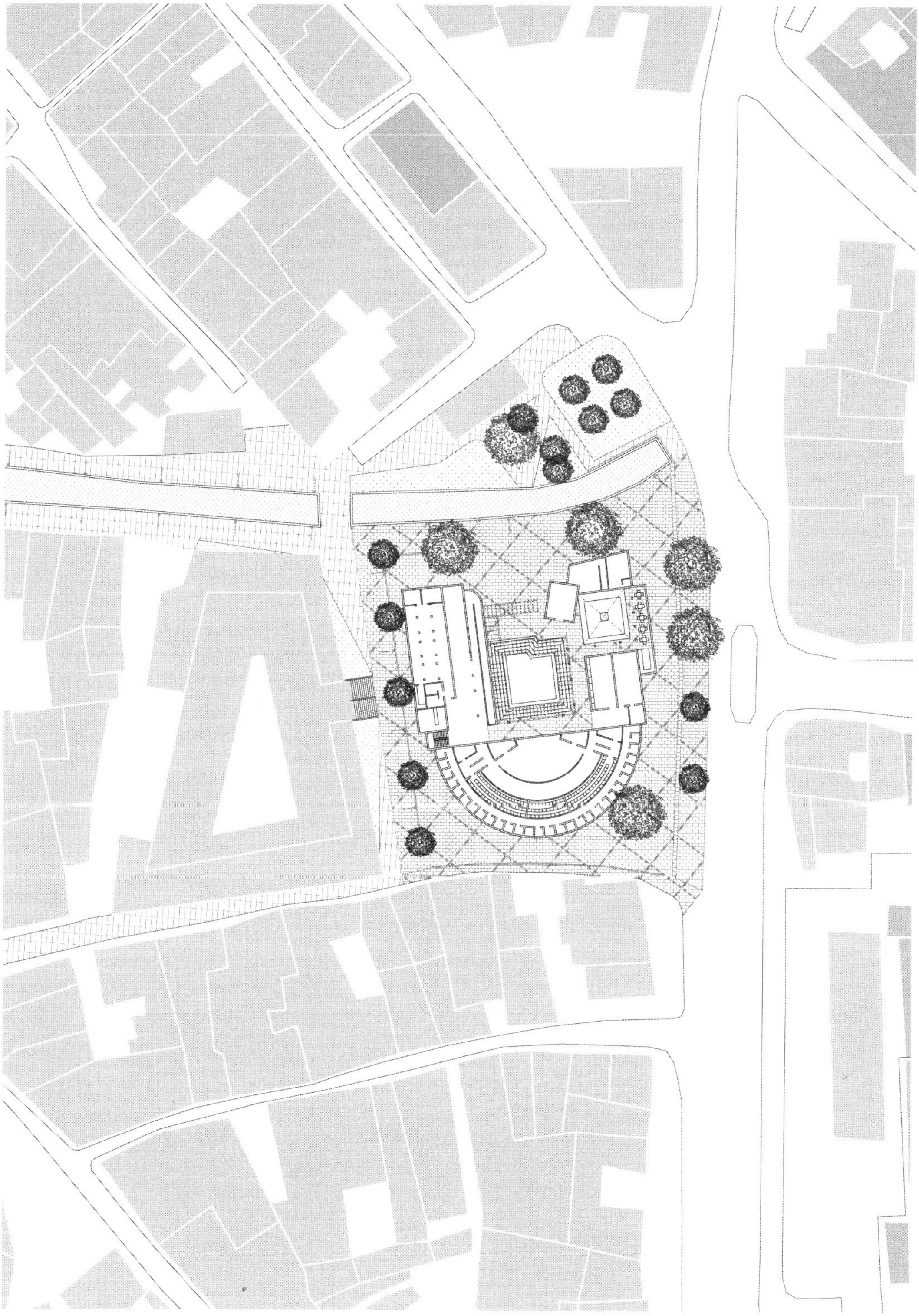

Scale:

0 2.5 5 10 25

ENVIRONMENTAL SITUATION

Moravia´s most pressing environmental concern was the presence of homes built directly over the waste dump. For that reason, most of them were removed, families were relocated and a park was created in its place (see the Moravia Ecological Park project). Another risk factor was the contamination of the Bermejala Creek, which traverses the Comunas 2, 3 and 4 and carries both sewage water and solid waste into the Medellin River. The segment of the creek that passes through Moravia is part of a pedestrian linear park, where the course of water remains open, making its presence felt by neighbors as a reminder of the lingering need to change the way the city uses its natural water systems.

URBAN SITUATION

Moravia enjoys a privileged location within Medellin. It is straddled by two important metropolitan roadways, Carabobo Avenue, to the east, and Regional Avenue, to the west. Its northern boundary is the Carrera 53 and its southernmost edge is 77th Street. The Moravia Cultural center, located on Carabobo Avenue, has become an important cultural facility for the neighborhood, but also for the city at large. It complements other nearby metropolitan destinations such as the botanical garden, the Explora Park, the Antioquia University, the North Transportation Terminal, and two metro stations.[8] The public space that surrounds the center is generous and directly linked to the Bermejala Creek linear park, which in turn leads to the Moravia Ecological Park and the Medellin River linear park system.

PROJECT FUNDING

Funding for the Moravia Cultural Center was donated by a private foundation. The construction company contributed its fees to the project.[9] The center´s operative costs are financed by the private sector. In the case of Moravia, it is managed by the Comfenalco Antioquia, an NGO that provides social security and other health related benefits as well as education and recreation to Colombian citizens.

RELATED PROGRAMS

The Cultural Center Moravia evolves from cultural activities that already existed in the community, and hosts several organizations predominantly centered around music and art. It was initially conceived to provide a formal space for the Moravia El Bosque School of Music, which is why the program includes an auditorium and practice rooms. The Moravia Cultural Network also operates at the Moravia Cultural Center. Both are community-based initiatives that helped generate an immediate appropriation of the center by neighbors. Other programs such as the toy library (Ludoteca), the Zonal Development Center (CEDEZO), where people can learn how to create or manage their own small businesses, and the Moravia Common Point program (Punto Común Moravia), are sponsored by the municipality and Comfenalco.

ACTIVITIES

The center is focused on increasing the community´s access to education and information. Activities are centered on three key areas: culture, the environment and social development. All three are addressed through various formats such as debates and workshops, movie forums and writing exercises. Dance, visual arts, theatre, music and artistic presentations are part of the center´s monthly programming which is open to both Moravia inhabitants and people from the rest of the city. Other programs include meetings with senior citizens to record the community's local history and cultural memory and activities to increase social cohesion, citizen participation, and community leadership.[10] The cultural center is equipped with an auditorium, practice rooms, classrooms, spaces for workshops and community gatherings, music halls, and multipurpose rooms. The central atrium acts as an extension of the exterior public spaces and functions as a place for more flexible and spontaneous programs such as dance choreography, playing music, reading, and social gatherings.

URBAN INTEGRATION

Wider sidewalks along the Carabobo Avenue, the creation of a linear park along the Bermeja Creek, and eventually the Medellin River Park are key interventions to increase connectivity and integrate diverse city fragments. The Moravia Cultural Center is located on one of these hinges, at the crossroad of Carabobo avenue and Bermejala Creek, signaling a point of entry for the community. The center is a cultural institution that shares the architectural and iconic value of the Explora Park and the botanical garden, just a few hundred meters down the road. The Moravia Cultural Center, and the programs and activities it hosts, reveal the latent artistic aptitudes in communities. Cultural institutions and public space are crucial in further developing and enhancing the talent and dedication of youth.

1 Gilberto Arango, "Moravia, una historia de mejoramiento urbano," *Procesos Urbanos Informales* 2012, 1. https://issuu.com/sem_proceso_urbanos_informales/docs/03_j-moravia_una_historia_de_mejoramiento__urbano (accessed January 19, 2019).

2 *Moravia, la ruta de la esperanza*. Dir. Matías Boero Lutz. YouTube, Moravia UAB-Unesco, 2013. https://www.imdb.com/title/tt5097092/ (accessed January 22, 2019).

3 Arango (2012).

4 Alcaldía de Medellín, *Plan de desarrollo local Comuna 4 Aranjuez* (Medellín: Alcaldía de Medellín, 2015).

5 Alcaldía de Medellín. *La memoria cultural como dispositivo para la intervención social en Moravia* (Medellín: Artes y Letras, 2011), 52.

6 Arango (2012), 3.

7 Alcaldía de Medellín (2015).

8 "Memoria Territorial, extensión de Moravia a la ciudad," *Historia de Moravia*, May 2, 2007. http://g4moravia.blogspot.com/2007/05/historia-moravia.html (accessed January 19, 2019).

9 Alcaldía de Medellín (2015).

10 Alcaldía de Medellín (2011), 50.

MORAVIA CULTURAL CENTER
MEDELLIN, COLOMBIA

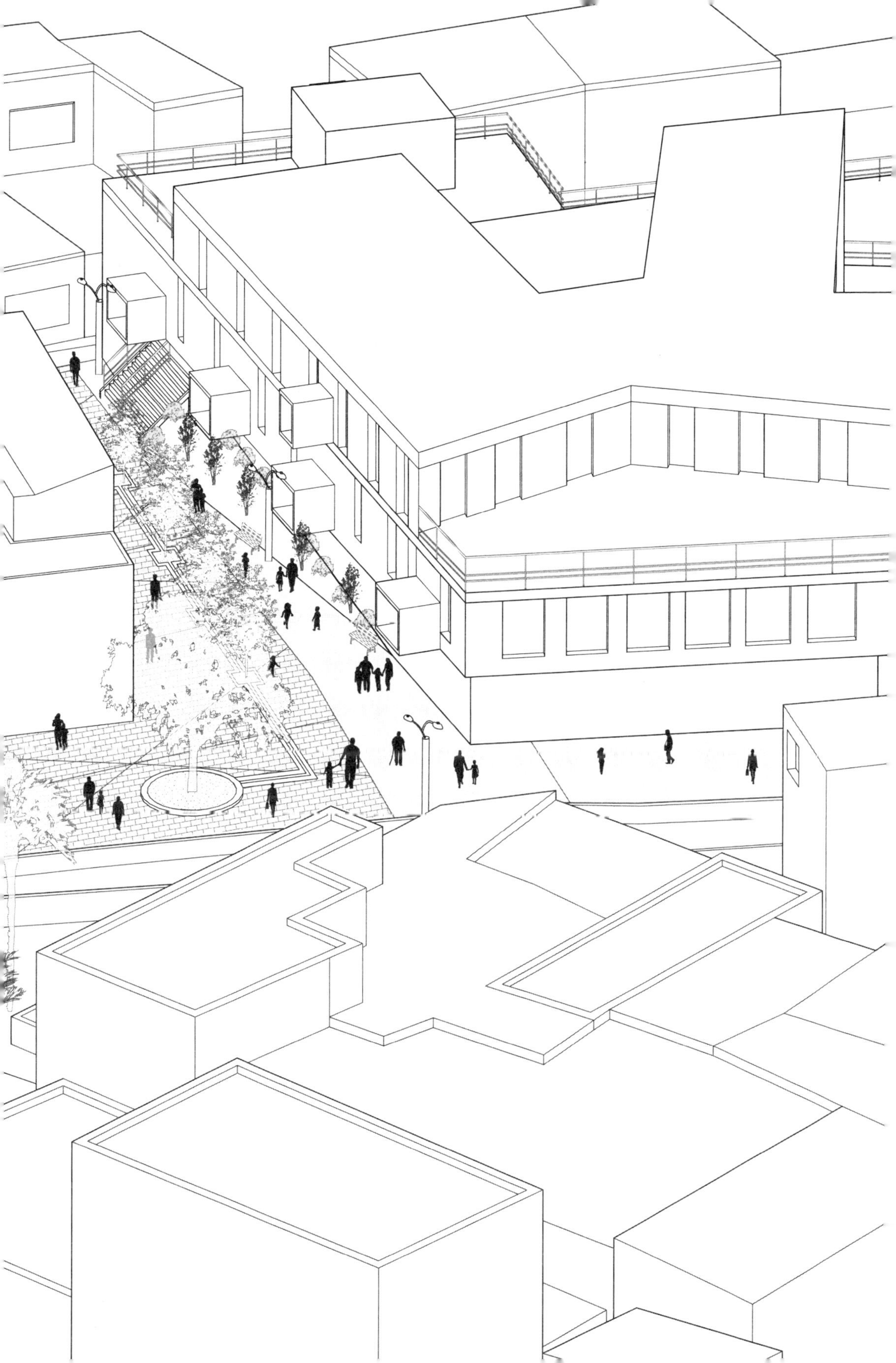

CANTAGALO HOTEL BUILDING ESPAÇO CRIANÇA ESPERANÇA

Cantagalo is located on a hill that rises between the beaches of Ipanema and Copacabana, in Rio de Janeiro. Toward the end of the ascent a very large building, once an unfinished, abandoned hotel, continues the path of the street into its interior hallway. The building has been appropriated by the community and hosts various programs including a library, a school, a cultural center, an auditorium, a nursery, a toy library for children, a restaurant and ball courts. Nearby, a police station known as the Police Pacification Unit (UPP), represents an institutional effort to help mitigate violence in the community.

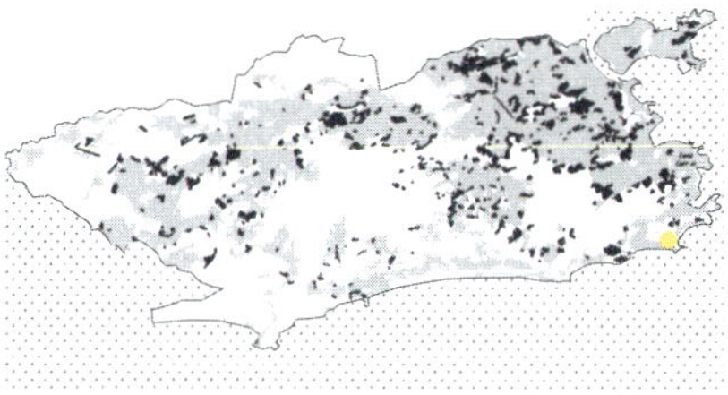

Location
Rio de Janeiro, Brazil

Project team:
Espaço Criança Esperança, Rede Globo, UNESCO, Governo do Rio de Janeiro, AfroReggae

Date 2001

Coordinates
22°58'49.61"S 43°11'53.30"O

Investment
30.2 million USD[1]

Public space area
18,004.76 m²

Urban density 356.97 hab / ha

Population benefited 13,626 hab

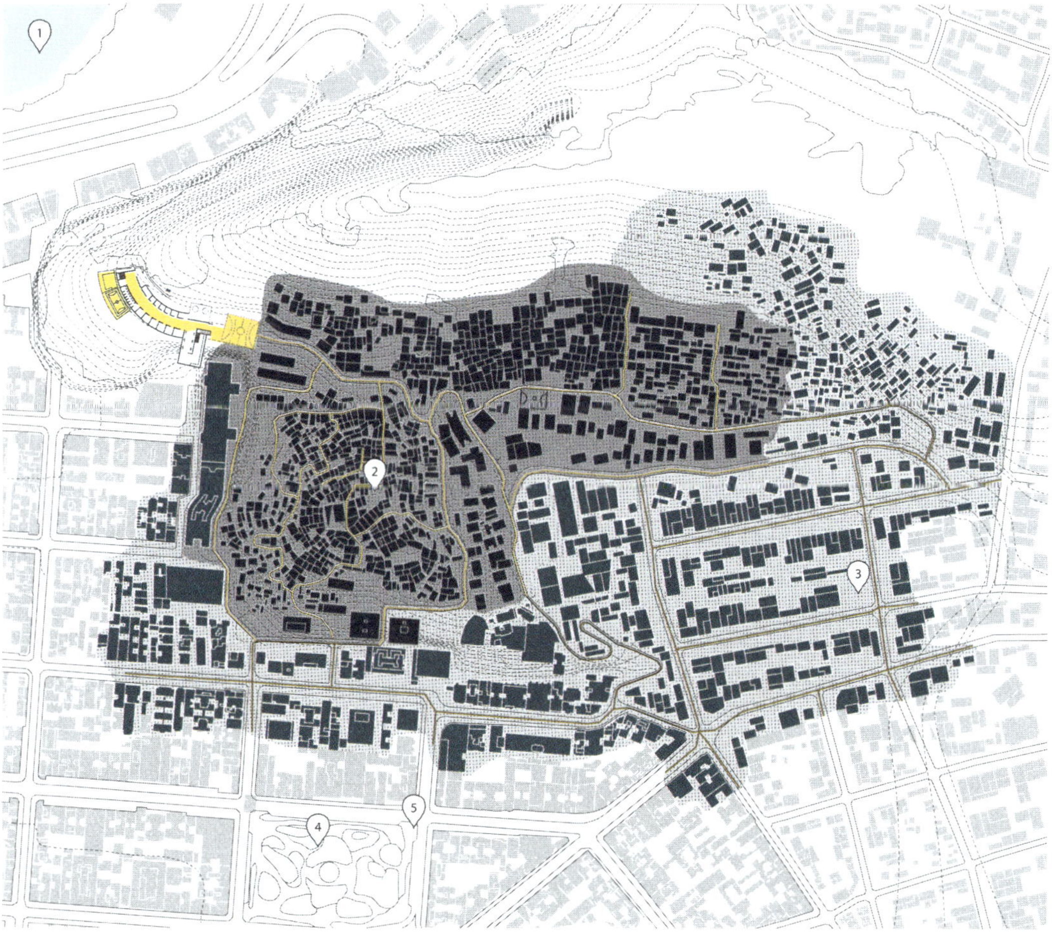

Distance traveled between 0m to 500m
Distance traveled between 500m to 800m
Public space
1,849 Structures
38.17 ha Area of influence 800m

Houses 500m
Houses 800m
Polygon 500m
Polygon 800m

1 Lago Rodrigo de Freitas
2 Museo de Favela
3 Parque Municipal Peter Pan
4 Plaza General Osorio
4 Estación de Metro General Osorio

Scale:
0 25 50 100 150

PUBLIC SPACE

The structure´s generous dimensions, allow it to host programs that have appeared organically, adapting to preexisting conditions. Hallways and exterior spaces function as public space, where the community gathers to chat, the way they would on an urban street. The project represents a unique experience of self-built public spaces.

HISTORY

The communities of Pavão-Pavãozinho and Cantagalo are the result of demographic growth and the displacement of people from the city center which was being "modernized" with new architectural and urban interventions during the 19th century.[2] Informal housing agglomerations were built by the displaced population on the hills near the city center, revealing a severe housing crisis in Rio.

At the top of the Cantagalo hill, a large concrete structure is known as the "Espaço Criança Esperança" (Child Hope Space). It is the most prominent institution in the building and people typically associate it with the entire structure. A mix of other programs, organized by local authorities, NGOs, foundations and the neighbors themselves, also reside in the building. The hotel was designed in the late sixties as the Hotel Panorama Palace. The project was not completed and the building was sold and transformed into a bar and panoramic restaurant for tourists. It was accessed using an elevator at the end of Nascimento Silva Street, in Ipanema. Toward the end of the seventies, as the *favelas* continued to expand in territory and population, the restaurant became less attractive for tourists. The property was then assigned to TV Rio and, in 1986, the government transformed the facilities into the João Goulart Integrated Center for Public Education (CIEP Centro Integrado de Educação Pública), which continues to serve children and youths in Cantagalo and Pavão-Pavãozinho. Between 1991 and 1994, the Community Center in Defense of Civic Culture (CCDC) also found its venue at the hotel building. The center's objective was to offer residents access to dentists, doctors, and legal assistance, as well as postal services identification cards and help with funerary expenses.[3] In 2000, the Police Group in Special Areas (GPAE Grupo de Policiamento em Áreas Especiais) also began operating in the building.[4] Espaço Criança Esperança enters the scene in 2001 with educational and cultural programs.[5] It is run by a foundation owned by the media group Rede Globo.

Other significant interventions include the Favela-Bairro program of the eighties, followed years later by the Growth Acceleration Program (PAC), in 2008, both focused on building infrastructure, providing basic services, and improving accessibility.

SOCIAL AND POLITICAL CONTEXT

In spite of its proximity to urban and tourist centers such as Ipanema and Copacabana, the inhabitants of Cantagalo and Pavão-Pavãozinho have been affected by social problems associated with poverty, violence, and drug trafficking.[6] Crime increased in the 1980s, creating a tense relationship between people living on the *morro*, the hill where the favelas are located, and those living on the *asphalt* bellow, which is how locals call the formally planned neighborhoods of Ipanema and Copacabana.

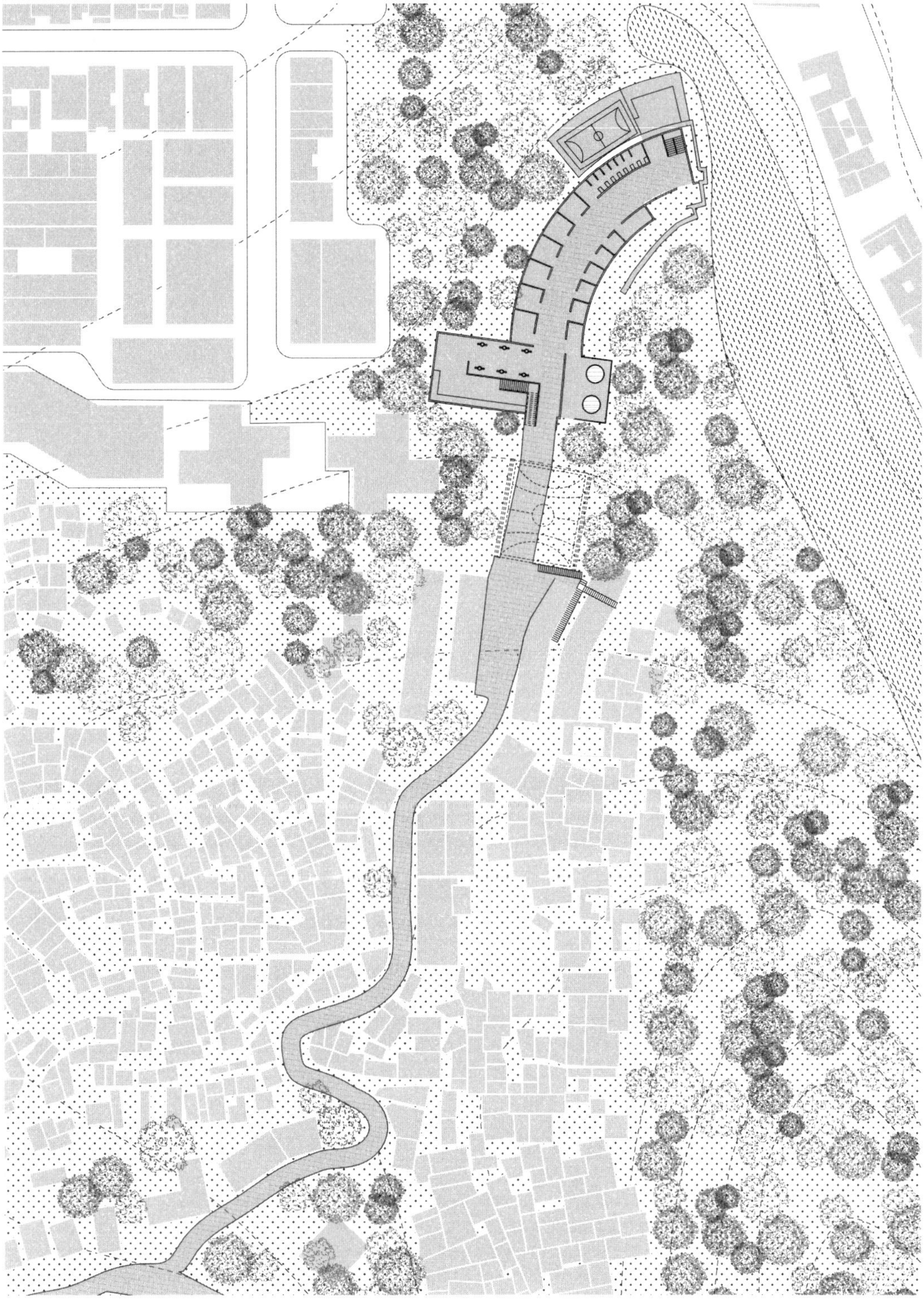

Scale:

0 10 25 50 100

Over the last two decades, the municipal government and NGOs have supported the community in their efforts to mitigate precarious economic and social conditions. The Growth Acceleration Program (PAC), implemented in 2008, created the conditions for physical urban renewal and the Police Pacification Units (UPP) displaced drug trafficking and criminal gangs, restoring security and tranquility among neighbors. The UPP program has been heavily criticized for its short-sighted approach to mitigate violence without considering the social circumstances that generate it and its lack of community participation.[7] Levels of crime decreased nonetheless, which opened the way for new programs. 70% of inhabitants between the ages of 4 and 24 participate in one or more of these programs.[8]

URBAN SITUATION

The communities of Pavão-Pavãozinho and Cantagalo are two *favelas* located in the center of the Rio de Janeiro Zona Sur, south of the Copacabana – Botafogo urban areas. They enjoy a privileged geographic location with views over the ocean and can be accessed from Ipanema and Copacabana. The PAC improvements created a system of sewage collection connected to formal networks and a new water cistern.[9] Mobility was improved with an elevator that leads to the General Osório metro station. New roadways were built to access the top of the *morro*, existing stairs and public spaces were improved, and new plazas were incorporated along pathways.[10] The Espaço Criança Esperança lies toward the top of the hill, at the end of the Criança Esperança Street.

PROJECT FUNDING

Rede Globo, a large media and communication group in Brazil founded in Rio de Janeiro, decided to create its first Espaço Criança Esperança experience in Cantagalo, in 2001. UNESCO "Viva Rio" is the organization that manages Rede Globo´s education and culture programs. The City of Rio de Janeiro also made a significant contribution to the project by giving Foundation Criança Esperança ownership rights over the building and by financing the construction of a library, a school, a basketball court and an auditorium. Over the course of the program´s first five years, TV Globo broadcasted Espaço Criança Esperança ´s activities on television. A diverse group of national and international athletes, intellectuals, and artists became interested in the program and contributed sizable donations.[11] Other organizations are financed through independent sources. For example, AfroReggae, which has one of its locations in the building (see the AfroReggae project), finances its activities through private companies and foundations. Also, 30% of their costs are covered with proceeds from their own programs.

RELATED PROGRAMS

The Favela-Bairro program began in 1993; it was the first to address urban deficiencies in Rio de Janeiro´s spontaneous settlements. It focused on building the infrastructure and public services that could transform *favelas* into formal neighborhoods by bringing order to urban space and improving the relationship of inhabitants with their surroundings.[12] Rio´s earliest UPPs were also conceived as part of the Favela-Bairro program. Later in 2007, the Growth Accelerator Program (PAC) developed by the federal government, intervened in Cantagalo and Pavão-Pavãozinho with improvements to the sewage collection network, access to potable water, rainwater drainage, street pavement, walkways and stairs.[13]

ACTIVITIES

The fact that a sizable structure was left unfinished and available to organically evolve into an agglomerate of multiple programs and institutions has been an important benefit to Cantagalo´s inhabitants. The building creates opportunities for young people and children to engage in sports, arts, culture, play, and education. The center´s educational programs include English courses, capacity building workshops for youths and support for children with homework assignments. Culture and sports programs are sponsored by the City of Rio de Janeiro. Facilities include a basketball court, an area for gymnastics, and the former hotel´s pool, used for swimming lessons and water aerobics. AfroReggae´s activities are focused on theatre, dance, photography, music, and performances.[14] There is also a computer center open to the entire community as well as a library with 38.000 donated books.

URBAN INTEGRATION

The concentration of so many activities within a single structure has generated a natural confluence of people that take advantage of the available open spaces within and around the building. Internal areas along corridors and passageways witness social dynamics typical of active public space. The community´s enthusiasm for the building´s institutions and their degree of participation in the activities they offer has created a vibrant atmosphere of social exchanges. As the number of activities increased and levels of personal security improved, social integration between the community and visitors has also been reinforced. This exchange helps dissolve social and territorial differences between the *favela* and the formal areas of Rio de Janeiro.

1 Total investment amount of the Growth Acceleration Program (PAC) in Cantagalo - Pavão-Pavãozinho.

2 Izaga (2014), 89.

3 "Pavão-Pavãozinho, una historia que comienza en la década de 1930." *O Globo* June 19, 2017. https://oglobo.globo.com/rio/pavao-pavaozinho-uma-historia-que-comeca-na-decada-de-1930-21532552 (accessed April 23, 2018).

4 Ibid.

5 M. Cardoso, *Como morre um projeto de policiamento comunitário: O caso do Cantagalo e do Pavão-Pavãozinho* (Brasilia: Universidade de Brasília, 2010).

6 TV Globo and UNESCO, "Criança Esperança 25 anos criando oportunidades," *Rede Globo* 2011. http://redeglobo.globo.com/criancaesperanca/noticia/2011/06/baixe-o-livro-crianca-esperanca-25-anos-criando-oportunidades.html (accessed January 19, 2019).

7 Ava Rose Hoffman. "Knowledge to Create Solutions in Complexo do Alemão: Instituto Raízes em Movimento,"*Rio On Watch* 2016.

8 TV Globo and UNESCO (2011).

9 Izaga, 91.

10 Izaga, 103.

11 Rede Globo, UNESCO. *Criança Esperança, mobilizando pessoas, transformando vidas* (Brasilia: UNESCO, 2009), 23.

12 Andreatta, 3.

13 Izaga, 96-97.

14 Q.G. Freire, "Espaço Criança Esperança no Cantagalo," *Diario do Rio* August 12, 2011. https://diariodorio.com/espaco-crianca-esperanca-no-cantagalo/ (accessed May 30, 2018).

CANTAGALO HOTEL BUILDING ESPAÇO CRIANÇA ESPERANÇA
RIO DE JANEIRO, BRAZIL

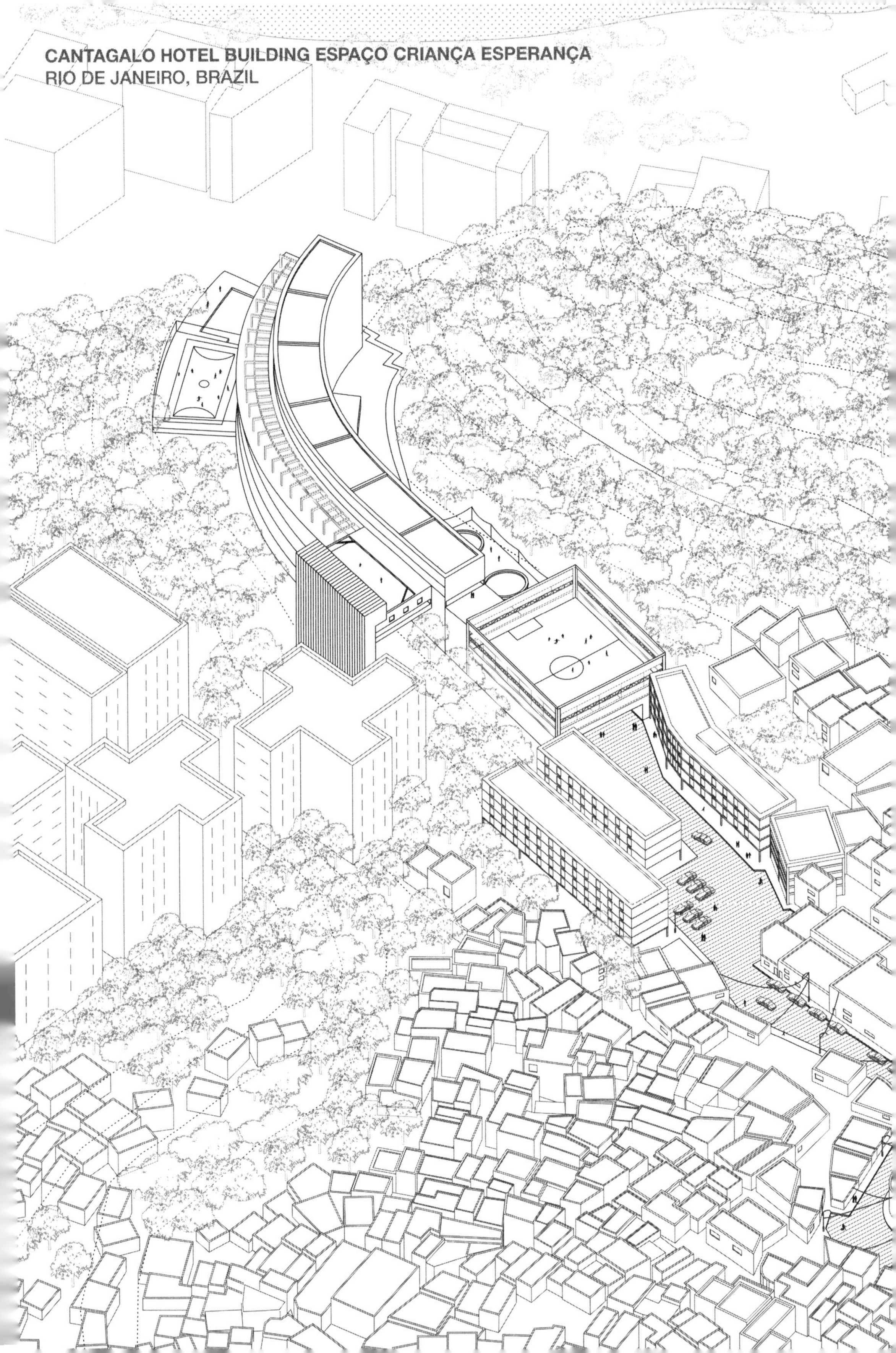

PUBLIC SPACE NETWORK IN VILLA TRANQUILA, VICENTE LÓPEZ PLAZA

Villa Tranquila is a spontaneous settlement in the municipality of Avellaneda and is part of the greater Buenos Aires metropolitan area. Migration during the country´s period of industrial development did not have a corresponding answer in terms of housing. Once employed, workers built their homes in undeveloped areas near the factories. Lack of planning, as the settlements formed, left them without provisions for public space. The Playspace initiative helped the community identify opportunities to insert public spaces through a participatory process. Urban analyses acknowledged the importance of the Estévez Street as a central corridor and a prominent public space. The projected interventions recognized the social dynamics associated with this street and located complementary public spaces for children along its length.

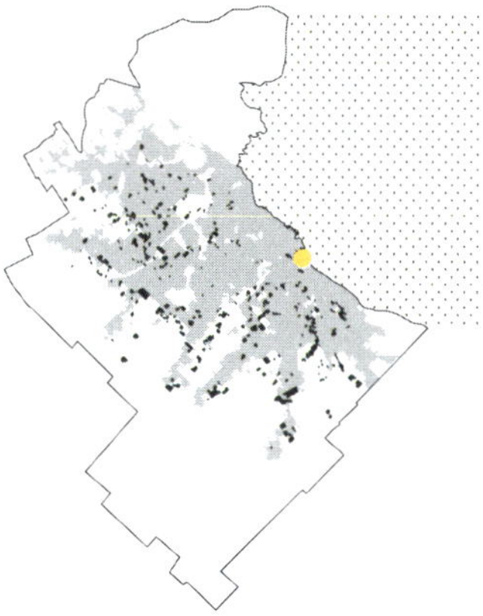

Location
Villa Tranquila, Partido de Avellaneda, Buenos Aires, Argentina

Project team:
Architects Flavio Jánches y Max Rohm, Social workers of Avellaneda Municipality, PlaySpace Foundation, students of the Buenos Aires University Faculty of Architecture, Design and Urbanism, Harvard University Graduate School of Design, Amsterdam Architecture Institute

Date 2009

Coordinates
34°39'13.24"S 58°21'36.13"O

Investment 64,000 USD

Public space area 788.87 m²

Urban density 62.30 hab / ha

Population benefited 7,727 hab

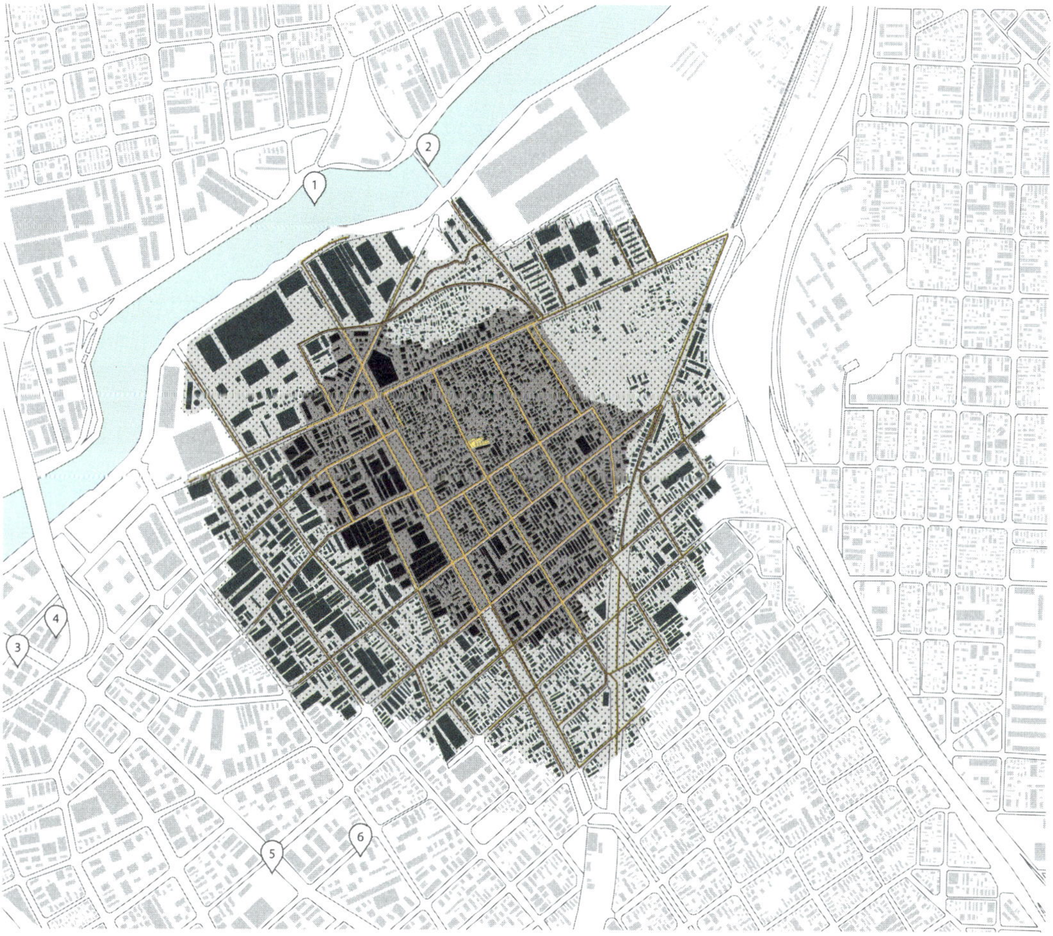

Distance traveled between 0m to 500m
Distance traveled between 500m to 800m
Public space
3,079 Structures
124.03 ha Area of influence 800m

Houses 500m
Houses 800m
Polygon 500m
Polygon 800m

1 Río Matanza
2 Puente Ferroviario Barranca Peña
3 Teatro General Roca
4 Teatro Colonial
5 Plaza Alzina
6 Teatro Municipal Roma

Scale:
0 50 100 200 400

PUBLIC SPACE

The Plaza Vicente López was built as part of a larger network of public spaces that would progressively weave the settlement´s periphery and center, thus integrating the community both internally and in relationship to other urban areas.

HISTORY

The spontaneous settlements of Buenos Aires or "misery villas" (villas miseria), as they are called in Argentina, developed together with the country´s industrialization processes. They were built by immigrants from the countryside and neighboring countries, who moved to the city looking for better employment opportunities in the industrial sector. The city did not have an adequate strategy to meet the rising demand for housing, and so between 1950 and 1970, the number of spontaneous settlements increased and so did their population density.[1] Then, in the mid-seventies, the military dictatorship implemented an eradication program that drastically reduced the population living in spontaneous settlements.[2] During the 1990s, neoliberal economic policies intensified social and urban differences in Buenos Aires. Industrial areas were moved out of the city, eliminating an important source of income for many families that worked there.[3] In time, spontaneous settlements grew and surpassed the formally planned areas of Buenos Aires in terms of size and population. Between 2001 and 2003, the municipality´s public policies began efforts to mitigate the urban problems of these territories through physical and social interventions.

Residents were able to attain some basic services through informal connections, potable water, drainage, sewer systems, and electricity remained problematic. It was not until 2005 that the federal government began financing rehabilitation projects in spontaneous settlements, through the Ministry of Federal Planning, Public Investment and the Services Neighborhood Improvement Program.[4] Substitution housing, investments in public spaces, flood mitigation, basic services and urban integration were addressed by this program.

SOCIAL AND POLITICAL CONTEXT

Villa Tranquila and other similar settlements in the Avellaneda district depended on the industrial economy of the 20th century. Most inhabitants were unskilled labor workers that earned small wages from factory jobs. When Buenos Aires´ industrial sector moved toward the new periphery, in the 1990's, buildings were left in disuse and most of the people living in spontaneous settlements found themselves without work.

Spontaneous settlement inhabitants are frequently discriminated. The "villeros," as they are known, are deemed violent, delinquent, poor and marginal by the rest of the city. The people of Buenos Aires consider the "poor" to be different from the "villero," the latter representing society´s lowest social rank.[5] The project developed through Playspace Foundation was conceived together with the community to question their relationship with neighboring areas. Physical transformations were designed to mitigate the negative and marginal conceptions typically associated with spontaneous settlements.

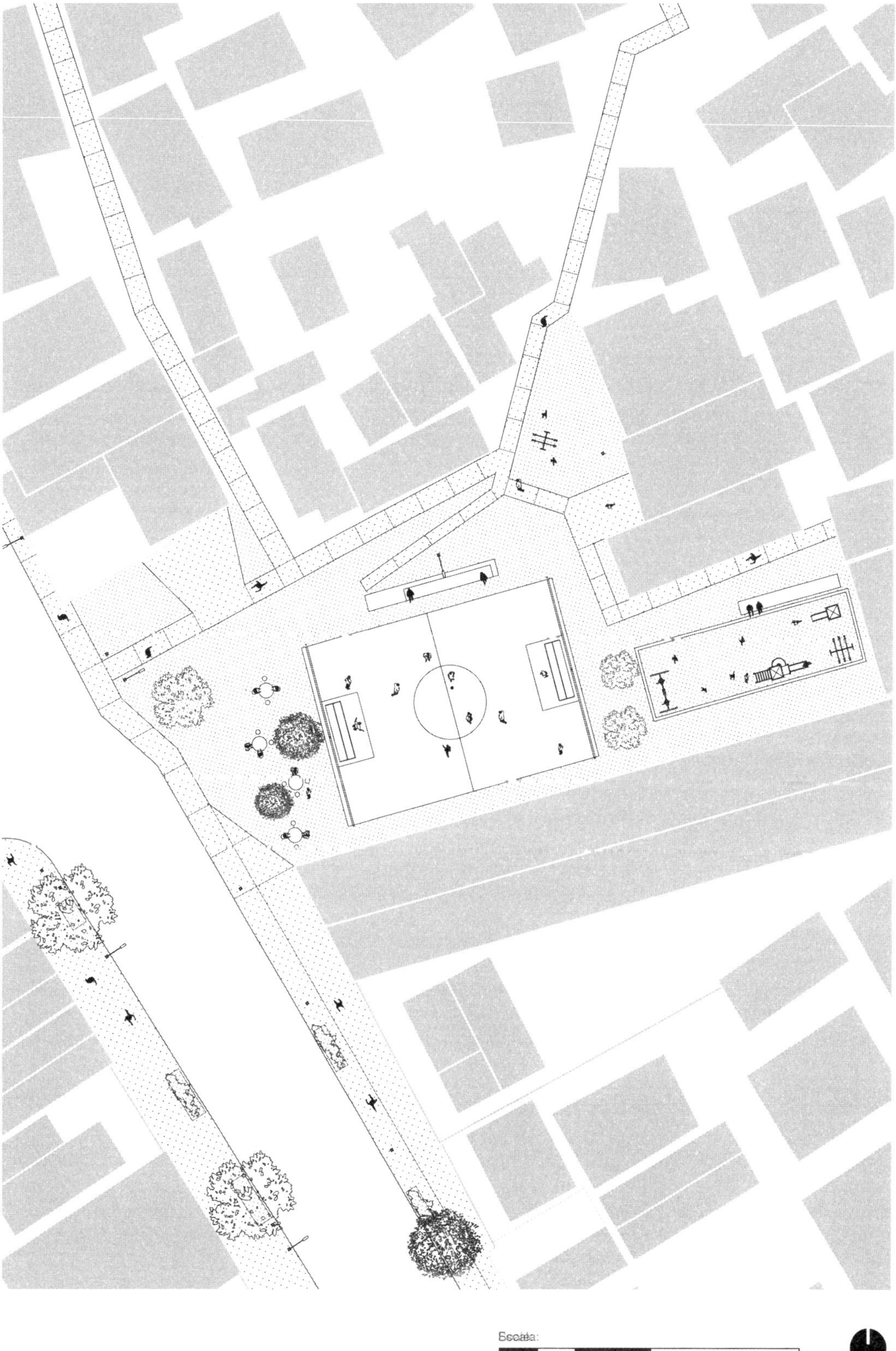
Escala:
0
2.5
5
10
20

ENVIRONMENTAL SITUATION

Villa Tranquila is a self-built settlement where inhabitants are exposed to flooding. Located near the southern margin of the Riachuelos River, the ground level is below the river water level, making Villa Tranquila very susceptible to floods. During periods of torrential rain, the topographical difference does not allow water runoff to enter the river´s course, inundating Villa Tranquila.[6]

URBAN SITUATION

Villa Tranquila is located in the Avellaneda district, Dock Sud, west of the Riachuelos River. It is known as one of the most dangerous and poor spontaneous settlements in greater Buenos Aires. For many years, the district´s main vocation was industrial, where the Riachuelos River provided easy transportation for materials all the way to the Río de la Plata. Many localities in Avellaneda are named after factories or important industrial parks that were located in this sector. Villa Tranquila began as a self-built, illegal settlement where more than half of its inhabitants were employed in nearby factories. Once situated on the outskirts of the city, later urban growth encircled these industrial sites. Settlers in the community were mostly unskilled workers that relied on the district´s industrial jobs. Economic changes motivated factories to move their headquarters to the new urban perimeter. Soon, settlements such as Villa Tranquila found themselves with high levels of unemployment, surrounded by abandoned structures, and isolated from the rest of the municipality.

As a way to begin creating opportunities to connect the community with the rest of the city, architects Flavio Jánches and Max Rohm, together with the City of Avellaneda and the PlaySpace Foundation, coordinated a project to recover and build a network of public spaces in Villa Tranquila.[7]

PROJECT FUNDING

PlaySpace Foundation is a non-for-profit organization founded by Argentine and Dutch professionals to build play spaces for children in disadvantaged communities. The Villa Tranquila project was the Foundation´s first initiative and began with resident workshops. Inhabitants were invited to become involved in the recovery, design and construction of a public space. The project included the participation of students from the Faculty of Architecture of the University of Buenos Aires, Harvard University and the Academy of Architecture of Amsterdam, who designed the urban proposal and intervention strategies.[8] Plans for the public space project were developed with the support of the Municipality of Avellaneda and became part of the city´ spontaneous settlement rehabilitation program.[9]

RELATED PROGRAMS

The community participated in the Vicente López plaza's recovery process. They helped clear the chosen space and build some of the plaza´s elements; they also contributed with the donation of an existing structure adjacent to the plaza, which was converted into a small reading room for children.[10] The community continued to lead cleaning initiatives for the plaza´s upkeep, while construction was organized through the human resources of PlaySpace Foundation and the Municipality.

ACTIVITIES

After the new public space was completed, the community helped build benches and paint elements of the square. One of the neighbors donated a space for a reading room in which children could play and learn. Months after the square´s inauguration, interviews with neighbors were conducted to gather their opinions. 90% of the people interviewed believed that the Vicente López Plaza encourages community engagement, social cohesion, play and informal encounters.[11]

URBAN INTEGRATION

The Vicente López Plaza was built as a pilot project. The main concern was to create a space for meeting, conversation, and play in an accessible location. The community workshops, developed by the universities, the PlaySpace Foundation, the municipality and the neighbors of Villa Tranquila, were an important component of the overall methodology that laid the ground for a successful project. Plaza Vicente López became the preferred meeting point for both the immediate neighbors and the rest of Villa Tranquila's inhabitants.

1 "Ciudades y localidades del partido Avellaneda," *La Ciudad: El Diario de Avelllaneda* 2012. http://laciudadavellaneda. blogspot.com/2010/02/9999999.html (accessed January 19, 2019).

2 M. Karlsson, "Informal settlements: the world's invisible communities," *Uppsala: SLU, Dept. of Urban and Rural Development* first cycle, G2E., 2012.

3 Flavio Jánches, *Public Space in the fragmented city* (Buenos Aires: Nobuko, 2012), 38-39

4 "Villas in Argentina: an overview," *Vamos Spanish Academy*, 2017. https://vamospanish.com/villas-buenos-aires-argentina/ (accessed January 10, 2019).

5 Ibid., 63.

6 "Ciudades y localidades del partido Avellaneda," *La Ciudad: El Diario de Avelllaneda*, 2012. http://laciudadavellaneda.blogspot.com/2010/02/9999999.html (accessed January 10, 2019).

7 Flavio Jánchez and Máximo Rohm, *Interrelaciones Urbanas* (Buenos Aires: Piedra, Papel & Tijera, 2012).

8 Ibid., 23.

9 Ibid.

10 Jánchez (2012), 42.

11 Ibid., 95.

PUBLIC SPACE NETWORK IN VILLA TRANQUILA, VICENTE LÓPEZ PLAZA
BUENOS AIRES, ARGENTINA

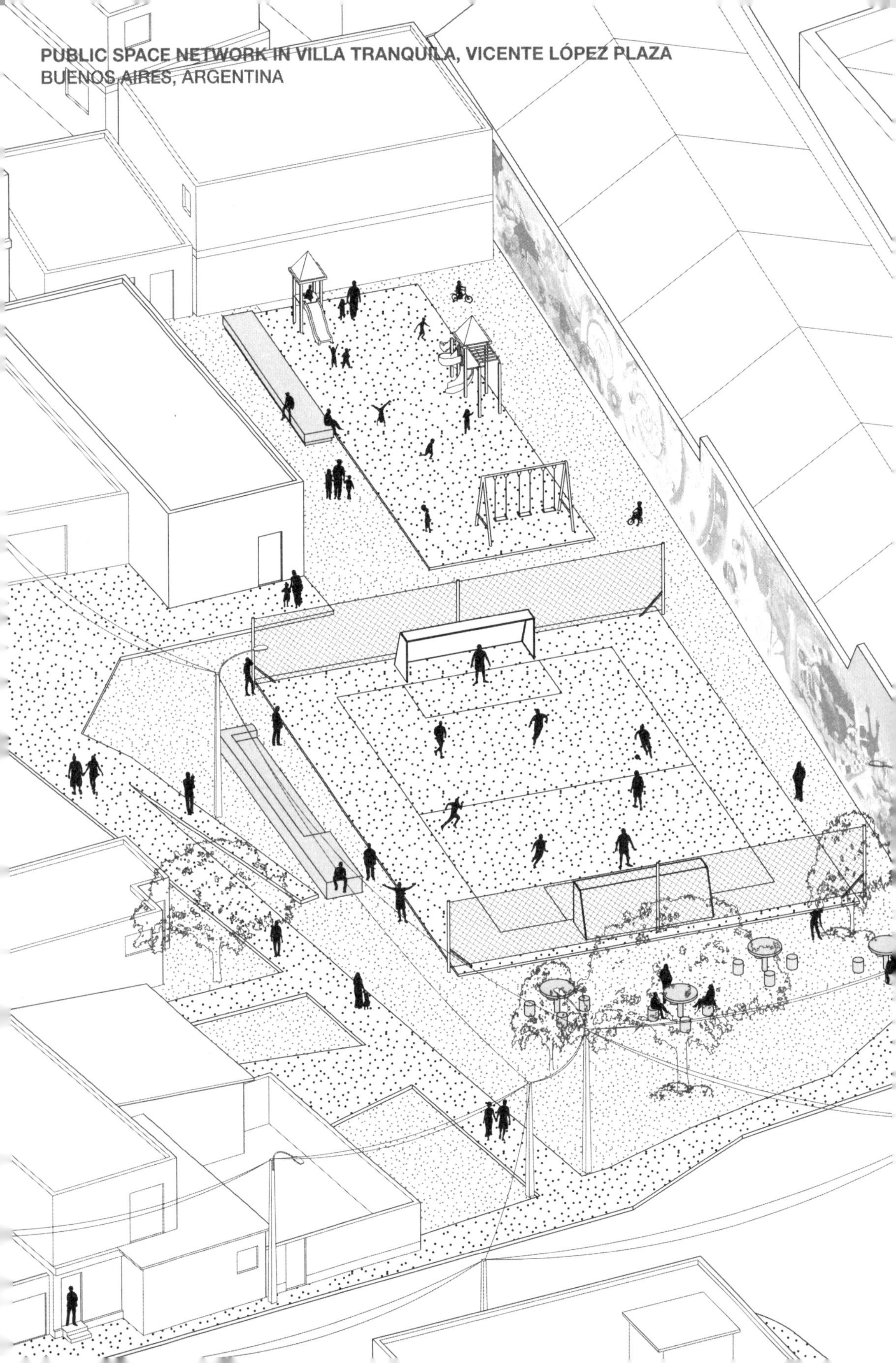

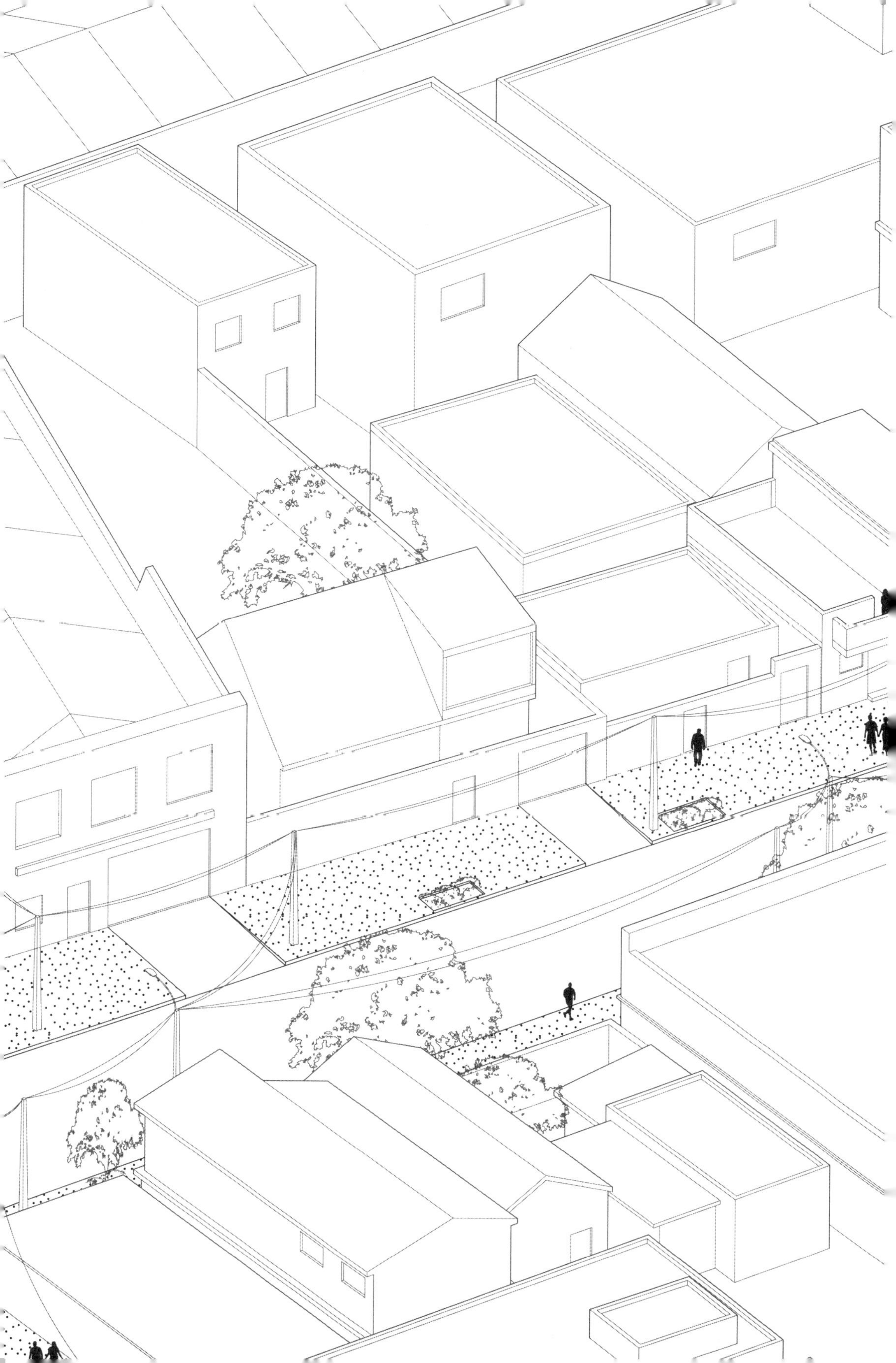

CASA KOLACHO

Casa Kolacho, formerly known as Pacharte, is a network of artists in the Comuna 13 of Medellín. It includes hip-hop musicians, graffiti artists, DJs, and performers who disseminate a common message against violence through urban art and music, using social media, the radio and cultural festivals. Perro, a graffiti artist, has painted several murals in the community including the wall of a playground named Sergio Pérez Cerna, after a child who died in cross fire between youth gangs. Casa Kolacho organizes an annual cultural event called "Revolution Without Weapons" (Revolución Sin Muertos) that calls on the neighborhood´s youth to join the artistic movement and distance themselves from violence.

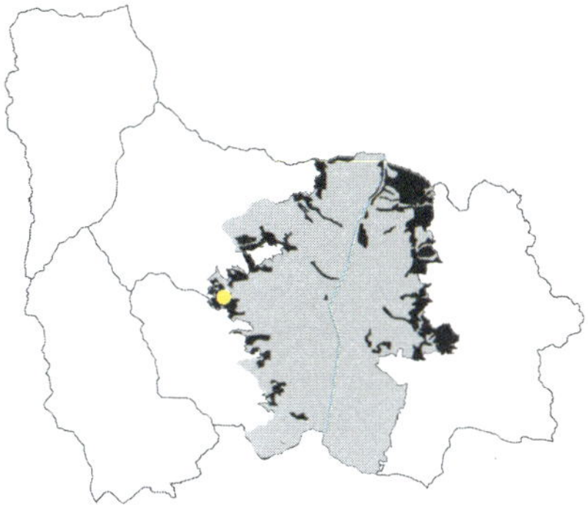

Location
Barrio Las Independencias, Comuna 13 San Javier, Medellin Colombia

Project team:
Hip Hop C15
and Producciones Camaleón

Date 2009

Coordinates
6°15'02.88"N 75°37'15.96"O

Investment 25,000 USD1

Public space area 3,600 m²

Urban density 199 hab / ha

Population benefited 7,713 hab

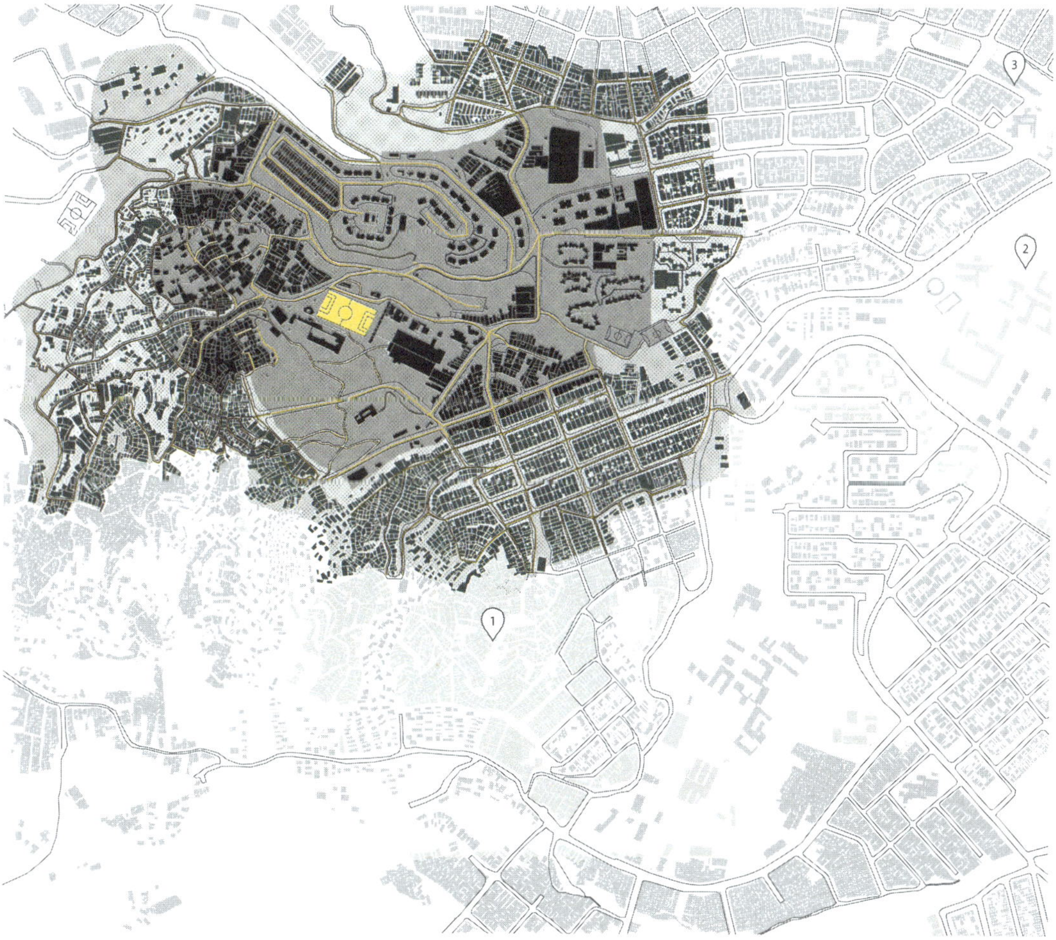

Distance traveled between 0m to 500m
Distance traveled between 500m to 800m
Public space
5,246 Structures
38.76 ha Area of influence 800m

Houses 500m
Houses 800m
Polygon 500m
Polygon 800m

(1) Escaleras Eléctricas Comuna 13
(2) Parque Biblioteca San Javier
(3) Estación de metro San Javier

Scale:
0 25 50 100 150

PUBLIC SPACE

Public space is interpreted by the Comuna 13 artists as an opportune place to register the neighborhood´s history during the times of the Medellin Cartel. Casa Kolacho artists create public space stages to reach the community´s youth and raise awareness regarding everyone´s human right to live peacefully and without violence.

HISTORY

Comuna 13 San Javier, where Casa Kolacho is located, is a spontaneous settlement on the slopes of Medellín, populated by migrants that guerilla violence forced out of the countryside.[2] Rapid population growth resulted in the emergence of spontaneous urban settlements along the slopes of the Aburrá Valley. They consist of self-constructed homes built on illegally sold plots of land that tend to concentrate poverty. Inadequate access to basic services, inequality and marginalization were rampant. The federal government and the municipality remained aloof for many years and did not address these unfolding urban, social and health problems.

As a result of local government´s disengagement, illegal armed groups, drug cartels and organized crime gangs took control of the city´s spontaneous settlements.[3] These territories became zones of war-like conflict between criminal bands, making conditions for institutional presence challenging. Since the seventies, spontaneous settlements were known for hosting the most wanted drug cartels in Colombia and the world.[4] The population was kidnapped by violence. The most affected were young men, obliged to join criminal gangs for lack of other opportunities and peer pressure. Many lost their lives in crossfires; many others were killed or received life threats. The streets, sidewalks and stairways were occupied by armed criminals that subjected families to live by the curfews they imposed. Groups of young artists in the Comuna 13 resorted to graffiti, dance and urban music to counteract the violent reality of their surroundings, and use urban cultural expressions as a way to mitigate both the damage of violence and the federal governments' interventions.

SOCIAL AND POLITICAL CONTEXT

Comuna 13 - San Javier went from being known as the most dangerous sector of Medellín to a destination for urban cultural expressions. In the 1980s, armed groups involved in drug trafficking were in control of the neighborhood´s streets.[5] Later, clashes between gangs created internal divisions within the settlement that restricted the mobility of neighbors. As illegal groups fought for control of the territory, families were constantly affected by violence and death. Children who grew up in this context witnessed assassinations and became used to shotgun sounds and curfews. Many youths joined the gangs and lost their lives, as did innocent people caught in cross fires. In 2002, the Colombian government conducted a military procedure, known as the Orion Operation, to eradicate the mafias settled in the spontaneous settlements of Medellín.[6] It resulted in the assassination and disappearance of numerous community members, a fact that remains embedded in the collective memory of Comuna 13 residents.

Artists in the community were also subjected to violence. Several rap leaders were killed and many others threatened with death by criminal bands. As a manifestation of solidarity and resistance,

Scale:
0 5 10 25 50 100

Casa Kolacho organized activities to promote peace and the end of violence against innocent people. It evolved from earlier youth groups such as Operation Hip Hop Elite, that hosted a musical festival in September 2002, to convey a message to authorities that the Comuna 13 is not just about violence.[7] Their motto was "in the 13th violence does not beat us" (en la trece la violencia no nos vence). In spite of the initiative, in October of that same year renewed state sponsored military interventions took place.

The military "pacification" process reduced violence in the community but also left scars of death and pain. The cultural youth groups played a fundamental role in the social reconstruction of the community. Their work has managed to keep children involved in artistic activities, away from violence and aware that they have a future that does not include crime.[8] Unfortunately, even after the occupation of Comuna 13 by the military forces, rappers and other artists continue to receive death threats from violent groups, albeit on a smaller scale. Casa Kolacho, nonetheless, maintains its motto that cultural expression is a weapon against violence, music is a form of activism and art is a tribute to memory.[9]

URBAN SITUATION

The activities organized by Casa Kolacho and other groups have allowed young artists and the community to intervene in spaces of the Comuna 13 with graffiti, performances, and music concerts. The nature of these activities and the public spaces intervened with art have been included in city tours known as "graffititours" that feature the murals of the El Salado soccer field and neighborhood sidewalks. The intention behind these artistic expressions is to pay homage to the deceased, emphasize a message of peace, and ensure that history is not forgotten nor repeated.

PROJECT FUNDING

Casa Kolacho was founded in honor of a young rap leader murdered in the Comuna 13 in 2009 named Héctor Pacheco, Kolacho was his nickname. The group is the result of many initiatives by young people in the community dedicated to urban art. The organization does not receive funds from municipal or national institutions, but is rather supported through direct donations from sponsors, income generated by the "graffitour," artistic presentations, brand representation, POP material, CDs, posters and paintings sold at the Casa Kolacho store.[10]

RELATED PROGRAMS

Casa Kolacho promotes groups dedicated to urban music and graffiti art. It is based on the premise that culture can fight violence by allowing artistic expressions to serve as a way of remembering and telling the history of the Comuna 13, while promoting peace, and creating an alternative outlet for young people to express themselves. The group also organizes concerts, musical improvisations, mural painting, and meetings that are part of Medellin´s cultural calendar. Today, one of the ways outside guests can get to know the Comuna 13 is through guided tours hosted by members of Casa Kolacho. They visit murals that recall the abuses of violence.

Casa Kolacho is located in the lower part of Comuna 13 San Javier, on the corner of 43th Street and Carrrera 97. A dance and music school, a recording studio available to musical artists, a space intended for concerts, and the hip-hop shop are housed at the Casa Kolacho headquarters.[11] Parcharte, which was absorbed by Casa Kolacho, organized the annual event "Revolution Without Deaths" in the El Salado neighborhood, which consisted of a concert series by local musicians and others from the rest of the city that disseminated a message of peace.

INTEGRATION

The concerts, tours, improvisations, and presentations staged by Casa Kolacho are directed both to the community of San Javier and the entire city of Medellin. Community spaces associated with these activities are visited by neighbors and visitors alike. Previously, San Javier was only known for violence. Now, it is also known for its cultural expressions thanks to the work of organizations such as Casa Kolacho and the municipality, which have allowed Comuna 13 to enter the mental map of Medellin citizens.

The layers of history embedded in public spaces through artistic expressions have become part of the community´s identity. In this case, public space goes beyond serving as a place for gathering; it becomes a place to record the cultural movements and events that marked the neighborhood´s history and represent an important step toward social reconciliation and ultimately toward urban integration.

1 One of the first donations to the group came from the Beyonce Foundation.

2 Alcaldía de Medellín (2012).

3 Sergio Acosta Tobón, "Una arqueología de la violencia en Medellín: de la 'la ambición rompe el saco' a 'la ocasión hace al ladrón'," *Revista Electrónica de Psicología Social Poiésis* January, 2012, 1-2.

4 Ibid.

5 Ibid.

6 "Operación Orión: 10 años de impunidad," *Verdad Abierta* 2012. http://www.verdadabierta.com/victimas-seccion/desaparecidos/4264-operacion-orion-la-verdad-diez-anos-despues (accessed January 19, 2019).

7 Catalina González, "El rapero de la Comuna 13 que le quita niños a la guerra," *El Espectador* February 12, 2015. https://www.elespectador.com/noticias/el-rapero-de-comuna-13-le-quita-ninos-guerra-articulo-543595 (accessed January 19. 2019).

8 Luisa Saldarriaga, María Camila Muñoz, Jenny Alejandra Echavarría, Ana María Londoño and Alejandro Arango, "El arte está amenazado en la Comuna 13," *De la urbe. Periodismo universitario para la ciudad* November 19, 2012. http://delaurbe.udea.edu.co/2012/11/09/el-arte-esta-amenazado-en-la-comuna-13/ (accessed January 19, 2019).

9 Lola Hierro, "Casa Kolacho: La violencia se cura con hip hop," *El País* June 30, 2016. https://elpais.com/elpais/2016/06/23/planeta_futuro/1466698760_170228.html. (accessed January 19, 2019).

10 Ibid.

11 Diego Londoño, "Casa Kolacho, donde el hip hop cobra vida," *Radionica* July 8, 2015. https://www.radionica.rocks/noticias/casa-kolacho-donde-el-hip-hop-toma-vida (accessed January 16, 2019).

CASA KOLACHO
MEDELLIN, COLOMBIA

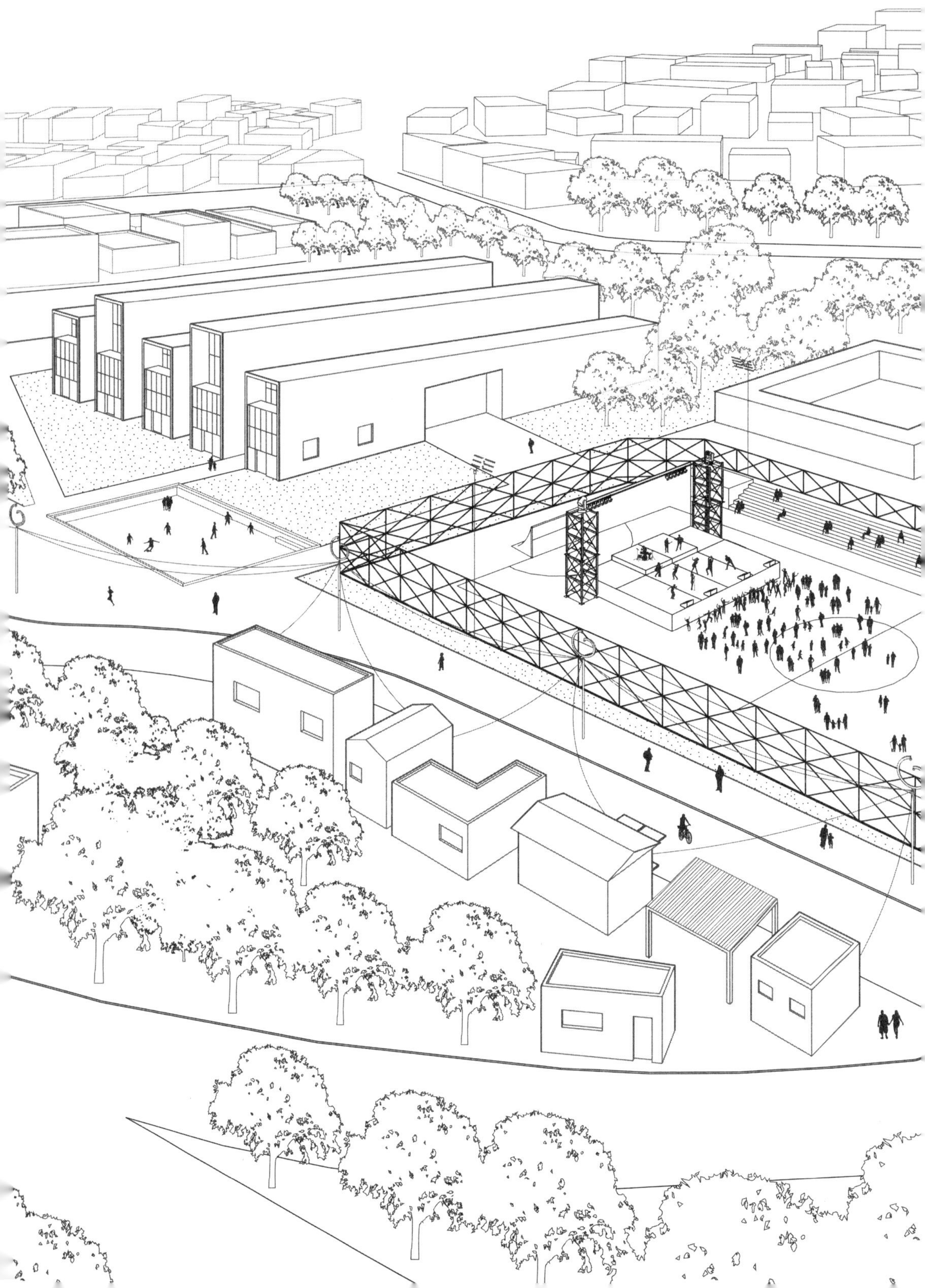

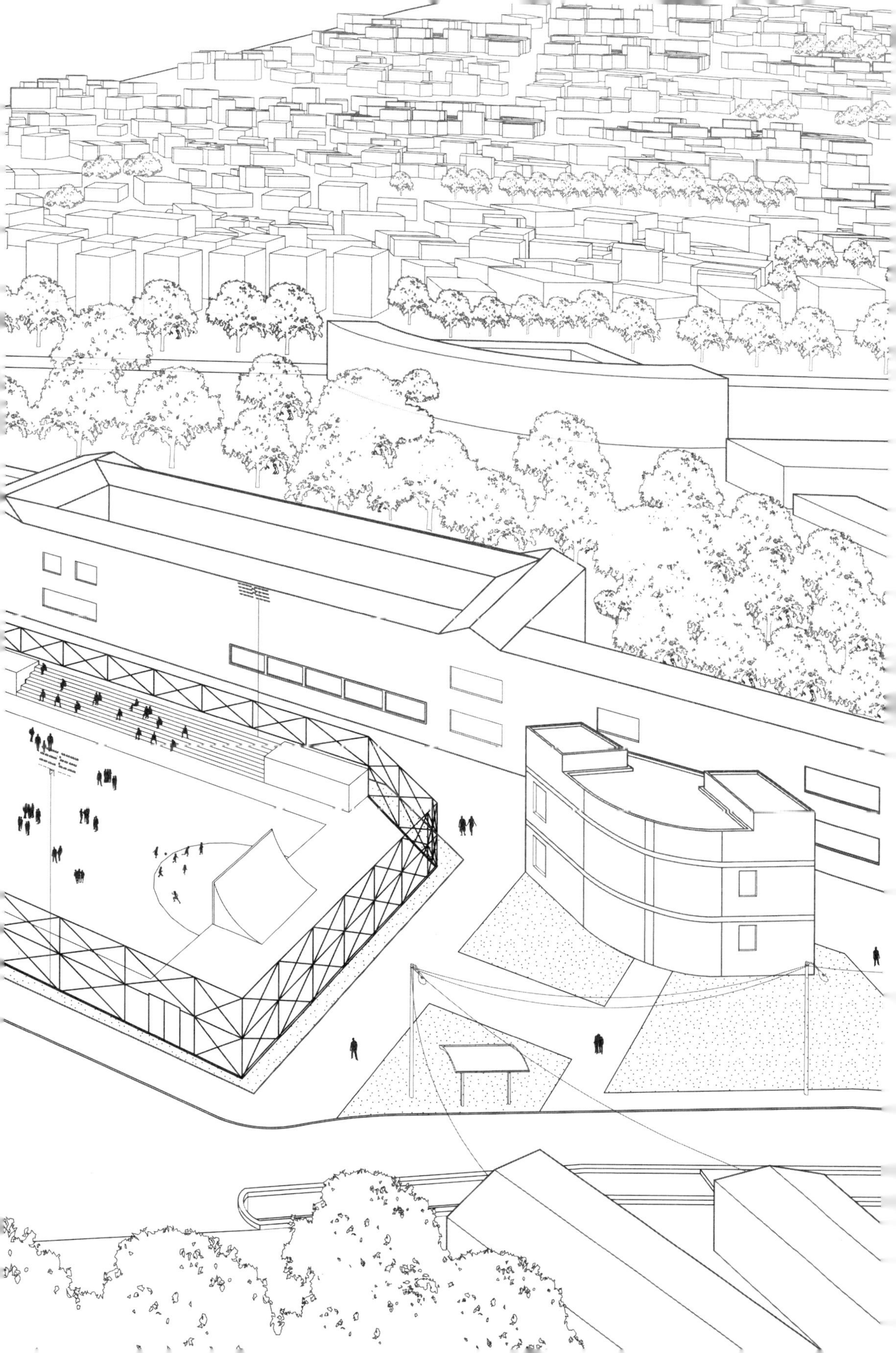

AFROREGGAE

AfroReggae is a cultural initiative in Rio de Janeiro and a privately sponsored NGO. It has several locations, the first was founded toward the northern section of the city, in Vigário Geral. The institution creates opportunities for children and youths to enjoy cultural activities, including dance, music and art, using state-of-the-art technologies in a high-quality facility, as a way of cultivating their interest in art and keeping them away from violence.

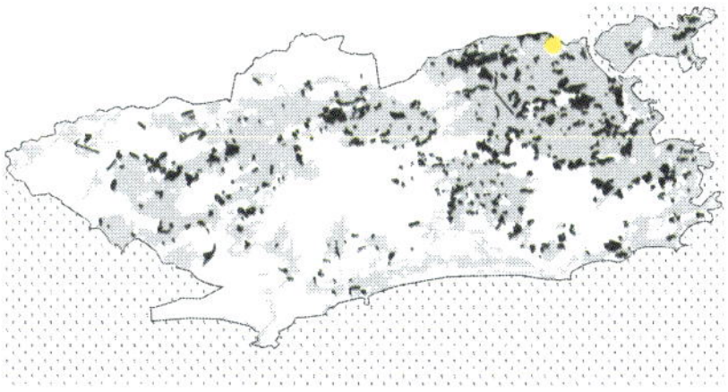

Location
Vigaário Geral, Rio de Janeiro

Project team:
Anderson Sa, José Junior and Altair Martins

Date
1992

Coordinates
22°48'15.47"S 43°19'06.99"O

Investment:
120,000 USD[1]

Public space area
2,062,77 m^2

Urban density
123.53 hab / ha

Population benefited
8,772 hab

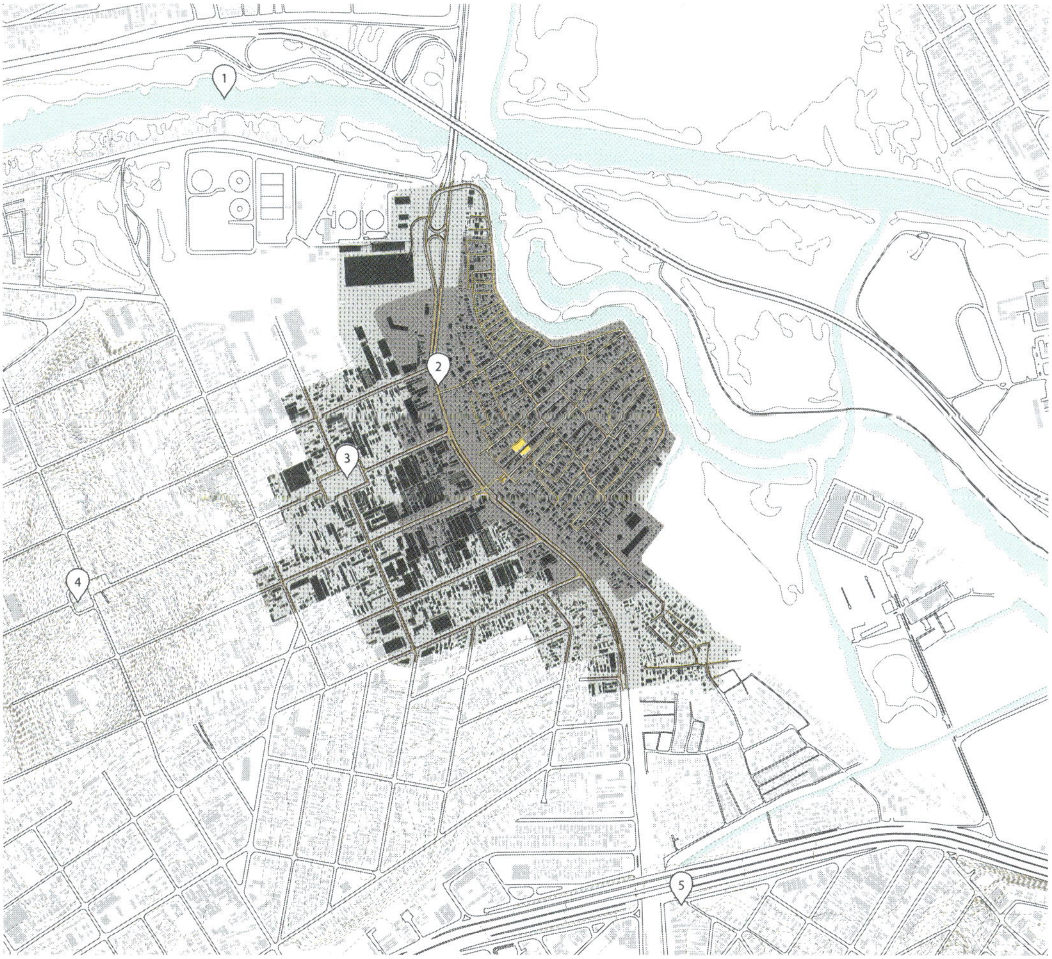

Distance traveled between 0m to 500m
Distance traveled between 500m to 800m
Public space
2,593 Structures
71.01 ha Area of influence 800m

Houses 500m
Houses 800m
Polygon 500m
Polygon 800m

1 Río Pavuna
2 Estación de tren Vigario Geral
3 Plaza Catole Do Rocha
4 Plaza Irineu Machado
5 Estación de tren Parada de Lucas

Scale:
0 50 100 200 400

PUBLIC SPACE

A covered amphitheater in front of AfroReggae´s entrance at Vigário Geral is used for performances by the children enrolled in the institution´s various activities. Since it is a public space, everyone in the community is invited to attend. Public recognition in turn encourages the children to continue pursuing art and culture instead of becoming members of gangs.

HISTORY

Vigário Geral is located in northern Rio de Janeiro. It was established as a proletarian neighborhood by local government to mitigate the emerging *favelas*.[2] The way these neighborhoods were created was to reserve land and create plots for people to legally build their own homes, while services and urban facilities were to be brought in by the city government.[3] Vigário Geral is defined by the Leopoldina rail line to the west and the Centro de Adestramento Almirante Marques de Leão to the east. Urban public policy in 1950 supported the elimination of Rio de Janiero´s *favelas*, increasing migration toward places such as Vigário Geral.[4] Scarce supervision from local authorities allowed construction to occur haphazardly in empty lots, just as people had done in the city´s *favelas*. People from the *favelas* Cidade Alta, Aterro Da Glória, and Morro de Santo Antônio were relocated by local authorities to Vigário Geral and their previous homes were razed. Other accounts affirm that many of Vigário Geral´s residents were railway workers, which makes sense given its proximity to the rail line.[5]

Over time, the inhabitants of Vigário Geral formed an organization to represent the community and negotiate basic service improvements in with the municipality. The Dwellers Association of Vigário Geral (Associação de Moradores de Vigário Geral) was constituted in the 1960s. It reflected the familiarity of the railway workers living there with syndicate organizations. During the seventies, inhabitants progressively replaced their wood homes with brick and cement structures. In 1980, the arrival of drug trafficking in Vigário Geral transformed the community. The neighborhood was controlled by drug cartels and violence was rampant. AfroReggae materialized as a social response to the community´s struggles with crime and violence.[6]

SOCIAL AND POLITICAL CONTEXT

The *favelas* on the hills of Rio de Janeiro's were seen as an urban and social problem that needed to be eliminated. In the 1960s, public policy supported eradication measures and moved many families to new territories called proletarian neighborhoods.[7] However, the very same urban and social problems present in *favelas* emerged once again in these neighborhoods, since public investment and institutional presence were weak. Urban public policy actively created ghettos, which like the *favelas*, were disconnected from the rest of the city, ignored by institutions and ruled by crime.[8]

Vigário Geral's early history boast a strong social organization, the Associaçao de Moradores, mentioned above that was able to coordinate urban improvements for the community. It was also tainted by the presence of drug cartels, which in the 1980's became the sole authority of Vigário Geral. Cartel leaders recruited youths to participate in criminal activities.[9] For a generation, it was normal for children to grow up admiring criminals, for whom they would willingly do small jobs related to drug trafficking, with the aspiration of joining the gang when they were old enough.

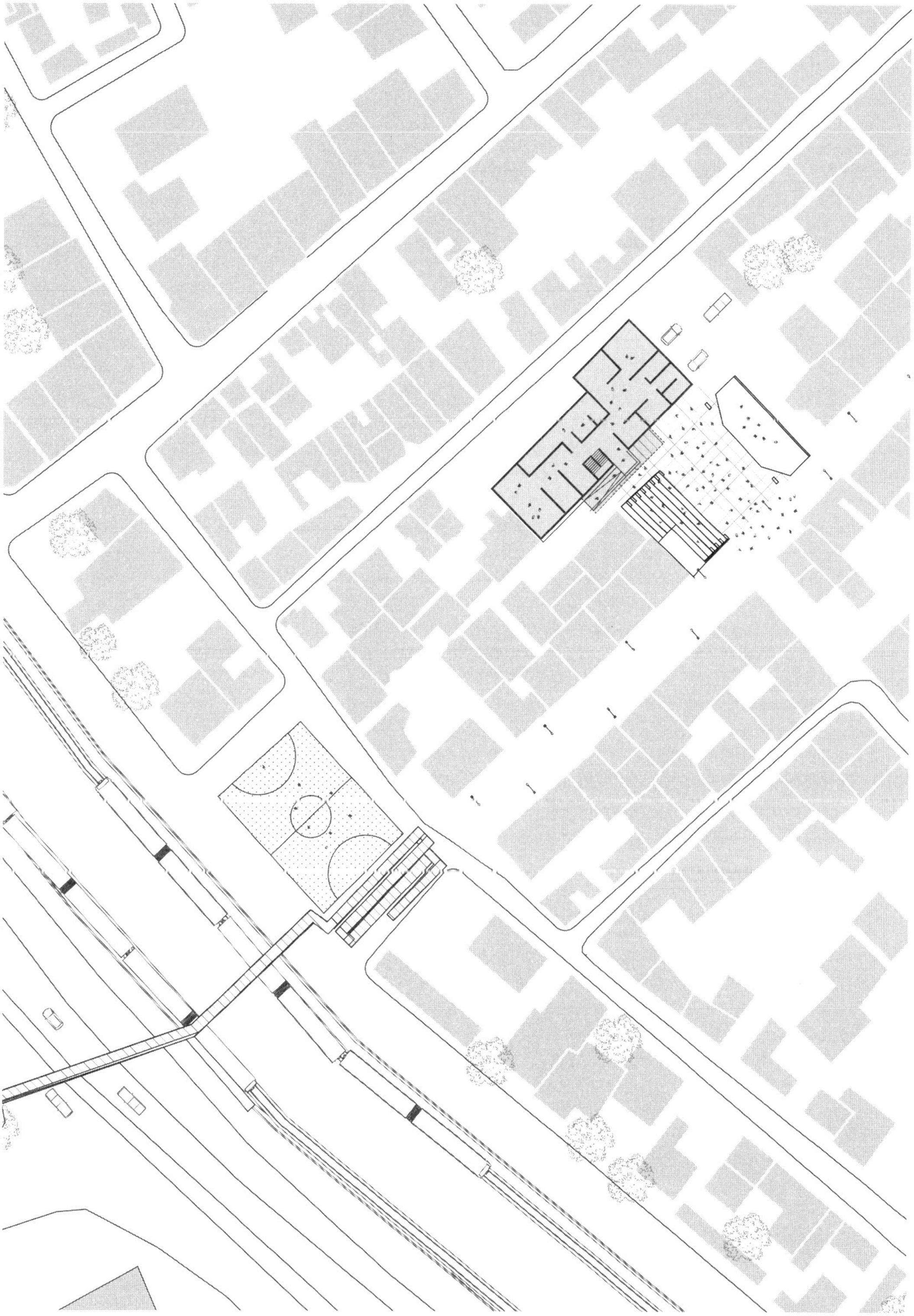

Scale:

0 5 10 25 50

In 1993, the Vigário Geral massacre took place: a violent act where police broke into the community and killed 21 innocent people in revenge for the murder of a policeman by criminals from the neighborhood. This event remains embedded in the community's collective memory. The constant threat of crime and violent confrontations motivated a group of community youths to build a collective pacification movement. That year, Anderson Sa and José Junior founded AfroReggae with the purpose of keeping the youth from entering criminal lifestyles through their engagement in art and dance.[10]

URBAN SITUATION

Vigário Geral is a proletarian neighborhood located on the northern limit of Rio de Janeiro, in what is known as the North Zone. Its construction began at the same time as the Leopoldina rail line, which ran through the city from north to south. North and east of Vigário Geral is the Duque Caixas district; Jardim América neighborhood is west, and Brazil Avenue marks its southern limit. As the Leopoldina rail was built, a strip of land between it and the Duque Caixas neighborhood, toward the east, was left unclaimed and became Vigário Geral. The neighborhood is isolated from its surroundings both physically and visually. Its western border is lined by a solid wall with a single access point, and the northern edge is marked by the river. Within these limits, Vigário Geral began as a regularly laid out grid with parceled land and self-built houses. Later, land set aside for communal facilities that were never built, was invaded, increasing the neighborhood's density.[11] Its houses tend to be two to three stories high. Urban improvements in the community in terms of public services, roads, and housing were negotiated with the municipality by the neighborhood association. More recently, Favela-Barrio further contributed to improving the community´s infrastructure.[12]

AfroReggae has helped recover open spaces in Vigário Geral by using them for concerts and improvisations. Presentations by renowned artists, including bands, singers, and DJs organized by the institution, have layered open spaces with a public and cultural use.

PROJECT FUNDING

AfroReggae began as a magazine edited by community youth after the 1993 massacre, and later evolved into a movement led by José Junior and Anderson Sa, using art and culture to contest violence.[13] In 1997, AfroReggae received a grant from the Ford Foundation for its work in human rights, citizenship and culture. The message caught the attention of national and international entities that came on board to support the initiative. Today it is an NGO that receives donations from private companies, foundations, institutions and non-governmental organizations. AfroReggae´s methodology and social work have been recognized internationally through awards and partnerships with organizations from other countries that have replicated the program. It manages an annual budget of approximately 500.000 USD, 30% of which is covered by self-generated income from events they organize. 100.000 USD have been invested in infrastructure.[14]

ACTIVITIES AND RELATED PROGRAMS

AfroReggae started as a group of young people who gave free music and dance lessons to children in the Vigário Geral community. It eventually became a sizable, privately owned, cultural institution that has expanded to other *favelas* including Cantagalo and Cidade de Deus. AfroReggae is also a social advisor to organizations in other countries. It serves 6.000 members in Rio de Janeiro's metropolitan area through eight programs for youth and children.[15] Combined they offer audiovisual media training, music, theater, art and circus workshops, *favela* mapping, defense of sexual diversity, reintegration of ex-offenders in society, social responsibility for businesses, and cultural activities in public spaces.[16] The organization also includes permanent artistic groups such as a percussion band, theater groups, traditional dance, samba and circus groups, as well as an orchestra and carnival performing artists.

INTEGRATION

AfroReggae' main objective is to keep vulnerable adolescents and children from entering criminal gangs. The organization operates in *favelas* and impoverished neighborhoods, once dominated by drug cartels. It promotes art and culture to inspire healthy civic behavior and mitigate violence. Its leadership has been instrumental in gaining the community´s support, which has allowed it to use and recondition public spaces to host music and dance events. The organization works with children and vulnerable youths to develop their talents and create venues in which they can share their abilities and receive recognition from the community. Art in public spaces and the street is used to tell the neighborhood's story and transmit messages of peace and non-violence.

AfroReggae´s ample national and international exposure in media has turned it into a prominent cultural institution in Rio de Janeiro. It has been able to replicate its operations in several sites throughout Rio, creating multiple cultural foci for art and culture. People from the entire city visit the AfroReggae sites in Vigário Geral, Cantagalo and Cidade de Deus to attend events and concerts. This fluid movement of people helps blur the perception of boundaries between urban and social fragments of the city.

1 Grant from Ford Foundation 2006-2007.

2 Rute Imanishi, "Os "Parques Proletarios" e os subúrbios do Río de Janeiro: aspectos da política governamental para as favelas entre 1930-1960," *Instituto de Pesquisa Económica Aplicada*, December, 2014, 8. http://www.ipea.gov.br/portal/index.php?option=com_content&view=article&id=24267 (accessed January 19, 2019)

3 Ibid.

4 M. P. Araujo and E. Salles, *História e memoria de Vigário Geral* (Río de Janeiro: Aeroplano Editora, 2009), 60.

5 Ibid., 62.

6 Maria Angela De Araújo, Eneida Maria de Souza and Danny José Almeida Costa. "Afroreggae: as "artes" do morro invadem o asfalto," *IPOTESI Juz de Fora*, v. 15, n.2, 2011, 133.

7 Imanishi, 14.

8 Ibid.

9 Araujo, p. 73.

10 *Favela rising.* Dir. J. Zimbalist, J. & M. Mochary, 2005.

11 Ibid.

12 World Bank, "Slum upgrading in Rio de Janeiro: Favela Bairro," *Healthy Cities* 2010. http://healthycities.berkeley.edu/uploads/1/2/6/1/12619988/brazil.pdf. (accessed January 5, 2018).

13 Ibid

14 A. J. Samuels, "The AfroReggae Cultural Group: A Rebirth Of Hope Within Rio De Janeiro's Favelas," *Culture Trip* January 24, 2018. https://theculturetrip.com/south-america/brazil/articles/the-afroreggae-cultural-group-a-rebirth-of-hope-within-rio-s-favelas/ (accessed February 15, 2019).

15 Ibid.

16 Ibid.

AFROREGGAE
RIO DE JANEIRO, BRAZIL

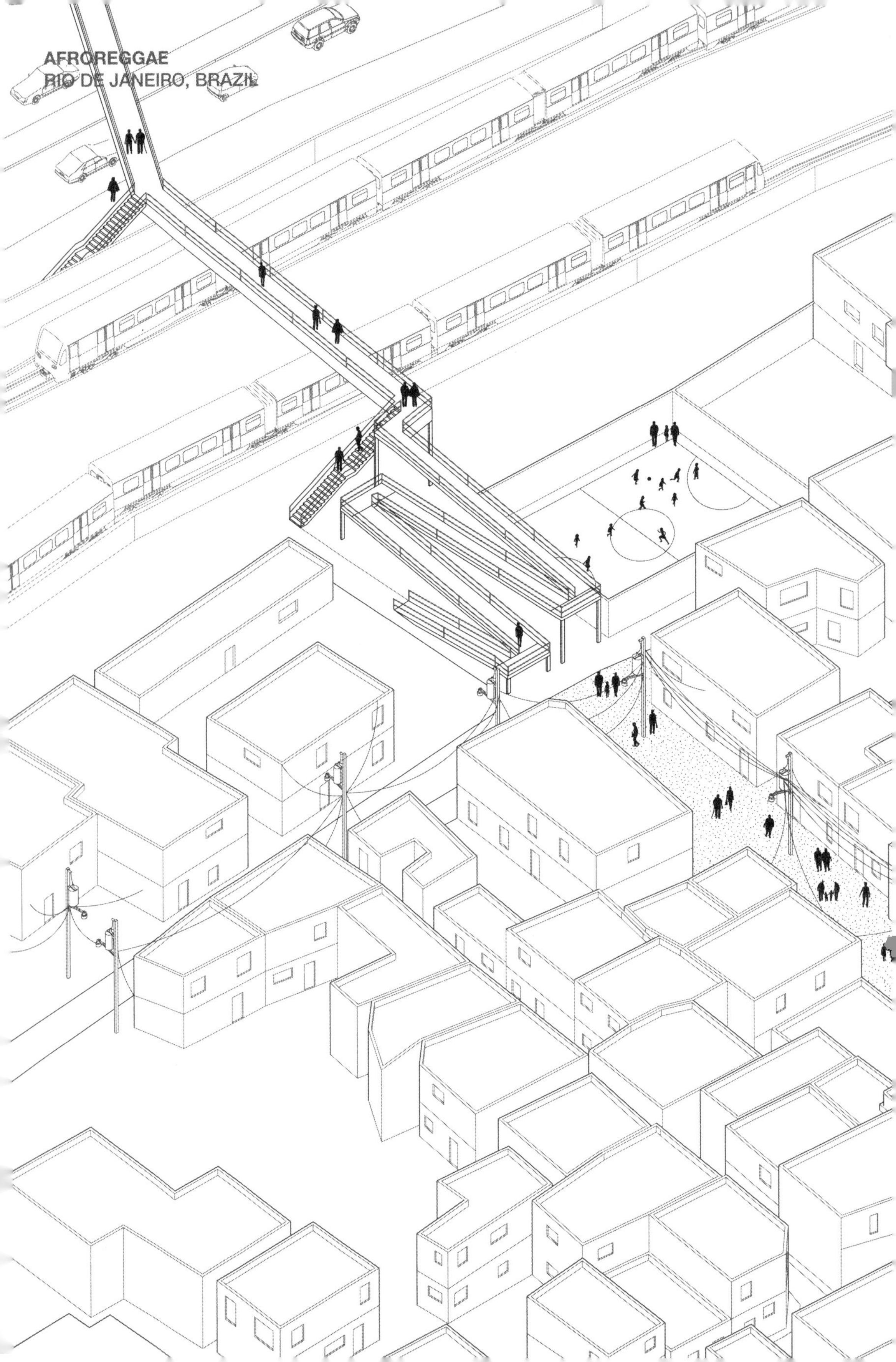

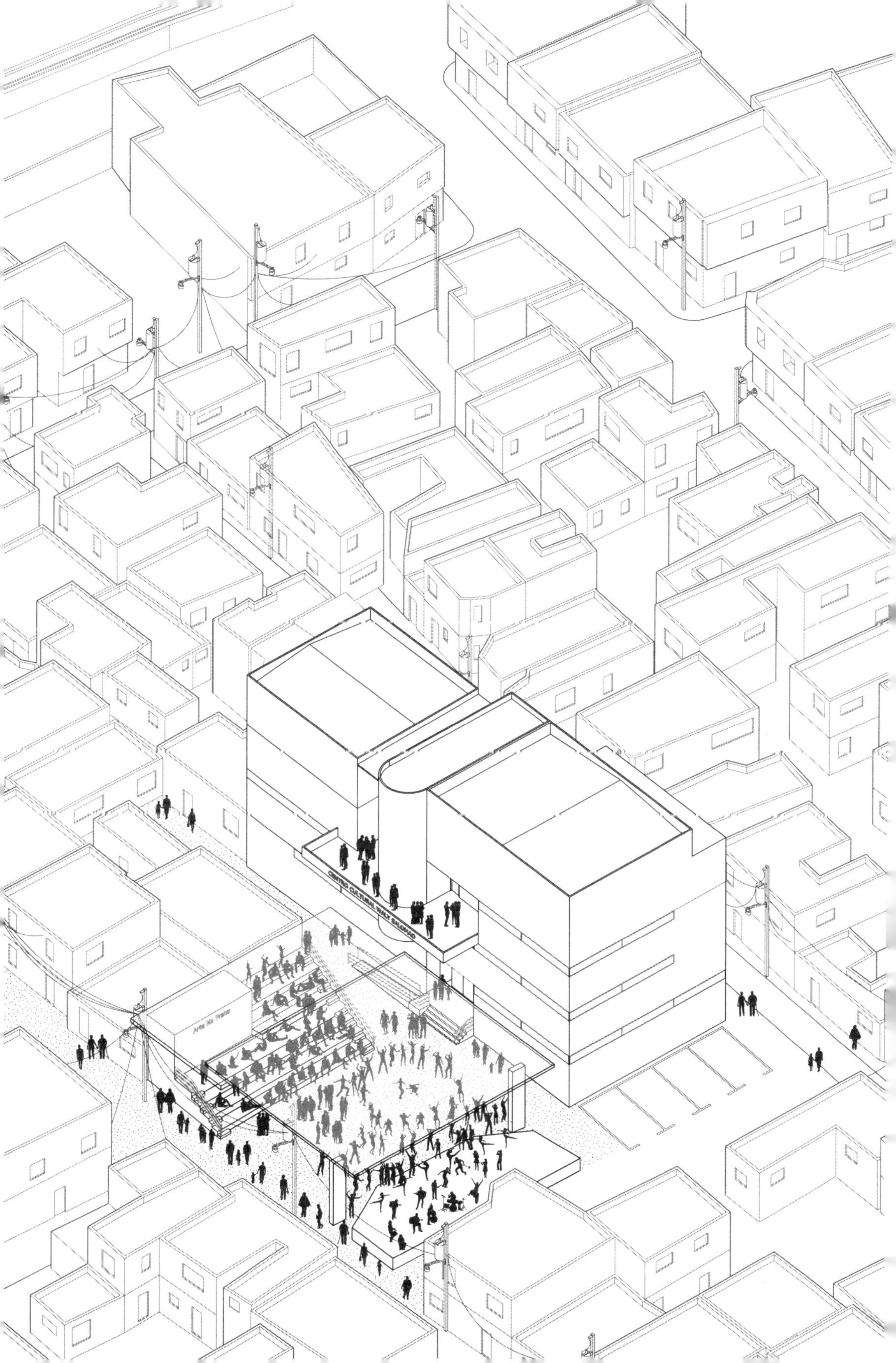
CENTRO CULTURAL WALY SALOMAO
Arte Na Praça

ALTO PERÚ

Alto Perú is a spontaneous settlement in Lima, located south of Chorrillos, along the Pacific coast. It is the site of a human development project that teaches youth to surf for free as a way of awakening in them a desire to have goals, live healthy lives and formulate more ambitious projects for themselves. Surfing is generally taught during the warm months. Other activities have also entered Alto Perú´s repertoire includes *muaythai,* a martial art practiced in Thailand, and *batucada,* a Brazilian percussion music, which is practiced during the winter months and performed in public spaces throughout Lima.

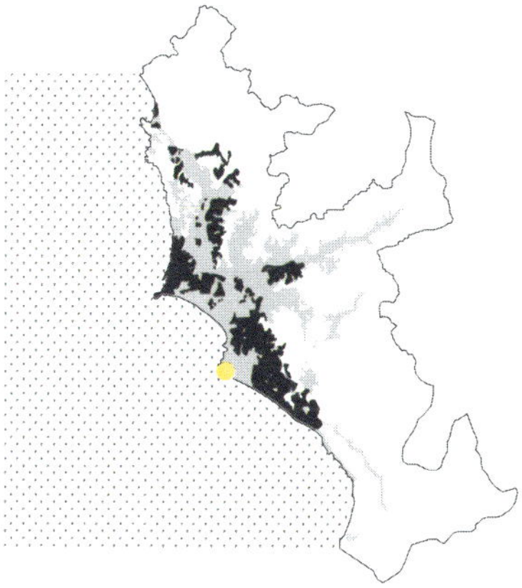

Location
Barrio Alto Perú, Distrito Chorrillos, Lima, Perú

Project team:
Diego Villarán and Matías Bayón

Date
2008

Coordinates
12°10'05.71"S 77°01'56.20"O

Investment
10,000 USD

Public space area
12,251,11 m^2

Urban density
89.34 hab/ha

Population benefited
7,830 hab

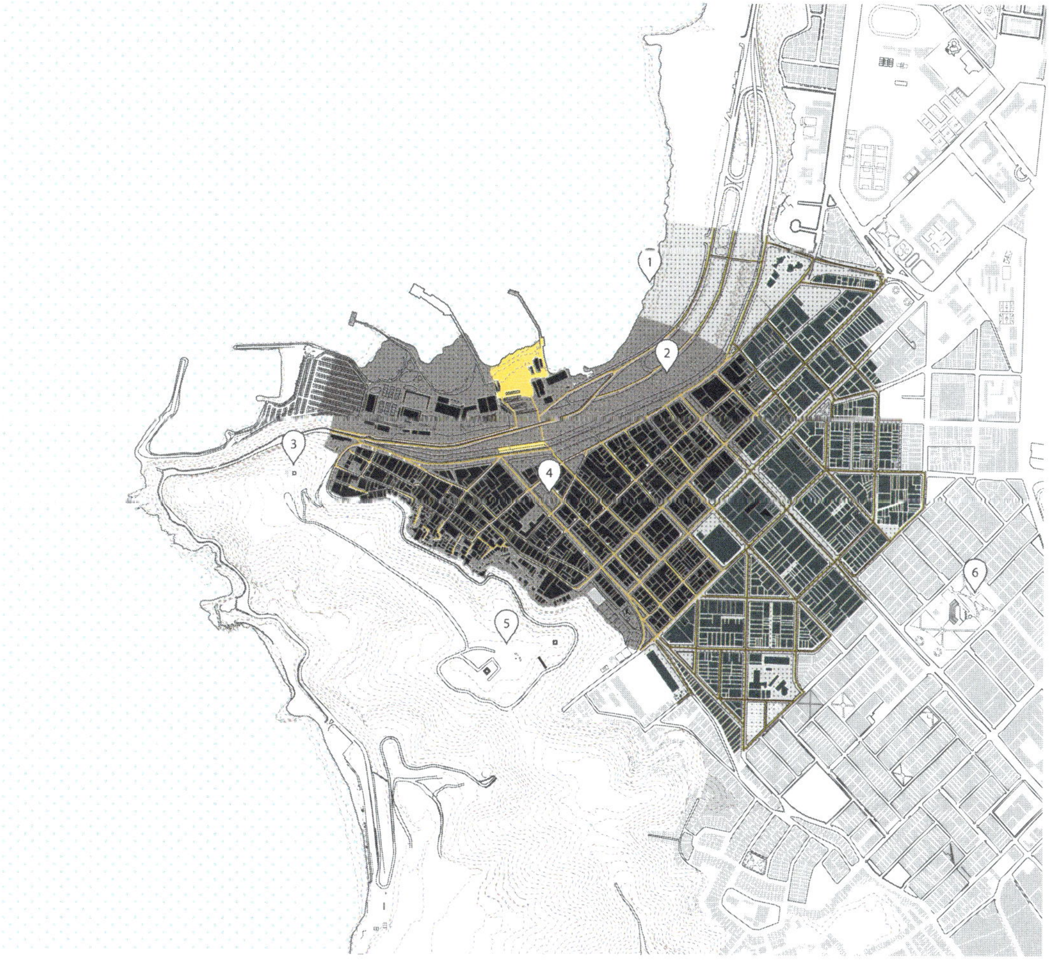

Distance traveled between 0m to 500m
Distance traveled between 500m to 800m
Public space
1,564 Structures
87.64 ha Area of influence 800m

Houses 500m
Houses 800m
Polygon 500m
Polygon 800m

1 Playa Agua Dulce
2 Malecón de Chorrillos
3 Santuario Virgen del Morro
4 Plaza San Pedro
5 Monumento al Soldado Desconocido
6 Parque Fátima

Scale:
0 50 100 200 400

PUBLIC SPACE

The use of public space to develop and practice the activities Alto Perú offers young people has been a constant in its evolution. *Batucada* concerts have given youths with precarious backgrounds an important sense of recognition when they perform in public. Alto Perú also hosts a festival every year, which takes advantage of the community´s public spaces to perform concerts and sell food, building bridges to integrate itself with the rest of the city.

HISTORY

Chorrillos is one of Lima´s 43 districts. It is located on the shores of the Pacific Ocean and has some of the most visited beaches in Peru. The earliest settlements date back to pre-Hispanic times and archeological remains of the Ichma culture can be found on the slopes of the Morro Solar.[1] Toward the end of the 17th century, a Spanish viceroy gave indigenous fishermen land to build their homes, which created a landscape of precarious structures along the ocean. [2] The beauty of Chorrillo´s beaches and views over the coast attracted Lima´s aristocracy, which began building summer houses there during the 19th century. Access was improved with the construction of railways and highways, and the modest homes of fishermen became dwarfed by the new mansions. Other transformations included the construction of a boardwalk, plazas, urban furniture, tree planting and improvement of the beach area.

In 1879, the Pacific War broke out between Chile and Peru with Bolivia as its ally. Chorrillos was among the sites most affected by the armed confrontations.[3] One of the war's bloodiest battles took place at Morro Solar, which essentially erased the structures that once stood there.

The district´s reconstruction and subsequent development continued to be marked by the contrast between elite residences and precarious housing. After the war, the Morro Solar became an important historical site in Lima, that also happens to enjoy a privileged view over the bay. Several landmarks were built on this hill including the Unknown Soldier monument, the Cross of the Pope, the Virgin of the Morro Sanctuary and the Planetary Museum.[4] The landscape is shared with Alto Perú, a spontaneous settlement, that begins at Mariscal Castillo Avenue, near the beaches and boardwalk, and climbs up the hillside. The gridded streets rise up the slopes as dirt paths reaching each of the self-built homes. The children and youths of this community are the target population for the Alto Perú program.

SOCIAL AND POLITICAL CONTEXT

In spite of its sea side views and the perception of privilege evoked by the luxurious multifamily homes and private regatta clubs along the shore, Chorillos has a very high poverty index and high levels of violence.[5] Alto Perú emerged as a spontaneous settlement, much like other settlements on hills near the center of Lima. It was built by low-income families who urbanized these territories themselves, extending streets from the city bellow. Poverty and insufficient access to public services, infrastructure, education and opportunities, together with the municipality´s disinterest in communities such as Alto Perú, leaves youths at risk of entering criminal lifestyles and joining violent gangs.

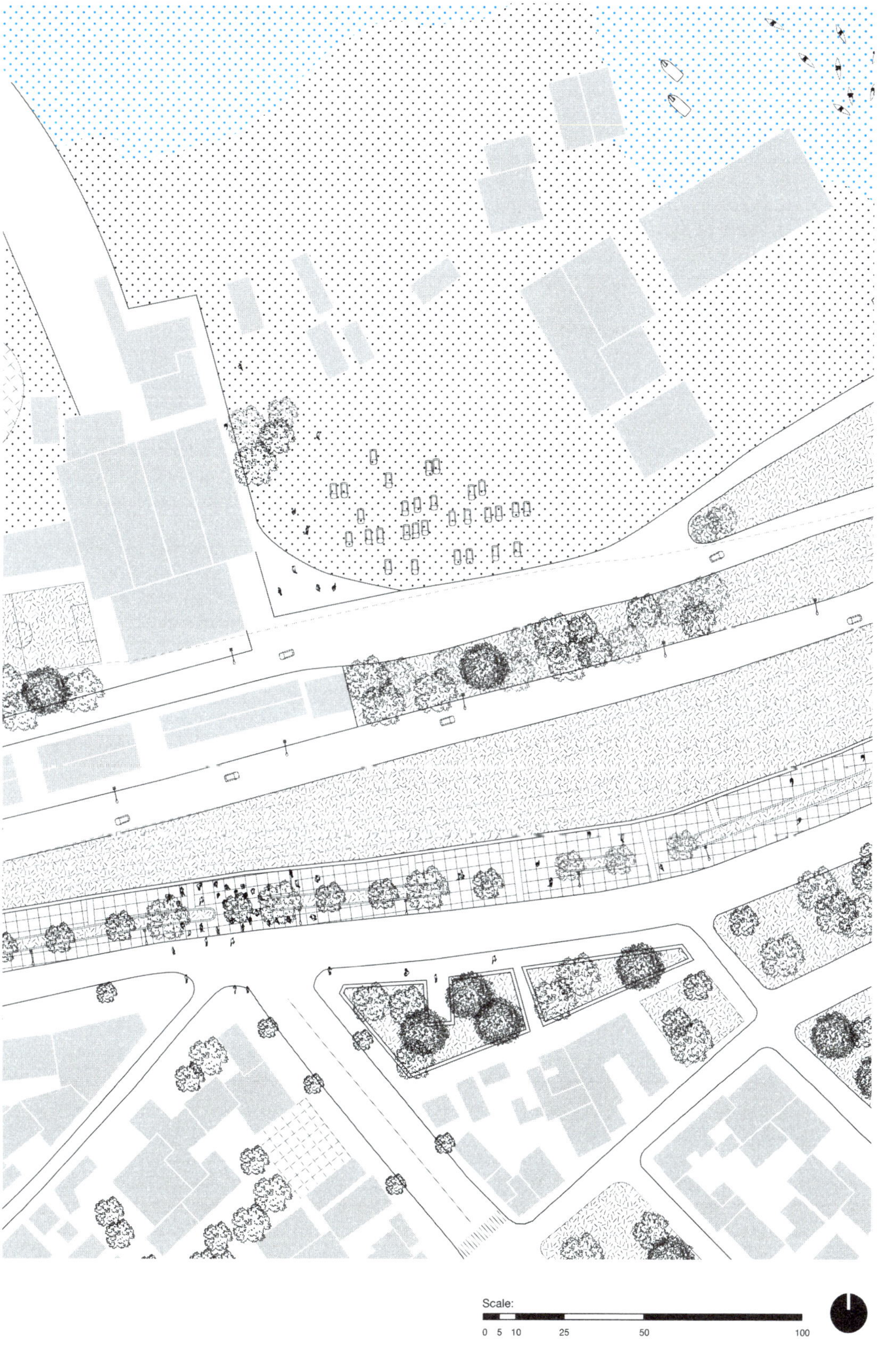
Scale:
0 5 10 25 50 100

The Alto Perú project began with surf lessons for a group of 15-year-old adolescents. In order for the program to be more effective at diverting kids from criminal lifestyles, the focus soon shifted to younger children that could still be influenced with new habits. Currently, the program incorporates children between the ages of 6 and 12 years of age.[6] Through sports, they build a closer relationship with nature, develop leadership skills, and learn the value of perseverance and team work. They are taught discipline, responsibility and respect, and are encouraged to be assertive in guiding the course of their lives. These values in turn are transmitted to children in the rest of the community. Alto Perú has also been a platform for professional development: some of its students have become amateur and professional athletes, teachers and instructors.

URBAN SITUATION

El Morro Solar is a hill southwest of Lima that overlooks the entire city, as a lookout point over the bay. It was considered a strategic location in colonial times and during the Pacific War.[7] Chorrillos is defined by three main axes: the Grau Malecón, parallel to the coast, Defensores del Morro Avenue and the Paseo de la República. The urban fabric of the district´s lower and flatter area is regular and gridded. As it meets the slope of Morro Solar, it becomes increasingly irregular. Several of its buildings are part of the city´s patrimonial heritage and tend to be between one and three stories high, while those along the Malecon Grau rise up to 8 stories high. In contrast, the houses of El Morro are self-built with varying degrees of informality including structures made of wood and zinc accessed by paths and stairs. The settlement is bounded by a parkway that leads to the Unknown Soldier monument. Access to basic services, including drinking water and electricity, diminish as the settlement progresses up the hill. Municipal urban policy has not addressed these issues and continues to favor localized and singular interventions.

PROJECT FUNDING

Alto Perú surf zone began as an individual project by Diego Villarán who decided to give free surf lessons to the children of Chorrillos. The number of kids grew so quickly that friends and collaborators joined the program and continued teaching for free.[8] Currently, Alto Perú is an organization supported by the sponsorship of private companies related to surfing, and donations from individuals and foundations. The events and festivals organized by Alto Perú are sponsored by private companies as part of their social responsibility and marketing strategies. Instructors generally donate their time and some of them were once students of Diego Villarán.[9]

RELATED PROGRAMS

Alto Perú´s efforts to make the program economically sustainable have led to the diversification of its activities to include corporate social responsibility programs. Companies can participate in the physical recovery of community spaces. They can also engage in dynamics to strengthen their own communication skills and aptitudes for teamwork through games and sports. Alto Perú has forged alliances with private schools and the Peruvian Sports Institute to help children with their homework and after school activities. They are also keen on building a closer relationship with the public sector, through the National Surf Federation and the Peruvian Muaythai Sports Federation, to serve children in communities of other neighborhoods in Lima.[10]

ACTIVITIES

The project began as a surf program for children, but quickly incorporated other disciplines such as paddle surf, *muaythai, batucada,* and *capoeira*. Alto Perú offers a weekly schedule of activities: surf is taught at the La Sombrilla beach; *muaythai, batucada* and *capoeira* are taught in the public spaces of the Chorrillo boardwalk; extracurricular help with school work is also offered.[11] Recitals are regularly performed in the community´s public spaces as well as in plazas throughout Lima. All teaching is done with an emphasis on helping children develop social and communication skills, and strengthen their self-confidence.

The Alto Perú festival is held annually. Neighborhood sidewalks, squares and the Malecón Grau are taken over with sports activities, cultural presentations and food vendors. Accessible public spaces located at the hinge between Alto Perú and the formal city allow the community to host events that attract people from nearby communities and the rest of Lima.

INTEGRATION

Alto Perú is a social initiative in which children of Chorrillos are given the opportunity to seek higher goals by practicing sports. This engagement keeps them from dropping out of school and entering lifestyles of crime and drug trafficking. Surfing and *muaythai* help kids and youth handle the frustrations associated with poverty and scarce resources. They focus instead on using their education and skills to build healthier and more productive lives. Furthermore, the social work with the children also benefits their families and the community in general. Parents and relatives participate in community initiatives organized by Alto Perú. A key event is their annual festival, where the children exhibit their talents to the entire city in public spaces. Other times of the year, the children visit parks and plazas in the rest of the city to perform *batucada* concerts. In this sense, Alto Perú not only acts as a prevention program for youth, but also connects and integrates the city through the activation of public space.

1 León Almenara, "Chorrillos: Invasiones no se detienen en zona arqueológica del Morro Solar," *El Comercio* 2017.

2 "Historia de Chorrillos. Mar del Sur." https://www.mardelsur.com.pe/historia-de-chorrillos/ (accessed January 19, 2019).

3 Ibid.

4 J. L. Orrego Penagos, "Chorrillos en el siglo XIX. Rumbo al Bicentenario," 2009. http://blog.pucp.edu.pe/blog/juanluisorrego/2009/06/29/chorrillos-en-el-siglo-xix/ (accessed January 10, 2019).

5 Historia de Chorrillos. Municipalidad Distrital de Chorrillos." http://www.munichorrillos.gob.pe/home/historia-chorrillos.php (accessed January 19, 2019).

6 Alto Perú. https://www.altoperu.org/proyecto-que-hacemos (accessed January 19, 2019).

7 J. Villalobos, "Chorrillos: nuestro pequeño Perú," *Coherencia* 2013. http://www.coherencia.pe/chorrilos-nuestro-pequeno-peru/ (accessed January 10, 2019).

8 "Diego Villarán, promotor de cultura y deporte en el Morro Solar de Chorrillos," *RPP Noticias* May 4, 2012.

9 Interview with Matías Ballón from Alto Perú by María Virginia Millán.

10 Alto Perú.

11 Ibid.

ALTO PERÚ
LIMA, PERÚ

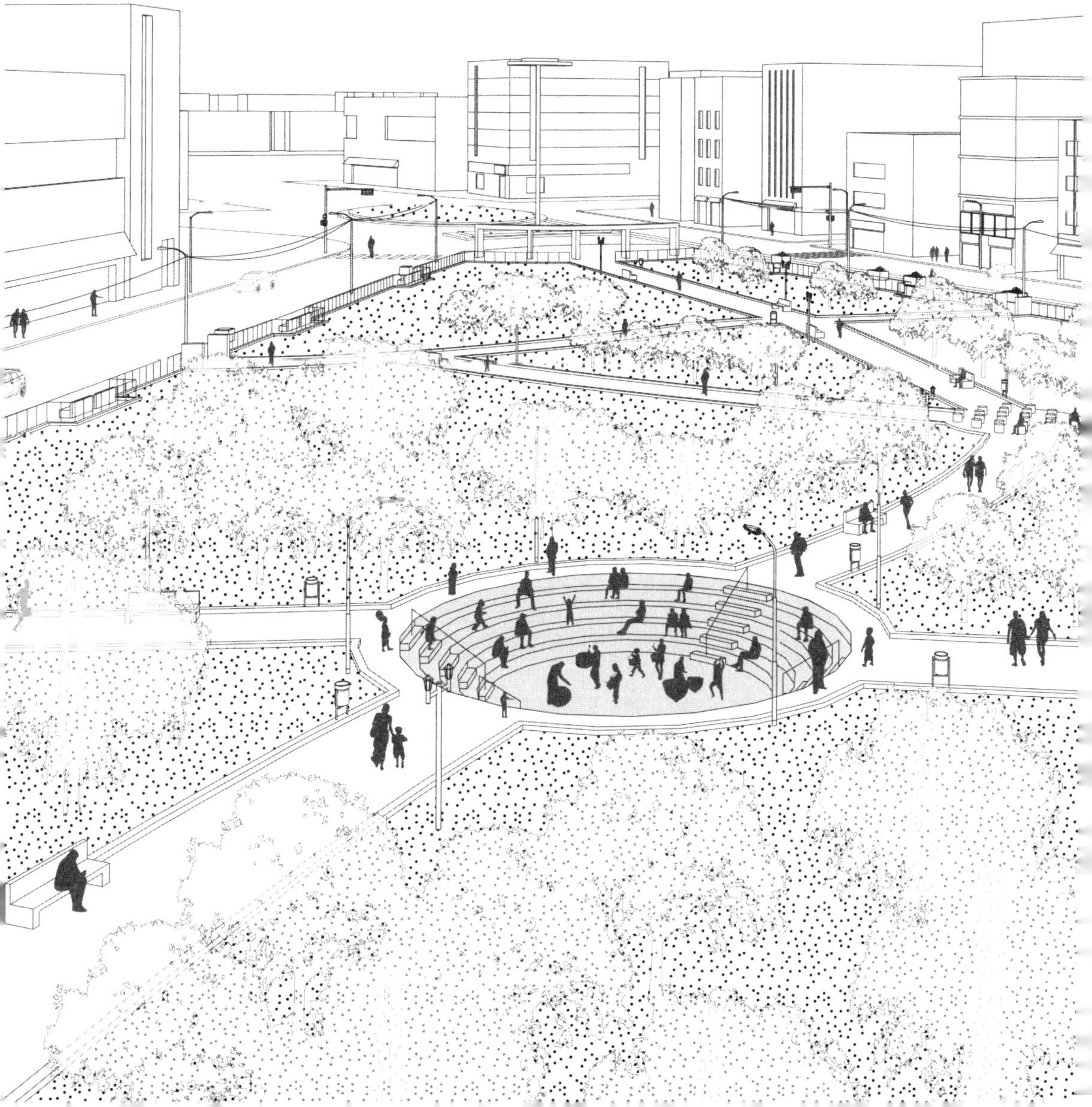

EL CALVARIO OPEN DOORS

El Calvario Open Doors (El Calvario Puertas Abiertas), is an event in which the community opens the neighborhood of El Calvario to the rest of the city with a one-day agenda of cultural and recreational events. It offers participants the opportunity to reflect on the stereotypes and prejudices that superficially divide the city. The local municipality helps promote the event. Various organizations participate and contribute to the roster of activities. Among the protagonists are artists who perform installations and members of the community who open their homes for book readings and concerts. An existing plaza is set up with a stage where several music groups perform live concerts, while audiences including locals and residents of Caracas at large listen to the music and dance. The event places El Calvario definitively on the map of Caracas as a place that is known by its participants.

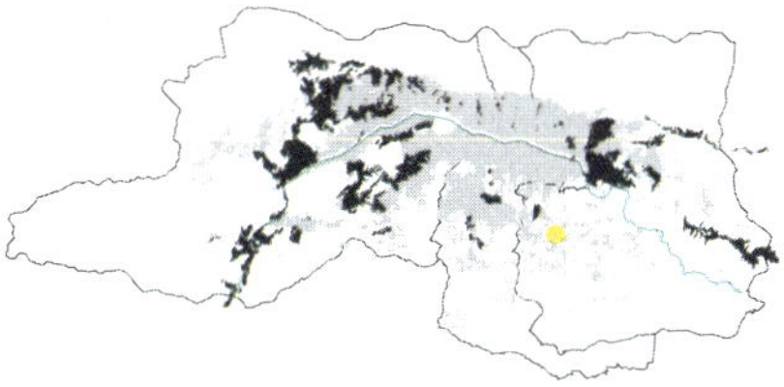

Location
El Calvario, municipio El Hatillo, Distrito Capital, Venezuela

Project team:
Ciudad Laboratorio, La Comunidad de El Calvario y el municipio de El Hatillo

Date
2015, 2015, 2017, 2018

Coordinates
10°25'47.24 "N 66°49'30.29" O

Investment
1.200 USD

Public space area
5.732,15m²

Urban density
395,43 hab/ha

Population benefited
6.005 hab

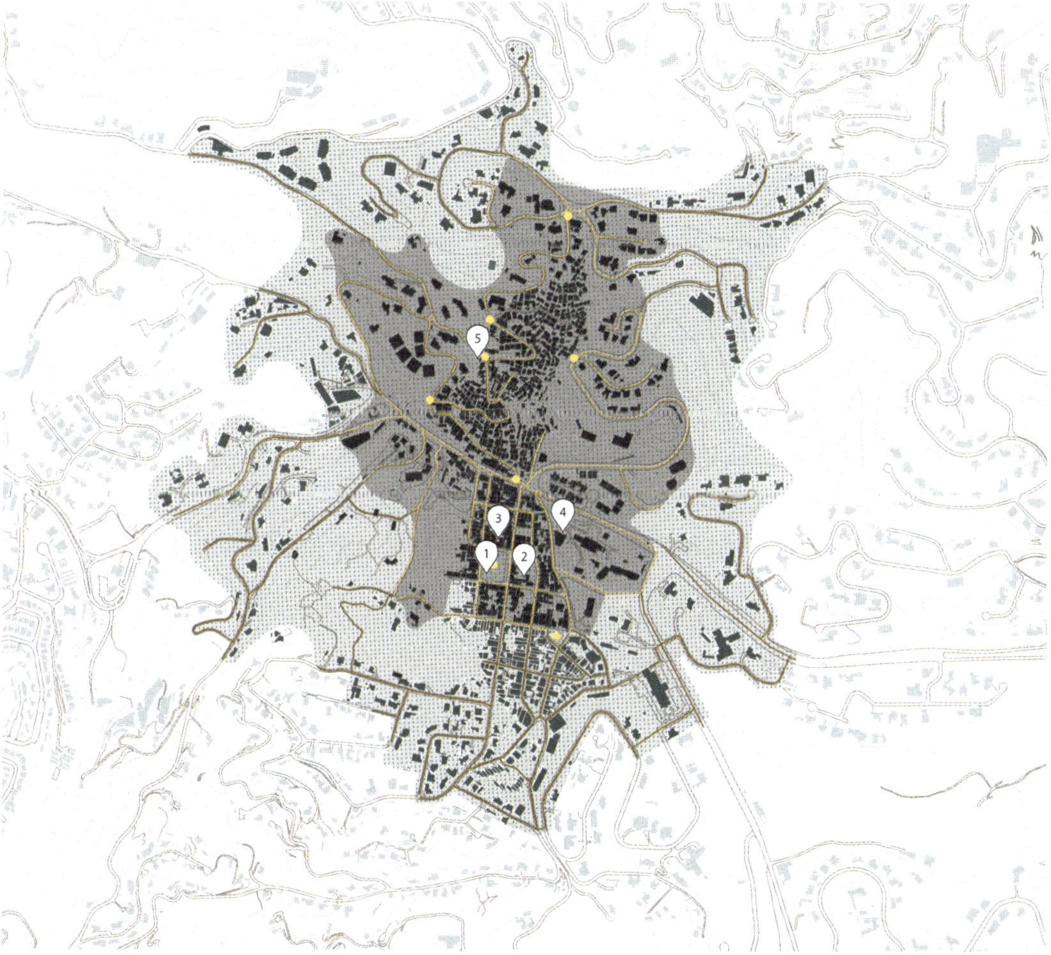

Distance traveled between 0m to 500m
Distance traveled between 500m to 800m
Public space
1,593 Structures
140.13 ha Area of influence 800m

Houses 500m
Houses 800m
Polygon 500m
Polygon 800m

1. Plaza Bolívar de El Hatillo
2. Iglesia Santa Rosalía de Palermo
3. Alcaldía de El Hatillo
4. Anfiteatro El Hatillo
5. Colegio María May

Scale:
0 2.5 5 10 25

PUBLIC SPACE

The agenda behind this event is for people from the entire city to become acquainted with El Calvario. As people walk through the neighborhood and participate in various activities, they reveal the neighborhood´s potential to be used and celebrated regularly. A latent map of plazas, park benches, and alleyways becomes visible as people occupy space while participating in the event.

HISTORY

El Calvario is located north of El Hatillo, in southeastern Caracas. It was founded as an agricultural town during Spanish colonial times, which was later registered in 1874 as a separate parish. El Calvario exists as an established settlement since the 1930s.[1] It is located north of El Hatillo an dwas inhabited by farmers. The El Calvario Chapel was built in 1884 and represents the community´s first church.[2]

El Hatillo was declared historic patrimony in 1960, confirming its vocation as a tourist and recreation center for Caracas. Its continued commercial growth began transforming the town and its residential colonial houses into stores, restaurants, and artisan shops. The town of El Hatillo became one of the most visited destinations in Caracas due to its mountainous climate, colonial architecture, art galleries, and cultural expressions. Caracas´ urban expansion during the second half of the twentieth century transformed the Municipality of El Hatillo into a satellite city through the construction of vast residential neighborhoods for middle- and upper-income families.

El Calvario became denser with new inhabitants that worked in the colonial town or on the construction sites of the new developments. The divide between formal neighborhoods became more pronounced. While the entertainment and recreational programs of the colonial center were widely visited, El Calvario remained a purely residential area that residents of El Hatillo and the rest of Caracas avoided because they considered it poor and ridden with violence. It seems to exist solely as the landscape background of the colonial houses that surround the El Hatillo Square. El Calvario Open Doors is an urban integration exercise that aims to dissolve the stigmas of spontaneous settlements by making them visible and creating an excuse to visit them.

SOCIAL AND POLITICAL CONTEXT

The community´s founding families feel strongly rooted in El Calvario. There are cultural groups with a long historical tradition within the community, such as the percussionists *Mina, Tambor and Clarín* or the group of dancers called *Apocalypse*.[3] Festivals and traditions, including the Virgen del Carmen, Carnival, the festivities of the Cruz de Mayo, and Christmas, are regularly celebrated.[4] El Calvario Open Doors allows artisans, visual artists, and musicians who live in El Calvario to share their talent with people outside the neighborhood. Neighbors are encouraged to open the doors of their homes for smaller events and act as hosts of their community for the day.[5]

Scale:
0 2.5 5 10 25

ENVIRONMENTAL SITUATION

El Hatillo Municipality is known for its abundant and wild vegetation; and yet very little is understood about the value of native species. Many are considered weeds and are regularly cut back or eliminated. A project pending for El Calvario Open Doors is to create scenarios for education on how to care for plants, trees, and greenery in the neighborhood and develop greater appreciation for what grows naturally in that particular landscape and climate.

URBAN SITUATION

El Calvario is located on a steeply inclined hill, north of El Hatillo. It is bound to the north and west by the Alto Hatillo neighborhood, by a ravine to the east, and by El Progreso Street, a busy artery within the municipality, to the south that divides El Hatillo from El Calvario. El Calvario Street is the only vehicular and pedestrian roadway that traverses the entire neighborhood. Stairs and alleys complete all internal pedestrian connections. For many years there was no proper pedestrian crossing between El Calvario and El Hatillo. People had to negotiate the heavy traffic of El Progreso Street and walk over a concrete divider until a proper crossing was installed by the municipality, as part of the activities linked to the second edition of El Calvario Open Doors.[6]

The community is divided into three sectors: El Calvario Bajo, Medio, and Alto. Noteworthy facilities and spaces within the neighborhood are El Calvario Chapel and its plaza, the María May School, the La Cruz Plaza, Callejón Guevara, a bocce court, and various convenience stores. The population density is high, 395 inhabitants per hectare, and most homes have four stories.[7]

PROJECT FUNDING

El Calvario Open Doors is a collaborative initiative between multiple organizations. Ciudad Laboratorio is responsible for coordination and the event´s overall structure. The Municipality of El Hatillo helps with advertisement, provides tour guides, organizes some of the activities, manages donations, and provides police surveillance. All other collaborators donate their time and the materials of their interventions. In general, the monetary investments are modest and the event's viability stems from everyone´s contributions of time and effort.[8]

RELATED PROGRAMS

The idea for El Calvario Open Doors came from mapping exercises Cheo Carvajal used to organize for school children in low-income neighborhoods of Caracas. A similar proposal was presented to the cultural department of the El Hatillo Municipality which evolved into El Hatillo Ciudad Laboratorio, with a series of tours along the streets of El Calvario. Walks through the neighborhood revealed the value of its spaces and its cultural activities as well as the neighbors' receptivity to outside visitors. This prompted the idea of making the experience more accessible to the entire city. The event came together through multiple visits and meetings with the community to identify the most relevant sites. People expressed interest in sharing their talents or opening their homes to guests.

ACTIVITIES

On the day of the event, visitors can either use a map provided by the organizers, indicating the activities, places of interest, and schedule of events, or choose to follow guided tours. Musical presentations, exhibitions, and recreational activities can be found all along the trajectory from El Calvario Chapel, in the lower part of the neighborhood, to Plaza La Cruz, in the highest part. Many of the houses leave their doors open, inviting visitors to see exhibitions, buy food, or enjoy the views over the landscape from their home. The program also includes readings for children, art exhibitions, photographic tours, city sketching, music concerts by famous Venezuelan artists, and art installations.

The event is organized by a team comprised of Cheo Carvajal, director of Ciudad Laboratorio, José González, a prominent community leader, and the Vive El Hatillo program of El Hatillo Municipality. Collaborators in the various editions have included students and professors of the Architecture and Visual Arts Department at the Simón Bolívar University, tourism students from the Nueva Esparta University, the Venezuelan American Fund for the Arts (VAEA), and FUNDARVIT (Fundación de Artistas Visuales Impulsores de Talento). Artist groups, such as La Rana Encantada and Escarabajos Cuentos Cuentos, organized a day of storytelling; Enlace Arquitectura designed and built ephemeral canopies for Plaza la Cruz and six other community spaces; architecture students of the Simón Bolívar University created a public space in the Guevara Alley; and Trazando Espacios invited attendees to participate in a mapping activity. Other artists and participants are Zaira Castro, La Pequeña Revancha, Los Colores de la Música, the Escuela de Saberes Miranda (which promotes joropo tuyero, a typical Venezuelan dance), Natalya Critchley, the editor of Portable Utopia, Vanessa Avendaño and Jesús Briceño. Music concerts by maestro Aquiles Báez have also been part of the roster of events.

INTEGRATION

El Calvario and El Hatillo are historically and culturally one entity. People that live in El Calvario have family members that live in El Hatillo; children from the spontaneous settlement study in schools located bellow in the town center, and many El Calvario inhabitants work in commercial spaces of El Hatillo. Nevertheless, El Calvario's marginal status remains unaltered mostly because it is an unknown territory to many. El Calvario Open Doors is a social experiment that instead of introducing foreign dynamics into the settlement, tries to create opportunities for the community to make itself known to the rest of the city from within. Tactical interventions through activities, programs, and exhibitions reveal spaces that work well for gathering and the public dimension of streets, walkways, and stairs. The event represents a pilot for an ideal city where people can traverse any territory and understand the urban artifact as the sum of different fragments. During the event visitors come to realize the natural continuity that exists between both neighborhoods and expand their mental map of the city.

1 Silva (2015), 190.

2 A. Suárez, "Plaza Bolívar de El Hatillo," Institutional Assets and Monumentos of Venezuela. https://iamvenezuela.com/2016/10/plaza-bolivar-de-el-hatillo/ (accessed January 15, 2018).

3 Interview with José Carvajal of Ciudad Laboratorio, June 12, 2018.

4 "El Calvario Puertas Abiertas regresa para el disfrute de los caraqueños." *Analítica* 2017. http://www.analitica.com/cultura/el-calvario-puertas-abiertas-regresa-para-el-disfrute-de-los-caraquenos/ (accessed January 19, 2019).

5 Cheo Carvajal (2018).

6 "Calvario Puertas Abiertas, un barrio para el encuentro caraqueño." *Tráfico Visual* 2015. http://www.traficovisual.com/2015/12/13/el-calvario-puertas-abiertas-un-barrio-para-el-encuentro-caraqueno/ (accessed January 19, 2019).

7 Silva (2015), 190.

8 Carvajal (2018).

EL CALVARIO OPEN DOORS
CARACAS, VENEZUELA

1

2

3

4

5

6

7

8

1-2 Estero Salado | 3-8 Chapéu Mangueira, Babilonia

9

10

11

12

13

14

15

16

9-12 Rimac River | 13-16 Moravia Ecological Park

17

18

19

20

21

22

23

24

17-20 La Palomera | 21-24 Guasmo Beach

25

26

27

28

29

30

31

32

25-28 Santa María El Triunfo | 29-32 Juan Bobo Creek

33

34

35

36

37

38

39

40

34-36 Medellin cable car | 38-40 Mechanical stairs and walkways Barrio Las Independecias

41

42

43

44

45

46

47

48

41-44 Funicular Santa Marta | 45-48 Complexo do Alemão

45

46

47

48

49

50

51

52

45-48 Ecotecnia Urbana Miravalle | 49-52 Cerro Santo Domingo and Cerro Toro

53

54

55

56

57

58

59

60

53-56 Cerro Santa Ana | 57-60 Fernando Botero Library

61

62

63

64

65

66

67

68

61-64 Moravia Cultural Center | 65-68 Espaço Criança Esperança Cantagalo

69

70

71

72

73

74

75

76

69-74 Villa Tranquila | 75-76 Casa Kolacho

77

78

79

80

81

82

83

84

77-80 AfroReggae | 81-84 Alto Perú

9

10

11

12

9-12 El Calvario Puertas Abiertas

BIBLIOGRAPHY

"16 zonas de Guayaquil se inundan cada vez que hay precipitaciones." *El Telégrafo* (2015).

"1828 Iglesia Santo Domingo." *Biblioteca del Congreso Nacional de Chile*. Retrieved January 19, 2019. https://www.bcn.cl/historiapolitica/congreso_nacional/edificios/detalle?sel=Iglesia_de_Santo_Domingo

Abla, Marcela Marques. Vivienda, favela y futuro: mejoría en favelas después de metodología de urbanización: el caso Santa Marta. A: Congreso Internacional de Vivienda Colectiva Sostenible. "I Congreso Internacional de Vivienda Colectiva Sostenible, Barcelona, February 25-27, 2014." Barcelona: Máster Laboratorio de la Vivienda Sostenible del Siglo XXI, (2014): 470-475. Retrieved January 29, 2019. http://hdl.handle.net/2099/15406

Abramo, Pedro. *Favela e Mercado Informal: a nova porta de entrada dos pobres nas cidades brasileiras*. Porto Alegre: Habitare, 2009.

Acosta Tobon, Sergio. "Una arqueología de la violencia en Medellín: de "la ambición rompe el saco" a "la ocasión hace al ladrón"." *Revista Electrónica de Psicología Social Poiésis* (2012): 1-2.

"Agricultura urbana y peri-urbana en Lima metropolitana: una estrategia de lucha contra la pobreza y la inseguridad alimementaria." *Urban Harvest* (2006). Retrieved January 10, 2019. https://www.scribd.com/document/260822079/Agricultura-Urbana-y-Peri-urbana-en-Lima-Metropolitana

AIVP. "Guayaquil (Ecuador): la espectacular metamorfosis urbana." *Red Mundial de Ciudades Portuarias*, (2013).

Alcaldía de Guayaquil. *Guayaquil es mi destino* (2018). Retrieved May 5, 2018. http://www.guayaquilesmidestino.com/es/historia-arte-y-cultura/cerro-santa-ana

Alcaldía de Guayaquil. *Rendición de cuentas 2000 - 2008*. Guayaquil: Wong y Wong Consultores Asociados, 2008.

Alcaldía de Guayaquil. *Rendición de Cuentas 2009 - 2010*. Guayaquil: Wong y Wong Consultores Asociados, 2010.

Alcaldía de Guayaquil. *Rendición de cuentas del Alcalde 2010 - 2011*. Guayaquil: Wong & Wong Consultores Asociados, Cía. Ltda, 2011.

Alcaldía de Medellín. *Medellín, Guía de la Transformación Ciudadana 2004-2011*. Medellín: Mesa Editores, 2011.

Alcaldía de Medellín. *Plan de desarrollo local Comuna 4 Aranjuez*. Medellín: Alcaldía de Medellín, 2015.

Alcaldía de Medellín. *Plan de Desarrollo Local Corregimiento San Cristóbal*. Medellín: Alcaldía de Medellín, 2015.

Alcaldía de Medellín. *La memoria cultural como dispositivo para la intervención social en Moravia*. Medellín: Artes y Letras, 2011.

Alcaldía de Medellín. *Medellín, Guía de la Transformación Ciudadana 2004-2011*. Medellín: Mesa Editores, 2011.

Alcaldía de Medellín. *Plan de Desarrollo local Comuna 1 La Popular.* Medellín: Alcaldía de Medellín, 2015.

Alcaldía de Medellín. *Plan de desarrollo local Comuna 13, San Javier*. Medellín: Alcaldía de Medellín, 2012.

Alcaldía de Medellín. *Plan de desarrollo local Comuna 4 Aranjuez*. Medellín: Alcaldía de Medellín, 2015.

Alcaldía de Medellín. *Proyecciones de población 2016 a 2020*. Retrieved August 19, 2019. https://www.medellin.gov.co/irj/portal/medellin?NavigationTarget=navurl://06bdb-4d911e35cb9d3de717115deedc3

Alcaraz, María Victoria. "Latinoamérica: reflexiones sobre las infraestructuras y equipamientos culturales." In "Manual Atalaya de apoyo a la gestión cultural" by Romero S. Catalán and A. J. Rueda González (2014). Retrieved January 19, 2019. http://atalayagestioncultural.es/capitulos/gestion-cultural/1

Alto Perú Zona Surf. "Proyecto." Retrieved January 19, 2019 https://www.altoperu.org/proyecto-que-hacemos

Andreatta, Verena. "Favela-Bairro, un nuevo paradigma de urbanización para asentamientos informales." *UPCommons. Portal del cneixement obert de la UPC* (2005). Retrieved January 10, 2019. https://upcommons.upc.edu/bitstream/handle/2099/1586/01_Favela-Bairro.pdf

Arango, Gilbertto. "Moravia, una historia de mejoramiento urbano." *Procesos Urbanos Informales* (2012): 1-8. Retrieved January 19, 2019. https://issuu.com/sem_proceso_urbanos_informales/docs/03_j-moravia_una_historia_de_mejoramiento__urbano

Araujo, M. P. and E. Salles. *História e memoria de Vigário Geral*. Río de Janeiro: Aeroplano Editora, 2008.

Aravena, Alejandro and Andrés Iacobelli. *Elemental*. Ostfildern: Hatje Cantz Verlag, 2016.

Arenas, Diana and María Margarita Arenas. "El Proyecto Urbano Integral Comuna 13 como modelo de transformación urbana. Antioquía," (2015).

"Arrancó la limpieza del estero Salado en etapas." *El Universo*, (July 6, 2003). Retrieved January 22, 2019. https://www.eluniverso.com/2003/07/06/0001/18/750613FBB-21447BAA896122CF68EF57B.html

Arruda, Ana Cristina. "Linguagem Audiovisual: Meio de construcao de memória e preservacao de identidade na comunidade do Chapéu Mangueira." *Revista Morpheus*, V. 4, n. 7 (2005). Retrieved January 19, 2019. http://www.seer.unirio.br/index.php/morpheus/article/view/4757

Autoridad Nacional de Lima. *Rimac: Historia del Río Hablador*. Lima: Perúcuadros Eirl, 2016.

Baldó, Josefina and Federico Villanueva. *Un plan para los barrios de Caracas*. Caracas: Consejo Nacional de la Vivienda, 1997.

Ballón, Diego and Diego Villarán. "Inspirando con el ejemplo: Diego y Matías de Alto Perú." *Conservamos por Naturaleza*. Retrieved July 19, 2018. http://www.conservamospornaturaleza.org/inspirate/inspirando-con-el-ejemplo-diego-y-matias-de-alto-peru/

Barahona, Sammy, Victoria González and Wendy Pereira. "Evaluación del uso turístico y recreativo de las escalinatas Diego Noboa." Thesis, Escuela Superior Politécnica del Litoral DSpace Repository Guayaquil, 2011.

Blinder, Ricardo and Falvio Janches. "Estrategias de intervención en villas de emergencia." *ARQA* (2010).

Bock, Marie Sophie. "Estudio macro-espacial de la arquitectura y de la sociedad guayaquileñas (1900-1940)." In *Guayaquil: Arquitectura, espacio y sociedad, 1900-1940*. Lima: Institut français d'études andines, 1992.

Borja, Jordi and Zaida Muxi. *El Espacio Público: Ciudad y Ciudadanía*. Barcelona: Electa, 2003.
Borja, Jordi. "Derecho a la ciudad, ciudadanía y actores sociales. O el Derecho libera y más tarde oprime." *Artículos* (2015).

Borja, Jordi. "Ciudades posibles, ciudades resistentes. Barcelona -Quito." In *Ciudades para cambiar la vida. Una respuesta a Habitat 3,* edited by Jordi Borja, Fernando Carrión and Marcelo Corti, 2016.

Breña-Naranjo, José Agustín et al. "World´s greatest rainfall intensities observed by satellite." *Atmospheric Science,* Letters 16 (2014): 420-424. Retrieved July 7, 2018. https://rmets.onlinelibrary.wiley.com/doi/pdf/10.1002/asl2.546

Brillembourg, Alfredo and Hubert Klumpner. *Torre David: Informal Vertical Communities*. Zurich: Lars Muller Press 2013.

Buchwald, J. V. "Guayaquil, una ciudad de cemento que desplazó al bosque tropical." *El Universo* (September 24, 2012).

Bullard, Arturo. "Comuna 13 de Medellín: Cuando la Violencia se Arrodilla ante la Cultura." *Arturo Bullard: fotografías de viaje* (March 28, 2015). Retrieved January 19, 2019. https://arturobullard.com/comuna-13-de-medellin-cuando-la-violencia-se-arrodilla-ante-la-cultura/

Cabezas, Constanza. "Primer Lugar Concurso Público Internacional del Anteproyectos Parque del Río en la ciudad de Medellín." *Plataforma*

Arquitectura, December 23, 2013. Retrieved July 10, 2018. https://www.plataformaarquitectura.cl/cl/02-320551/primer-lugar-concurso-publico-internacional-de-anteproyectos-parque-del-rio-en-la-ciudad-de-medellin

CAF. *Equidad e inclusión social en América Latina: acceso universal al agua y el saneamiento*. Bogota: Panamericana Formas, 2013

CAF. "Casos emblemáticos de desarrollo urbano: temas." (2015). Retrieved January 7, 2018. http://scioteca.caf.com/handle/123456789/779

CAF and UN-Habitat. *Construcción de ciudades más equitativas*. Bogotá: UN Habitat, 2014.
Caixeta, Fernanda and Flavia Damásio. "Tourism and slums: A study about Favela Santa Marta and the role of the Pacification Police Units in Rio de Janeiro." *Cuadernos Proarq 19* (2018): 250-264.

"Calvario Puertas Abiertas, un barrio para el encuentro caraqueño." *Tráfico Visual*, (December 13, 2015). Retrieved January 19, 2019. http://www.traficovisual.com/2015/12/13/el-calvario-puertas-abiertas-un-barrio-para-el-encuentro-caraqueno/

Cámara Inmobiliaria de Venezuela. "Cámara Inmobiliaria de Venezuela: Cifras de viviendas anunciadas por el gobierno son irreales." Retrieved January 15, 2019.
http://www.camarainmobiliaria.org.ve/camara-inmobiliaria-de-venezuela-cifras-de-viviendas-anunciadas-por-el-gobierno-son-irreale/

Cano, C. M. "Internet es arma secreta contra violencia de la Comuna 13 en Medellín." *El Tiempo* (March 15, 2013).

Cano, C. P. "Viviendas con corazón en la quebrada Juan Bobo Medellín, Colombia." *Ciudades para un Futuro más Sostenible* (November 13, 2018). Retrieved January 19, 2019. http://habitat.aq.upm.es/dubai/08/bp1982.html

Cardoso, M. *Como Morre um Projeto de Policiamento Comunitário: O caso do Cantagalo e do Pavão-Pavãozinho*. Brasilia: Universidade de Brasília, 2010.

Carvajal, Cheo. "El Calvario tiene las puertas abiertas." *Contrapunto* (2015).

Carvajal, Cheo. "El Calvario con las puertas abiertas, otra vez." *Contrapunto* (2016).

Carvajal, Cheo. "Katiuska Camargo: "Entendí que yo era dueña del barrio"." *Prodavinci* (February 14, 2018). Retrieved July 10, 2018. https://prodavinci.com/katiuska-camargo-entendi-que-yo-era-duena-del-barrio/

Carvajal, Jorge (member of Miravalle Council). Interview by Elisa Silva, Mexico City, Mexico, September 22, 2018.

Centro Cultural Moravia. Retrieved November 28, 2018. http://www.centroculturalmoravia.org/

Chauvet, D. W. *Del caos al orden. Guayaquil y su desarrollo urbano actual*. Guayaquil: Ciudades, 2005.

Cheo Carvajal (director of Ciudad Laboratorio). Interview by María Virginia Millán, Caracas, Venezuela, June 12, 2018.

"Ciudades y localidades del partido Avellaneda." *La Ciudad: El Diario de Avelllaneda* (2012). Retrieved January 19, 2019. http://laciudadavellaneda.blogspot.com/2010/02/9999999.html

"Ciudad Maravillosa: Una guía para conocer Río de Janeiro." *Una favela por dentro* (April 6, 2012). Retrieved January 19, 2019. https://ciudadmaravillosa.wordpress.com/2012/04/06/una-favela-por-dentro/

"Con jornada ecológica se motiva cuidado de estero." *De Estero Salado a Estero Salvado* (March 23, 2015). Retrieved April 7, 2018. http://esterosalado.blogspot.com/

Confama. https://www.comfama.com/webinicio/default.asp

Comfenalco. http://www.comfenalcoantioquia.com/Cultura.aspx

Correa, C. A. "Proyecto Urbano Integral en la zona nororiental de Medellín." I Congreso Internacional sobre Desarrollo Humano, Madrid 2006.

Cortés Puentes, Luisa Fernanda and Oscar Hernando Guiot Martínez. "Quebrada Juan Bobo y el Faro: Procesos de mejoramiento barrial en asentamientos informales." *Universidad de La Salle* (2016): 1-29. Retrieved January 19, 2019. http://hdl.handle.net/10185/20746

Creaven, Jackie. "A Low-Cost Housing solution for Haiti Earthquake Victims." *ThroughtCo* (June 9, 2018). Retrieved January 7, 2019. https://www.thoughtco.com/low-cost-housing-solution-haiti-earthquake-178073

Crosgrove, Dennis. ed. *Mapping*. London: Reaktion Books Ltd, 1999.

Cuadros, J., J. Valencia and A. Valencia. "Las bibliotecas públicas como escenario de participación ciudadana e inclusión social." *Rastros y rostros* (2013): 73-81.

Da Luz Moreira, Pedro. *Cidade Integrada debate com a sociedade*. Rio de Janeiro: Instituto de arquitetos do Brasil – Departamento do Rio de Janeiro, 2012.

Da Silva, E., B. Boy, C. Franco and V. Fialho. "Favela e Preservacao de áreas verda na cidade do Río de Janeiro: é póssivel coexistirem." *Reviste científica ANAP*, vol. 8, n. 12 (2015): 42-56.

DASE. *Dirección de Acción Social y Educación*. Guayaquil, 2014.

Davis, D., J. Castillo and Y. Luo. *Housing and Habitus: Craft, Politics, and the Production of Housing in Oaxaca, Mexico*. Cambridge: Harvard University Graduate School of Design, 2015.

De Araújo, Maria Angela, Eneida Maria de Souza and Danny José Almeida Costa. "Afroreggae: as "artes" do morro invadem o asfalto." *IPOTESI, Juz de Fora*, v. 15, n. 2 (2011): 133-141.

De Souza Pereira, Luiz. "Pacificação do Complexo do Alemão em tempos de megaeventos esportivos na cidade do Rio de Janeiro." *Revista Geográfica de América Central*, special edition EGAL (2011): 1-13.

"Dedication ceremonies for First Houses, December 3, 1935 – First Lady Eleanor Roosevelt cuts the ceremonial ribbon at the landmark opening of the first public housing development in the United States." *Voices of the West Village News* (January 8, 2015).
Retrieved June 5, 2018. http://westviewnews.org/2015/01/the-birth-of-public-housing/the-birth-of-public-housing-2/

Delgado, D. E. *Estudio del impacto del plan de regeneración urbana en la calidad de vida de los habitantes del cerro Santa Ana, escalinatas Diego Noboa y Arteta*. Guayaquil: Universidad Católica de Santiago de Guayaquil, 2012.

Desco Centro de Estudios y Promoción del Desarrollo. "Programa Urbano / Premio Internacional a las buenas prácticas para mejorar condiciones de vida." Retrieved January 19, 2019. http://www.desco.org.pe/programa-urbano-premio-internacional-a-las-buenas-practicas-para-mejorar-condiciones-de-vida

"Diego Villarán, promotor de cultura y deporte en el Morro Solar de Chorrillos." *RPP Noticias* (May 4, 2012).

Dreher, Douglas. "La regeneración urbana de la ciudad de Guayaquil." Douglas Dreher Arquitectos (June 2017). Retrieved March 10, 2018. http://www.douglasdreher.com/noticias/noticia.asp?id=271&sc=9

Duarte, Patricio and Isabel Zúñiga. "Valparaíso cosmopolita: los efectos de la disposición hacia la técnica como parte de un espíritu progresista." *Revista de Urbanismo*. No. 17 (December 2017).

Echeverri, Alejandro and Francesco Orsini. "Informality and Social Urbanism in Medellin." In *Medellin Environment, Urbanism and Society* (2008): 132-156. Retrieved January 10, 2018.
https://pdfs.semanticscholar.org/0fcb/410c512f443d7455c461bbc7c560849ef0a5.pdf

Edgar Pichardo (director Miravalle Cultural Center). Interview by Elisa Silva, Miravale, Mexico City, Mexico, September 22, 2018.

"El Calvario Puertas Abiertas regresa para el disfrute de los caraqueños." *Analítica* (December 1, 2017). Retrieved January 19, 2019. http://www.analitica.com/cultura/el-calvario-puertas-abiertas-regresa-para-el-disfrute-de-los-caraquenos/

"El cuidado de parques está bajo la responsabilidad de los vecinos." *El Telégrafo* (October 11, 2013). Retrieved May 07, 2018. https://www.eltelegrafo.com.ec/noticias/guayaquil/10/el-cuidado-de-parques-esta-bajo-la-responsabilidad-de-los-vecinos

"El Guasmo, la hacienda que se convirtió en micro ciudad. *El Telégrafo* (January 29, 2017). Retrieved May19, 2018. https://www.eltelegrafo.com.ec/noticias/septimo/1/el-guasmo-la-hacienda-que-se-convirtio-en-una-microciudad

"El Parque Biblioteca Fernando Botero partió la historia de los corregimientos." *Periódico de la Alcaldía de Medellín* (2011): 8-9.

Empresa Constructora Pukara. Síntesis diagnóstico: Memoria proyecto Cerro Santo Domingo, Valparaíso, 2010.

Empresa de Desarrollo Urbano. *Medellín: Modelo de transformación urbana.* Medellín, 2015.

Enlace Arquitectura. "Cubiertas El Calvario - Calvario Puertas Abiertas," 2017. Retrieved January 19, 2019 http://www.enlacearquitectura.net/proyectos/2017/12/cubiertas-el-calvario/

Enlace Arquitectura. "Sembrando Ciudad La Palomera," 2017. Retrieved January 19, 2019 http://www.enlacearquitectura.net/projects/2017/08/citi-planting-la-palomera/

Escallón, Clemencia. *Arrendamiento y vivienda popular en Colombia como alternativa habitacional*. Bogotá: Ediciones Uniandes, 2010.

Escobar, C., C. Borja and L. M. Arredondo. "Informe especial construcción de la Biblioteca San Cristóbal de la Empresa de Desarrollo Urbano," 2011.

"Favela rising." Directed by J. Zimbalist and M. Mochary, 2005.

"Fewer Chileans living in poverty despite economic slowdown." *Reuters* (September 22, 2016). Retrieved October 7, 2018 https://www.reuters.com/article/chile-poverty/fewer-chileans-living-in-poverty-despite-economic-slowdown-idUSL2N1BY1B4

Fitzmaurice, Rosie. "An Italian architect has designed an eco-friendly flat pack home that costs £25,000 and only takes 6 hours to build." *Business Insider UK* (November 23, 2017). Retrieved January 7, 2018. http://uk.businessinsider.com/eco-friendly-flat-pack-tiny-home-takes-six-hours-to-build-2017-11

Fomento del Desarrollo Popular Fudep. "'Sembrando ciudad' en la comunidad La Palomera del Municipio Baruta." Retrieved January 10, 2019. http://fudep.org/2017/10/sembrando-ciudad-en-la-comunidad-la-palomera-del-municipio-baruta/

Fondo Nacional de Vivienda Fonvivienda en Colombia. https://www.fna.gov.co/vivienda

Freire, Q. G. "Espaço Criança Esperança no Cantagalo." *Diario do Rio* (August 12, 2011). Retrieved May 30, 2018. https://diariodorio.com/espaco-crianca-esperanca-no-cantagalo/

Freitas, C. "Comissária da ONU vai ao Alemão ver estragos da chuva." *Jornal Do Brasil*, (2013).

Fudep Fomento para el Desarrollo Popular. http://www.fudep.org

Fuenmayor, Jesús. "The Tower of David." *Domus* April 27, 2011. Retrieved March 15, 2019. https://www.domusweb.it/en/architecture/2011/04/28/the-tower-of-david.html

Fundación Malecón 2000. http://malecon.org.ec/quienes-somos

Gaceta Oficial. "Ley Orgánica de Ordenación Urbanistica," n. 33.868, December 16, 1987.

Ganem, Daniel. "Cinco anos de UPP: Um breve balanço." *Dilemas.* v. 7, n. 3 (2014).

García, Teresa. "Puertas Abiertas en El Calvario." *El País* (January 10, 2017).

GEF Small Grants Programme. "Mission and History." Retrieved January 22, 2019. https://sgp.undp.org/index.php?option=com_content&view=article&id=98&Itemid=223#.WsuKAi5ublU

Gehl, Jan and Birgitte Svarre. *How to Study Public Life*. Washington: Island Press, 2013.

"Pavão-Pavãozinho, una historia que comienza en la década de 1930." *O Globo* (June 29, 2017). Retrieved April 23, 2018. https://oglobo.globo.com/rio/pavao-pavaozinho-uma-historia-que-comeca-na-decada-de-1930-21532552

Gomes, Q. "História do Morro da Mangueira." *Diario Do Río Do Janeiro* (February 21, 2016).

"Gondola in Complexo do Alemão Favelas." *The Rio Times* (July 12, 2011). Retrieved June 8, 2018. http://riotimesonline.com/brazil-news/rio-politics/gondola-in-complexo-do-alemao-favelas/

González, Catalina. "El rapero de la Comuna 13 que le quita niños a la guerra." *El Espectador* (February 12, 2015). Retrieved January 19, 2019. https://www.elespectador.com/noticias/el-rapero-de-comuna-13-le-quita-ninos-guerra-articulo-543595

Gouverneur, David. *Diseño de Nuevos Asentamientos Informales*. Bogotá: Ediciones Unisalle, 2016.

Governo do Rio de Janeiro. "Estado recupera áreas de risco dentro do Complexo do Alemão." Rio de Janeiro, 2011.

Gobierno de Chile. "Plan de inversiones. Reconstrucción y rehabilitación urbana. Valparaíso," August, 2014. Retrieved January 10, 2019. https://www.interior.gob.cl/media/2014/09/PLAN-DE-INVERSION-VALPO-2014-2021.pdf

"Gran Santiago: estudio indica que hay 3,7 metros cuadrados de áreas verdes accesibles por persona." *Fundación Terram* (May 30, 2017). Retrieved November 24, 2018. http://www.terram.cl/2017/05/gran-santiago-estudio-indica-que-hay-37-metros-cuadrados-de-areas-verdes-accesibles-por-persona/

Habermas, Jurgen. *The Structural Transformation of the Public Sphere: An Inquiry into a Category of Bourgeois Society*. Cambridge, Massachusetts: MIT Press, 1991.

Harvey, David. "The right to the city." *New Left Review* 53 (2008): 23–40.

Hermelin M., A. Echeverri and J. Giraldo. *Medellín Medio-Ambiente Urbanismo Sociedad*. Medellín: Fondo Editorial Universidad EAFIT, 2010.

Hernández-García, Jaime. *Public Space in Informal Settlements: The Barrios of Bogotá*. Newcastle upon Tyne: Cambridge Scholars Publishing, 2013.

Hetch, Romy. "Una discusión sobre el espacio público." *Ediciones ARQ* (August 2014).

Hierro, Lola. "Casa Kolacho: La violencia se cura con hip hop." *El País* (June 30, 2016). Retrieved January 19, 2019. https://elpais.com/elpais/2016/06/23/planeta_futuro/1466698760_170228.html

"Historia. Villa Maria Lima." Retrieved January 19, 2019. http://villamarialima.galeon.com/productos1689543.html

"Historia Comuna 13." Retrieved January 19, 2019. https://es.slideshare.net/adrima0204/historia-comuna-13

"Historia de Chorrillos. Mar del Sur." Retrieved January 19, 2019. https://www.mardelsur.com.pe/historia-de-chorrillos/

"Historia de Chorrillos. Municipalidad Distrital de Chorrillos." Retrieved January 19, 2019. http://www.munichorrillos.gob.pe/home/historiachorrillos.php

Hoffman, Ava Rose. "Knowledge to Create Solutions in Complexo do Alemão: Instituto Raízes em Movimento." *Rio On Watch* (July 11, 2016). Retrieved January 10, 2019 http://www.rioonwatch.org/?p=30158

Imanishi, Rute. "Os "Parques Proletarios" e os subúrbios do Río de Janeiro: aspectos da política governamental para as favelas entre 1930-1960." *Instituto de Pesquisa Económica Aplicada* (December 2014). Retrieved January 19, 2019. http://www.ipea.gov.br/portal/index.php?option=com_content&view=article&id=24267

INDECI, PNUD, ECHO, MDVMT. *Escenario de riesgo sísmico y medidas de mitigación en Villa María del Triunfo.* Lima: INDECI, 2011.

Infonavit. *Vivienda Infornavit*. Mexico: Centro de Investigación para el Desarrollo Sostenible CIDS del Infonavit Instituto de Fondo Nacional de la Vivienda para los Trabajadores, 2016.

Instituto de Estudios Regionales y Urbanos. *Proyecto de Habilitación Integral de La Palomera*. Caracas: Universidad Simón Bolívar, 2002.

Izaga, Fabian and Margareth Da Silva Pereira. "A mobilidade urbana na urbanização das favelas no Rio de Janeiro." *Cadernos do Desenvolvimento Fluminense* (2014).

Jánchez, Flavio and Max Rohm. *Urban interrelations*. Buenos Aires: Piedra Papel & Tijera, 2012.

Jánchez, Flavio. *Public Space in the Fragmented City: Strategy for Socio-Physical Urban Intervention in Marginalized Communities*. Buenos Aires: Nobuko, 2012.

Jovchelovitch, S. and J. Priego-Hernández. *Underground Sociabilities: identity, culture and resistance in Rio de Janeiro's favelas*. Paris: UNESCO, 2013.

"Juan Bobo, en Medellín, ganó Premio Dubai." *Portafolio* (December 4, 2008). Retrieved January 10, 2019. http://www.portafolio.co/economia/finanzas/juan-bobo-medellin-gano-premio-dubai-319834

Karlsson, M. "Informal settlements: the world's invisible communities." *Uppsala: SLU, Dept. of Urban and Rural Development* first cycle, G2E. (2012): 1-24.

"Las Comunas de Medellín" *Insumisos*. Retrieved January 19, 2019. https://www.insumisos.com/lecturasinsumisas/MEDELLIN%20FRONTERAS%20INVISIBLES%20III.pdf

Lefebvre, Henri. *The Production of Space*. Translated by Donald Nicholson-Smith. Oxford: Blackwell, 1991.

Leguía, Mariana. ed. "Latin America at the Crossroads Architectural" *Design AD* No. 221 (June, 2011).

León Almenara, J. P. "Chorrillos: Invasiones no se detienen en zona arqueológica del Morro Solar." *El Comercio* (September 11, 2017).

Lipthay, Antonio. "Reparación de tejido urbano Cerro Toro y Cerro Santo Domingo." *Revista ARQ*. no. 73 (2009): 28-35.

Lombard, Melanie. "Constructing ordinary places: Place-making in urban informal settlements in Mexico." *Progress in Planning* volume 94 (November 2014): 1-53. Retrieved September 30, 2018. http://dx.doi.org/10.1016/j.progress.2013.05.003

Londoño, Diego. "Casa Kolacho, donde el hip hop cobra vida." *Radionica* (July 8, 2015). Retrieved January 16, 2019. https://www.radionica.rocks/noticias/casa-kolacho-donde-el-hip-hop-toma-vida

Luttenbarck, M. *Vulnerabilidade familiar: concepções dos agentes*. Río de Janeiro: Ministerio de Saúde, 2015.

Maasho, Aaron. "Ethiopia 80% of urban population live in slums in Ethiopia." *Sapa-AFP* (January 18, 2017). Retrieved January 19, 2019. http://nazret.com/blog/index.php/2007/01/18/ethiopia_80_of_urban_population_live_in

Magalhaes, F. and F. Di Villarosa. eds. *Urbanizaçao de Favelas*. Washington: Interamerican Development Bank, 2012

Magrini, Claudio. Presentation at Limapolis 2017, Facultad de Arquitectura y Urbanismo de la Pontificia Universidad Católica del Perú. Lima, Peru, March 5, 2017.

Maglione, Hernan. "Una favela por dentro." *Ciudad Maravillosa* (April 6, 2012). Retrieved January 19, 2019. https://ciudadmaravillosa.wordpress.com/2012/04/06/una-favela-por-dentro/

Maldonado, Elena. "Parque Biblioteca Fernando Botero San Cristóbal." *Caminos y Memorias*, No. 1 (2017): 16-19.

Matías Ballón (co-director of Alto Perú). Interview by María Virginia Millán, Lima, Peru, July 19, 2018.

"Medellín, Colombia: Proyecto Urbano Integral zona Nororiental." Observatorio de Ciudades Inclusivas Comisión de Inclusión Social, Democracia, Participación y Derechos Humanos de CGLU (2011): 1-12.

Medellín Como Vamos. "Movilidad y espacio público en Medellín." Retrieved November 24, 2018. https://www.medellincomovamos.org/movilidad-y-espacio-p-blico/

"Medellín se vive a través del graffitour." *Radiónica* (June 04, 2014). Retrieved February 20, 2019. https://www.radionica.rocks/noticias/medellin-se-vive-traves-del-graffitour

Merzthal, G. "Agua y agricultura urbana." *Agricultura Urbana* (December 20, 2008).

Mesinas, S. "Miravalle en la azotea del DF." *El Mirón: periódico comunitario* (2013): 6-8.

"Mexico City: Miravalle Community Council." *UrbanXChanger*. Retrieved January 10, 2019. http://www.urbanxchanger.com/eng/conteudos/visualizar/Miravalle-Community-Council

Ministerio de Desarrollo Urbano y Vivienda. "Generación de áreas verdes y espacios recreativos públicos para provincia de Guayas." *Habitat y Vivienda* (2015). Retrieved January 10, 2019 https://www.habitatyvivienda.gob.ec/wp-content/uploads/downloads/2015/06/PROYECTO-GUAYAS-ECOLOGICO-FINAL29-ENERO-V3-en-formulacion.pdf

Ministerio de Tecnologías de la Información y las Comunicaciones de Colombia, "Población de Medellín 2018-2020," 2019. Retrieved December 9, 2019. https://www.datos.gov.co/Estad-sticas-Nacionales/Poblacion-Medellin-2018-2020/j8ze-v9z6

Minoja, Livia. "Favelascape: tools of integration for the favela Santa Marta in Rio de Janeiro." Thesis Politecnico di Milano. In *Abitare,* edited by Silvia Franceschini, (November 11, 2010). Retrieved February 10, 2019. http://www.abitare.it/en/archive/2010/11/11/politecnico-di-milano-10-2010-livia-minoja-favelascape-tools-of-integration-for-the-favela-santa-marta-in-rio-de-janeiro-2/

Molina Verdejo, Ricardo. "Valparaiso: Glimpses to a soiciourban and identitary construction process." *Revista austral de ciencias sociales*, n. 28 (2015). Retrieved January 10, 2019. http://mingaonline.uach.cl/scielo.php?pid=S0718-17952015000100010&script=sci_arttext

Montoya, Jorge. I., Oihana Cuesta Gómez, Óscar Flecha Quintanilla, Daniel Viandé Andavert, et al. "Moravia como ejemplo de transformación de áreas urbanas degradadas: tecnologías apropiadas para la restauración integral de cuencas degradadas." *Publicación Científica en Ciencias Biomédicas*, Vol. 9, No. 15 (January – June, 2011): 1-120.

"Moravia, la ruta de la esperanza." Directed by Matías Boero Lutz. YouTube, Moravia UAB-Unesco. December 3, 2013. Retrieved January 22, 2019. https://www.imdb.com/title/tt5097092/

Mpe, R. and A. Ogra. "Making Great Places in Slums/ Informal Settlements." Conference Proceedings: *Planning Africa 2014*. Conference paper - International Convention Centre (ICC), Durban, South Africa, October 19, 2014.

"Morro de Babilonia, un lugar lleno de historias que regala una imagen diferente de Río de Janeiro." *Imaginario de Janeiro*. Retrieved January 22, 2019 https://imaginariodejaneiro.com/morro-de-babilonia/

Mumford, Eric. *The CIAM Discourse on Urbanism, 1928-1960*. Cambridge: MIT Press, 2000.

"Moravia: el barrio que floreció sobre una montaña de basura." *Historias Kien y Ke* (December 7, 2014). Retrieved January 26, 2018. https://www.kienyke.com/historias/moravia-medellin-el-barrio-que-florecio-sobre-una-montana-de-basura

Municipalidad de Villa María del Triunfo. https://munivmt.gob.pe/portal/distritos/

Muñóz, Camila. "Medellín sale de su infierno." *ABC* (June 3, 2012). Retrieved February 15, 2019. https://www.abc.es/internacional/abci-medellin-sale-infierno-201206030000_noticia.html

BIBLIOGRAPHY

Nietzche, Friedrich. *Thus Spoke Zarathustra*. London: Penguin Books 1978, First published 1891.

"Nueva Esperanza: Mejoramiento de nuevos barrios en Villa María del Triunfo a través de la participación en la gestión urbana," *Desco Programa Urbano*, 2006. Retrieved January 19, 2019. http://urbano.org.pe/project/nueva-esperanza-mejoramiento-de-nuevos-barrios-de-villa-maria-del-triunfo-a-traves-de-la-participacion-en-la-gestion-urbana/

Olmsted, Frederick Law. "Public Parks and the Enlargement of Towns." In *Frederick Law Olmsted: Writings on Landscape, Culture and Society*, edited by Charles Beveridge. Baltimore: John Hopkins University Press, 2015.

"Operación Orión: 10 años de impunidad." *Verdad Abierta* (October 16, 2012). Retrieved January 19, 2019. http://www.verdadabierta.com/victimas-seccion/desaparecidos/4264-operacion-orion-la-verdad-diez-anos-despues

Organización de las Naciones Unidas para la Alimentación y la Agricultura. Retrieved January 22, 2019. http://www.fao.org/ag/agp/greenercities/es/cmvalc/lima.html

Orrego Penagos, J. L. "Chorrillos en el siglo XIX." *Rumbo al Bicentenario* (June 29, 2009). Retrieved January 10, 2019. http://blog.pucp.edu.pe/blog/juanluisorrego/2009/06/29/chorrillos-en-el-siglo-xix/

Orsini, Francesco and Alejandro Echeverri. "Informalidad y urbanismo social en Medellín." *Sensible* (2009): 11-24. Retrieved January 10, 2019. https://upcommons.upc.edu/bitstream/handle/2099/11900/111103_RS3_AEcheverri_%20P%2011-24.pdf

Paulus Bosole, I. "Comprehensive Exploration of Public Space in Informal Settlement as a Tool for Sustainable Development Strategies." *Informal Settlement and Affordable Housing* (2009): 109-122. Retrieved March 10, 2018. www.irbnet.de/daten/iconda/CIB_DC25380.pdf

"Pavão-Pavãozinho, una historia que comienza en la década de 1930." *O Globo* (June 29, 2017). Retrieved April 23, 2018. https://oglobo.globo.com/rio/pavao-pavaozinho-uma-historia-que-comeca-na-decada-de-1930-21532552

Peattie, Lisa. *The view from the Barrio*. Ann Arbor: University of Michigan Press, 1970.

Peña Gallego, L. E. "Las bibliotecas públicas de Medellín como motor de cambio social y urbano de la ciudad." *Textos universitatris de biblioteconomía i domentació* (December 31, 2011).

Peregrino, Miriane. "Tram, Tourism, History and Resistance: "Each Brick has its Story"." *Agência de Notícias das Favelas* (March 6, 2015). Retrieved January 5, 2018. http://www.rioonwatch.org/?p=20388.

Pérez, P. "Huir de las pandillas sobre una tabla de surf." *El País* (February 14, 2017).

Perrone, G. N. *Malecón 2000 El inicio de la regeneración urbana de Guayaquil: un enfoque proyectual*. Quito: Flacso, 2012.

"Plan Masa del Guasmo Sur elevará los índices de acceso a espacios verdes en Guayaquil." *El Ciudadano* (May 10, 2014).

"Playita del Guasmo." In Guayaquil es mi destino. Retrieved January 30, 2019. http://www.guayaquilesmidestino.com/es/diversion-y-esparcimiento/balnearios/playita-del-guasmo

Pontes, Fernanda. "Pesquisadoras traçam a história da ocupação do Complexo do Alemão. Pioneiro da região veio da Polônia" *O Globo* (October 4, 2013). Retrieved June 14, 2018. https://oglobo.globo.com/rio/pesquisadoras-tracam-historia-da-ocupacao-do-complexo-do-alemao-10247995

Prakinson, C. "Reborn from a trash heap, with women at the helm." *Next City: inspiring better cities* (March 19, 2014). Retrieved January 10, 2019. http://nextcity.org/daily/entry/reborn-from-a-trash-heap-with-women-at-the-helm
Programa Urbano DESCO. *Concurso Participativo de Proyectos: gestión participativa del territorio y movilización social en la mejor del barrio*. Lima: DESCO, 2008.

Programa Urbano DESCO. *Concursos Participativos de Proyectos Sociales: fortaleciendo capacidades de desarrollo para una gestión participativa*. Lima. DESCO, 2009.

"Proyecto de desarrollo de las zonas urbano marginales de Guayaquil." In *Programas de desarrollo social*. Guayaquil: Unidad de gestión, ZUMAR, 2006.

"Proyecto Urbano Integral (PUI) Nororiental, Comunas 1 y 2 - Áreas de influencia sistema metrocable de Medellín." *Archivo BAQ Arquitectura Panamericana* (September 27, 2018). Retrieved January 10, 2019. http://www.arquitecturapanamericana.com/proyecto-urbano-integral-pui-nororiental-comunas-1-y-2-areas-de-influencia-sistema-metrocable-medellin/

"¿Qué es el PUI." In "Proyectos Urbanos Integrales: Empresa de Desarrollo Urbano," 2010. Retrieved January 10, 2019. http://proyectosurbanosintegrales.blogspot.com/p/que-es-el-pui.html

Rede Globo, UNESCO. *Criança Esperança, mobilizando pessoa, transformando vidas*. Brasilia: UNESCO, 2009.

Reimerink, L. "Medellín popularizó las escaleras mecánicas, pero, ¿han tenido algún impacto?" *Citiscope* (July 24, 2014).

"Reurbanização do Dona Marta sai do papel e esta em fase de licitação." *Licitacao.net* (April 22, 2004). Retrieved January 10, 2019. https://www.licitacao.net/noticias_mostra.asp?p_cd_notc=704#

Robinson, Jennifer. *Ordinary cities: between modernity and development*. London, Routledge, 2006.
Rosa, Marcos L. and Ute E. Weiland, eds., foreword by Richard Sennett. *Handmade Urbanism: From Community Initiatives to Participatory Models*. Berlin: Jovis Verlag GmbH, 2013.

Roy, Ananya. "Urban informality: toward an epistemology of planning." *Journal of the American Planning Association*. Volume 71, 2005 - Issue 2 (November 26, 2007). Retrieved January 10, 2019. https://doi.org/10.1080/01944360508976689

Rubio Vollert, R. *Ciudades Urgentes: Intervención en áreas urbanas de crecimiento rápido*. Bogotá: Editorial Uniandes, 2006.

Sáez Giraldez, E., J. García and F. Roch Peña. Conference paper, "Laboratorio de urbanismo emergente: Una mirada sobre los barrios informales de Lationoamérica." Sustainable Building Conference, 2010.

Saldarriaga, Luisa, María Cecilia Muñóz, Jenny Alejandra Echeverría, Ana María Londoño and Alejandro Arango. "El arte está amenazado en la Comuna 13." *De la urbe Periodismo universitario para la ciudad* (2012). Retrieved January 19, 2019. http://delaurbe.udea.edu.co/2012/11/09/el-arte-esta-amenazado-en-la-comuna-13/

Samper, Angel. *La ciudad –region: el paisaje intermedio – Casos de studio: La Sabana de Bogotá – La region capital de Caracas*. Bogotá: Ediciones Uniandes, 2007.

Samper, Jota. "Repensando la informalidad. Estrategias de Co-producción del Espacio Urbano." *Issue* (August 13, 2004). Retrieved November 24, 2018.
https://issuu.com/coproduccion/docs/informe_aug_13_web_version

Samuels, A. J. "The AfroReggae Cultural Group: A Rebirth Of Hope Within Rio De Janeiro's Favelas." *Culture Trip* (January 24, 2018). Retrieved February 15, 2019. https://theculturetrip.com/south-america/brazil/articles/the-afroreggae-cultural-group-a-rebirth-of-hope-within-rio-s-favelas/

Sánchez, Alfredo, Joaquín Bosque and Cecilia Jiménez. "Valparaíso: su geografía, su historia y su identidad como Patrimonio de la Humanidad." *Estudios Geográficos*. Vol. 20, No. 266 (2009): 269-293.

Santana, F. "El Guasmo cumple 25 años de asentamiento popular." *El Universo* (July 18, 2003).

"Sert, Josep Lluís and the Town and Planning Associates (TPA)." Harvard University Loeb Library. CIAM Collection. Folder: E003.

SHF Sociedad Hipotecaria Federal. https://www.gob.mx/shf

Silva, Elisa and Pablo Vaggione. *Políticas Pro Inclusión. Herramientas prácticas para el desarrollo integral de las ciudades en América Latina*. Bogotá: CAF, 2016.

Silva, Elisa, Maximo Sacchini, Valentina Caradonna et al. *CABA Cartografía de los barrios de Caracas 1966-2014*. Caracas: Fundación Espacio, 2015.

Souza, R. "Plano inclinado do Morro Santa Marta, Estación 1." *TGBR Ferrovías Brasil* (May 29, 2009). Retrieved January 10, 2019. http://www.tgvbr.org/viewtopic.php?t=2843

Spector, Julian. "Another Reason to love Urban Green Space: It Fights Crime." *Citylab* (April 15, 2016).

Srivastava, Rahul and Matias Echanove. "'Slum' is a loaded term. They are homegrown neighbourhoods." *The Guardian* (November 28, 2014). Retrieved June 24, 2018. https://www.theguardian.com/cities/2014/nov/28/slum-loaded-term-homegrown-neighbourhoods-mumbai-dharavi 06.10.2018

Steiker-Ginzberg, K. "Morar Carioca: The Dismantling of a Dream Favela Upgrading Program." *Rio On Watch* (September 10, 2014).

Suárez, A. "Plaza Bolívar de El Hatillo." In *IAM Institutional Assets and Monuments of Venezuela*. Retrieved January 15, 2018. https://iamvenezuela.com/2016/10/plaza-bolivar-de-el-hatillo/

"Sur y arte para ganarle a la pobreza" *Perú 21* (May 26, 2016). Retrieved January 10, 2019 https://peru21.pe/cultura/surf-arte-ganarle-pobreza-219047

Swiss Contact. http://www.swisscontact.org

Tarchópolus, Doris. "La Unidad Vecinal: Objeto de investigación de Josep Lluís Sert." Doctoral dissertation, Department of Urbanism and Land Use Planning at the Universidad Polítectnica Cataluña, 2018. Retrieved January 29, 2018 https://upcommons.upc.edu/bitstream/handle/2099/14896/132_137_Doris_Tarchopulos_.pdf

Taylor, Charles. *Multiculturalism: Examining the Politics of Recognition*. Princeton: Princeton University Press, 1994.

Toche Medrano, E. ed. *Perú Hoy, Ajustes al modelo económico: La promesa de la inclusión*. Lima: DESCO, 2011.

Trazando Espacios Públicos. "El Calvario," 2017. Retrieved January 10, 2019 http://trazandoespacios.org/es/trazando-espacios-el-calvario/#

Turner, J. "Uncontrolled urban settlement: Problems and policies." In *The city in newly developing countries: Readings on urbanism and urbanization*, edited by G. Breese. Englewood Cliffs: Prentice Hall, 1968.

Turner, J. and R. Fichter, R. eds. *Freedom to build: Dweller control of the housing process*. New York: Collier-Macmillan, 1972.

TV Globo and UNESCO. "Criança Esperança 25 anos criando oportunidades." *Rede Globo* (June 8, 2011). Retrieved January 19, 2019. http://redeglobo.globo.com/criancaesperanca/noticia/2011/06/baixe-o-livro-crianca-esperanca-25-anos-criando-oportunidades.html

"Un parque lineal termina con la insalubridad del estero Las Ranas." *El Telégrafo* (July 28, 2017)vf. Retrieved May 7, 2018. https://www.eltelegrafo.com.ec/noticias/guayaquil/10/elcuidado-de-parques-esta-bajo-la-responsabilidad-de-los-vecinos

"Una ciudad dentro de otra ciudad, así lo ven al Guasmo, a los 40 años." *El Universo* (March 1, 2015).

UNESCO. "Regional Report about Education for all in Latin America and the Caribbean," April 09, 2014. Retrieved February 25, 2018. www.unesco.org/fileadmin/MULTIMEDIA/HQ/ED/ED_new/pdf/LAC-GEM-2014-ENG.pdf/

UN Habitat. *New Urban Agenda Habitat III*. Quito: UN Habitat, 2016

UN Habitat. *Slum Almanac 2015/2016. Tracking Improvement in the Lives of Slum Dwellers*. Nairobi: UNON Publishing Service Section, 2016.

UN Habitat. "World Cities Report 2016." Retrieved January 15, 2019. http://wcr.unhabitat.org/

United Nations. Millennium Goals. https://www.un.org/millenniumgoals/bkgd.shtml

United Nations Population Fund. http://www.unfpa.org/urbanization.

Universidad Pontificia Bolivariana. *Mejoramiento Integral del Hábitat para la Región Metropolitana del Valle de Aburrá*. Medellín: Editorial Artes y Letras Ltda, 2007.

"Valparaíso, la ciudad del mar y los cerros lindos." *El Diario* (May 7, 2016).

Van den Bosch, Matilda ed. *Oxford Textbook of Nature and Public Health: The Role of Nature in Improving the health of a population*. Oxford: Oxford University Press, 2018.

Vargas, N. *Indicadores de calidad de vida en un barrio del municipio Baruta. Caso de estudio: La Palomera*. Caracas: Universidad Simón Bolívar, 2006.

"Vecinos y visitantes de El Hatillo entraron por las Puertas Abiertas de El Calvario." *RunRunes* (December 20, 2016). Retrieved January 19, 2019 http://runrun.es/relax/291306/vecinos-y-visitantes-de-el-hatillo-entraron-por-las-puertas-abiertas-del-calvario.html

Velasco, Alejandro. *Barrio Rising: urban popular politics and the making of modern Venezuela*. Oakland: University of California Press, 2015.

Velásquez, R. "El páramo más pequeño del país está en el Aburrá." *El Colombiano* (December 30, 2017).

Verdejo, Ricardo Molina. "Valparaíso: miradas a un proceso de construcción socio-urbano e identitario." *Revista austral de ciencias sociales*, n. 28 (2015): 183-192.

Villalobos, J. "Chorrillos: nuestro pequeño Perú." *Coherencia* (July 3, 2013). Retrieved January 10, 2019. http://www.coherencia.pe/chorrilos-nuestro-pequeno-peru/

Villarán, Diego. "Diego Villarán - Pecha Kucha Night Lima," Volume 4. Lima, Peru, October 21, 2009, video. Retrieved January 19, 2019. https://www.youtube.com/watch?v=g_TVCdGvx74

Villavicencio, G. "Políticas públicas y renovación urbana en Guayaquil: las administraciones social cristianas 1992-2000." *Universitas* (December 30, 2012).

Vivas, A. C. *Ambiente violento, infancia perdida*. Río de Janeiro: Pontificia Universidade Católica do Río de Janeiro, 2011.

"Vulnerabilidad de los cerros, otro problema latente en los inviernos." *El Comercio* (April 1, 2013). Retrieved July 18, 2018, https://reliefweb.int/report/ecuador/vulnerabilidad-de-los-cerros-otro-problema-latente-en-los-inviernos

World Bank Data, http://data.worldbank.org

World Bank. "Slum upgrading in Rio de Janeiro: Favela Bairro." *Healthy Cities* (2010). Retrieved January 5, 2018 http://healthycities.berkeley.edu/uploads/1/2/6/1/12619988/brazil.pdf.

BIOGRAPHY

Elisa Silva is principal and founder of Enlace Arquitectura and Enlace Foundation, established in Caracas, Venezuela. The two entities work in tandem to raise awareness of spatial inequality, advance the integration of informal settlement communities and address the social and environmental challenges of rural landscapes in Venezuela and parts of Mexico. Their work has received awards in numerous design competitions and international architecture and urban design biennials. Elisa is visiting professor at the Princeton University School of Architecture and has taught at the Harvard University Graduate School of Design, the Daniels Faculty of Architecture, Landscape Architecture and Design at the University of Toronto, the Simón Bolívar University and the Central University of Venezuela in Caracas.

The research and publication of *Pure Space: Expanding the Public Sphere through Public Space Transformations in Latin American Informal Settlements* was made possible by the Graham Foundation, the Wheelwright Fellowship from Harvard University and CAF development bank of Latin America.

Pure Space

Expanding the public sphere through public space transformations in Latin American spontaneous settlements

Elisa Silva

Published by

Actar Publishers, New York, Barcelona

CAF Banco de desarrollo de América Latina

Edited by

Elisa Silva

Contributions of:

Enlace Arquitectura:
María Virginia Millán,
Sergio Dos Santos,
Verónica González,
Sofía Paz
Vanesa Malpica,
Valentina Caradonna,
Jeniree Calderón,
Eduardo Mouhtar
Gabriela Alvarez,
Jaeson Montilla

Graphic Design: Actar

Editing and proofreading:
Luis Miguel Isava, Josefina Berrizbeitia, Daniela Díaz and Ery Valero de Marcano

Printing and Binding:
Arlequin

With the contribution of:

BANCO DE DESARROLLO DE AMÉRICA LATINA

Distribution:
Actar D, Inc. New York, Barcelona.

New York

440 Park Avenue South, 17th Floor
New York, NY 10016, USA
T +1 2129662207
salesnewyork@actar-d.com

Barcelona

Roca i Batlle 2-4
08023 Barcelona, Spain
T +34 933 282 183
eurosales@actar-d.com

ISBN: 978-1-948765-42-8

PCN: 2019951127

Publication date: 2020